Praise for *Successful Business Plan: Secrets & Strategies*

" User-friendly and exhaustive…highly recommended. Abrams' book works because she tirelessly researched the subject. Most how-to books on entrepreneurship aren't worth a dime; among the thousands of small business titles, Abrams' [is an] exception. **"**

— *Forbes Magazine*

" There are plenty of decent business-plan guides out there, but Abrams' was a cut above the others I saw. *Successful Business Plan* won points with me because it was thorough and well organized, with handy worksheets and good quotes. Also, Abrams does a better job than most at explaining the business plan as a planning tool rather than a formulaic exercise. Well done. **"**

— *Inc. Magazine*

" We are again using *Successful Business Plan* in my business honors course this semester. Must be working, as Penn State was just named (by Kaplan and *Newsweek* magazine) as the 'hottest school in the U.S. for student entrepreneurs!' **"**

— *Greg Pierce, Penn State University*

" *Successful Business Plan* enables my Entrepreneurship students at the University of Vermont to develop really great business plans. The book's easy-to-follow, step-by-step format makes preparing a plan logical and understandable. Over the years…several students have actually launched their businesses successfully. Our son used the book at St. Michael's College in Vermont to develop a plan for airport fitness centers, winning the school's annual business plan competition for business majors…with a hefty cash prize! His plan was so thorough, especially the financials, that he was flown to the West Coast to present his plan to a prospective buyer. The bottom line, there is no better road map to business plan success than *Successful Business Plan*! **"**

— *David Kaufman, University of Vermont*

"If you'd like something that goes beyond the mere construction of your plan and is more fun to use, try *Successful Business Plan: Secrets & Strategies*, by Rhonda Abrams…this book can take the pain out of the process."

— *"Small Business School," PBS Television Show*

"*Successful Business Plan* is easy to follow and comprehensive. From the first chapter to the last, it guides you through the business planning process with a proven systematic approach."

— *Sean S. Murphy, Ernst & Young LLP*

"As a 20+ year veteran SBDC director, consultant and entrepreneurship instructor, I have assisted thousands of individuals and business owners through the planning process. Having reviewed tens of thousands of plans and critiquing hundreds of planning texts, programs and tools, *Successful Business Plan: Secrets & Strategies* remains my hands-down favorite text/ workbook/guide. The content and construction is comprehensive, practical and "do-able" for the serious small business owner/entrepreneur."

— *David Gay, Illinois Small Business Development Center at College of DuPage*

"In my opinion, your book is the definitive guide for successful business plans. I particularly appreciate and recommend the use of the Flow-Through Financial worksheets. Each is a great device to illustrate the connection between the qualitative and quantitative elements of a plan."

— *Gene Elliott, Business Consultant, New Mexico*

"I've been using and promoting *Successful Business Plan* since 1993, and it's great! I've taught business plan writing in several local SBDCs, as well as nationally, through the Neighborhood Reinvestment Training Institute. My course is designed and delivered around your book."

— *Ransom S. Stafford, Business Consultant, Twin Cities, MN*

"*Successful Business Plan* was an excellent learning tool for me at the University of Vermont and proved to be incredibly valuable as I started my own business after graduation. The step-by-step guidance through business planning ensures that you have all your bases covered before investing time and money in a new enterprise. The book helped me start a promotional products business and I have since recommended this book to dozens of other entrepreneurs who have used it for everything from restaurants to fashion boutiques. If you are considering starting your first, second, third or tenth business you need to look at *Successful Business Plan*!"

— *Issa Sawabini, University of Vermont, '99 Partner, Monitor Premiums LLC*

" In December 1991, I came upon the book *Successful Business Plan: Secrets & Strategies*. It is the closest to what I know works in the real world, at least in high-tech industries. **"**

— *Barb Tomlin, e-Business Strategy Consultant and President/CEO, Westward Connections, Inc.*

" One of the best books on business planning. The overall quality of this book is excellent, but three things make it stand out: First, it contains worksheets that walk you through the information-gathering process. Fill them out, and even the financials—always the hardest part of a plan—will fall right into place. Second, it has a sample plan that reads like a real business plan, written by a real person for a real business. You can use much of the wording in your own plan. Third, it has tips from successful managers, leaders, and business owners, large and small. I was especially fascinated reading the tips from ex-49er head coach Bill Walsh. You can't go wrong following his advice on planning and organizing! **"**

— *Economic Chamber of Macedonia*

" *Successful Business Plan* is thorough, well-organized, and a very useful tool for business planning and development. It's an excellent guide to the details involved with creating a solid, useful business plan. **"**

— *Jim Jindrick, The Institute of Electrical and Electronics Engineers and the University of Arizona*

" I chose *Successful Business Plan* because of its ease of use, its clarity and its good examples. I have used the book for a number of years now... **"**

— *Jean Morris, The Culinary Institute of America*

" It has a clearly defined, comprehensive approach. **"**

— *Zane Swanson, Emporia State University, KS*

" Here at the SBDC we offer clients an 8-week business planning counseling program called Business Plan Expedited (BPE). BPE is structured around *Successful Business Plan*—the end result is a well-written business plan that can be used as a part of a business loan application package. I specifically chose this text because I used it, per recommendation from my graduate school advisor, for my MBA project in graduate school 13 years ago! **"**

— *Indria Gillespie, Sierra College SBDC*

" Your book has been both an inspirational read as well as a comprehensive guide for starting my business. Since I am relatively inexperienced with entrepreneurship, your book has not only given me the ability to create a solid road map for planning, but has also provided an encouraging and easy way to cope with the enormous amount of information and organization needed. I particularly enjoy the various quotes from business professionals who have had experience in business planning. They give precious insight and different viewpoints that I would not have seen. Thank you for writing this book! "

— *Simon Lee, Entrepreneur*

" It combines, in a very clear way, both aspects of business planning and effective writing of business plans. The book is very well written. The forms are very useful. "

— *Eyal Yaniv, Bar-Ilan University, Israel*

Other Recognition for *Successful Business Plan*

- ◼ Ranked one of the Two Best Books for small business by *Forbes*.
- ◼ Ranked one of the Six Best Books for start-ups by *Inc.*
- ◼ Ranked one of the 20 Essential Books for Entrepreneurs by *Home Office Computing*.
- ◼ Main Selection, BusinessWeek Book Club.
- ◼ Main Selection, Executive Book Club.
- ◼ Used in colleges, universities, and business schools nationwide, including Stanford Business School; Haas School of Business, UC Berkeley; Northwestern University; Cal Poly, San Luis Obisbo; MIT; Cornell University; Temple University; Texas A & M; University of Massachusetts, Amherst; Southern Oregon University; Arizona State; University of Washington; and dozens of others.

Praise for Books from PlanningSho

Entrepreneurship: A Real-World Approach

"What separates Rhonda Abrams from the crowd? She is an expert in building successful small businesses. And she continues to create timely, meaningful, and (most importantly) useful content for academics, students, and business owners like myself. This book is the definitive guide for anyone who either wants to be an entrepreneur or just wants to grow their own business."

— *Gene Marks,* New York Times *Small Business Columnist*

Business Plan In A Day

"A business plan is something every business needs, but too many fail to create one because it seems intimidating. Rhonda Abrams is on a mission to change that. With this book she shows you how to create a professional business plan that will seem like it took weeks to write instead of 24 hours."

— *Anita Campbell, Publisher of* Small Business Trends

"I'm growing my business this year by purchasing a commercial building, and I needed a real estate loan to make the purchase. *Business Plan In A Day* was THE source I used for writing my plan, and the bankers and brokers I spoke with all commended my plan as being very strong and well-written. Thanks to you, I've secured my loan and the transaction is going through. I feel so fortunate to have found this book."

— *Lisa Stillman, Garden Walk Massage Therapy, St. Louis, MO*

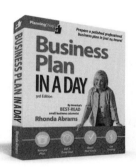

Bringing the Cloud Down to Earth

"No matter how you refer to it, working in the Cloud is a fundamental business practice these days and Abrams has done a terrific job of making this sometimes confusing subject relevant and practical for businesses of all shapes and sizes."

— *John Jantsch, Author of* Duct Tape Marketing *and* The Referral Engine

Successful Marketing: Secrets & Strategies

"*Successful Marketing* encourages students to think through standard marketing concepts while applying them directly to their business idea."

— *Meredith Carpenter, Entrepreneurship Instructor, Haywood Community College, NC*

To my clients, who've shared with me their enthusiasm for the entrepreneurial spirit and have shown me that business can be a career for people of integrity, intelligence, and honor.

To my employees, who've helped me grow a sustainable business and who share with me their intelligence, commitment, ideas, hard work, and their continual good humor.

To the memory of Eugene Kleiner, my mentor and friend, who taught me so much more than just what made a good business and a good business plan.

To my family, who has been with me every step of the way. They are more than family—they are friends.

To the memory of my parents, who would have been proud.

PlanningShop
Palo Alto, California

Successful
Business
Plan *Secrets & Strategies*

America's Best-Selling Business Plan Guide!

Rhonda Abrams

essful Business Plan: Secrets and Strategies™
991, 1993, 2000, 2003, 2010, 2014 by Rhonda Abrams

ished by PlanningShop™
er editions published by Running 'R' Media and The Oasis Press/PSI Research

rices for our readers:

leges, business schools, corporate purchasing:

ningShop™ offers special discounts and supplemental teaching
erials for universities, business schools, and corporate training.
tact: info@planningshop.com or call 650-364-9120.

business tips and information:

eceive PlanningShop's free email newsletter on starting and growing
ccessful business, sign up at www.PlanningShop.com.

PlanningShop
555 Bryant Street, #180
Palo Alto, CA 94301 USA
650-364-9120

Fax: 650-364-9125
Email: info@PlanningShop.com
www.PlanningShop.com

ningShop™ is a division of Rhonda, Inc., a California corporation.

h Edition Copy Editor: Mark Woodworth Editorial Services
h Edition Editor: Anne Marie Bonneau
h Edition Indexer: Theresa Duran
h Edition Cover and Interior Design: Diana Russell, DianaRussellDesign.com
stration: Paulina Cioce, PaulinaArt.com

-1-933895-46-8 (Trade)
-1-933895-48-2 (Academic Bundle)
-1-933895-47-5 (eBook)
rary of Congress Control Number: 2014904392

is publication is designed to provide accurate and authoritative information
egard to the subject matter covered. It is sold with the understanding that the
lisher and author are not engaged in rendering legal, accounting, or other pro-
ional services. If legal advice or other expert assistance is required, the services
a competent professional person should be sought."

*— from a Declaration of Principles jointly adopted by a committee of the
American Bar Association and a committee of publishers*

nted in the United States of America

9 8 7 6 5 4 3 2 1

About Rhonda Abrams

Entrepreneur, author, and nationally syndicated columnist Rhonda Abrams is widely recognized as one of the leading experts on entrepreneurship and small business. Rhonda's column for *USA Today*, "Successful Strategies," is the most widely distributed column on small business and entrepreneurship in the United States, reaching tens of millions of readers each week.

Rhonda's books have been used by millions of entrepreneurs. Her first book, *Successful Business Plan: Secrets & Strategies*, is the best-selling business plan guide in America. It was named one of the Top Ten business books for entrepreneurs by both *Forbes* and *Inc.* magazines. She is also the author of more than a dozen other books on entrepreneurship and has sold more than a million copies of her books. Rhonda's other books are perennial bestsellers, with three of them having reached the nationally recognized "Top 50 Business Bestseller" list.

Rhonda not only writes about business—she lives it! As the founder of three successful companies, Rhonda has accumulated an extraordinary depth of experience and a real-life understanding of the challenges facing entrepreneurs. Rhonda first founded a management consulting practice working with clients ranging from one-person start-ups to Fortune 500 companies. Rhonda was an early Web pioneer, founding a website for small business that she later sold. In 1999, Rhonda started a publishing company—now called PlanningShop—focusing exclusively on topics of business planning, entrepreneurship, and new business development. PlanningShop is America's leading academic publisher focusing exclusively on entrepreneurship.

A popular public speaker, Rhonda is regularly invited to address leading industry and trade associations, business schools, and corporate conventions and events. Educated at Harvard University and UCLA, where she was named Outstanding Senior, Rhonda now lives in Palo Alto, California.

Rhonda Abrams:

facebook.com/
RhondaAbramsSmallBusiness

twitter.com/RhondaAbrams

PlanningShop:

facebook.com/PlanningShop

twitter.com/PlanningShop

What's New in the Sixth Edition...

The business world is constantly evolving, and this edition of *Successful Business Plan: Secrets & Strategies* takes into account many of the latest trends of today's changing business world. New in this edition, you'll find:

- **Crowdfunding and Other New Ways to Raise Money for Your Venture**—Crowdfunding is dramatically changing the fund-raising landscape for new companies and new products. This edition helps you determine whether your company is a good candidate for crowdfunding and provides tips on how to conduct a successful crowdfunding campaign. This edition also includes new information on another increasingly popular source of funding innovative new companies—corporate venture capital.

- **New Social Media Platforms**—Social media continues to change and evolve, with new social media sites and tools emerging on a sometimes-overwhelmingly-fast basis. This edition includes updated information on these essential marketing tools.

- **Sample PowerPoint Slide Presentation**—Most investors, especially the most sophisticated ones such as venture capitalists, want to see a PowerPoint overview of your business plan before they look at the whole plan. This edition provides a complete Sample PowerPoint presentation for you to use as a guide when developing your own electronic presentation.

- **Lean Start-Up**—New approaches, as well as new technologies, make it easier for you to start faster, using fewer resources. This edition outlines what types of companies lend themselves to this approach and how to start faster. This edition also discusses the "Business Model Canvas"—a method for sketching out an overview of a business concept.

- **The Cloud**—Running critical business services over the Internet, rather than on-premise or on-computer, has created a fundamental shift in business operations, often dramatically lowering costs and increasing a company's speed and power. This edition provides guidance on running crucial business processes in the cloud.

- **Updated Resources**—*Successful Business Plan* provides resources to help you find the information you need to complete your plan quickly, from U.S. and international resources for the latest statistics, to funding sources, to resources that support entrepreneurs.

■ **A New Look and Infographics** — This latest edition includes a fresh layout, graphics throughout to help you digest important concepts easily, and icons to direct you to the specific worksheets you'll use to quickly complete every segment of your business plan. This design will make it easier — and more enjoyable — to create your business plan.

Icons

The following icons appear throughout the book in the margins. Look for a page number in the text near the icon to find the corresponding worksheet, sample plan, or sample electronic presentation.

Worksheet

When this icon appears in the margin next to text, it signals a nearby worksheet related to the topic under discussion.

Sample Plan & Plan Preparation Form

This icon indicates both the sample plan sections of the fictitious company ComputerEase and the Plan Preparation Forms you will fill out for the various sections of your own business plan (Executive Summary, Company Description, Target Market, and so on). Use the sample plan as a guide to help you fill out the Plan Preparation Forms. These completed forms will become the basis of your business plan.

Flow-Through Financial Worksheet

This icon indicates a Flow-Through Financial worksheet (which is also marked with a dollar-sign logo). Transfer the figures from each of these completed worksheets to their appropriate line(s) on the financial forms in Chapter 16. For more information on using the Flow-Through Financial Worksheets, see page 287.

PowerPoint Presentation

This icon indicates a sample PowerPoint Presentation.

Foreword to the Fifth Edition

By John Doerr

Partner, Kleiner Perkins Caufield & Bryers

Ideas Are Easy, but Execution Is Everything and "Teams Win"

Ideas Are (Relatively) Easy

I love innovation, great new ideas and businesses, and the entrepreneurs who create them. Probably you do, too. Innovation is the source of America's great wealth and leadership position, and the way lives are improving around the world.

Innovation can be everywhere. It is a high-tech, magical iPad, or a breakthrough life-saving drug. Or innovation can be a better local yogurt store, or helping Realtors list homes, or one of hundreds of thousands of programs in a smartphone app store.

Now, more than ever, we need the power of new ideas, new businesses, and the resulting new jobs.

But, relatively speaking, new ideas are easy. New ideas are necessary, but insufficient. What's more difficult and even more important is execution.

Execution Is Everything

Thomas Edison is one of the great innovators of all time. He invented the light bulb, the phonograph, and the motion picture camera. But just as important, Edison understood well the importance of execution. He famously said, "Vision without execution is hallucination."

On this topic my friend Bill (Coach) Campbell is blunt and direct: "John, we've gotta focus to achieve operational excellence. Execution is everything."

The best entrepreneurs are the ones who really go the distance with their companies, who are always learning. They don't know what they don't know, so they attempt to do the impossible. And they often succeed.

Entrepreneurs do more than anyone thinks possible, with less than anyone thinks possible.

Teams Win

Unless you are Einstein, or an author, your work is not alone. Most ideas worth pursuing take a Team to Win.

Great entrepreneurs are great team leaders. They motivate their teams with the promise of more than money. They inspire their teams with their plan for winning. The plan clearly says **who** and **how** the team wins (**what**)—how who wins what.

The Plan

Why write a business plan? Particularly in this age of 24/7 tweeting, friending, and blogging? Won't PowerPoint and a smooth elevator pitch work just as well?

You may think business plans are fund-raising documents for investors, and indeed they are.

But the best plans are much more. They are the road map so your team can execute with excellence. Writing them disciplines your thinking, and establishes priorities. Your plan clearly, concisely defines the mission, values, strategy, and measurables—objectives and key results. If you don't know where you're going, and how, and why, you won't get there.

Your plan is for more than investors. In 1974, my partners Gene Kleiner, Tom Perkins, and Brook Byers invested in Tandem Computers. Tandem's business plan was written in Kleiner's offices by a junior partner, Jim Treybig. Jim became the CEO and grew the business to great global success. (Compaq acquired Tandem for $3 billion in 1997.)

Treybig was a great communicator. Every Friday he held popular "beer busts," which were actually company meetings. And once a year Jim gathered all of Tandem's employees, spouses, and families for a picnic with beers and burgers. He presented Tandem's business plan, in its entirety, to all of them. Jim said, "I don't care if my competition knows our plans. I want to be sure our executives and families get it."

Plan to Win

There's never been a better time than now to start a new business. Innovation is everywhere—in how we communicate, how we buy things, how we sell things, how we learn, how we live. Now is a great time to be an entrepreneur. And this book can help you take your good idea and make it great business.

Good luck. Plan on it.

Foreword to a Previous Edition

By Eugene Kleiner

Founding Partner, Kleiner Perkins Caufield & Byers

In today's environment, a business plan is an entrepreneur's most crucial business document. No company can expect to articulate its goals or to secure financing without a well-conceived and well-presented business plan. Without a convincing business plan, no one will seriously consider your business idea.

This wasn't always the case. The first business plan I ever wrote as an entrepreneur was not a business plan at all; it was just a letter. Eight of us from Shockley Laboratories for various reasons wanted to start a semiconductor company on our own, and we needed the money to make it possible. We drafted a letter, perhaps four or five pages long, describing what we proposed to do and sent that letter along with our resumes to an investment banker.

Fortunately for us, that letter found its way to the desk of a young business school graduate named Arthur Rock who felt that we might have promise. As a result, we were able to get our funding, and Fairchild Semiconductor was born. From Fairchild, the eight of us branched out and went on to form or fund such companies as Intel, Tandem Computer, and many other leading Silicon Valley firms.

Today, our letter might never be completely read. Investors now are far more structured and expect a far higher level of expertise and preparation from the entrepreneurs they choose to fund. When examining a proposal, they want to see much more than just a good idea and a bright young man or woman; they want to see a business plan showing that the concept has been rigorously assessed and that the entrepreneur has carefully thought through the issues for steps necessary to take the idea and fashion it into a successful company.

At Kleiner Perkins Caufield & Byers, the venture capital firm I cofounded in 1972, we had a diligent system of evaluating business plans. A plan had to stand up to the most exacting scrutiny and toughest standards. Most plans, of course, never made it past the initial screening phases. Only the most interesting and well-conceived plans warranted the allocation of resources necessary for a more thorough examination. From that group, we narrowed our selection down even further, spending a great deal of time investigating each plan's merits. Finally, before deciding to invest in a company, part of the staff would serve as "devil's advocate," suggesting all the pitfalls. Only the plans that made it through that process were considered for final funding.

In this book, Rhonda Abrams has given you the tools you need to create a successful business plan. Working with Rhonda over the years, I've developed a strong appreciation and respect for her grasp of the business planning process. We have had many sessions evaluating what it takes to make a successful company, and I've seen her take what I've shared with her about long-term and strategic planning and expand upon that knowledge, bringing to bear her own experience with clients and her intelligent, practical approach to the entrepreneurial process.

About the Contributors

John Doerr
Partner, Kleiner Perkins Caufield & Byers

Famed venture capitalist John Doerr is a Partner at Kleiner Perkins Caufield & Byers, the nation's premier venture capital firm. Doerr began his career with a summer job in 1974 at what was then a small chipmaker, Intel, and in 1980 he joined KPCB. With KPCB, Doerr has funded some of the world's most innovative companies, including Google, Amazon, Intuit, Twitter, Symantec, and Zynga. Passionate about sustainability and social issues, Doerr has backed entrepreneurs working to combat global warming, poverty, and health issues. He is active in public policy, covering issues from public school funding to preparedness for pandemic flu. Doerr serves on the President's Council on Jobs and Competitiveness. He also serves on several company boards, including Coursera, Flipbook, and Google.

Eugene Kleiner
Founding Partner, Kleiner Perkins Caufield & Byers

Eugene Kleiner was a legend—in venture capital and in Silicon Valley. Kleiner was one of the country's first venture capitalists: In 1972, he founded what would become the country's foremost venture capital firm, Kleiner Perkins Caufield & Byers. He was an early investor in companies such as Intel and Genentech. Kleiner was one of the so-called "Traitorous Eight"—the eight young men who broke away from Nobel Prize winner William Shockley to form the first silicon semiconductor company, Fairchild Electronics, in 1957, and who are considered to be the "fathers" of Silicon Valley.

Andrew Anker
CEO, Tugboat Yards

A veteran of several start-ups, Andrew Anker is the CEO of Tugboat Yards and the executive chairman of PandoMedia. As an angel investor, Anker has invested in a wide range of companies, including LinkedIn, TCHO Ventures, and Ebates. He was the cofounder and CEO of Wired Digital, Inc., a pioneering Internet news and media organization that launched the first advertising-supported website, www.hotwired.com, in 1994. Anker led Wired Digital from its founding through 1998 and built it into what was one of the 20 largest networks of websites at the time. After leaving Wired Digital, he was a Partner at August Capital—one of the nation's most respected venture capital firms—and then served as vice president of corporate development at Six Apart.

Damon Doe
Vice President, Technology Banking Group, U.S. Bank

A former Partner at Montage Capital, Damon Doe has extensive experience in financial services, corporate banking, fund management, corporate finance, and equity investment. Prior to working in a senior-level capacity for several banks in the San Francisco Bay Area, Doe cofounded Sand Hill Capital, a $150 million venture debt and equity fund located in Menlo Park, California, where he managed a large part of the venture firm's portfolio and also served as CFO. Before that, Doe financed early-stage and middle market high-tech companies at both Silicon Valley Bank and Bank of the West. Doe's past clients include Advanced Fiber Communications and JDS Uniphase.

Lauren Flanagan
Angel Investor, BELLE Capital USA

Lauren Flanagan is cofounder and Managing Director of BELLE Capital USA, an early-stage angel investment fund, located in the Greater Chicago area. Belle invests solely in companies with women in leadership positions. Flanagan has more than 25 years' experience founding and operating technology companies, and she was the founder of four technology companies. She is also cofounder and Managing Director of the Phenomenelle Angels Fund. In 2010, BusinessWeek named her one of the top 25 angels in technology. She is Executive Chairman of the Current Motor Company.

Nancy Glaser
Management Consultant, The Glaser Group

Nancy Glaser is founder and President of The Glaser Group, a consulting firm specializing in early-stage business strategies and turn-arounds for troubled companies. Her focus is in specialty retailing and in consumer-based and service businesses. Previously, Glaser was a Partner at the venture capital firm U.S. Venture Partners. Some of the companies she has invested in and helps direct are Gymboree, Fresh Choice, and PetsMart. Earlier in her career, Glaser helped take The Gap from a 35-store chain to 350 stores in less than five years, and served with Macy's and Lord & Taylor. Glaser was active in international venture capital, both in Poland and as a founder of the Apparel Innovation Center in St. Petersburg, Russia.

Seth Goldman

President and CEO, Honest Tea

With his partner and former Yale School of Management professor, Barry Nalebuff, Seth Goldman cofounded Honest Tea in 1997. He began his entrepreneurial career at the age of six by retrieving stray golf balls from a course near his home, and selling them back to golfers along with lemonade. Honest Tea was acquired by the Coca-Cola Company in 2011 and today, more than 100,000 retail outlets carry the company's beverages. In addition to his role as President and CEO of Honest Tea, Goldman also serves on several boards, such as Bethesda Green, Beyond Meat, the Yale School of Management, the American Beverage Association, and the Maryland Economic Development Commission.

Mark Gorenberg

Founder and Managing Director, Zetta Venture Partners

Mark Gorenberg has the rare distinction of having been a judge in three of the country's leading university business plan competitions, at MIT, Stanford University, and the Haas School of Business at the University of California, Berkeley. As founder and Managing Director of Zetta Venture Partners, Gorenberg invests in the fast-growing analytics market. Prior to launching Zetta Venture Partners, he served as Managing Director at Hummer Winblad. He has over 20 years' experience in venture capital and serves on the boards of start-up and public companies. Gorenberg also serves on the President's Council of Advisors on Science and Technology (PCAST), the Board of Trustees for MIT, the National Venture Capital Association, and the FCC's Technological Advisory Council.

Kay Koplovitz

Chair, Kate Spade

When Kay Koplovitz founded USA Network, she became the first female network president in television history. She served as Chairperson and Chief Executive of the network until it was sold in 1998 for $4.5 billion. President Bill Clinton appointed Koplovitz to head the National Women's Business Council, after which she helped found Springboard Enterprises in 2000 to showcase women-led entrepreneurial ventures. Since its founding, Springboard has helped women entrepreneurs raise more than $6 billion in venture capital, creating tens of thousands of jobs. To further encourage women entrepreneurs, Koplovitz also cowrote *Bold Women, Big Ideas*. In 2007, Koplovitz joined the board of what was then Liz Claiborne Inc. (now Kate Spade & Company) and long served as Chairperson of the Board. She is the Chairperson and CEO of Koplovitz & Company, and serves on several other boards.

Larry Leigon
President, Leigon Associates

As President of Leigon Associates, Larry Leigon is a corporate trainer and executive coach. He consulted with Hewlett-Packard globally for six years, during which time the company merged with Compaq. Previously, Leigon cofounded Ariel Vineyards in 1985 to produce and market premium de-alcoholized wines. In its first four years of operation, Ariel grew to be larger than 95% of all the wineries in the United States. Leigon was one of the four founding principals of Ariel and served as its first President, with primary responsibility for all marketing and distribution strategies—a unique challenge since Ariel was creating a new product category. By the time it had been acquired, Leigon had grown Ariel Vineyards to a valuation of $15 million.

Robert M. Mahoney
Former Executive Director of Corporate Banking, Bank of Boston

In this leadership position, Robert Mahoney was responsible for commercial lending services throughout the New England states for the Bank of Boston, a bank that earned a reputation as one of the nation's most receptive to entrepreneurial companies. During his two decades with the bank, Mahoney served as President of Massachusetts Banking and Vice President for corporate banking in the United Kingdom.

F. Gibson "Gib" Myers, Jr.
Venture Capitalist, The Mayfield Fund

Gib Myers is well known as a General Partner (Emeritus) of the prestigious Mayfield Fund, a venture capital firm with over $1.5 billion of capital under management. Myers joined Mayfield in 1970 and has participated in virtually all of the firm's portfolio company investments, including 3Com Corporation. He has nurtured companies in diverse areas of technology through every phase of growth, from start-up to maturity. In 1997 Myers and Mayfield Fund created the Entrepreneurs' Foundation, dedicated to bringing the entrepreneurial spirit and commitment to societal and community activities. The Entrepreneurs' Foundation is a nonprofit organization that assists entrepreneurs and young companies in developing a community involvement plan and in participating in unique philanthropic giving programs.

Bill Rancic
Entrepreneur and Inaugural Winner of *The Apprentice*

By the time he won the first season of the reality TV show *The Apprentice*, Bill Rancic was already a seasoned entrepreneur. After he graduated from college, he founded the Cigar of the Month Club. Today, Rancic travels across the U.S. and around the world as motivational and business speaker. He has written two business books, develops real estate, runs restaurants, and makes guest appearances on shows such as *Today, The Tonight Show, The View*, and various CNBC programs. A television producer, Rancic appears with his wife on their weekly reality TV show, *Giuliana & Bill*.

Premal Shah

President, Kiva

Premal Shah first began dreaming of "Internet microfinance" while working at PayPal, the online payments company. In late 2004, Shah took a three-month leave from PayPal to develop and test the Internet microfinance concept in India. When he returned to Silicon Valley, he met other like-minded dreamers and quit his job at PayPal to help bring the Kiva concept to life and eventually to scale. Kiva today raises over $1 million each week for the working poor in over 50 countries worldwide and was named a Top 50 Website by *Time Magazine* in 2009. For his work as a social entrepreneur, Shah was named a Young Global Leader by the World Economic Forum and selected for *Fortune* magazine's "Top 40 under 40" list in 2009. Shah began his career as a management consultant.

Andre S. Tatibouet

Founder and Former Owner, Aston Hotels and Resorts

Andre S. Tatibouet's first exposure to the hotel business in Hawaii began in his parents' 14-room hotel in Waikiki in the 1940s. At the age of 19, Tatibouet developed his first hotel and has been a force in the hospitality industry ever since. He built the largest condominium resort and hotel chain in Hawaii, which also included properties in California and Mexico. He was named one of the top five entrepreneurs in the hotel industry and is active in numerous philanthropic and civic organizations. Today, he works with other hotel owners as a consultant.

Bill Walsh

Former Coach and President, San Francisco 49ers

When Bill Walsh was hired as head coach of the San Francisco 49ers football franchise in 1979, the team was hardly taken seriously. But within three years, under his innovative management, the 49ers had won a Super Bowl. He went on to win two additional world championships and was named "Coach of the Eighties." His management style was marked by intelligent, strategic planning of every detail and contingency. Formerly a commentator on NBC Television, he was a frequent speaker to business audiences.

Ann Winblad

Partner, Hummer Winblad Venture Partners

In high-technology circles, Ann Winblad is a well-known software entrepreneur and venture capitalist. In 1976, she cofounded Open Systems with a $500 investment and sold the company in 1983 for $15.1 million. Prior to starting her venture capital firm with partner John Hummer, she served as a consultant to clients such as IBM, Microsoft, Apple, Price Waterhouse, and numerous start-up companies. Hummer Winblad has invested in companies such as Central Point Software, Powersoft, and Liquid Audio.

Table of Contents

Starting the Process   SECTION I

Business Plan Components   SECTION II

Putting the Plan to Work   SECTION

References & Resources   SECTION

Sample Plans

Worksheet, Examples, and Charts in This Book

Introduction

*If you don't know where you are going, how will you
know when you are lost?*

Over the past two decades, *Successful Business Plan: Secrets & Strategies*
has been used by entrepreneurs to launch hundreds of thousands of businesses. I am incredibly proud of helping entrepreneurs to achieve their
dreams—and, as importantly, create new jobs. It is my life's work.

It's led to some wonderful moments in my life. Like the time I was
speaking at a conference in Pittsburgh and a man, surrounded by a gaggle
of his employees, told me that he had been homeless, found this book in his
local library, and used it to help start a small business, which eventually grew
to having more than 100 employees.

Or the time a woman came rushing out of a store in Boise, Idaho. She
had somehow recognized me, and pulled me into her beautiful home goods
store. "I built this store following your book—just look around." And I
did—not only at the lovely products she was selling and the employees she
had working, but at the immense pride she had in her accomplishment.

Or meeting some of the hundreds of thousands of students who have
used this book to better understand the possibilities and opportunities of
entrepreneurship. Many have used what started as a class assignment to actually launch their own businesses.

It's been immensely gratifying to hear from entrepreneurs from all walks
of life, from all over the globe, about the businesses they've started, the
money they've raised, the jobs they've created—and knowing that this book
has been a part of that.

> " With the first edition
> of your plan, you shouldn't even
> think about getting money. Use
> the planning process to decide
> if the business is really as good as
> you think it is. Ask yourself if you
> want to spend five years of your
> life doing this. Remember, that's
> about 10% of your active working
> life, so seriously examine whether
> the enterprise could really be
> worthwhile to you."
>
> *Eugene Kleiner*
> *Venture Capitalist*

> "The intensity in football incorporates, in one season, what a corporation must have over five years or so. You deal with people under stress; performance is measured by the bottom line; success is what the group accomplishes. To succeed, you must set goals, define roles, recognize excellence, acknowledge failure, recover from disappointment, and stay abreast of the competition. You must always be evolving systematically, improving the mechanisms for developing progress, and bringing along younger players."

Bill Walsh
Former Coach and President,
San Francisco 49ers

Creating a business plan helps you:

■ Think through your entire business

■ Better understand your true financial needs

■ Secure funding

■ Attract key management

■ Develop marketing messages and materials

■ Identify key strategic partners and customers

Remember, it's the PLANNING and not the PLAN that's really important. The process of developing a business plan is what helps you succeed. The greatest benefits come from examining all the critical aspects of your business, looking at the factors and trends that can affect your success or threaten your livelihood, and then asking yourself the tough questions.

During the process of developing a business plan, you're almost certainly going to change several facets of your business—perhaps even some major components of it. It's far better to make your mistakes on paper instead of with your real money and precious time.

I sincerely hope this book helps you achieve your dreams.

—*Rhonda Abrams, Palo Alto, California*

SECTION I

Starting the Process

CHAPTER 1

The Successful Business

*It is not enough merely to survive;
the goal is to succeed.*

Factors of a Successful Business

The ultimate purpose of developing a business plan is to have a successful business. In the long run, it is fruitless to write a business plan that can raise the funds you seek if your enterprise is so poorly conceived it is bound to fail. So, as you create your plan, be certain to address the long-term needs of your business and devise strategies that enhance both the overall performance of your company and your personal satisfaction.

The following factors, discussed in detail in this chapter, contribute most to business success and should guide your planning process:

- The Business Concept
- Understanding the Market
- Industry Health and Trends
- Clear Strategic Position and Consistent Business Focus
- Capable Management
- Ability to Attract, Motivate, and Retain Employees
- Financial Control
- Anticipating Change and Adaptability
- Company's Values and Integrity
- Responding to Global Opportunities and Trends

The Business Concept

Meeting needs is the basis of all business. You can devise a wonderful new machine, but if it doesn't address some real and important need or desire, people won't buy it, and your business will fail. Even Thomas Edison recognized this fact when he said, "Anything that won't sell, I don't want to invent."

Typically, entrepreneurs get their original business inspiration from one of four sources: 1) previous work experience; 2) education or training; 3) hobbies, talents, or other personal interests; or 4) recognition of an unanswered need or market opportunity. Occasionally, the impetus comes from the business experience of a relative or friend.

As you refine your business concept, keep in mind that successful businesses incorporate at least one of these elements: something new, something better, underserved or new market, new delivery or distribution, and increased integration.

SUCCESSFUL BUSINESS ELEMENTS

Include at least one of these as you refine your business concept.

Something New	Something Better	Underserved or New Market	New Delivery or Distribution	Increased Integration
Create a new product, service, feature, or technology.	Improve on existing product or service: more features, lower price, greater reliability, faster speed, or increased convenience.	Find a market with greater demand than competitors can satisfy, an unexploited niche market, or an unserved location.	Provide products or services less expensively, to a wider geographic area, or with greater choice.	Both manufacture and sell your product, or offer more services and products in one location.

Your business should incorporate at least one of these factors — more than one if possible. Ideally, you can bring a new or better product or service to an identifiable but underserved market, perhaps using a more efficient distribution channel. Evaluate the ways your business concept addresses the elements described above. Your concept should be strong in at least one area. If not, you should ask yourself how your company will be truly competitive. *The Basic Business Concept worksheet on page 6 helps you evaluate the strengths and weaknesses of your basic business idea.*

Understanding the Market

It is not enough to have a great idea or new invention as the basis of your business; you must also have a market that is sufficiently large, accessible, and responsive. If your market isn't large enough, you can't reach it efficiently, or it isn't ready for you. Your business will fail, no matter how good your business concept. Consider the automatic teller machine (ATM) seen on virtually every street corner. It was invented more than 10 years before it became popular, but the company that initially marketed the ATM was unsuccessful—people weren't yet willing to trust their banking to machines.

First, evaluate whether market demand is adequate to support your company. For instance, if you are opening a flower shop in a neighborhood where none currently exists, what indications are there that the neighborhood residents are interested in buying flowers? Do they currently purchase flowers at a nearby supermarket? Does national data on the demographics of flower purchasers coincide with neighborhood demographics? Perhaps you should conduct a survey of the neighborhood's residents, asking about their flower-buying habits and preferences.

Next, if you are creating a new product or service, what indications are there that the market will be receptive to you? Market readiness is one of the most difficult and most unpredictable aspects to measure. That is why

Success key terms

Barriers to Entry
Those conditions that make it difficult or impossible for new competitors to enter the market: Two barriers to entry are patents and high start-up costs.

Cash Flow
The movement of money into and out of a company; actual income received and actual payments made out.

Strategic Position
A company's distinct identity that separates it from the competition and helps it focus on its activities.

Basic Business Concept

Using this worksheet as a guide, outline your business concept as you presently conceive it.

Is yours a retail, service, manufacturing, distribution, or online business? _____
_____

What industry does it belong to? _____
_____

What products or services do you sell? _____
_____
_____

Who do you see as your potential customers? _____
_____
_____

Describe your basic overall marketing and sales strategy: _____
_____
_____

Which companies and types of companies do you consider to be your competition? _____
_____
_____

List your competitive advantages, if any, in each area listed below.

New Products/Services: _____
_____
_____

Improved Features/Services and Added Value: _____
_____
_____

New or Underserved Markets Reached: _____
_____
_____

New/Improved Delivery or Distribution Method: _____
_____
_____

Methods of Increased Integration: _____
_____
_____

companies spend substantial amounts of money on market research before launching a new product.

You may not have the funds to undertake extensive market research, but even a small amount of analysis can help you gauge the receptivity of a particular market to your idea. Methods of conducting market research and evaluation in a practical, economical fashion are discussed in Chapter 2. When gathering information for your business plan, spend considerable time learning about your market. The more you understand the various factors that affect your market, the more likely you are to succeed.

Industry Health and Trends

Your business does not operate in a vacuum; generally, your company is subject to the same conditions that affect your overall industry. If consumer spending declines nationally, there's a good chance your retail business—whether a neighborhood boutique or an online shopping mall—will also experience poor sales.

As you develop your plan, you need to respond to the industry-wide factors affecting your own company's performance. While it is certainly possible to make money in an industry that is experiencing hard times, you can only do so if you make a conscious effort to position your company appropriately. For example, if you are in the construction business and the number of new-home starts is down, you may want to target the remodeling market or the commercial real estate market rather than the new-home construction market.

Investors and lenders are particularly sensitive to issues of industry health. It is much harder to raise money to start or expand businesses in troubled industries. Even though opportunities exist in such fields, investors and bankers are concerned about the increased risks an enterprise faces in an unhealthy industry. Conversely, if your business is in a healthy and expanding industry, investors are likely to be more receptive.

What direction is your industry going? It is important to look at the major trends that will influence industry health in the future as well as examining its current condition. Is the industry consolidating as big companies merge into huge businesses? What is happening with pricing pressures, consumer demand, availability of parts and supplies, and global competition? *Several worksheets included in Chapter 6 help you identify and anticipate trends in your industry.*

If you are seeking outside funds, your business plan must reassure investors or bankers that you understand the industry factors affecting your company's health and that you have taken those factors into consideration when developing your business strategy.

Clear Strategic Position and Consistent Business Focus

A crucial factor for a successful business is the development of a clear **strategic position** that differentiates you from your competition—and then maintaining focus on that position. All too often businesses fail because management loses sight of the central character of the enterprise.

> " The main thing is to keep going back and talking to the people who actually use what you're making. See if what you're making is truly helpful to your customers."
>
> *Larry Leigon*
> *Founder, Ariel Vineyards*

> " What tips me off that a business will be successful is that they have a narrow focus of what they want to do, and they plan a sufficient amount of effort and money to do it. Focus is essential; there can be the possibility of the business branching out later, but the first phase of a company should be quite narrowly defined."
>
> *Eugene Kleiner*
> *Venture Capitalist*

Defining a clear strategic position enables you to capture a particular place in the market and distinguish yourself from your competitors. Different companies may sell a similar product, but each may have a very different sense of what its business is really all about.

For example, suppose four companies are making jeans. Company A defines itself as selling work clothes; Company B sees itself as a sportswear manufacturer; and Company C defines itself as being in the business of selling youth and sex appeal. But Company D has never clarified its mission—it just sells jeans.

These different positions affect the way each company markets itself, how it designs its jeans, what subsequent products it produces, and even the employees it hires. The first three companies may all succeed and rarely be in competition with one another. But Company D, which misses the big picture, is almost certain to fail over time as it flounders in its attempts to compete with all of the other, more-focused companies.

A second aspect of positioning your company and maintaining focus is the development of a company style or corporate culture. By creating a consistent style that permeates every aspect of your enterprise, from the design of your stationery to personnel policies, you give your customers and employees a sense of trust in your company.

Imagine two different restaurants on the same street, both with basically the same business mission: providing good, fast food, priced at only a few dollars a meal.

The first restaurant is a national burger chain. Its style is characterized by consistency, cleanliness, and impersonal friendliness. A strong corporate image is important, which is reinforced through the restaurant's decor, the food's packaging, and the employees' uniforms. The meals are prepared by standardized routines, and every customer is given the same greeting.

The second restaurant is a diner. Management characterizes its corporate culture as that of a friendly neighbor. To help make sure that employees know customers' names and food preferences, management aims to retain employees for many years. A bulletin board features notices of local events. This restaurant's target market is the neighborhood regulars who know they will feel at home there.

With a strong company style, each restaurant clearly distinguishes itself from its competitors and gives its target customers a precise understanding of what to expect. Every business needs to consider its style as it relates to the company's overall mission, and then infuse that style into virtually all its undertakings.

To help clarify your company's position and focus as part of the business plan process, you should define a Statement of Mission. This Mission Statement should guide your company's short-term activities and long-term strategy, position your marketing, and influence your internal policies. *A Statement of Mission worksheet is in Chapter 5.*

Capable Management

Perhaps more than any other factor, competent management stands out as the most important ingredient in business success. The people in key positions are crucial in determining the health and viability of your business. Moreover, because of the importance of capable management to business success, many investors and venture capital firms place the single greatest emphasis on this factor when evaluating business plans and deciding on loans or investments. They'll review the management section of a business plan with special scrutiny. Your business plan must inspire confidence in the capabilities of your management, and you should put your management team together carefully.

Before submitting your business plan to investors, conduct your own analysis of your management team. Evaluate each individual (and yourself) to see if he or she fits the profile of a successful manager. Some of the traits shared by successful managers are:

- **Experience.** They have a long work history in their company's industry and/or they have a solid management background that translates well to the specifics of any business in which they become involved.

- **Realism.** They understand the many needs and challenges of their business and honestly assess their own limitations. They recognize the need for careful planning and hard work.

- **Flexibility.** They know things go wrong or change over time, and they are able to adapt without losing focus.

- **Ability to Work Well with People.** They are leaders and motivators with the patience necessary to deal with a variety of people. They may be demanding, but they are fair.

In developing your business plan, determine whether key members of your management team possess these characteristics. If not, perhaps you can increase training, add staff, or take other measures to enhance your management's effectiveness. For instance, if you have little or no experience in your chosen field, perhaps you should first take a job with an existing company in that field before opening your own business.

In addition to evaluating the traits of each individual, look at the overall balance of your management team. Do you have people who are capable and experienced in the various aspects of your business — marketing, operations, technology, finance, and so on? Are some managers better at dealing with internal issues and others at handling external relations? Or do the talents and traits of your managers duplicate each other?

Ability to Attract, Motivate, and Retain Employees

A company is only as good as its people. The ability to find, attract, and keep outstanding employees and managers is crucial to a company's long-term viability and competitiveness.

Demographic trends indicate a tight labor market in the United States well through the early part of the 21st century. Companies will have a difficult time competing for the relatively limited number of outstanding job

> "The most successful entrepreneurs tell you they have a great team, but lots of small business owners let ego get in the way. Many people helped me along the path. You've got to remember the people who were loyal to you. Don't forget them when you become successful."
>
> *Bill Rancic*
> *Serial Entrepreneur*

> " We don't just want to make secure loans; we want to make good loans. A good loan is a loan with a high probability of being repaid from the primary source, such as the business, without interrupting the lifestyle of the borrower. Collateral makes a loan 'safe,' not necessarily good. It's not fair to make a loan if the collateral is good BUT the business plan is shaky. We're not interested in getting people's homes; we're interested in successful businesses."
>
> *Robert Mahoney*
> *Corporate Banker*

applicants. Your company's reputation for treating employees well directly enhances both the number and the quality of job applicants and your company's ability to retain employees once hired.

Employee morale also has a significant impact on a company's productivity, the quality of its products or services, and its ability to provide outstanding customer service. Unhappy employees are less motivated to do excellent work. Satisfied employees are far more likely to want to see their company succeed, and they can dramatically alter a company's bottom line.

Examine your management style and policies as part of your overall business planning process. Develop management practices that treat employees fairly, offer opportunities for advancement, afford reasonable job security, and provide fair pay and benefits.

Financial Control

Key to any business is how it handles money. Not fully anticipating start-up costs can immediately place impossible pressures on a new business. Poor **cash flow** management can bring down even a seemingly thriving business. One of "Rhonda's Rules" is "Things take longer and cost more than anticipated." Build financial cushions in your plan to allow for unanticipated expenses and delays.

As you develop your business plan, make sure you have the information to understand your financial picture on an ongoing basis. What does it take to open your doors each month? Where is your real profit center? How much expansion do you need to maintain growth? What are the hidden costs of marketing your company? What are the consequences of your credit policies?

Build in mechanisms to keep you continually informed as your business develops. It is easier to establish good financial procedures right from the start than to wait until you face a financial crisis. How frequently will you do your billing? What kinds of credit policies will your business follow?

How will you keep informed on inventory?

Make certain you receive detailed financial statements at least monthly and that you understand them thoroughly. Examine financial reports for any deviations from your plan or any indications of impending cash flow problems.

Controlling and understanding your finances makes decisions easier. And you'll sleep better at night.

Anticipating Change and Adaptability

Change is inevitable, and the rate of change gets ever faster. In today's world, your company needs to anticipate and respond to change quickly and train its employees to be adaptable. Nimble companies that can quickly evaluate and respond to changing conditions are most likely to be successful.

In planning for change, keep in mind the kinds of conditions that will affect your business' future. They include:

■ **Technological Changes.** It's impossible to predict the exact technological developments that will affect your industry, but you can be sure that you will be faced with such changes. Even if you make old-fashioned chocolate chip cookies, you'll find that advancements in oven design, food storage, or inventory control software will place competitive pressures on your business. Competitors' technological advances may cause significant downward pricing pressures on you.

■ **Sociological Changes.** Evaluate demographic and lifestyle trends in light of their potential influence on your business. In the cookie business, for example, consumer interest in natural foods or the number of school-age children in the population may influence the number and kinds of cookies you sell. What sociological factors have the greatest impact on your company? Keep your eye on trends that represent true change; be careful not to build a business on passing fads.

■ **Competitive Changes.** New businesses start every day. How hard is it for a new competitor to enter the market, and what are the **barriers to entry**? The Internet makes it possible for companies all over the world to compete against each other, increasing the number and type of competitors you may face.

When developing your business plan, consider how your company deals with these outside changes. Also anticipate major internal changes, such as growth, the arrival or departure of key personnel, and new products or services.

No business is static. Planning a company responsive to change will make the inevitable changes easier. See Chapter 6, for more on anticipating change.

A Company's Values and Integrity

Every company must make money. You can't stay in business unless you eventually earn a profit. However, studies of business success over time have shown that companies that emphasize goals in addition to making money succeed better and survive longer than companies whose sole motivation is monetary.

As you develop your business plan, keep in mind those values you wish to have characterize the company you are creating or expanding. These values can be aimed externally (at achieving some business, social, or environmental goal) or they can be aimed internally (at achieving a certain type of workplace or quality of product or service) or both.

Articulating your company's values to employees, suppliers, and even your customers can strengthen their commitment to your business. Values-driven companies often have greater success in attracting and retaining good employees, and they can usually better weather short-term financial setbacks because employees and management share a commitment to goals in addition to financial rewards.

> " You need to be able to fail fast and fail forward. At PayPal, our business started out as sending money between Palm Pilots, then we had the idea of sending money over email. We saw the need for electronic payments, but we weren't wedded to the idea of something that wasn't working."
>
> *Premal Shah*
> *President, Kiva*

> " Passion is a prerequisite. If you don't have passion, you're not going to be successful. Entrepreneurship is not purely a numbers game. But you can't be stupidly passionate, you have to do your homework."
>
> *Damon Doe*
> *Managing Partner*
> *Montage Capital*

A company is likewise strengthened by maintaining integrity in all aspects of its dealings—with employees, customers, suppliers, and the community. Certainly, you will face situations where it appears that you will be at a disadvantage if you are more honest than your competitors or more fair than other employers. However, the long-term benefits of earning and keeping a reputation for integrity outweigh the perceived immediate disadvantages. A clear policy of honesty and fairness makes decision-making in difficult situations easier, inspires customer and employee loyalty, and helps avoid costly lawsuits and regulatory fines. It's also the right thing to do.

Responding to Global Opportunities and Trends

Today's business world is a global world. In all aspects of your business, you may find it possible to be working internationally. Even a small company with an online presence may be selling its products internationally. Certainly, your raw materials or inventory may come from global sources. You may have competitors, suppliers, employees, contractors, and partners worldwide. A successful business in this environment must at least evaluate international opportunities and consider international threats when constructing a business plan.

Some of the global considerations to keep in mind as you develop your business plan are:

■ **Target market.** Because of the electronically connected world, it's possible to target a market even halfway around the globe, and that can be a way to significantly expand your market opportunities. If you have a highly niche product, your customers may be widely scattered internationally, and you may need to or want to serve a wide geographic area. Even if you plan to concentrate on a local or domestic market, you must address how you'll serve international customers who find you online. Successful companies today at least evaluate international market opportunities when choosing which markets to target.

■ **Competitors.** It's far easier than ever for global competition to enter local markets. Certainly, if you are selling a product—even a fairly mundane one—you may find yourself competing with online international companies.

■ **Suppliers.** Whether for raw materials for production/manufacturing or inventory for sale, it is likely that at least some of your supplies will come from countries other than your own. You should certainly be considering sourcing material and inventory globally as you grow your company.

■ **Labor.** It is no longer necessary for your employees or contractors to be located in the same office, same city, or even same country as you. Finding workers—especially technology or manufacturing labor—in other countries may offer significant labor cost reduction. It is now typical for companies to "offshore" many tasks, and flexible companies evaluate some of those opportunities. Of course, managing a far-distant

> " *Getting sufficient supplies can be challenging. When we launched our Honest Kids organic drink pouch, we had to buy half the world's supply of organic, kosher grape juice.*"
>
> *Seth Goldman*
> *Cofounder, Honest Tea*

labor supply has significant challenges, and you must think those through as you plan the global aspects of your business.

- **Legal issues.** Whether protecting your intellectual property, ensuring that you are following all necessary laws and regulations, or dealing with international tax or finance issues, you will certainly need to understand the legal issues affecting you as you work globally.

- **Partners.** As you think about expanding your business internationally, one approach is to find existing companies "on the ground" in those markets to partner with. This can make your entry far easier, help you understand local business customs and practices, and better serve your market.

- **Social responsibility.** The best international companies are good global citizens. As you work globally, make certain that you are always acting in a socially responsible manner—whether dealing with labor issues, human rights, the environment, bribery, or corruption.

What Motivates You?
Personal Satisfaction: The Four Cs

For smaller enterprises, sole proprietorships, or businesses in which one or two key members of management have primary control, issues of personal satisfaction can be a central element in determining long-term success. Some businesses fail, and others flounder, because their founders, owners, or key managers are uncertain what they really want to achieve or because they did not structure the company and their responsibilities in ways that satisfy their personal needs and ambitions.

It is useful to evaluate and consider your personal goals when deciding on the nature of your business development. For most entrepreneurs, these goals can be summed up by the Four Cs: Control, Challenge, Creativity, and Cash.

Control

How much control you need to exercise on a day-to-day basis influences how large your company can be. If you prefer to be involved in every business decision or are uncomfortable delegating or sharing authority, your business should be designed to stay small. Likewise, if you need a great deal of control over your time (because of family or personal demands), a smaller business without rapid expansion is more appropriate.

In a large company, you will have less immediate control over many decisions, and others will share in decision-making. Structure your management reporting systems to ensure that as the company grows, you continue to have sufficient information about and direction over developments to give you personal satisfaction. If you are seeking outside funding, understand the nature of control your funders will have and be certain you are comfortable with these arrangements.

> "First and foremost you have to have passion. You've got to understand why you're in the business, you have to understand why you're going to be wildly successful, and you have to be able to sell it to people. It's very easy to write a business plan with lots of pretty charts and graphs and research quotes, and if you can't present it to coworkers, employees, investors, and ultimately to the customer, you're not going anywhere. You always have to have the passionate person who lives and breathes, eats and sleeps the idea."
>
> *Andrew Anker*
> *Venture Capitalist*

> "   Writing a business plan forces you into disciplined thinking if you do an intellectually honest job. An idea may sound great in your own mind, but when you put down the details and numbers, it may fall apart."
>
> *Eugene Kleiner*
> *Venture Capitalist*

Challenge

If you are starting or expanding a business, you are likely to be a problem-solver and risk-taker, enjoying the task of figuring out solutions to problems or devising new undertakings.

It is important to recognize the extent of your need for new challenges and develop positive means to meet this need, especially once your company is established and the initial challenge of starting a company is met. Otherwise, you may find yourself continually starting new projects that divert attention from your company's overall goals. As you plan your company, establish personal goals that provide you with sufficient stimulation, while also advancing the growth of your business.

Creativity

Entrepreneurs want to leave their mark. Their companies are not only a means of making a living, but a way of creating something that bears their stamp. That's why many businesses carry the founder's name.

Creativity comes in many forms. For some, it is the creativity involved with designing or making a new "thing"—a fashion designer creating a line of clothes, a software developer writing a new program, a real estate developer erecting a new building. For others, it may be the creativity of coming up with a new business process. Creativity also comes into play in finding new ways to make sales, handle customers, or reward employees.

If you have a high need for creativity, make certain you remain involved in the creative process as your company develops. You'll want to shape your business so it is not just an instrument for earning an income but also a mechanism for maintaining creative stimulation and making a larger contribution to society. But don't overpersonalize your company, especially if it is large. Allow room for others, particularly partners and key personnel, to share in the creative process.

Cash

Understand how your personal financial goals have an impact on your business plan. For instance, if you require substantial current income, you may need investors so you have sufficient cash to carry you through the lean start-up time. This means you will share ownership interest with others, and the business must be devised for substantial profit potential to reward those investors appropriately.

Likewise, if your aim is to build a very large company and accumulate substantial income or wealth quickly, you will need outside investors to finance such rapid development or expansion. Once again, this means giving up more control over your company.

If, on the other hand, your current income needs are less demanding or your overall financial goals more modest, you may be able to forego giving up a piece of your company to investors and instead expand your business more slowly through sales or through loans or credit lines. Keep in mind there is sometimes a trade-off between personal goals: Wanting more cash often means having less control.

Examine your personal goals and those of key personnel using The Four Cs worksheet on page 16.

Chapter Summary

A successful business plan not only ensures that you achieve your short-term objectives, it also helps secure the long-term viability of your business. When developing your plan, keep in mind the underlying factors affecting business success and personal satisfaction. Make sure your business concept is clear and focused and your market is well-defined. Understand the key trends in your industry, both nationally and globally, and develop responsive, disciplined management procedures.

The Four Cs

Each founder or key employee in small or new companies should complete their own copy of this worksheet. Check the level of importance to you in each area.

	Extremely Important	Somewhat Important	Somewhat Unimportant	Not Important
CONTROL				
Over own work responsibilities	☐	☐	☐	☐
Over own time, work hours, etc.	☐	☐	☐	☐
Over company decisions and directions	☐	☐	☐	☐
Over products/services	☐	☐	☐	☐
Over other employees	☐	☐	☐	☐
Over work environment	☐	☐	☐	☐
Over social/environmental impact of products/services	☐	☐	☐	☐
Over own future and business' future	☐	☐	☐	☐

Other:_____

	Extremely Important	Somewhat Important	Somewhat Unimportant	Not Important
CHALLENGE				
Long-term problem solving	☐	☐	☐	☐
Critical problem solving (putting out fires)	☐	☐	☐	☐
Handling many issues at one time	☐	☐	☐	☐
Continually dealing with new issues	☐	☐	☐	☐
Perfecting solutions, products, or services	☐	☐	☐	☐
Organizing diverse projects & keeping the group goal-focused	☐	☐	☐	☐

Other: _____

	Extremely Important	Somewhat Important	Somewhat Unimportant	Not Important
CREATIVITY				
Determining the design or look of products/packaging	☐	☐	☐	☐
Creating new products or services	☐	☐	☐	☐
Devising new business procedures/policies	☐	☐	☐	☐
Identifying new company opportunities	☐	☐	☐	☐
Creating new business materials	☐	☐	☐	☐
Devising new ways of doing "old" things	☐	☐	☐	☐

Other: _____

CASH

List approximate dollar ranges for each of the following. Measure wealth as the value of stocks or the company.

Income needed currently_____   Wealth desired in 2–5 years_____

Income desired within 12–24 months_____   Wealth desired in 6–10 years_____

Income desired in 2–5 years _____   Wealth desired in 10+ years_____

CHAPTER 2

Getting Your Plan Started

You find easy answers only by asking tough questions.

> " You must have ongoing contingency plans to allow for miscalculations, disappointments, and bad luck. It's assumed that if you're a leader, you don't make mistakes. But it's not so; if you're decisive, you'll sometimes miscalculate, and sometimes just be unlucky. You need to openly discuss the possibility of mistakes, so people are prepared and aren't crestfallen when they occur. You need to rehearse your contingency plans."
>
> *Bill Walsh*
> *Former Coach and President*
> *San Francisco 49ers*

The Business Plan Process

Once you determine that a business plan is a necessary tool for your company, you may wonder, "Where do I start?" Because a plan requires detailed information on almost every aspect of your business, including industry, market, operations, and personnel, the process can seem overwhelming.

The business plan process entails five fundamental steps:

1. Laying out your basic business concept.

2. Gathering data on the feasibility and specifics of your concept.

3. Focusing and refining the concept based on the data you compile.

4. Outlining the specifics of your business.

5. Putting your plan in compelling form.

The first step is to lay out your basic business concept. In the previous chapter, you were provided a worksheet on which to delineate the various components of your business. With an existing operation, it may be tempting to skip over this step, but if you wish to develop strategies for future success, you must first examine the assumptions underlying your current efforts.

The focus of this chapter is on steps 2 and 3: gathering and interpreting the data you need. Solid information gives you a realistic picture of what happens in businesses similar to yours, as well as a better understanding of your own company. *You can then evaluate and refocus your concept in light of your newly acquired information; a worksheet provided on pages 39–40 will help you with this evaluation.*

Once you have compiled sufficient information and reevaluated your business concept, you can begin to actually write your plan. By following the chapters of this book and completing the Plan Preparation Forms, you can shape your plan into a compelling document.

Developing a business plan is much more a business project than a writing assignment. The process itself—not just the document produced—can positively affect the success of your business. During the everyday operation of your business, you seldom have time to think through the kinds of issues you'll examine while putting together your business plan; the planning process gives you a rare opportunity to enhance your knowledge of how your company, market, and industry work.

Gathering Information

Knowledge is power. With accurate information at your fingertips, you make better business decisions as well as a more persuasive presentation of your plan when meeting with a banker, potential investor, or divisional president. Savvy investors use a business plan not merely to learn about a new business concept but as a means to judge whether an entrepreneur has the knowledge and exercises the **due diligence** necessary to run a business. So take time to do your homework. Sufficient research prevents you from placing inaccurate information in your plan—a mistake that can keep you from getting funded—and enables you to make informed decisions.

If you're new to an industry or to business management, allow yourself more time on your research efforts and start with general background information. Use the research project as an opportunity to educate yourself on the key issues of your industry, not merely as a way to find the specific details you need for your particular company.

To begin your information-gathering efforts, start by checking the resources listed later in this chapter and in the References & Resources chapters at the back of the book. First, seek general information about each of the areas you've identified in your Basic Business Concept worksheet from Chapter 1. As you progress, focus your research on more-specific issues, compiling the details necessary to make operational and financial decisions. Chapters 4 through 17 outline the data you need to complete each section of your business plan, and in some cases include suggestions of possible sources of such information.

How Much Information Is Enough?

It is relatively easy to get a great deal of information online; it is likewise easy to feel overwhelmed with so much of it. Conversely, you will also feel frustrated because some critical data is proprietary and unavailable. The difficult challenge is determining which information is important and how much information is enough to put in your plan, especially if you are seeking funding.

Don't try to be exhaustive in your research efforts; it's not necessary or possible. You are merely looking for information that will answer the key questions about your business. At the same time, your research must be thorough enough to give you, and those reading your plan, confidence that the answers are accurate and from reliable sources.

For example, if you are manufacturing dolls, you might identify your target market as girls between the ages of 4 and 10. One of the questions you need to address in your plan is, "How large is the market?" For this, you may have to consult only one source, the U.S. Census Bureau, to find a reliable answer. However, other questions that arise, such as, "What are the trends in doll-buying habits?" may require consulting three or four industry sources or undertaking your own market research to compile information you can trust.

> *A lot of entrepreneurs don't pay attention to the financial side of the house, and that's where we see a lot of them fail. They relegate finance and accounting to the back seat."*
>
> *Damon Doe*
> *Managing Partner*
> *Montage Capital*

Start Your Research by Asking Questions

Start your research by making a general statement that is the basis of your business (or a portion of your business). For example, if you are planning to open a sporting goods store in Chandler, Arizona, your statement might be: "There is a substantial need for a sporting goods store to serve the city of Chandler."

Next, make a list of questions that logically follow from and challenge that statement. Here are some questions you might then ask:

- How many sporting goods stores now serve the area?
- How profitable are the current sporting goods stores in the area?
- Are residents generally satisfied with the current sporting goods stores?
- Is there more business than current sporting goods stores can handle?
- What are the trends in the sporting goods industry nationally?
- What are the demographic trends in Chandler?
- How do Chandler demographics relate to national sporting goods trends and statistics?

As another example, your statement might be: "There is a profitable way to provide psychological counseling online." The questions following from and challenging that statement could include:

- What companies are already providing such a service?
- What is the size of the market for psychological counseling now?
- What indications are there that consumers would be willing to get counseling online?
- What portion of the existing psychological counseling market is it reasonable to expect would transfer to online counseling?
- How many consumers who do not currently get counseling could reasonably be expected to be attracted to online counseling?
- What are the key technology issues necessary to conduct such counseling, securely, online?
- What laws or regulations would affect the ability to offer such services?

After formulating your list of questions, look for answers. You will find some of your answers by searching government and trade associations' websites. Others you'll find by consulting reference material through a library or business development center or by contacting industry associations or hiring paid research services. To get some answers, you will have to conduct your own market research by talking to potential customers, meeting with other business owners, or observing foot traffic at similar or nearby establishments.

As you start the business plan process, use the Research Questions worksheet on page 21 to record the general questions you have at this point and the issues you will investigate. Look not only for specific current details but also for trends and patterns.

Research Questions

List the questions you will examine in each area of your business, using the categories below as guidelines.

Industry/Sector: _____
_____
_____
_____

Products/Services: _____
_____
_____

Target Market: _____
_____
_____
_____

Competition: _____
_____
_____
_____

Marketing and Sales Strategy: _____
_____
_____
_____

Operations/Technology: _____
_____
_____
_____

Long-Term Considerations: _____
_____
_____
_____
_____
_____
_____
_____

How much information you gather will be, to a large extent, a result of your resources, of both time and money. If you are working on a business plan for a one-person business while holding down a full-time job, you don't need to compile the same amount of information appropriate for a large corporation with a market research budget and staff.

Staying on Top of Your Material

During the course of your planning process, you will accumulate a great deal of information and many documents. Set up a way to organize the material you gather, such as your notes, ideas, and contact information, right as you begin.

Make individual files, either on your computer or in paper files, of the different topic areas corresponding to the chapters of this book. Add information to the files as you go along. Otherwise, you may find yourself unable to locate specific details you need when you are actually preparing your written document. As you gather data, write down the source and date of information; otherwise you may later find yourself with data and no way to verify or attribute it.

The planning process also enables you to meet many people who can be very helpful to you later, when you run your business. It is likely that you will interview potential customers, suppliers, competitors, and strategic partners, as well as other industry sources. Keep a file of all these contacts as you do your research, so you easily know how to reach them.

Sources of Information

If this is your first time conducting business research, you may be surprised at just how much information exists. Mountains of statistics and bookshelves of studies are available concerning virtually every endeavor and activity of American life. Without difficulty, you can find data revealing the average purchase in a fast-food restaurant, how many laptops and tablets were sold last year, and the likely number of new housing units that will be built in your community in the coming year.

You can locate most of the general information you require from government sources, business publications, and trade associations. To find more specific information relative to your particular business or industry, you may have to undertake some market research. In a limited number of cases, when you either lack the time to do the research yourself or are involved in a new industry or one in which data is mostly proprietary, you may have to utilize paid sources of information.

Sources of general information are listed in this chapter and in the References & Resources chapters at the end of the book. Sources of more particular information relating to costs, equipment, or other specific areas of your business are listed in the appropriate chapters of this book.

Keep in mind that contact information, particularly website addresses, changes frequently.

> "The first thing I did when I got serious about starting a business was delete the solitaire program on my computer. I had to get to work."
>
> *Seth Goldman*
> *Cofounder, Honest Tea*

Online

The best, easiest, and least expensive place to start your research is online.

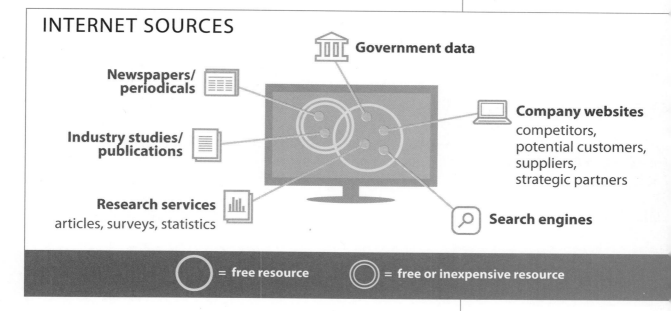

INTERNET SOURCES

- Government data
- Newspapers/periodicals
- Company websites
  competitors,
  potential customers,
  suppliers,
  strategic partners
- Industry studies/publications
- Research services
  articles, surveys, statistics
- Search engines

◯ = free resource   ◎ = free or inexpensive resource

Government Sources and Statistics

As a taxpayer, you've already paid for your government to collect vast quantities of information, so you'll be able to get more data free from government sources than from private research services or other sources. This is true not only for the United States as a whole, but for most state and some local governments, and many other countries as well.

Most of the information collected by the U.S. Government, as well as most states, is available online. As you begin your research, you may find it helpful to know your NAICS code. This may make finding specific information relating to your type of business easier.

NAICS CODES

www.census.gov/eos/www/naics

NAICS is the abbreviation for North American Industry Classification System. It replaces the older Standard Industrial Classification (SIC) codes. Each industry—and subsector of each industry—is assigned a specific NAICS number.

U.S. CENSUS BUREAU

www.census.gov

The U.S. Census Bureau, part of the Department of Commerce, is the government agency with the primary responsibility for collecting and disseminating in-depth data on all aspects of American life. You may be aware that the Census gathers data on the American people: population, income, housing patterns, levels of education, and so on. But it also accumulates an enormous amount of data on the economic activity of the United

U.S. Research Sources

U.S. Government	U.S. Census Bureau	Small Business Administration
	U.S. Department of Commerce	Securities and Exchange
	U.S. Department of Labor	Commission (Edgar database)
	Internal Revenue Service	
	Other government departments appropriate to your industry	
State Government	Sales Tax	Planning Departments
	Franchise Business Tax	New Business Licenses
	City and County Governments	
Quasi-Governmental Sources	Regional Planning Associations	
Industry & General Business	Trade Associations	Corporate Annual Reports
	Trade Publications	ThomasNet
Community Services	Chambers of Commerce	Merchants Associations
	Banks	Real Estate Agents
	Universities	Yellow Pages
	Newspaper and Online Libraries	
	Entrepreneurs Associations	
Computer Databases	Business and Trade Information	
	Individualized Research Services	
Market Research Sources	Customers	
	Suppliers	
	Distributors	
	Independent Sales Representatives	
	Managers of Related Businesses	
	Loan Officers/Factors/Venture Capitalists	
	Competitors	
Paid Services	Industry-Related Research Firms	
	Survey/Polling Firms	
	Market Research Consultants	
Internal Data	For existing businesses	

Canadian Research Sources

Statistics Canada
Canada Business
Canadian Industry Statistics (CIS)

International Research Sources

The World Bank
International Data Base (IDB)

States, right down to the number, type, and average sales of businesses, by particular business type, zip code by zip code.

Because Census Bureau data covers such a huge number of people and businesses, and because it is so detailed, such data is considered among the most reliable information you can use. Those reading your business plan (for example, potential investors or bankers) will generally consider Census Bureau data reliable and conservative.

The Census Bureau has done an excellent job of making that vast resource of data easily available online. And remember—all that data is *free*.

ECONOMIC CENSUS

www.census.gov (click on "Economic Census")

If you are looking for information about specific industries or types of businesses, from the Census Bureau's homepage, click on the "Data" tab and look for "Economic Census." From there, choose the link to the latest results (left-hand column) or the years that you are interested in. A full Economic Census of the United States is conducted every five years; the last one covered the year 2012.

By exploring the tables, you can find data on the number of businesses by industries in any zip code, county, metropolitan area, or state in the U.S. You'll also be able to find a vast amount of other information, such as distribution of business expenses and **receipts** by industry, data on women-owned and minority-owned businesses, and product shipments. Be certain to search using the options in the left-hand column for much greater detail in any report you select.

COUNTY BUSINESS PATTERNS

www.census.gov/econ/cbp

The Census Bureau produces annual reports on the number of business establishments—detailed by industry, business size, and payroll—throughout the United States and Puerto Rico. This data is available on the national, state, county, metropolitan area, and zip code levels. County Business Patterns are very useful in evaluating how well-served or underserved specific geographic areas are by particular business types.

Other ways to access Census data online include:

CENSTATS

http://censtats.census.gov

This site provides access to databases including Census Tract Street Locator, County Business Patterns, Zip Business Patterns, International Trade Data, and more.

AMERICAN FACTFINDER

http://factfinder2.census.gov

This has an easy-to-use pull-down interactive menu that allows you to find a range of demographic information about the American people—down to city or census tract level.

QUICKFACTS

http://quickfacts.census.gov

Quickfacts offers easy access to frequently requested demographic data at national, state, or local level.

CURRENT INDUSTRIAL REPORTS

www.census.gov/manufacturing/cir

The U.S. Census Bureau publishes more than 100 *Current Industrial Reports,* providing extremely detailed data on tens of thousands of manufactured products—everything from baby clothes to consumer electronics to airplane engines. This information accounts for more than 40% of all goods manufactured in the United States. CIRs provide information on production, shipping, inventories, consumption, and the number of firms manufacturing each product. The data is reported on a monthly, quarterly, and annual basis.

For other websites with federal U.S. statistics, visit these useful sites:

FEDSTATS—GATEWAY TO U.S. GOVERNMENT FEDERAL STATISTICS

www.fedstats.gov

This main gateway to national statistics has links to statistics compiled by over 100 government agencies as well as government statistical agencies. It is a very good entry-point to all U.S. statistics.

EDGAR DATABASE—U.S. SECURITIES AND EXCHANGE COMMISSION

www.sec.gov/edgar.shtml

You can find annual, quarterly, and other financial reports required from publicly traded companies by selecting "Search for Company Filings." You need the name of the corporation, not the brand name of the product, to find reports. For information about *USA Today,* for instance, enter the parent company, "Gannett Company."

INTERNAL REVENUE SERVICE

www.irs.gov/uac/Tax-Stats-2

Tax statistics are generally harder to maneuver than Census Bureau statistics. However, if you are seeking a specific income or tax-related statistic, this might be a source of that data.

Individual U.S. State and Local Sources

Each U.S. state, as well as many individual counties and cities, collects and maintains information that can be useful to you in planning your business. For instance, state sales tax receipts may be a good indicator of the health of your local economy, and local planning department information regarding building permits can indicate where population growth is occurring.

Use a search engine to locate your state and local government websites.

STATE DATA CENTERS

www.census.gov/sdc

The U.S. Census Department maintains links to individual U.S. states data/statistics programs. This will help you locate state-wide economic statistics.

BUSINESS.GOV

http://business.usa.gov

Operated by the U.S. Small Business Administration, this is a portal to government—federal and state-by-state—legal and regulatory information. Keep in mind this is a site for legal information, not statistics.

Statistics for Canada

The Canadian government not only collects extensive data about Canadian businesses and population, but also it provides a number of sites to make accessing and using that information relatively easy.

STATISTICS CANADA

www.statcan.gc.ca

This is the primary entry point for statistical information about all aspects of Canada, including demographics and economic conditions.

CANADA BUSINESS

www.canadabusiness.ca/eng

This site provides a single access point to all the Canadian government services and information to start, run, and grow a business in Canada.

CANADIAN INDUSTRY STATISTICS (CIS)

www.ic.gc.ca

This well-organized site makes readily available the resources and data of the Canadian government department Industry Canada.

BMO CAPITAL MARKETS

www.bmonesbittburns.com/economics

BMO Capital Markets is a good nongovernmental source of Canadian and North American economic statistics, including economic outlooks.

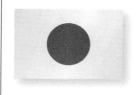

International Statistics

Most developed, and many developing, countries have substantial statistical information available online, and international economic organizations also make data available.

U.S. CENSUS BUREAU LIST OF FOREIGN STATISTICAL WEBSITES

www.census.gov/aboutus/stat_int.html

The U.S. Census Bureau maintains links to locate statistical sites of countries throughout the world.

THE WORLD BANK

www.worldbank.org

This international organization compiles data worldwide. It offers free data by topic or country and links to online databases, as well as publishing its own economic reports.

EXPORT.GOV

www.export.gov

A rich resource of information, designed primarily for American companies engaged in international trade, this site provides substantial, in-depth information about markets and industries throughout the world.

STATE DEPARTMENT COUNTRY BACKGROUND NOTES

www.state.gov/r/pa/ei/bgn

The U.S. State Department prepares background papers on virtually every country in the world. These background papers include statistics and overviews of each country's economy as well as useful links.

INTERNATIONAL DATA BASE

www.census.gov/population/international

The International Data Base (IDB) contains statistical tables of demographic and socioeconomic data for over 200 countries and areas of the world.

Nongovernmental Free Online Resources

In addition to the sources listed below, be certain to use search engines such as Google (www.google.com) and Bing (www.bing.com), and online directories, such as Yahoo (www.yahoo.com), to find information from many sources about the topics you're interested in. Other good sources are listed below.

LOUISIANA STATE UNIVERSITY

www.lib.lsu.edu/gov

LSU maintains a very well-organized index to research and data available on the Web, including government sources and subject-specific search engines.

NATIONAL ASSOCIATION OF MANUFACTURERS

www.nam.org

This large industry association provides substantial information to manufacturing companies, as well as collecting data about manufacturing. Click on the "Statistics & Data" link to find data as well as economic analysis and reports on manufacturing topics.

SOCIETY FOR HUMAN RESOURCE MANAGEMENT

www.shrm.org

The leading organization for human resource executives, this site has some good information on personnel issues available to nonmembers (and a lot more information for members). However, it also has some excellent links to general business resources online.

THOMASNET

www.thomasnet.com

This site is the ultimate resource for locating suppliers and vendors. Not only does it list suppliers by product category, but also it names many suppliers that have detailed product/part/equipment lists, some with prices.

You can also find information about industries, trends, and companies from publications, which may charge a fee for archived stories. A few to try:

WALL STREET JOURNAL

www.wsj.com

BUSINESS WEEK

www.businessweek.com

RED HERRING

www.redherring.com

THE ECONOMIST

www.economist.com

FORBES

www.forbes.com

Fee-based Online Resources

Some of the websites listed below offer certain information free, but for more in-depth information, you will have to pay a fee.

LEXISNEXIS

www.lexisnexis.com

This service provides a wealth of information and should be the first place you start when you are ready to pay for information. It is indispensable to researchers and includes comprehensive company, country, financial, demographic, market research, and industry reports. LexisNexis offers access to hundreds of databases, thousands of worldwide publications, public and legislative records, data on companies and executives, and more. Payment for access to the LexisNexis database is available on a per article, per day, per week, or subscription basis.

HOOVER'S ONLINE

www.hoovers.com

From Hoover's, you can get free, basic information on individual companies, particularly public companies, as well as more detailed information for a fee. Look at Hoover's Publications for more information relating to your industry. Hoover's also has links to other sources of specific information on companies, mostly fee-based.

DUN & BRADSTREET

www.dnb.com

D&B maintains credit reports and financial information on tens of thousands of companies. You can purchase a report about a competitor, customer, or supplier. You can also buy targeted marketing lists and industry reports.

For statistics and trends in technology-related industries, the following websites are sources for fee-based research reports and data:

FORRESTER

www.forrester.com

> "You need to have numbers. If I ask you a question, you better know the answer. If you say you're going to sell shoes to people with very wide feet, you better know the number of people with very wide feet."
>
> *Andrew Anker*
> *Venture Capitalist*

GARTNER

www.gartner.com

Offline Research Resources

While you will most likely start your research online, you may find that some data is not available or is too expensive to access. A number of "real-world" sources may provide additional information.

Libraries

Many public and university libraries subscribe to an array of paid online research services and/or purchase expensive statistical research publications. Visiting a library may give you access to this fee-based data for free. Choose the largest library convenient to you; the larger the library, the more likely it is to subscribe to these services or purchase these publications. You might want to make an appointment with a reference librarian at a nearby university. Many universities gather their own statistical data about regional economic performance.

Ask the librarian if they have access to any of the paid online services listed above, such as LexisNexis.

Other services to ask about include:

PREDICASTS F&S FORECASTS AND PREDICASTS PROMT (PREDICASTS OVERVIEW OF MARKETS AND TECHNOLOGY)

Predicasts PROMT provides summaries and full text of articles from trade and industry publications. It is especially useful for finding detailed information on specific companies, industries, products, and brands.

Predicasts F&S Forecasts provides an index to articles, full text of brief articles, and excerpts from nearly 1,000 journals, newspapers, research studies, and so on, covering all manufacturing and service industries and a wide range of business-related subjects.

INFOTRAC

Many libraries subscribe to an online database service called InfoTrac (published by Gale Group), which allows you to search for magazine and journal articles, as well as have access to substantial **proprietary information**.

STANDARD & POOR'S INDUSTRY SURVEYS

While designed for investors, this can be a source of insight about your overall industry and major competitors. It provides overviews of industry trends and reports revenues of more than 1,000 companies.

WILSON BUSINESS FULL-TEXT

This provides full-text access to articles from more than 350 business publications, and in-depth abstracting of articles from more than 600 publications. If your library has access to the Wilson Business database, it may be a less expensive way to get archived articles from publications such as *The Wall Street Journal* than from other sources.

GALE'S BUSINESS INSIGHTS: ESSENTIALS

www.cengagesites.com/Literature/782/gale-business-insights-global-essentials/

SBDCs and Other Support Organizations

Small Business Development Centers (SBDCs) are located in many American communities and are an excellent source of information and assistance. In addition to maintaining a library of reference materials, SBDC staff can usually direct you to sources appropriate to your planning process. They may be able to help you in identifying local resources for your particular business, and they often conduct workshops on business topics and skills. Many SBDC centers are located at community colleges or universities.

SBDC DIRECTORY ONLINE

www.sba.gov/about-sba/sba_locations

This is where you can find an online listing of all SBDC centers.

Many communities have other private or quasi-governmental entrepreneurial support organizations and centers. These may be run by minority enterprise organizations, women's entrepreneur groups, regional industry associations, or your local Chamber of Commerce. To find such organizations, check the business section of your local newspaper, inquire at the SBDC or your local economic development office, or ask other entrepreneurs.

CHAMBER OF COMMERCE LOCATOR

www.uschamber.com/chamber/directory

Trade and Industry Associations

There are over 35,000 trade and industry associations in the United States alone. These associations are frequently the best source of current data relating to specific industries. Many of them conduct surveys, track market trends of their industry, and publish research papers relating to industry topics. There is almost certainly at least one association serving your company's industry.

Industry trade shows (conventions, exhibits, and the like) are an outstanding source of information and market research. In a brief time, in one location, you can identify potential competitors, customers, and suppliers. Seminars held concurrently with trade shows can help you learn about the key trends and issues in your industry. Most industries have at least one major trade show per year. Contact your industry association(s) to find out when shows are being held, and how you can get accredited to attend. Some industries hold regional or local trade shows as well as national conventions.

To find your industry association, in addition to using an online search engine (www.google.com) and directory (www.yahoo.com), you might also want to check:

PLANNINGSHOP

www.PlanningShop.com/associations

PlanningShop, publisher of this book, maintains a list of major trade associations on its company website.

THE CENTER FOR ASSOCIATION LEADERSHIP

www.asaecenter.org

This national association of directors of trade, industry, and professional associations also provides a "Gateway" on its site that can help you locate associations related to your business.

GALE'S ENCYCLOPEDIA OF ASSOCIATIONS

This publication lists over 135,000 membership organizations worldwide. You may be able to find it at a good library.

INTERNET PUBLIC LIBRARY—ASSOCIATIONS ON THE NET

www.ipl.org

The Internet Public Library is a valuable resource maintained by the University of Michigan. In addition to this directory of associations, you can find a variety of other useful business information by searching elsewhere on this well-organized site.

TSNN.COM

www.tsnn.com

This database lists more than 25,000 trade shows, exhibitions, events, and conferences worldwide.

Paid Research Services

In some cases, you will want to use a private research firm as a source of data. Private firms gather information (sometimes from confidential sources), provide more detailed competitor-sales estimates, and undertake market research projects. These firms are all relatively expensive, so you should use them only when your time is very limited, when undertaking an unusually large or expensive enterprise, or when the information you are seeking is hard to find, is proprietary, or has never been compiled.

Check with your industry trade associations for research firms that are particularly knowledgeable about your industry. Each firm provides different services, and costs vary dramatically. Sometimes these firms have reports or surveys they prepared for private corporate clients that, after a few months, they are able to sell to the general public. The reports may be a good source of information and a relative bargain.

Historical Performance of Your Company

If yours is an ongoing business (not newly established), you also need to gather historical data about your own company. In particular, you should examine your past internal financial records. Here is some of the financial information you may need to locate:

■ Past sales records, broken down by product line, time period, store, region, or salesperson;

- Past trends in costs of sales;
- Overhead expense patterns;
- **Profit margins** on product lines; or
- Variations from budget projections.

If you cannot gather this information easily, change your reporting system so that in the future you will be able to have the data you need for adequate planning.

If you have created business plans or set goals or objectives in the past, you should also track how well your business has performed in terms of meeting your objectives. Have you consistently underperformed or exceeded your goals? Have you reached key **milestones** within the time period originally projected? *A Milestones Achieved to Date worksheet is included in Chapter 15.*

How to Conduct Your Own Market Research

Some of the most important information you need will not be available from any published source, particularly information that is quite specific to your market or new product. To obtain this data, you will have to undertake your own research. For most businesses, even very large ones, this research needn't be expensive or prohibitively time consuming.

Personal Observation Is an Easy Method

One fundamental way to gather information — and also one of the easiest — is through personal observation. Watching what goes on in other businesses or the way people shop gives you insight into factors affecting your own business. You can observe auto and foot-traffic patterns near a selected location, how customers behave when shopping in businesses similar to yours or for similar products, and how competitors market or merchandise their products or services. Personal observation is a vital tool in your planning process and applicable for almost every business, large or small.

Informational Interviews Can Be Structured or Informal

The second principal method of market research is informational interviewing. Since the amount of information you can garner from personal observation is limited and colored by your own perceptions, you should talk with as many people as possible who can provide you with information relating to your business.

Some of these interviews may be highly structured. For instance, you might make personal appointments with those you want to interview and have a prepared list of questions. In other cases, such as when you go into a competitor's store and chat with a salesperson, your questions will appear to be more casual.

> " We taste-tested our product in all the places we wanted to sell it eventually: hotels, restaurants. We wanted to see what our potential consumers wanted and spent an enormous amount of time talking to them. We tested at supermarkets, parties, polo matches. We watched how people reacted physically and listened to what they told us. We changed the product a dozen times in the first couple years in response to consumers. You have to be willing to make radical changes."
>
> *Larry Leigon*
> *Founder, Ariel Vineyards*

Surveys Help You Spot Trends

If you decide you need information from a large number of people, you may want to conduct a survey, whether by phone, by mail, online, or in person. Surveys are a good way to spot trends and are particularly useful in assessing customer needs and desires. You can conduct in-person surveys by going to an appropriate location and interviewing subjects on the spot. Develop a questionnaire of the most important concerns to ascertain from interview sources. Don't make your survey too long or people will refuse to participate. Mail surveys have a notoriously low response rate, so if you conduct one, it is a good idea to include some kind of incentive, such as discounts or free gifts, to encourage people to respond.

Focus Groups Offer Candid Opinions

A popular form of market research is the focus group, a small group of people brought together to discuss a product, business concern, or service in great detail. For example, a few joggers might be brought in to examine and evaluate a new pair of running shoes. Focus group participants are often paid a small fee.

Market research firms conduct focus groups for businesses, bringing together the participants and leading the group discussion in a room with a one-way mirror, so that the businessperson involved can observe and listen in. However, if you do not have the funds to hire a market research firm, you might still consider assembling a focus group of your own, perhaps a gathering of potential consumers. Try, however, to find focus group participants you do not know personally.

Accessible Sources for Market Research

Consider the sources in the graphic below for your market research.

MARKET RESEARCH SOURCES

 Potential customers, both end-users and buyers or distributors, if you are in a wholesale business

 Banks, real estate agents, universities, local or regional Chambers of Commerce, merchant groups, or others observing the local economy

 Potential suppliers

 Your competitors

 Businesses related geographically or by product line

 Entrepreneurs' groups

 Similar businesses serving different cities and others in your industry

Suppliers, **distributors**, and independent sales representatives can give you a great deal of information about industry trends and what your competition is doing without violating confidentiality. Because they are in touch with the market, they know which products and services are in demand.

Learn from Other Businesses

Those in related businesses often know about conditions affecting your company. For example, if you are considering locating a retail store in a mall, managers of other mall shops can give you a realistic idea of foot traffic, slow periods, and shopper demographics.

Try talking to people who are in the same industry or business as yours in a different city; they are an excellent source of information. If you are starting an on-site computer repair company in San Antonio, Texas, for instance, you might arrange to meet with a similar company in Houston. Since you will not be competing with Houston businesses, they may be very helpful in providing information not only on marketing but on operations and financial considerations.

In addition, large banks and universities frequently maintain information about the health of the local economy and particular industries. They are a good and reasonably reliable source of future-growth forecasts. Don't overlook real estate agents. They often have more up-to-date information about neighborhood trends than any other source.

Talk to Your Competition

Sometimes you can even talk to your competitors. In many industries and professions, and in instances where there is more work than the market can handle, your competitors may be willing to talk with you directly. In other cases, you need to use less-direct ways of approaching them.

However, be careful not to use illegal or unethical methods of dealing with your competitors; not only is it wrong, but you'd be surprised at how such activities can come back to haunt you. Today's competitor may one day be a source of referrals, a strategic partner, or possibly, in a merger or acquisition, the owner of your company.

Getting Help

Many people realistically feel they need assistance in researching, developing, and then preparing their business plan. You may also. Fortunately, there are many places to turn.

You may want to begin with one of the many sources of assistance available free or at little charge. In many communities, you might want to start with a Small Business Development Center (see above). There is also assistance offered by the Service Corps of Retired Executives (SCORE), minority or women's economic development centers, or local economic development agencies. Many universities offer extension or evening courses to assist entrepreneurs.

> " If you're truly creating something new, it doesn't show up in trends."
>
> *Larry Leigon*
> *Founder, Ariel Vineyards*

One of the best sources of assistance may be local organizations of entrepreneurs or industry support groups. Many entrepreneurs' groups hold business planning seminars or offer "Special Interest Groups" (SIGs) in particular industry or topic areas.

You may also want to turn to a paid consultant to offer more personal, in-depth assistance. Consultants are available in business planning, graphic design and desktop publishing, research services, writing and editing, accounting, and many other fields.

Evaluating the Data You've Collected

Once you start compiling information, you might feel you have more facts than you know what to do with. Here are a few tips to keep in mind about the information you gather:

- Use the most recent data you can find; printed information is often at least two years old and a lot can change in two years.

- Translate data into units rather than dollars whenever possible. Due to inflation, dollars may not give you consistent information from year to year.

- Give the most reliable source the most credence. Generally, the larger the group sampled for information, or the more respected the organization that conducted the research, the more trustworthy the numbers you collect.

- Integrate data from one source with another in order to draw conclusions. However, make sure the information is from the same time period and is consistent; small variations can lead to vastly inaccurate results.

- Use the most conservative figures. Naturally, you'll be tempted to paint the brightest picture possible, but such information often leads to bad business decisions.

A Quick Feasibility Analysis

Once you complete your initial research efforts, but before you lay out the specific components of your plan, it's time to reexamine your business concept to see if it appears to be feasible. Of course, at this early stage, you'll not have all the required information to know whether you can completely execute on your business plan or even how much money you can reasonably expect to make. You will not, for instance, at this point have done a financial analysis, so you won't know what your costs and profits are likely to be. That's why you're going to develop a complete business plan.

Nevertheless, a feasibility analysis is a chance to begin to flesh out your initial business idea, see which components are already in place to make it possible, see which are not, and do a quick assessment of whether you can pull this off successfully. Before you develop the specific components of your business plan in depth, take time to see if it seems feasible—and identify the likely roadblocks you're going to face.

Doing a feasibility analysis is a chance to open your eyes, ask yourself some very tough questions, then check to see whether your idea, as originally conceived, needs to be modified, refocused, or changed dramatically. (Or perhaps even scrapped altogether. It's better to drop an unworkable idea early on and move on to pursuing one of your other, potentially more successful, ideas.)

How does a feasibility analysis differ from a business plan? Think of developing and planning your business as entailing a few components:

1. **Vision.** Identifying and articulating your business idea and concept.

2. **Feasibility analysis.** Challenging your concept, identifying which components are in place to make it realistic to easily execute, recognizing the biggest obstacles you're likely to face.

3. **Business plan.** Clarifying your business strategy in detail, describing how you're going to execute on your vision, developing the major components of your business, projecting detailed financial forecasts.

4. **Marketing/operations/technology plans.** Describing in detail and developing budgets for the internal aspects of how you'll run your business day-to-day.

How involved your feasibility analysis is will depend a bit on how unusual your idea is or how hard your market is to reach. The more novel your concept, or the more unproven your marketing and sales channel, the more investigation you'll need to do to see whether the necessary building blocks are available to you or whether you'll have to create those too.

Let's say you've got an idea for a new product—tasty meals that come in packages that are self-heating—and you plan to sell them to airline passengers so they can bring hot meals to eat while they fly. There are a lot of things you can look at fairly quickly to test the feasibility of this idea. Does such packaging already exist and is it proven? Would airlines allow such packages on planes? How expensive is it for you to get space in airports to sell these? That's on top of the bigger question: Would flyers even want this?

But if you're doing something more proven—let's say you're opening an Italian restaurant on a street that's already a major destination for diners—your feasibility analysis will be much less involved. Is there space available in that neighborhood? Are the rents low enough to operate profitably? Do you personally have the restaurant experience necessary to make this a success? Can you find a great Italian cook?

With every feasibility analysis, start by evaluating yourself. Are you really suited to run a business? Do you yourself have the knowledge and skills to pull this off? Can you assemble a winning team?

A feasibility analysis is only a beginning to your business plan—and to your questioning and exploring. You should continually be challenging your assumptions. It's the entrepreneurs most willing to ask themselves the tough questions who are most likely to succeed.

The Feasibility Analysis worksheet on pages 39–40 helps you evaluate your basic business concept. Be sure to complete it only after finishing your initial research.

> " I happen to gravitate to things that are disruptive and transformational. I love the scope of new ideas and think how to make them happen. Lots of people see a problem and want to solve it. I gravitate to the big, disruptive idea."
>
> *Kay Koplovitz*
> *Chair, Kate Spade*

Business Model Canvas

One tactic some have used to sketch out a basic overview of a business concept is called the **business model canvas**. On one page, in a visual format, a novice entrepreneur who has come up with an idea for a product or technology can begin to think about some of the considerations necessary to turn an idea into an actual business.

A business model canvas can be particularly useful for someone who has a number of ideas and wants to outline those various ideas to see which seem most viable before beginning an actual plan for their business. Tools such as these, however, can easily lead the aspiring entrepreneur to treat assumptions as facts. They are no substitute for doing the real business planning—researching data, investigating markets and industries, developing detailed financial forecasting, challenging assumptions—necessary to launch a successful company. Users with significant business experience or knowledge may find a business model canvas more useful than novice entrepreneurs.

Chapter Summary

A thorough business planning process gives you ammunition to use when looking for money to fund your business and an outstanding opportunity to better understand your business concept, market, and industry, thus increasing your chance of success. Keep in mind that this process is a business activity, *not* a writing assignment. The process itself—not just the document you produce—can positively affect the success of your business.

After you complete your research, but before you develop your business plan in depth, take the time to do a feasibility study on your concept. This will save you time and give you a better idea of what kind of roadblocks you may face.

Feasibility Analysis Worksheet

Complete this worksheet after conducting your initial research to identify which areas of your business are the strongest and which are likely to present major challenges. Rate each of the following areas on a scale of 1–10 — with 1 being "not at all" to 10 being "completely." The higher your scores in each area, the less risk you are likely to face. Those areas with very low scores are likely to make it more difficult for your business to be developed and, ultimately, successful. You will need to spend more time on those areas as you develop your complete business plan.

Your Industry

_____ Is economically healthy.

_____ Is new, expanding, or growing signficantly.

_____ Is characterized by a large number of competitors rather than a few entrenched, large companies.

_____ Is able to withstand downturns in economic cycles.

_____ Has positive forecasts for significant growth in the immediate future.

Your Product or Service

_____ Is proven and not unique.

_____ Is already in demand.

_____ If unique, there are significant barriers to keep others from competing with you.

_____ Is currently developed or can be developed in the near future.

_____ Has a clear source of suppliers for the necessary materials or inventory.

_____ Can be produced at a cost significantly lower than the future sales price.

_____ Is not burdensome — in terms of cost or time — for new customers to convert to.

_____ Is consumable — meaning customers will use your product or service repeatedly.

Your Market

_____ Is clearly identifiable.

_____ Is large enough to be able to support your business.

_____ Is small enough to be able to be reached affordably for marketing purposes.

_____ Has shown it is already interested in your product or service.

_____ Is growing.

_____ Has forecasts for significant growth in the immediate future.

_____ Has existing sales channels to sell to your customers.

Your Competition

_____ Exists.

_____ Is clearly identifiable.

_____ Has market share that is widely distributed and is not dominated by a few major companies.

_____ Does not have deep pockets to come after you.

Feasibility Analysis Worksheet (continued)

Your Operations

_____ Does not entail significant initial capital investment.

_____ Does not require the purchase of substantial, expensive inventories.

_____ Does not require new or unproven technologies.

_____ Is not reliant on one or two suppliers or distributors.

_____ Does not entail unusual production or operational challenges.

_____ Has a ready source of skilled labor.

_____ Does not require expensive insurance or entail significant liability.

Your Leadership Abilities

_____ You have started or run a company previously.

_____ You have had training in entrepreneurship and/or business management.

_____ You have previous experience in this industry.

_____ You are open to suggestions and guidance from others.

_____ You are able to be flexible and change course if the situation demands.

_____ You have prior experience leading a team.

_____ Others naturally find you to be a leader.

_____ You have the personal capability to develop your product or service.

_____ You have the personal capability and willingness to go out and make sales.

_____ You have a good credit history.

Your Management Team

_____ You have identified and/or secured others with the capability to develop your product or service.

_____ You have identified and/or secured others who can make sales.

_____ You have clearly identified/secured others to be part of your team.

_____ Members of your team have previous industry experience.

Financial/Business Model

_____ You will be able to finance all start-up costs and become profitable without any outside funding.

_____ There exist funding sources (angel investors, venture capitalists) who actively invest in your industry.

_____ The business does not require high start-up costs.

_____ The business does not require high annual operating costs.

_____ You will be able to be profitable within the first 12 months.

_____ You are able to forecast continued, significant growth for at least 36 months.

_____ A clear, proven business model already exists on how you'll charge customers for your product or service.

CHAPTER 3

Making Your Plan Compelling

People don't read.

Five Crucial Minutes

Time is valuable for businesspeople. Rarely can they give any one matter the attention it deserves. This is especially true of bankers, **venture capitalists**, and other investors who are inundated with business plans and proposals; a typical venture capitalist can expect to see more than 1,000 business plans a year.

Although you may spend five months preparing your plan, the cold, hard fact is that an investor or lender can dismiss it in less than five minutes. If you don't make a positive impression in those critical first five minutes, your plan will be rejected. Only if it passes that first cursory look will your plan be examined in greater detail.

The most important aspects of your plan must jump out at even the most casual reader. Even if your plan is intended for internal company use only, it will be more effective if it is presented in a compelling, vivid form. Highlighting specific facts, goals, and conclusions makes your plan easier to review, more effective as a working document, and more likely to make a positive impact.

As you start your business plan process, keep in mind the kind of information, statistics, and graphics your readers expect to see and that will enable your plan to make a greater impact. Capture charts and graphs that you turn up in your research. When it comes time to put your plan into final form, you will then have this information handy.

How Your Business Plan Is Evaluated

When evaluating a business plan, experienced business plan readers generally spend the first five minutes reviewing it in this order: first, the Executive Summary; second, the Financials; third, the Management section; and next, the **Exit Plan** and/or Terms of the Deal, if applicable.

The Most-Asked Questions

Funding sources primarily look for answers to these questions concerned with the heart of the plan:

- Is the business idea solid?

- Is there a sufficient market for the product or service?

- Are the financial projections healthy, realistic, and in line with the investor's or lender's funding patterns?

- Is the key management described in the plan experienced and capable?
- Does the plan clearly describe how the investors or lenders will get their money back?

Within the first five minutes of reading your business plan, readers *must* perceive that the answers to all these questions are favorable.

Increasing the Reader's Interest

Three sections—the Executive Summary, the Financials, and the Management description—must spark enough interest and inspire sufficient confidence to make the reader decide it is worthwhile to spend additional time reading other sections of your plan. You may have done a bang-up job of describing how your company will operate, but it is unlikely the Operations section will even be read if your Executive Summary and Financials fail to entice the reader.

Some venture capitalists and investors have specific areas of interest, or are known for giving certain aspects of a plan more weight than others. If you know this information, highlight those areas that are consistent with the particular investor's funding patterns when sending out your plan; do this in the Executive Summary and in your cover letter, too.

For instance, if you know a venture capital firm is especially interested in new technology, emphasize any patents you have secured and the aspects of your company that represent ground-breaking technological developments. Or, if a member of your management team (or of the Board of Directors) is known and respected by a particular investor, you may want to discuss management near the beginning of your Executive Summary.

You can tailor the order of the Executive Summary, even the entire plan, for individual recipients. More information about how to research your intended funding sources and how to prepare your plan to be sent out is discussed in Chapters 18 and 19.

Getting Your Facts Right

The worst mistake you can make in a business plan *is* to make a mistake. If the reader of your plan knows a statement you have made is not true, you have lost credibility, even if you were just mistaken, not trying to mislead. Make certain your facts are correct.

Your facts must not only be correct, but must also be attributable to a reputable source. As you do your research and prepare your plan, keep track of the sources of your information. You may want to indicate the source of your data in your plan, but even if you do not include the source in your written plan, you need to be able to quickly tell a reader or potential funder where you found your information.

> " If I've learned anything, it's that you have to look where your idea has organic traction — where it really gets people excited."
>
> *Premal Shah*
> *President, Kiva*

> " As an entrepreneur, you've got to have more skepticism than I will have. You've got to question the numbers. Someone is going to question those numbers; if you haven't you're going to look foolish."
>
> *Andrew Anker*
> *Venture Capitalist*

Success key terms

Exit Plan
The strategy for leaving an investment and realizing the profits of such investment.

Venture Capitalist
Individual or firm that invests money in new enterprises; typically this is money invested in the venture capital firm by others, particularly institutional investors.

Length of the Plan

How long should the perfect business plan be? No magic number exists, but below are some guidelines.

IDEAL LENGTH

15–35 pages (not including financials or appendices)

<10
seems unsubstantial

20
sufficient for most businesses

30+
only for complicated business/product

APPENDICES:
< or = to length of plan

TRAVEL-FRIENDLY:

Plan needs to fit into a briefcase — so investors can read it on a trip

Break any of these rules if your business requires something different

> "I don't like a plan that's too long. To avoid that, put detailed plans in the appendices so that people can refer to them only if they want to. A well-written plan should be no more than 25 pages, 100 pages total or less with appendices. If an investor is interested, they'll ask for more details."
>
> **Eugene Kleiner**
> *Venture Capitalist*

These guidelines apply to most business plans. But if you are confident that your business requires a different configuration, go ahead!

What Period Should Your Plan Cover?

Most plans should project three to five years into the future, or until you have reached your anticipated exit strategy, whichever is earlier. However, you need only include monthly financials for the first year or two, depending on development time. For the second and third years, quarterly financials are usually adequate; annual projections suffice for the fourth and fifth years.

Similar time guidelines apply to how much detail you should include when describing your business operations. Quite thorough information should be provided for the first year or two; for subsequent years, a more general Operations description is acceptable.

Plans for existing businesses and in-house corporate use should include historical performance information for the past five years, or the duration of your business, if less than five years. If your business is longstanding, you may want to examine trends over the life of the business, or the last 10 years; this gives you insight into cyclical patterns and helps you anticipate events that are likely to recur.

Use Language to Convey Success

The language you use in your plan can give the impression you are thoughtful, knowledgeable, and prudent, or, conversely, it can make you seem naive and inexperienced. Your fundamental goal is to convey realistic optimism and businesslike enthusiasm about your prospects.

Use a straightforward, even understated, tone. Let the information you convey, rather than your language, inescapably lead to the conclusion that your business will succeed. Avoid formal, stilted language. Instead be natural, as if you were speaking to the reader in person; however, avoid slang and don't be chatty. Always be professional.

Listed below are some other pointers to keep in mind when writing your business plan.

Be Careful with Superlatives

Readers are naturally skeptical of overreaching self-promotion. Avoid using words such as "best," "terrific," "wonderful," or even "unmatched." They reduce credibility. Rather, use factual descriptions and specific information to make positive impressions.

Instead of saying, "Our widget will be the best on the market, clearly superior to all others," say, "Our widget will not only handle all the functions of existing widgets, but will also add features x, y, and z, and sell for $3 less than our closest competitor's widget. No competitor of ours offers these features at any price."

When trying to get additional financing for your restaurant, don't tell the reader that the food and atmosphere are "terrific." Instead provide specific information that proves you are doing something right: "Due to the restaurant's popularity, there is an average 45-minute wait for a table on Friday and Saturday nights, and a wait of 15 to 30 minutes on other evenings."

The only exception to this rule is when you use superlatives as part of your goal in a Statement of Mission. Then it is appropriate to state, "We intend to make a dog food unmatched in quality by any national brand." Even then, however, it is important to include the specifics of what you mean by such a goal.

Use Positive Comments from Third-Party Sources

Everyone expects you to think your product or service is outstanding; thus, your own glowing comments about your company are meaningless in your plan. Instead, as you do your research, look for statements by outside sources to give readers confidence in your business.

For instance, a reader of your plan is likely to tune out when encountering a comment such as: "Adeena's fashions are equal to those by top designers," or "Our restaurant serves the best food in the city." However, the same comment, when made by an authority, becomes quite powerful: "*Women's Wear Daily* states that Adeena's fashions are equal to those of the top designers," or "The newspaper's annual survey rated our restaurant among the top 10 in its price category."

You don't even have to quote a well-known authority; anyone with credible, related experience will do, as this example shows: "The breeder of the winner of last year's Tri-County Dog Show tested our dog food and concluded, 'This will be the best dog food on the market, superior to any national brand.'"

> "The important thing about a business plan is believability. I want to see a simple logic to the whole plan. The more a plan relies on leaps of faith, the less believable it is."
>
> *Robert Mahoney*
> *Corporate Banker*

Use Business Terms

Although it is certainly not necessary to be a business school graduate to develop a business plan, you should know and use appropriate basic business terms. You don't want to be discredited or misunderstood by using words improperly. If business is new to you, familiarize yourself with the Business Terms Glossary at the back of this book.

Become familiar also with the terms of your specific industry and use those words when appropriate in your plan. If you don't know these already, you should be able to pick many of them up while doing background work for the Industry Analysis section of your plan. However, do not fill your plan with a lot of technical jargon in the hope of sounding impressive; there is a good chance that someone unfamiliar with your industry will be reading it, especially if you are seeking outside funding.

Certain terms and trends are more popular at one time than another. You may find it helpful to include these "buzzwords" in your plan. As you do your research, keep track of the terms and practices that are currently "hot" with investors or industry leaders. Look to see what they are talking and reading about. Even if you do not include these buzzwords in your plan, you may be asked about them in a meeting with potential funders.

Points of Style

In addition to using the most beneficial and appropriate language in your plan, you should pay attention to the elements of style discussed below.

Use Numbers for Impact

People tend to put great faith in numbers, and using numbers to support your plan can add significant credibility. If the figures come from a reputable source, they have even more power.

One particularly good technique for making your plan stronger is to state, "Our _____ is supported by...," followed by specific figures relating to demographics, growth of market, information from other businesses, or market research. For example: "Our foot-traffic projections are supported by figures that show neighboring stores average 22 customers an hour on weekdays and 43 customers an hour on Saturdays," or, "Our choice of the young adult market is supported by U.S. Census Bureau figures projecting a growth of 32% in that age category over the next five years."

It is vital to bring data from your Financials into the text of your plan to indicate specifically why you will be able to achieve certain goals. For instance, state: "Our new production method will reduce each unit cost by 43% (currently projected savings: $1.57 per unit), thus allowing us to offer additional features at a competitive price while still maintaining our profit margin." Do not expect the reader to pick out these kinds of specifics simply from looking at your Financials; the information must be incorporated into the text.

> "Style shows thoroughness. Use lots of white space, so I can make notes in the margins. Use a binder that keeps the document together, preferably one that keeps the plan open to the page I'm on. Use bullet points. Use a block style rather than indented paragraphs. Don't misspell my name, and don't address me as 'Mr.' Imagine that you have to hand your plan to a customer. So if you don't know how to make a document look good, get some help."
>
> *Ann Winblad*
> *Venture Capitalist*

Use Bullet Points

Bullets are symbols that precede information offset from the text (such as the small boxes before the three sentences below). Bullets:

■ Draw attention to specific information.

■ Make long material more inviting to read.

■ Eliminate the need to write whole sentences.

Bullet points are an excellent way to convey information, and they make writing your plan somewhat easier. Because they are read faster than text and quickly get the reader's attention, use bullet points only with information you particularly want the reader to notice.

Be careful not to clutter a plan with too many bullets; use them selectively. Bullets seem to work better with short items than with long ones. Also, each list of bulleted items must be presented in a consistent manner, such as starting with a verb or being a complete sentence. Keep in mind that lists can be as few as one item or as many as 10, though a long list weakens effectiveness.

Your bulleted items also become excellent candidates for slides in an electronic presentation, such as a PowerPoint presentation, that you may later put together for meetings with potential investors, department heads, or other readers of your plan.

Know How and When to Be Redundant

Writing a business plan gives you the rarely granted right to repeat yourself. People do not read a plan from start to finish; they turn first to the sections that most interest them and then skip around. For this reason, it may be beneficial to refer in one section to conclusions you have reached in another.

For instance, when addressing the issue of staff training in your Operations section, you can refer to the importance of high-quality service to your target market, and underscore the wisdom of choosing this market by restating information provided earlier in your plan: "Surveys indicate high-quality service is demanded by our target market—women ages 35 to 49—who, as shown in the market analysis, spend the most per capita on our product."

Two cautions about repetition, however: 1) only repeat information that is important and impressive; and 2) don't repeat information within the same section.

Using Visuals in Your Plan

In the case of your business plan, a picture may be worth more than a thousand words. A thousand words, after all, most likely will not be read, but a picture will definitely be looked at. Graphs, charts, and illustrations also are visually appealing; they catch the reader's attention, forcefully explain concepts, and break up the monotony of the text.

> " The physical appearance of a plan (layout, binder, etc.) isn't significant in making the investment decision. But it sets your mind in a certain frame if it is well done. And it is certainly a negative if it's done wrong or poorly."
>
> *Eugene Kleiner*
> *Venture Capitalist*

> " Quantity is not a virtue in a plan. Quantity of thought is important in an entrepreneur. But in some cases, there's an inverse correlation between the size of the plan and the quality of the plan."
>
> *Andrew Anker*
> *Venture Capitalist*

Examples of Charts to Use in Your Business Plans

Here are some different types of charts you can use to help convey specific information.

Bar charts work especially well when making comparisons:

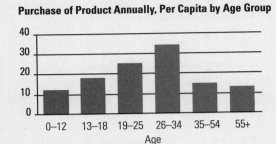

Purchase of Product Annually, Per Capita by Age Group

Line charts are useful when demonstrating trends or drawing comparisons:

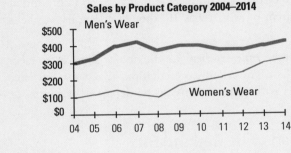

Sales by Product Category 2004–2014

Pie charts are ideal for showing the specific breakdowns of products sold, markets, and so on:

Store Sales by Product Category

Flow charts illustrate development patterns and organization of authority:

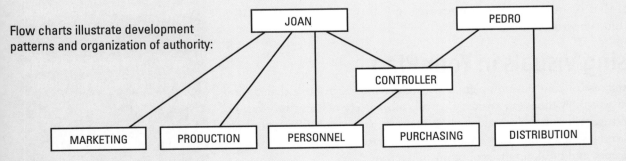

As you do your research and prepare your plan, look for items that can have a strong impact if presented in a more visual form, such as positive statistics on the growth or size of market. You may also want to include some of these in any electronic presentation you later put together.

An electronic presentation will make your plan more compelling. For detailed instructions on what to include in such a presentation, see Chapter 18.

Photographs and Illustrations

Photographs can be extremely effective in your plan, especially if your company is producing a product that is unusual or difficult to understand. You can include pictures of your location, specialized equipment, or packaging but not of yourself or individual members of your management team. Photographs should be placed in the Appendix only.

Illustrations help present information about products or marketing materials still in development. While generally placed in the Appendix, a small illustration can be inserted directly into the text. If an illustration is not of good quality, don't use it; a business plan is not the place for exhibiting amateur art.

Graphs and Charts

Graphs and charts are excellent tools for communicating important or impressive information, so you should find ways of including them in your plan. Place charts, particularly of half-page size or less, in the text rather than in the Appendix; this will engage the reader with your plan, as many readers pay minimal attention to the Appendix.

A number of inexpensive computer software programs are available for generating graphs and charts (the Excel-based Business Plan Financials package available as a supplement to this book will automatically generate professional charts based on your financial projections. Visit www.planningshop.com). Do not draw charts and graphs by hand. The four examples on page 48 help you identify various types of charts and judge when each would most appropriately be used in your business plan.

For even more impact, produce and reproduce some or all of your charts and graphs in color.

Chapter Summary

When researching and preparing your plan, look for information and statistics that will enable you to make the most positive impression on a reader quickly—you only have five crucial minutes to do so. Find items that will be visually interesting and attractive; use photographs and images, charts and graphs to bring attention to your most impressive information. Attention-grabbing bullet points turn long passages into more readable snippets. Use numbers to support your conclusions. Keep your language believable, and use supportive comments from credible and authoritative sources. In every case, be accurate and do not make mistakes of fact.

SECTION II

Business Plan Components

CHAPTER 4

The Executive Summary

> *If they don't get it at first, they won't get it at all.*

> " A good Executive Summary gives me a sense of why this is an interesting venture. I look for a very clear statement of their long-term mission, an overview of the people, the technology, and the fit to market. Answer these questions: 'What is it? Who's going to build it? Why will anyone buy it?' To paraphrase the movie *Field of Dreams*, we want to know, 'If we fund it, will they [buyers] come?'"
>
> *Ann Winblad*
> *Venture Capitalist*

The Executive Summary Is Crucial

Without a doubt, the single most important portion of your business plan is the Executive Summary. Only a clear, concise, and compelling condensation of your business right up front will persuade readers to wade through the rest of your plan. No matter how beneficial your product, how lucrative your market, or how innovative your manufacturing techniques, it is your Executive Summary alone that persuades a reader to spend the time to find out about your product, market, and techniques.

Write Your Summary Last

Because of this, it is imperative that you prepare the Executive Summary last. Although it appears first in your completed document, the Summary reflects the results of all your planning and should be crafted only after careful consideration of all other aspects of your business.

The Executive Summary is so important, in fact, that some venture capitalists prefer to receive just a Summary and Financials before reviewing an entire plan. If you want to send out only a "concept paper" to gauge investor interest before submitting a complete business plan, the Executive Summary should serve as that document. As important as the financial considerations are to investors and bankers, it is the Executive Summary that first convinces them that yours is a well-conceived and potentially successful business strategy.

Even if your business plan is for internal use only, the Executive Summary is still crucial. The Summary is the place where you bring all your thoughts and planning together, where you make a whole out of the disparate parts of your business, and where you sum up all that you propose. So, if you have not yet completed the other sections of your plan, proceed to the next chapter and return to the Executive Summary when you have finished the rest of your plan.

What to Convey in Your Executive Summary

The Executive Summary gives the reader a chance to understand the basic concept and highlights of your business quickly, and to decide whether to commit more time to reading the entire plan. Therefore, your goal in the Executive Summary is to motivate and entice the reader.

To do so, you want to convey your own sense of optimism about your business. This does not mean using "hype"; it simply means using a positive, confident tone and demonstrating that you are well-positioned to exploit a compelling market opportunity.

In a short space, you must let the reader know that:

- Your basic business concept makes sense.
- Your business itself has been thoroughly planned.
- The management is capable.
- A clear-cut market exists.
- Your business incorporates significant competitive advantages.
- Your financial projections are realistic.
- Investors or lenders have an excellent chance to make money.

If someone reading your Executive Summary concludes that all the above elements exist in your business, that person will almost certainly commit to reading the rest of your business plan.

Targeting the Summary

Ask yourself: "Who will be reading my business plan?" You can improve your chances for a positive reception if you know the answer to that question before you prepare your Executive Summary. Since the Summary is what the reader reads first (and perhaps is the only portion read at all), try to find out what "buttons" to push. Is the bank mostly interested in managers who have had previous business successes? Is the venture capital firm particularly interested in patentable new technology? Does the division president like to see new markets for existing products?

Do a little homework on your potential recipients (see Chapters 18 and 19) and then organize your Executive Summary so the issues most important to each recipient are given precedence.

Be careful, however, not to tailor the Executive Summary for just one person at a bank or venture capital firm; your plan is likely to end up in the hands of someone else. Target your Summary to address institutional concerns rather than individual preferences.

The Two Types of Executive Summary

Depending on the nature of your business and the capability of the writer, you can approach the Executive Summary in one of two ways: the synopsis Summary or the narrative Summary.

The Synopsis Summary

A synopsis Summary is the more straightforward of the two: It simply relates, in abbreviated fashion, the conclusions of each section of the completed business plan. Its advantage is that it is relatively easy to prepare and less dependent on a talented writer. The only disadvantage is that the tone of a synopsis Summary tends to be rather dry.

The synopsis-style Executive Summary covers all aspects of your business plan and treats each of them relatively equally, although briefly. In addition, it tells the reader what you are asking for in the way of financing—which you also state in your cover letter.

> " In a business plan, I want to know the answers to these questions: 'What are they going to sell, to whom, and how?' In other words, what is the marketing aspect of the business? What sales force, advertising, and other marketing techniques are they going to use? And secondly, what are the costs? I want to know manufacturing or sourcing costs. How reliable and stable are these costs? At what costs will they sell their products or services? I want to see believable costs and believable pricing."
>
> *Robert Mahoney*
> *Corporate Banker*

> " You need a business plan so you have a bible of what you're going to do in your business, a clear statement of your company's mission. The important thing in a business plan is to tell the truth. If there's a problem, we [the venture capitalists] are going to learn it anyway, so it's better if you don't try to hide it."
>
> *Ann Winblad*
> *Venture Capitalist*

The Narrative Summary

The narrative Summary is more like telling the reader a story; it can convey greater drama and excitement in presenting your business. However, it takes a capable writer to prepare a narrative Summary that communicates the necessary information, engenders enthusiasm, and yet does not cross over the line into hyperbole.

A narrative Executive Summary is useful for businesses that break new ground, either with a new product, a new market, or new operational techniques that require considerable explanation. It is also more appropriate for businesses that have one dominant element—such as holding an important patent or the participation of a well-known entrepreneur—that can be highlighted. Finally, the narrative Executive Summary works well for companies with interesting or impressive backgrounds or histories.

A narrative-style Executive Summary has fewer sections than the synopsis Summary. Greater emphasis is placed on the business' concept and distinctive features, and less attention is given to operational details.

With a narrative Summary, you want to get the reader excited about your company; you do this by taking the one or two most impressive features of your company and giving the reader an understanding of how those features will lead to business success.

A narrative Summary may do more "scene-setting"—recounting the sociological or technological changes that have led to the development of your company's products or services—than a synopsis Summary. It may be more personal, telling how the founders' relevant experiences motivated them to start the company.

You may place the topics of a narrative Summary in any order that best showcases your company. The topics do not have to be covered equally; the business concept may be described in three paragraphs and the management team in only one or two sentences. Using topic headings is not necessary, although you may do so if you wish.

You may likewise place the topics of a synopsis Summary in the most advantageous order. Most businesses are well-served by a synopsis Summary, especially if the business concept is easily understood and the marketing and operations are relatively standard. A synopsis is a very businesslike approach, and experienced business plan readers are comfortable reviewing such straightforward Executive Summaries.

Writing the Summary

Clear, strong writing pays off in the Executive Summary more than in any other section of your business plan. A dynamic, logical writing style can make the difference between a plan's being considered or being discarded.

If you are unsure about your own writing ability, consider hiring a professional writer for the Summary or asking help from a friend or family member who is a good writer. Writing style is less important in a synopsis than in the narrative approach to an Executive Summary, and if your writing ability is limited, use the synopsis form for your Summary.

Length and Design of the Summary

The great advantage to the reader of the Executive Summary is that it is short. A busy funder must be able to read your Summary in less than five minutes. Thus, an Executive Summary should be no more than two to three pages in length. A one-page Summary is perfectly acceptable.

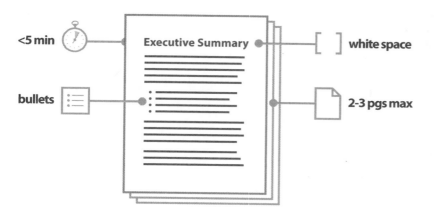

> **An Executive Summary should be short: two pages at most, one page if possible. Spell out the company's objectives, what you plan to do. Do not attempt to describe details. Describe the need for the product and exactly what it is. Tell the qualifications of the principals as they relate to the business."**
>
> *Eugene Kleiner*
> *Venture Capitalist*

Refer to Chapter 18 for tips on page layout. Use white space to make the page less intimidating. Bullet points can also be used effectively in the Summary. Since you are limited to so few pages, it may seem frustrating to have to give up space for visual considerations, but these techniques make your plan more inviting to the reader.

Use the Plan Preparation Forms on pages 58–61 to develop your Executive Summary; there is one for the synopsis type of Summary and one for the narrative type. A Sample Plan of each kind of Executive Summary is also provided.

Chapter Summary

Your Executive Summary, the single most important part of your business plan, quickly outlines your basic business concept; it must motivate the reader to consider your plan as a whole. Know who will be reading your plan and target it to that audience accordingly. Use the style of writing—synopsis or narrative—best suited for your business and writing abilities. While synopsis is more straightforward, a narrative style can create more drama. Whichever style you choose, use clear, dynamic, and logical writing. Prepare your Executive Summary last, only after your entire plan is completed.

Synopsis Executive Summary Plan Preparation Form

Take highlights from each section of your completed plan and address the areas listed below. Remember to be brief and clear. Cover each topic in no more than one to three sentences. Describe only the most important and impressive features of your business. After the first two topics, Company Description and Statement of Mission, place the remaining sections in any order that gives the best impression of your business to your target reader. For the reader's quick comprehension, use topic headings at the beginning of each paragraph (see the Sample Plan at the end of this chapter); if you'd like a Summary that seems less like a list, omit the headings. Feel free to combine related topics, such as "Target Market" and "Marketing Strategy," to create a more fluid document.

Company Description: List the company name, type of business, location, and legal status, e.g., corporation, sole proprietorship, partnership._____

_____

_____

Statement of Mission: Write the concise statement of company purpose you developed in Chapter 5._____

_____

_____

_____

Stage of Development: State whether your company is a start-up or continuing business, when it was founded, how far along the product or service is in its creation, and if you've already made sales or started shipping._____

_____

_____

Products and Services: List the products or services your company sells or plans to sell; this can be generic for a company with many products—e.g., women's sportswear—or specific for a company with just a few. _____

_____

_____

_____

Target Market(s): List the markets you intend to reach and why you chose them; indicate the results of any market analysis or market research._____

_____

_____

Marketing and Sales Strategy: Briefly describe how you intend to reach your target market(s), and the advertising, direct mail, trade shows, and other methods you will use to secure sales._____

_____

_____

_____

Competitors and Market Distribution: Indicate the nature of your competition and how the market is currently divided.

_____

_____

_____

Competitive Advantages and Distinctions: Show why your company will be able to compete successfully; list any important distinctions, such as patents, major contracts, or letters-of-intent. _____

_____

_____

_____

Management: Briefly describe the histories and capabilities of your management team, particularly those of company founders. _____

_____

_____

_____

Operations: Outline your key operational features, such as locations, crucial distributors or suppliers, cost-saving production techniques, etc._____

_____

_____

Financials: Indicate your company's expected revenues and profits for years one through three. _____

_____

_____

Long-Term Goals: Describe the expected status—e.g., sales, number of employees, number of locations, market share of your company—five years from now. _____

_____

_____

_____

Funds Sought and Exit Strategy: Indicate how much money you are seeking, how many investors you plan to have, how the funds raised will be used, and how investors or lenders will get their money out. _____

_____

_____

_____

Use this information as the basis of your plan's synopsis Executive Summary.

Narrative Executive Summary Plan Preparation Form

This form provides you an opportunity to outline the Executive Summary portion of your business plan if you choose to write a narrative type of Summary.

The Company: Describe how your company is organized, its stage of development, stage of product creation, legal status, location, and company mission._____

_____

_____

_____

_____

_____

_____

The Concept: Explain the background of your company, how the product came about, how the market opportunity was recognized, and the products and services. _____

_____

_____

_____

_____

Market Opportunity: Describe your target market, market trends that exist, why there was a need for the company, the results of market research, the competition, and market openings. _____

_____

_____

_____

_____

_____

Competitive Advantages and Distinctions: Indicate why your company can compete successfully; list important distinctions such as patents, major contracts, and letters-of-intent; specify barriers-to-entry for new competitors.

_____

_____

_____

_____

_____

_____

Management Team: Describe the background and capabilities of your key managers, and relate past successful business experiences. _____

_____

_____

_____

_____

_____

_____

_____

_____

Milestones: List the milestones by which you will measure success and at what date you expect to reach them; these might include specific revenue or profit levels, the percentage of market share reached, shipments of first product, and the number of employees or locations. _____

_____

_____

_____

_____

_____

_____

_____

_____

Financials: Specify the amount of funds sought, the number of likely investors, the use of funds secured, and how investors or lenders will get their money back—through an exit plan (acquisition, public offering, merger) or security (collateral) for a loan. _____

_____

_____

_____

_____

_____

_____

_____

_____

Use this information as the basis of your plan's narrative Executive Summary.

SAMPLE PLAN: SYNOPSIS EXECUTIVE SUMMARY

EXECUTIVE SUMMARY

The Company

ComputerEase, Incorporated, provides computer software and software-as-a-service (SaaS) training services, primarily to the corporate and business market. In addition to offering local training at its own dedicated facilities, the firm delivers on-premises training to corporations located in the Greater Vespucci, Indiana, area. It also offers online versions of its courses that can be accessed from anywhere with an Internet connection. The technology business services industry is one of the fastest growing in the United States, and ComputerEase intends to capitalize on that growth. The company's stock is currently held by President and CEO Scott E. Connors and Susan Alexander, Vice President, Marketing.

States legal status, location, stock ownership, and industry opportunity.

The Company's Mission

ComputerEase views its mission as increasing the corporate community's productivity by helping them realize the maximum benefit from their personnel and computers through software training. ComputerEase is dedicated to building long-term relationships with customers through quality training and support, to being known as the premier software training company in the Greater Vespucci area, and to expand online course offerings globally to English-speaking countries throughout the world. The goal is steady expansion, becoming profitable by the third year of operations. Computer-Ease also is dedicated to contributing back to the Vespucci community by providing free computer training programs for inner-city youth, low-income residents, and "welfare-to-work" program participants.

Provides a sense of how the company views itself and its long-term goals.

Products and Services

The company provides software training programs targeted to the corporate market, and currently has a portfolio that covers a broad range of leading business software programs. There are two ways that training is delivered. On-premise training is provided by in-person instructors, either at the customer's place of business or at ComputerEase's Corporate Training Center. Online training is offered via the Internet. In addition to providing training for the most-used enterprise and business software and Web-based business services, ComputerEase also creates custom programs at corporate customers' request for both on-premise and online delivery. The online training programs incorporate some video training segments, enhancing the learning experience.

Marketing and Sales Strategy

ComputerEase differentiates itself in its marketing by emphasizing the needs of the corporation, not merely of the students taking the classes. Locally, the firm employs highly regarded sales professionals with extensive ties to the target market who secure sales predominantly through face-to-face solicitations. For customers who access ComputerEase's online training, the company has an aggressive online marketing strategy that includes advertising on prominent training websites, exhibiting at training industry trade shows, publishing a monthly email newsletter on best practices in corporate training, and using search engine marketing by purchasing keywords. To support its customer base, ComputerEase also maintains an active Facebook business page, a LinkedIn profile, and a YouTube channel.

The Competition

No market leaders have yet emerged in the corporate software training field — either in the Vespucci region or online. Competition is diverse and uneven, creating substantial market opportunities. ComputerEase maintains the following advantages over existing competition: strategic partnerships with leading software publishers; formal certifications from those publishers; a growing reputation for delivering highly effective training and superior customer support; a company-owned, state-of-the-art computer Training Center; a local sales staff with strong ties to target customers; and a national network of third-party consultants and computer retailers that bundle ComputerEase's courses with their own services.

Shows market opportunity.

Target Market

ComputerEase's "brick-and-mortar" business operates in the Greater Vespucci, Indiana, area. Vespucci is the 16th-largest city in the United States, with a diverse and healthy economy. U.S. Census Bureau data shows that more than 10,000 organizations with more than 50 employees each (ComputerEase's primary target market) are located in the area. ComputerEase's online market is composed of English-speaking countries where a high percentage of businesses are automated or in the process of becoming automated. The market for online computer training has grown by more than 33% each year for the past five years, and is projected to sustain this rate of expansion for the remainder of the decade.

Management

President and Founder Scott E. Connors brings significant technology-related management experience to this position. Immediately before starting ComputerEase, Connors served as regional vice president for Wait's Electronics Emporium, a large computer hardware and electronics retail chain. Previously, he was a sales representative for IBM. Vice President Susan Alexander brings direct experience in marketing to the target market from her prior position as assistant marketing director for AlwaysHere Health Care Plan, and sales experience as sales representative for SpeakUp Dictation Equipment.

Emphasizes past business ownership and directly related experience.

Operations

ComputerEase owns its Corporate Training Center with 20 PCs fully equipped with all the latest versions of the most popular business software programs. The company offers corporate training sessions at the Center, as well as at local corporations' place of business. It plans to open a second Training Center with some of the funds currently being sought. ComputerEase utilizes the excess capacity of the Training Center by offering Saturday and evening classes to consumers. Additionally, ComputerEase has three development PCs for creating the interactive course content based on the instructor-led courses and documentation. All equipment is leased,

SAMPLE PLAN: SYNOPSIS EXECUTIVE SUMMARY (continued)

resulting in lower capital expenses and ensuring the latest equipment at all times. All data center operations, including the servers that host the online training applications and student data, are outsourced to a local managed services provider. Video production is outsourced to a local company experienced in creating instructional videos.

Stage of Development

ComputerEase began operations in January 2014, and opened its first software Training Center classroom in August 2014.

Financials

Tells investors there is no return on capital for at least three years.

The financial strategy of ComputerEase emphasizes reinvestment of income for growth during the first few years of operation, with the company reaching profitability within the next three years. Annual revenue projections for the current year are $466,000; for year two, $987,750; and for year three, $1,637,230.

Funds Sought and Utilization

Cites specific numbers and uses for funds.

The company is currently seeking $160,000 in investment financing. These funds will be used for expansion, primarily opening an additional Training Center, hiring new staff, and increasing marketing activities. Long-term plans are for the company to aggressively market and expand its online business into English-speaking countries outside the U.S.; work with customers to develop interactive online custom training programs for employees; and either develop a franchise operation or expand to become a regional company-owned chain, adding at least one training location annually.

SAMPLE PLAN: NARRATIVE EXECUTIVE SUMMARY

EXECUTIVE SUMMARY

The Concept

The technology business services industry is one of the fastest growing in the United States. The use of computers, tablets, and mobile devices in virtually every business setting has provided unprecedented opportunities to companies offering training services to business clients, both in person and online. Because no market leader has emerged in this field, either in Vespucci, Indiana, or online, a well-conceived and well-executed company can secure a leading position.

Provides a sense of the health and opportunities of the industry.

Background

Scott E. Connors, President and Founder of ComputerEase, Incorporated, recognized this opportunity when, as Regional Vice President for Wait's Electronics Emporium, he conducted a study of the potential market for corporate software training in the Indiana, Ohio, and Illinois areas. As a result of this study, he realized that a professionally managed software training company could quickly become the region's market leader. When developing an online component to ComputerEase's training classes, Connors discovered a huge potential for online training services.

Gives history of motivation for business.

The Company

ComputerEase is positioned to become the premier provider of software training targeted to the corporate market. The company began operations in January 2014, and was quickly able to secure corporate clients with software training programs offered at the customers' location.

The client base expanded when ComputerEase opened its first Training Center in August 2014, with 20 personal computer stations. At this same time, ComputerEase launched its software-as-a-service (SaaS) training services, accessible from any computer with an Internet connection. Both of these initiatives offer greater flexibility to corporate employees. ComputerEase offers software training for all leading software programs, as well as custom programs at corporate customers' request.

Tells developmental stage, products and services, long-term goals, legal status, and ownership.

ComputerEase is incorporated in the state of Indiana and stock is currently held by President Scott E. Connors and Vice President Susan Alexander.

The Market

The company targeted large corporations in the Greater Vespucci, Indiana, area as the base of its initial operations. As the 16th-largest city in the United States, Vespucci offers a diverse and healthy economy with more than 10,000 companies employing over 50 employees each. ComputerEase's online market includes an even larger pool—English-speaking countries with a high percentage of automated businesses.

Competitive Position

Currently, corporate software training programs are offered in the Vespucci area by small, local, underfunded, and generally poorly managed companies and through national online programs, with no leader having yet emerged in either space. Market

SAMPLE PLAN: NARRATIVE EXECUTIVE SUMMARY (continued)

research indicates an extremely high level of dissatisfaction with current providers among current customers of software training. ComputerEase's growing reputation for delivering highly effective training and superior customer support both in person and online, along with its company-owned, state-of-the-art computer Training Center, local sales staff with strong ties to target customers, and national network of third-party consultants and computer retailers, sets the company apart from its competition.

Management Team

Emphasizes previous business ownership and related experience.

The current management of President Scott E. Connors and Vice President of Marketing Susan Alexander gives ComputerEase an excellent team with which to begin operations. Mr. Connors brings extensive technology-related management and sales experience from his years with Wait's Electronics Emporium and IBM.

In her positions as assistant marketing director for AlwaysHere Health Care Plan, and sales representative at SpeakUp Dictation Equipment, Ms. Alexander gained significant experience in sales and marketing to ComputerEase's target market: corporate human resource directors. Her personal connections with this target audience are extensive, giving ComputerEase immediate access to the potentially most lucrative clients.

The Future

Provides investors with a sense of growth opportunities.

The company has many opportunities for growth now and in the future. First, the company plans to expand its online offerings beyond the U.S. to English-speaking countries around the world. Second, the company may become a franchise operation, selling franchise licenses, materials, and training for independent operations under the ComputerEase name.

Financials

The company projects rapid growth, with sales revenues of $466,000 in the current year, $987,750 for year two, and $1,637,230 in year three. It emphasizes the reinvestment of income for expansion rather than profit taking, funding growth internally rather than through additional investment beyond that currently sought.

Funds Sought

Gives specific numbers and uses of funds.

The company anticipates only one round of financing (unless franchising is later undertaken) with $160,000 being sought from one investor. These funds will be utilized to add a new training center, hire staff, and expand marketing activities.

CHAPTER

5 Company Description

The reason most businesses fail is that they don't understand the business they are in.

Conveying the Basics of Your Business

Before you can discuss the more-complex aspects of your business and the meatier sections of your business plan, such as marketing strategy or new technology, you must first inform the reader of the basic details of your business. The object of this section is to convey information such as your legal status, ownership, products or services, company mission, and milestones achieved to date.

The Company Description may be relatively simple to complete, especially if you have been in business for some time. However, the simplicity may be deceptive, particularly if yours is a new company. Many of these basic issues require a lot of thought and planning. For instance, you may find yourself spending a great deal of time trying to choose a business name or deciding on which legal form your company should take.

If yours is a start-up company, you may feel you don't have the information to complete each category. As an example, you may not yet have rented an office or legally incorporated. In that case, write down what you intend to do. You might include information about your current situation as well. Thus, you might say, "Rocket Science Technology will be headquartered in Austin, Texas, with a manufacturing facility in Luckenbach, Texas. Currently, the company's address is 1234 Bruce Springsteen Street, San Antonio, TX 78216."

The most challenging aspect of the Company Description section is likely to be developing a "Mission Statement," which concisely describes the goals, objectives, and underlying principles of your company. A Mission Statement enables you and readers of your business plan to get a better picture of where you intend to go with your business, and it helps you more clearly articulate exactly what business you are in.

The following topics should be addressed in the Company Description section of your business plan.

> " [Our mission is] To continually provide our members with quality goods and services at the lowest possible prices. In order to achieve our mission we will conduct our business with the following five responsibilities in mind: obey the law, take care of our members, take care of our employees, respect our vendors, reward our shareholders."
>
> *Mission Statement of Costco*

Company Name

In many cases, the name of your company or corporation is not the same as the name(s) you use when doing business with the public. You may actually have a number of different "names" associated with your business, including:

- Your own name
- The legal corporate or company name
- A "**dba**" ("doing business as")
- Brand name(s)
- Model name(s)
- Subsidiary company name(s)
- Domain name(s)

SAMPLE COMPANY "NAMES"

YOUR OWN NAME	COMPANY NAME	DOING BUSINESS AS	BRAND NAME
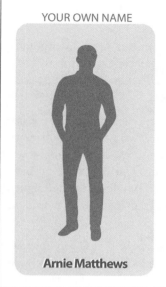			
Arnie Matthews	**AAA, Incorporated**	**Arnie's Diner**	**Arnie's Atomic**

	MODEL NAME	SUBSIDIARY COMPANY	DOMAIN NAME

	Atomic Hot Sauce	**Rosie's Catering Service**	**www.arniesatomic.com**

Success key terms

Advisory Committee
A nonofficial group of advisors; has no legal authority or obligation.

Board of Directors
The members of the governing body of an incorporated company. They have legal responsibility for the company.

Capital
The funds necessary to establish or operate a business.

Copyright
Legal rights covering any type of work that is "fixed" and "tangible" and granting protection from others who would copy, imitate, or steal that work.

dba
"Doing business as…" a company's trade name rather than the name by which it is legally incorporated; a company may be incorporated under the name XYZ Corporation but do business as " The Dew Drop Inn."

Licensing
The granting of permission by one company to another to use its products, trademark, or name in a limited, particular manner.

Market Share
The percentage of the total available customer base captured by a company.

Partnership
A legal relationship of two or more individuals to run a company.

Patent
A government-issued protection of an invention, protecting the inventor for an extended period from letting others copy or sell imitations of the invention.

Sole Proprietorship
Company owned and managed by one person.

Strategic Partnership
An agreement with another company to undertake business endeavors together or on each other's behalf; can be for financing, sales, marketing, distribution, or other activities.

Trademark (or Service Mark)
A word, phrase, symbol, or design (or a combination of these) that identifies and distinguishes the maker of a product (or service) from makers of other, similar, products (or services).

The number and types of names you need depend on the kind of business you are in, how you interact with the public, whether you are incorporated, what kinds of and how many products/services you have, and your own personal taste.

For instance, a company might list its legal name as AAA, Incorporated, doing business as Arnie's Diner, operating the subsidiary business Rosie's Catering Service, selling products under the trade name "Arnie's Atomic," and operating the website www.arniesatomic.com.

If yours is a new business, and you have not yet chosen a name, consider one that meets your current needs but also gives you flexibility over the years. If you plan a company where most customers will do business with you because they know of you or your reputation, you may have no better name than your own. Many consultants, service providers, and designers, use just their own name. You can also combine your name with words that describe what you do, such as Erin's Editing Services.

However, using your own name or a business name that is very narrowly descriptive may limit your ability to grow, change focus, or sell the company in the future. Al's Airplane Repair is more confining than Take-off Aviation Services, or even Take-Off Transportation Services.

Having the legal rights to a memorable website or "domain" name may be a competitive business advantage, and if you have secured the rights to such a name, you may want to highlight this fact in your business plan.

In your business plan, include the legal name of your company and any brand or trade names, **dba**'s, subsidiary company name, and domain name.

Company's Objectives/Statement of Mission

Many, if not most, successful large companies describe the main goal of their internal planning process as articulating and clarifying their "philosophy" or "mission." The best, most effective Mission Statements are not mere empty words, but principles and objectives that guide all other aspects and activities of the business.

You should be able to sum up the basic objectives and philosophy of your company in just a few sentences. One statement should encapsulate the nature of your business, your business principles, your financial goals, your "corporate culture," and how you expect to have your company viewed in the marketplace.

A Statement of Mission provides focus for your company and should be the defining concept of your business for at least the next few years. It should be the result of a meaningful examination of the foundations of your company, and virtually every word should be important.

A finished Mission Statement might be: "AAA, Inc., is a spunky, imaginative food products and service company aimed at offering high-quality, moderately priced, occasionally unusual foods using only natural ingredients. We view ourselves as partners with our customers, our employees, our community, and our environment, and we take personal responsibility in our actions toward each. We aim to become a regionally recognized brand

> " We are a mission-driven business. We are democratizing organic and fair trade."
>
> *Seth Goldman*
> *Cofounder, Honest Tea*

name, capitalizing on the sustained interest in Southwestern and Mexican food. Our goal is moderate growth, annual profitability, and maintaining our sense of humor."

The Statement of Mission worksheet on pages 72–73 helps you outline your company's objectives.

Legal Issues

In forming a business, you must address many critical legal issues. One of the first is which type of legal entity to choose for your company. Businesses often start as a **sole proprietorship** or a **partnership**. This has the advantage of being easy, since there may be no papers to file with your state. Being incorporated, on the other hand, provides you and your investors with much greater protection from personal liability. Most investors (and some lenders) are usually more comfortable dealing with an incorporated entity.

If you choose to incorporate, you will still have many decisions. What form of corporation will you choose? In which state will you incorporate? How many shares in your corporation will be issued, and to whom? Legal concerns and agreements will have a profound impact on the future of your company.

In addition to the legal form of your business, there are many other legal considerations and issues to address in your business plan. Have you entered into **licensing** or distribution agreements? Have you secured **trademarks**, **patents**, **copyrights**, or other legal instruments that may protect your proprietary business assets?

Every company has certain intangible assets that are, or can be, extremely valuable. Most of them come under the heading of intellectual property (IP)—assets that have value because of the knowledge, recognition, and inventiveness they consist of. Some businesses, such as software companies, publishers, inventors, consultants, app developers, and so on, only have products composed of intellectual property.

While protecting intellectual property is always a challenge—it is, after all, intangible—there are methods to protect a company's IP from being copied, imitated, stolen, or used.

■ Copyrights cover any type of work that is "fixed" and "tangible" even if it's only computer code, words spoken on an audiotape, or images "fixed" in a movie.

■ Trademarks (or service marks) are words, phrases, symbols, or designs—or a combination of these—that identify and distinguish the maker of a product (or service) from makers of other, similar, products (or services).

You'll need to include in your business plan what you've done to protect your intellectual property—especially for businesses with IP that may be of significant value. Such companies include technology firms developing apps or software. Investors will want to know how you have ensured the security of these assets.

Statement of Mission

Describe your company's philosophy in terms of the areas listed below.

Range/Nature of Products or Services Offered: _____
_____
_____
_____
_____
_____
_____

Quality: _____
_____
_____
_____
_____

Price:_____
_____
_____
_____
_____

Service:_____
_____
_____
_____
_____

Overall Relationship to Customer: _____
_____
_____
_____

Management Style/Relationship to Employees: _____
_____
_____
_____
_____

Nature of Work Environment: _____

_____

_____

_____

_____

Relationship to Rest of Industry: _____

_____

_____

_____

_____

Incorporation of New Technology/Other New Developments: _____

_____

_____

_____

_____

Growth/Profitability Goals: _____

_____

_____

_____

_____

_____

Relationship to Community/Environment/Other Social Responsibility Goals: _____

_____

_____

_____

_____

_____

Other Personal/Management Goals:_____

_____

_____

_____

_____

_____

_____

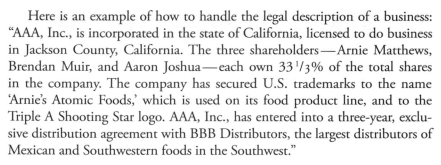

Here is an example of how to handle the legal description of a business: "AAA, Inc., is incorporated in the state of California, licensed to do business in Jackson County, California. The three shareholders—Arnie Matthews, Brendan Muir, and Aaron Joshua—each own 33 1/3% of the total shares in the company. The company has secured U.S. trademarks to the name 'Arnie's Atomic Foods,' which is used on its food product line, and to the Triple A Shooting Star logo. AAA, Inc., has entered into a three-year, exclusive distribution agreement with BBB Distributors, the largest distributors of Mexican and Southwestern foods in the Southwest."

The worksheet Legal Issues is included on pages 76–77 to help you identify key legal concerns.

If you plan to work globally—either selling your products or services internationally, importing or exporting products or supplies, or signing agreements with international companies to handle aspects of your business like distribution, support, or software development—you'll need to educate yourself about the legal requirements and issues that can affect your business.

For example, if you sell products that entail significant IP, you'll want to make certain that the countries where you'll sell your products provide adequate legal protection against piracy. If you are entering into international contracts, you'll want to understand typical contractual terms, but even more importantly, you'll want to determine where any disputes/lawsuits will be settled.

Be on the lookout for some countries' limits on the activities and ownership rights of foreign companies. Many countries, for instance, require companies in some industries to be at least majority-owned by locals. They may also limit foreign ownership of land or assess tariffs on imports. Be certain to understand those limits before entering an international market.

Use the worksheet on page 78 to capture your findings relating to the legal issues you need to consider when working internationally.

Products and Services

This part of your business plan can be relatively short, or it can be an entire section of its own. If your products or services are particularly technical, complicated, innovative, or proprietary, you will want to spend considerable time describing them. This is especially true if you are seeking funding for a new product or service and if potential funders are likely to be motivated by the specifics.

In this part of your plan, clearly identify and describe the nature of the products or services you provide. Be fairly specific, but if you have a large line of products or services, you do not need to list each one, as long as you identify the general categories. Also list future products or services planned by your company and when you expect to introduce them.

If you are developing an innovative product or service, particularly a technology product, you must walk a fine line in describing its details. While you must provide sufficient detail both to give a clear idea of what your product does and to inspire confidence that it actually achieves its intended purpose, you do not want to disclose sensitive information. Even if a reader of your

> *What is the market problem? What is the urgency of the problem you are trying to solve for your customers? Is your solution a 'must have' rather than a 'nice to have?'"*
>
> *Lauren Flanagan*
> *Cofounder and Managing Director, BELLE Capital USA*

business plan has signed a Nondisclosure Agreement (see Chapter 18), be extremely wary of putting highly proprietary or technical details in your written document. These can be disclosed at a later stage of discussions.

Once again using the fictional AAA, Inc., the "Products/Services" section might read: "Arnie's Diner is a full-service restaurant specializing in Mexican and Southwestern cuisine. Rosie's Catering Services provides catering for both business and personal occasions. The Arnie's Atomic food line currently consists of seven shelf-stable chili and salsa products. We anticipate releasing a line of four packaged Southwestern spice mixtures in the next six months. In the second year of this plan, we anticipate introducing a line of tortilla chips."

Management/Leadership

Next, include the name of the chairperson of the **Board of Directors**, president, and/or chief executive officer. If there are other key members of management, especially those that might be known to potential investors, list their names here. Also, if you have a Board of Directors, **Advisory Committee**, or other governing entity, indicate how many people serve on that body and how frequently it meets. If the membership of these bodies is particularly impressive, include their names; otherwise, it is not necessary to do so.

Business Location

List the location of your company's headquarters, main place of business (if different), and any branch locations. If you have more than one or two branches, you can list just the total number (although you might want to include a complete list in your plan's Appendix). If you have not yet secured a location but intend to do so, indicate the general whereabouts of your intended operation. Also, it is very important to describe the geographical area your company serves.

For instance, state: "The corporate offices of AAA, Inc., are located at 123 Amelia Earhart Drive, Jackson, California. Arnie's Diner is located at 456 Lincoln Street in Jackson. Rosie's Catering Services operates from the diner and serves the entire Jackson County area. Arnie's Atomic food products will be produced at a plant to be leased in Jackson and will be sold in five Southwestern states."

Development Stage and Milestones Achieved to Date

Someone reading your business plan should be able to get a clear sense of how far along your company is in its development, and what progress you have made in building the company.

Even start-up companies often have a record of accomplishments. You may have already developed technology, raised seed funding, lined up **strategic partnership**s, or secured indications of interest from key customers. Showing the progress you've achieved to date inspires confidence in your ability to develop your company further and indicates the level of commitment you have made to your business. You will want to clearly indicate any positive milestones you've achieved.

> " Some potential milestones a business plan could indicate include product completion, product testing, first customer shipment, unit volume goals, company infrastructure developments, core agreements reached, and second product shipping."
>
> *Ann Winblad*
> *Venture Capitalist*

Legal Issues

LEGAL FORM

What is the legal form of your company currently?

☐ Sole proprietorship

☐ Partnership

☐ Subchapter S Corporation

☐ C Corporation

☐ Other, describe:_____

☐ Limited Liability Company

☐ B corporation

☐ Not-for-profit corporation

☐ No legal entity/status

What is the intended legal form if different from above?

☐ Sole proprietorship

☐ Partnership

☐ Subchapter S Corporation

☐ C Corporation

☐ Other, describe:_____

☐ Limited Liability Company

☐ B corporation

☐ Not-for-profit corporation

☐ No legal entity/status

OWNERSHIP

If a sole proprietor or partnership, list the owners: _____

_____

_____

_____

If incorporated, how many shares of stock have been issued?_____

_____

_____

_____

Who owns the stock and in what amounts? _____

_____

_____

In which state(s), province(s), country(s), etc., are you legally incorporated or registered to do business? List dates

and specifics: _____

_____

_____

Have you secured written agreements between/with:

☐ Principals, partners

☐ Suppliers

☐ Investors

☐ Key employees/management

☐ Customers

☐ Strategic partners

List which of the following you have secured; include dates and specifics:

Trademarks:_____
_____

Copyrights: _____
_____

Patents: _____
_____

Domain names: _____

List investments to date, including dates and terms:_____
_____
_____
_____

List loans or any other debts, including dates and terms: _____
_____
_____
_____

List property leases, purchase agreements, etc., including dates and terms:_____
_____
_____
_____

List equipment leases, purchase agreements, etc., including dates and terms: _____
_____
_____
_____

List any distribution or licensing agreements, etc., including dates and terms: _____
_____
_____
_____

List other strategic partnerships, arrangements, etc., including dates and terms: _____
_____
_____
_____
_____

Globalization: Legal Issues

For each country in which you plan to do business, research and list the legal issues that may have an impact on you and your company.

COUNTRY _____

Contracts/jurisdiction: _____

_____

Import/export licenses: _____

_____

Intellectual property protections: _____

_____

Global distribution agreements: _____

_____

Partnership agreements: _____

_____

Other licenses or regulations: _____

_____

Export tariffs: _____

_____

Tax incentives/advantages: _____

_____

Corporate ownership: _____

_____

Trade agreements: _____

_____

Facilities and property ownership/leases: _____

_____

Other legal issues: _____

_____

_____

_____

_____

_____

_____

_____

_____

Begin by stating when the company was founded. Next, indicate your phase of development: a seed company (with a business concept but without a product or service finalized); a start-up (in early stages of operation); expansion (adding new products, services, or branches); retrenchment (consolidating or repositioning product lines); or established (maintaining **market share** and product positioning).

Indicate how far along your plans have progressed. Has the product been developed or tested? Have orders been placed or the product shipped? Are leases signed or suppliers secured? What have been the past milestones and successes of current operations? If you earlier set specific goals with target dates, indicate if you met those objectives.

A Milestones Achieved worksheet is included in Chapter 15. You may wish to take highlights from that worksheet to include in the Company Description section of your business plan.

Using the above example of AAA, Inc., this section might read: "Arnie's Diner opened in 2010, and the company began packaging food products used in the restaurant in 2012. These were initially sold in grocery stores on a local basis. In January 2013, the company set an annual sales goal of $60,000 for the 'Arnie's Atomic' line of packaged food and exceeded that goal, achieving $103,000 in gross sales in 2013. In 2014, sales of packaged food products rose to $237,000. A leading distributor has been secured to sell 'Arnie's Atomic' products to grocery and specialty stores in five Southwestern states. The first orders have been received, placed, and renewed, and the company now plans to expand its production facilities to accommodate increased sales and develop new products."

Financial Status

You also want to give a brief idea of the status of your company in financial and personnel terms. For example, readers will want to know how you have been funded to date and any major financial obligations. You should also indicate any loans or investments you have received and on what terms. If you are seeking funding, briefly indicate how much money you seek and for what purpose. You will expand on your financial obligations and use of funds sought in the Financials section of your plan.

Thus, this section might read: "AAA, Inc., has maintained overall profitability through slow, careful expansion of its component companies. Total gross revenue for the previous year was approximately $1,247,000. Rosie's Catering is presently the most profitable, last year showing a profit of $128,000 on sales of $525,000; Arnie's Diner showed a profit of $81,000 on sales of $485,000; Arnie's Atomic Foods projects a current year loss of $77,000 on sales of $237,000. Currently the total workforce is five full-time employees and seven part-time employees. We are now seeking to expand the production facilities, add employees, and increase our sales and marketing efforts. To do so, we are seeking an additional $500,000 in **capital**."

> " I launched Cigar of the Month Club with two other guys. We each had $8,000 . We started in a 400-square-foot studio apartment, and my brother-in-law gave us used chairs and desks for free."
>
> **Bill Rancic**
> **Serial Entrepreneur**

Company Description Plan Preparation Form

List facts about your business according to the categories below.

NAMES

Legal/Corporate Name: _____

Doing Business As: _____

Brand/Trade/Domain Names: _____

_____

Subsidiary Companies: _____

LEGAL FORM

Legal Form of Business: _____

State in Which Incorporated (if incorporated): _____

County in Which Business Is Licensed: _____

Owner(s) of Company or Major Shareholders: _____

MANAGEMENT/LEADERSHIP

Chairperson of the Board: _____

President: _____

Chief Executive Officer: _____

Other Key Management Members: _____

_____

Governing/Advisory Bodies: _____

_____

Number of Members: _____

LOCATION

Company Headquarters: _____

Place of Business: _____

Branches: _____

Geographic Area Served: _____

DEVELOPMENTAL STAGE

When Company Was Founded: _____

Stage of Formation or Immediate Goals: _____

When Product or Service Was Introduced: _____

Progress of Current Plans and Milestones Reached: _____

_____

_____

Other Developmental Indicators: _____

_____

FINANCIAL STATUS

Last Year's Total Sales: _____

Last Year's Pretax Profit: _____

Sales and Profitability by Division or Product Line: _____

_____

Current Number of Employees: _____

Amount of Funds Sought: _____

Basic Use of Funds Sought: _____

Previous Funding and Major Financial Obligations: _____

_____

_____

PRODUCTS AND SERVICES

General Product/Service Description: _____

_____

Number and Type of Lines: _____

_____

Number of Products or Services in Each Line: _____

_____

PATENTS AND LICENSES

Patents Held/Pending: _____

Trademarks Held/Pending: _____

Licenses Held/Pending: _____

Copyrights Held/Pending: _____

Tells company basics: incorporation, location, services.

States how the company intends to distinguish itself to customers.

Shows how the company has grown and established revenues.

Provides specific financial development data.

SAMPLE PLAN: COMPANY DESCRIPTION

COMPANY DESCRIPTION

ComputerEase, Inc., is an Indiana-based company providing computer software training services — both on-premises in the Greater Vespucci, Indiana, area, and online — to business customers. It operates under the name "ComputerEase."

Corporate headquarters and the company's software training classroom are located at 987 South Main Street, Vespucci, Indiana. ComputerEase also offers software training classes at its corporate clients' offices.

The Company's Mission

ComputerEase views its mission as increasing the corporate community's productivity by helping them realize the maximum benefit from their personnel and computers through software training. ComputerEase is dedicated to building long-term relationships with customers through quality training and support, to being known as the premier software training company in the Greater Vespucci area, and to expanding online course offerings globally to English-speaking countries throughout the world. The goal is steady expansion, becoming profitable by the third year of operations. ComputerEase also is dedicated to contributing back to the Vespucci community by providing free computer training programs for inner-city youth, low-income residents, and "welfare-to-work" program participants.

Services

ComputerEase offers training classes for users of all leading business software programs. The company also devises customer training programs for corporate clients. ComputerEase's classes are targeted primarily to the corporate market. Training classes can be taken online, or on-site at the customers' offices or at ComputerEase's Training Center in downtown Vespucci. To fully leverage the company's investment in hardware and software, the company offers online training courses to corporate clients in markets throughout the U.S.

Prior to opening the Training Center and developing online courses, the company was limited in the services it could offer potential clients. The most lucrative business, continuing corporate contracts, was severely restricted, and no public seminars could be offered. Nevertheless, in the first nine months of operation, the company conducted 184 training programs, and secured ongoing training contracts with 11 primary target corporate customers in its local geographic area. And despite investing very little in marketing its online programs during the first two months of offering them, ComputerEase acquired three national accounts. Combined, these activities produced revenues of $171,000 through August 2014.

The company projects deficits for the first two years of operation, with income reinvested for expansion. We anticipate that the company will be profitable by the third year. In these three years, our goal is to become the premier software training company in the Greater Vespucci area, and to increase our market share of the online training services sector. Trends in training, however, are toward nationally known providers, so the company anticipates either joining or starting a national franchise by year three.

The company owns the trademark to the name ComputerEase, under which it does business, and to the slogan "We Speak Your Language."

Development to Date

Founded in January 2014 by Scott E. Connors, ComputerEase began operation by providing software training at corporate customers' offices.

In March 2014, Susan Alexander became Vice President for Marketing. Ms. Alexander immediately began an extensive sales campaign, targeting 200 large companies in the Vespucci area.

In August 2014, ComputerEase opened its software Training Center at its present location in downtown Vespucci, enabling the company to significantly expand its offerings.

Also in August 2014, ComputerEase released its first online training classes, accessible over the company's website. Site licenses were offered to larger corporations with more-extensive ongoing training needs.

In its first nine months of operation, the company conducted 184 training programs, and secured ongoing training contracts with 11 primary target corporate customers in its local geographic area. During the first two months of offering online programs, ComputerEase acquired three national accounts.

Legal Status and Ownership

ComputerEase was incorporated in the state of Indiana one year ago. Ten thousand shares in the company have been issued: 6,000 are owned by President and CEO Scott E. Connors; 1,000 are owned by Vice President of Marketing Susan Alexander; and 3,000 shares have been retained by the company for future distribution.

The company was granted the trademark "ComputerEase" by the U.S. Patent and Trademark Office.

Funding of the company to date has come from the personal savings of Mr. Connors. This has amounted to a $60,000 investment and $40,000 in loans. In addition, the company has received a $30,000 loan from Mr. Connors' family members. All other funding has come from the income generated by sales.

The company is now seeking $160,000 from outside investors. These funds will be used to open an additional Training Center, hire trainers, add staff, and expand marketing activities, especially for online courses.

Gives clear picture of current ownership and equity available.

Preparing the Company Description Section of Your Business Plan

You need to inform your readers of your company's basic information early in your plan. While the Executive Summary creates a compelling case for why your business will succeed, the Company Description fills in the necessary specifics. While much of this information seems mundane, providing these facts is the foundation of the picture you paint of your company.

Use the worksheets throughout this chapter to help you fill out the Company Description Plan Preparation Form on pages 80–81.

Chapter Summary

Your plan's Company Description communicates the basic details of your business in a brief form. From this section, a reader gets a clear idea of what your company does, its legal status, types of products and services, your management and leadership, the business location, and how far you have developed. The Statement of Mission shows that you understand the focus of your company and can articulate your objectives concisely.

CHAPTER

6 Industry Analysis & Trends

*A company must know both how it is like,
and how it is unlike, other businesses.*

Your Business and Industry

No company operates in a vacuum. Every business is part of a larger, overall industry; the forces that affect your industry as a whole will inevitably affect your business as well. Evaluating your industry increases your own knowledge of the factors that contribute to your company's success and shows potential investors that you understand external business conditions.

An industry consists of all companies supplying a similar product or service, other businesses closely related to that product or service, and supply and distribution systems supporting such companies. For example, the apparel industry comprises companies making finished clothing, including the fabric and notion suppliers, independent sales representatives and clothing marts, trade publications, and retail outlets.

In this chapter, you are given the tools to examine your industry. Most of the forms are for your internal planning use, and once you complete them, you will have the information necessary to prepare your Industry Analysis. In your plan, you want to focus on:

■ A description of your industry;

■ Trends in your industry; and

■ Strategic opportunities that exist in your industry.

Naturally, you will need to do some research to get this information. For guidance in your research endeavors, see Chapter 2.

If you have been in your industry for a long time, and if both you and the probable readers of your business plan are well aware of industry conditions, you may not need to spend much time on this section.

Your Economic Sector

The broad category into which your industry or business falls is called its economic sector. The four general sectors are 1) service, 2) manufacturing, 3) retail, and 4) distribution. Your business may belong to more than one sector; for example, you could both manufacture products for resale by others and sell them yourself at the retail level.

Economic sectors experience trends, and it's useful to note your sector's patterns. Because an economic sector is large and diverse, your business can vary dramatically from overall sector performance and trends. It is unnecessary to do a detailed analysis of your sector, but you should understand its past performance and growth projections. ***Study articles in business publications, and then fill in the worksheet on page 87.***

Past and Future Growth of Your Economic Sector		
Economic Sector	Past Growth (Low, Med., High)	Future Growth (Low, Med., High)
1. _____	_____	_____
2. _____	_____	_____
3. _____	_____	_____

Your Industry

Your business may intersect two or more industries. For instance, you may produce electronic devices used in new and used automobiles. Thus, you are part of three industries: electronics, new automobiles, and the automobile after market. (The used car industry has many different issues than does the new car industry.) If your business falls in more than one industry, research each of the applicable industries, giving particular weight to issues most relevant to your business. ***Below list the industry or industries in which your company operates.***

Your Company's Industries
1. _____
2. _____
3. _____

Size and Growth Rate of Your Industry

Pay particular attention to the rate at which your industry is expanding; this gives you insight into the opportunities available for your business. How does the growth rate for your industry compare with the growth of the gross domestic product (GDP), which measures the national economy? This comparison will give you an idea of the current health of your industry.

For example, if your industry is growing at 2% a year, and the GDP at 5% a year, your industry is losing ground, and opportunities will be few. However, if your industry is growing at 15% a year, while the GDP is at 5%, you are in an industry with far greater potential.

If information for your overall industry is difficult to find, you may be able to estimate its approximate size and growth by evaluating the largest companies in your field. Get copies of their annual reports or analyses from stock brokerages and read articles about them in trade and business publications.

After obtaining these basic facts about your industry, fill in the worksheet on page 88, indicating the industry's past and projected future growth. Of course, your own company's development may differ greatly from industry averages—statistics may show that on a national scale, fewer people are dining out, yet your restaurant could be booming.

Past and Future Growth of Your Industry

Factor	2 Years Ago	Past Year	This Year	Next Year	Next 5 Yrs (Avg.)
Total Revenue					
Total Units Sold/Volume					
Total Employment					
Industry Growth Rate					
GDP Growth Rate					
Rate Compared to GDP (+ or %)					

If your business plan's figures are far out of line with industry averages, you need to explain in your plan how you account for the variation.

Industry Maturity

Industries don't remain static; they may change dramatically over time. Generally, the life cycle of an industry comprises four phases: 1) new, 2) expanding, 3) stable, and 4) declining. The last phase, decline, is not inevitable; many long-standing, stable industries show no sign of decline.

Industries have distinct attributes in different stages of maturity. Even industries that seem closely related are quite dissimilar based on their development stage. For instance, the soft drink industry is relatively stable, and a few major companies dominate the field. Little room exists for newcomers, and it would be extremely expensive to try to compete. On the other hand, the newer bottled water industry has lots of competition and variation.

The Industry Maturity Chart on page 90 describes characteristics of industries in the four different stages. Examine the chart and the descriptions of the growth stages, then list the maturity characteristics of your industry and the opportunities and risks they represent on the worksheet on page 89.

Maturity Characteristics of Your Industry and Associated Opportunities/Risks

Growth Rate: _____

Opportunities/Risks: _____

Competition: _____

Opportunities/Risks: _____

Market Leaders/Standards: _____

Opportunities/Risks: _____

Marketing Goals: _____

Opportunities/Risks: _____

Market Share Strategy: _____

Opportunities/Risks: _____

Product Range: _____

Opportunities/Risks: _____

Customer Loyalty: _____

Opportunities/Risks: _____

Sensitivity to Economic Cycles

Some industries are heavily dependent on strong economies, either nationally or internationally, and it is crucial to understand how vulnerable your industry is to economic conditions.

PROSPER IN GOOD ECONOMY

Construction

Autos

Furniture

Tourism

Office Equipment

Technical Equipment

PROSPER IN POOR ECONOMY

Discount Department Stores

Used Car Dealerships

Fairly Immune to Economic Cycles

Personal Care

Low-cost Entertainment

Construction, large consumer items (autos, furniture), and tourism all prosper when the economy is healthy. Industries dependent on new business formation or business expansion, such as office and technical equipment, also perform far better in good times.

Industries such as discount department stores and used-car dealerships are counter-cyclical, doing relatively better in poor economies than in strong ones. And some industries, such as personal care products and low-cost entertainment, are fairly immune to economic cycles.

Industry Maturity Chart

CHARACTERISTIC	DEVELOPMENT STAGE			
	New	**Expanding**	**Stable**	**Declining**
Growth Rate	Very High	Very High	Plateau	Minimal/None
Competition	Increasing	Shakeout	Entrenched	Decreasing
Market Leaders/ Standards	None	In Flux/Emerging	Fixed	Contracting
Marketing Goals	Exposure and Credibility	Differentiate from Competition	Industry Leadership	Survive
Market Share Strategy	Gain Foothold	Build Market Share	Maintain Share	Cannibalize Weakened Competitors
Product Range	Limited	Expanding	Wide	Reduced
Customer Loyalty	None	Hardening	Strong	Weakening

The four stages of an industry's life cycle are described below.

New industries provide excellent entrepreneurial opportunities. Smaller companies are well suited to respond to rapid changes, and larger companies have not yet recognized the field's potential. The market, however, is limited because customers are not yet comfortable with the product or service.

Expanding industries enjoy rapidly growing markets as customers begin to recognize the need for the product or service. Competition is brisk as well-funded companies begin to enter the field. All companies are vulnerable, even those that looked strong when the industry was new.

Stable industries have arrived at a plateau with markets leveled off at a reasonably high level. The rate of growth is slow, and customers maintain strong brand loyalty. It is relatively difficult to enter these industries.

Declining industries result from technological, demographic, and sociological changes, and from overwhelming foreign competition. Corporations leave the field or go bankrupt, and the few major companies fight to survive by stealing remaining customers from weakened competitors.

If your business is located in a smaller community that is heavily dependent on one industry or one major employer, take into account the effect of the economy on that industry or company and, thus, your own business.

Considering the economic conditions or cycles that affect your business helps you anticipate and plan for growth in good times and belt-tightening in difficult times. *On the worksheet below, describe the effect, if any, of each of the listed factors on your industry.*

Effects of Economic Conditions on Your Industry and Business

High Business Expansion/Formation: _____
_____
_____

Low Business Expansion/Formation:_____
_____
_____

High Unemployment/Low Unemployment: _____
_____
_____

Low Interest Rates: _____
_____
_____

High Interest Rates:_____
_____
_____

Low Inflation:_____
_____
_____

High Inflation: _____
_____
_____

Strong Dollar/Weak Dollar: _____
_____

High/Low New Home Construction: _____
_____
_____

> " You've got to be agile. Be able to adapt and react to the changing world. In the [2008] economic downturn, those who survived were those who adapted."
>
> *Bill Rancic*
> *Serial Entrepreneur*

Seasonality

For many industries, certain times of the year produce higher revenues than others, and many industries fluctuate based on holidays.

SEASONALITY

 Spring: An important season for any wedding-associated industry.

 Summer: The big season for bathing suit manufacturers and many tourism-related businesses.

In your financial forms, particularly cash flow projections, understand and account for the seasonal factors that affect your income and expenses. You may sell your product in December, but pay for its raw materials in June.

 Fall: Halloween is now the second largest holiday in the U.S. in terms of retail sales.

 Winter: The holidays may account for one-third to one-half of retail and consumer products sales. While toy companies depend on the holidays, nonessential products and services may actually suffer, as consumers reduce nongift expenses. Construction-related industries may experience slowdowns in winter months, especially in colder climates.

On the worksheet below, describe the impact, if any, that the various seasons or holidays have on the economic health of your industry.

How Seasonal Factors Affect Your Industry

Christmas/Holiday: _____

_____

_____

_____

Summer: _____

_____

_____

_____

Winter: _____

_____

_____

_____

Other: _____

_____

_____

Technological Change

Technological advances affect every industry. Technology changes the way products are made and sold, how information and communication is managed, and how costs are reduced. The Internet has dramatically affected many aspects of even the most traditional industries, including sales and distribution channels, customer service, and relationships with suppliers.

It is, of course, impossible to imagine all the technological developments that may affect your industry over the next five years. But it is useful to take note of the trends of the last five or 10 years. If yours is an industry in which technology changes rapidly, assume that you will need to be positioned to respond to change, and indicate in your business plan your strategy to do so and the financing required. Some technological developments in your industry provide you with strategic opportunities that you want to emphasize when writing your plan.

On the checklist below, indicate the rate of technological change each area of your industry has experienced over the last five years.

Technological Change in Your Industry Over the Last Five Years

Product/Service Features	High	Moderate	Low	None
Manufacturing/Production	☐	☐	☐	☐
Billing/Administration	☐	☐	☐	☐
Information Management	☐	☐	☐	☐
Inventory Control	☐	☐	☐	☐
Delivery Time/Method	☐	☐	☐	☐
Marketing/Communication	☐	☐	☐	☐
Sales Channels	☐	☐	☐	☐
Customer Service	☐	☐	☐	☐
Other: _____	☐	☐	☐	☐
_____	☐	☐	☐	☐

> " In 2011, we converted all of our remaining teas to Fair Trade Certified, helping to ensure that workers on tea gardens receive a fair share of profits, and that the tea gardens comply with specific workplace criteria for equality and fairness."
>
> *Seth Goldman*
> *Cofounder, Honest Tea*

Regulation/Certification

Certain industries are particularly affected by the actions of governmental authorities. While all businesses are influenced by regulation to some degree, regulation, licensing, and certification can dictate in large part how certain industries conduct business. Take time to think about how, if at all, your business and industry are influenced by governmental regulations.

Consider the actions of governmental entities at all levels—national, state, county, municipal, or special regional bodies—when analyzing the regulatory trends in your industry. Some regulatory measures actually create strategic opportunities. In the environmental field, for instance, increased governmental regulation over pollution has led to whole new industries dealing with waste management and energy conservation.

You may also find your business is subject to certification, by either a governmental body or an industry association. You may be required to take state tests to qualify to conduct your business. If your company benefits from regulatory actions, in your plan emphasize how you intend to capitalize on these opportunities.

Indicate your industry's sensitivity to regulation and certification on the checklist below.

How Sensitive Is Your Industry to Government Regulation?

Area of Sensitivity	High	Moderate	Low	None
Environment	☐	☐	☐	☐
Health and Safety	☐	☐	☐	☐
International Trade	☐	☐	☐	☐
Performance Standards	☐	☐	☐	☐
Licensing/Certification	☐	☐	☐	☐
Fair Trade/Deregulation	☐	☐	☐	☐
Product Claims	☐	☐	☐	☐
Other: _____	☐	☐	☐	☐
_____	☐	☐	☐	☐

Supply and Distribution Channels

The supply and distribution channels in your industry can be crucial in determining your company's success. In some industries it is notoriously difficult to gain access to distribution, and in others there are few reliable sources of supply. In industries with a large number of suppliers and distributors, costs remain lower and entry is relatively easy.

Be cautious when entering industries with extremely limited supply or distribution systems. Imagine, for instance, that you are considering starting a new print magazine. While the lines of supply present little or no problem (many sources of paper, printing plants, writers), distribution may be problematic. One or two companies may control all magazine newsstand distribution in your area, making costs extremely high, if they are willing to carry your magazine at all.

In some industries or businesses, the company itself can control its supply or distribution channels. Many companies distribute their products online, directly to their customers without intermediaries. However, this may not necessarily be the most advantageous business choice.

> We started with the technology; we didn't really know what we were going to make. We could have used our process to produce low-alcohol wine, nonalcoholic wine, bottled water, or a soft drink. In taste tests, we got a very high response to the soft drink, but it would have been beyond our resources to get distribution for a soft drink. We had contacts and experience in distribution in the wine industry, and an excellent response to our nonalcoholic wine, so we went with the plan we could execute. I would hate to start a product in a distribution system I didn't know."

Larry Leigon
Founder, Ariel Vineyards

Below, indicate the relative numbers of supply and distribution channels in your industry.

Supply and Distribution Channels in Your Industry				
Number of Channels	**High**	**Moderate**	**Low**	**Self-Control**
Supply	☐	☐	☐	☐
Distribution	☐	☐	☐	☐

Financial Characteristics

No area of your Industry Analysis is more important than an evaluation of the financial patterns characterizing your industry, especially if you are new to the field. Knowing the standards of such aspects as markups, commissions, and returns on sales will substantially help your own budgeting process.

Much of this information may seem difficult to locate if you are just now entering the industry. Perhaps the best way to get this information is to interview those already in the industry, especially those who are not your direct competitors. But make certain the information is industry-specific; knowing the retail markup on apparel won't tell you the markup on food, consumer electronics, or fashion accessories, for example.

The Financial Patterns worksheet on page 98 helps you keep crucial financial specifics handy when preparing budgets. Established businesses should complete this worksheet with actual company data.

Global Industry Concerns

Because of the global nature of business today, you need to consider not only industry trends in your own country, but also industry trends worldwide. This is particularly true if you hope to sell your products or services internationally, but it is even true if you are sourcing materials/inventory worldwide, are using labor across national borders, or are hoping to take advantage of global industry advances to improve your own company's performance.

Use the worksheet on page 96 to identify the global trends that may affect your company.

Preparing the Industry Analysis Section of Your Business Plan

Once you have analyzed your industry for your internal planning purposes, coordinate that information and incorporate the highlights in the Industry Analysis Plan Preparation Form on page 99. This form, when completed, will contain information that will serve as the basis for the Industry Analysis segment of your business plan.

Globalization: Industry Concerns

Which global industries are you a part of? _____
_____
_____
_____

What are the size and growth rates of your industry in countries where you hope to do business? _____
_____
_____
_____

In which countries is your industry new or rapidly developing? _____
_____
_____

In which countries is your industry experiencing high growth rates? _____
_____
_____

Are there seasonality concerns in the countries in which you'll be operating or sourcing supplies or labor? _____
_____
_____
_____

Are other countries introducing technological improvements in your industry? _____
_____
_____

Are government regulations a substantial factor for your industry in countries where you'll be doing business? _____
_____
_____

What other trends or changes are affecting your industry globally? _____
_____
_____
_____

Are international suppliers a significant source of your raw materials or inventory? _____
_____
_____

If you are selling internationally, are there established distribution channels to enable you to reach your market? _____
_____
_____

Chapter Summary

Evaluating the standards, trends, and characteristics of your industry helps you ensure your own company's success and assists you in planning your budgets. Although each company is unique, no business completely escapes the realities and constraints of the industry in which it operates. Anticipating changes in your industry can help you position your company for future developments. You need to understand the larger environment before you can successfully differentiate your own business.

> " This [winemaking] is a capital-intensive industry; inventories are expensive to maintain. You get a low asset turnover because your inventory has to sit around in barrels for a long time. Profit margins are not good. You must determine what are the key ratios in the business, even if the formal financials don't follow for six months. Stay on top of the payables and receivables turnover, the gross profit margin, the inventory turnover ratio."
>
> *Larry Leigon*
> *Founder, Ariel Vineyards*

Financial Patterns

$ ➤ $$ ➤ $$$

Fill in this worksheet with figures representative of the financial standards in your industry.

Normal Retail Markup of Goods: _____
_____
_____
_____

Normal Distributor Markup of Goods: _____
_____
_____
_____

Typical Sales Commission Percentage:_____
_____
_____
_____

Standard Credit Terms: _____
_____
_____
_____

Days of Inventory Maintained: _____
_____
_____
_____

Average Percentage of Return on Sales: _____
_____
_____
_____

Other Financial Patterns of Note: _____
_____
_____
_____

Percentage of Merchandise Price due to

Cost of Labor: _____   Fixed Costs: _____

Cost of Materials: _____   Shipping:_____

Energy: _____   Other: _____

Industry Analysis Plan Preparation Form

Using this form as a guide, summarize the main points you wish to convey in your Industry Analysis.

Industry Description:_____

_____

_____

_____

_____

_____

_____

_____

_____

_____

_____

Industry Trends:_____

_____

_____

_____

_____

_____

_____

_____

_____

_____

_____

_____

Strategic Opportunities: _____

_____

_____

_____

_____

_____

_____

_____

_____

_____

_____

_____

_____

Use this information as the basis of your plan's Industry Analysis.

SAMPLE PLAN: INDUSTRY ANALYSIS & TRENDS

INDUSTRY ANALYSIS

ComputerEase is well-positioned to take advantage of the significant opportunities presented by the rapidly expanding industry of computer-related business services.

Computer-Related Services on the Rise

Cites statistics, showing real knowledge of industry.

Service industries represent the fastest-growing sector of the national economy, and computer-related business services reflect that continued growth. These services as a whole grew in excess of 62% over the five years from 2009 to 2013, compared to an overall GDP of approximately 2% during that period.

Rapidly Evolving Industry

Computer software training is a rapidly evolving industry, as technologies advance and develop. The industry is in a state of flux, with no market leaders, nationally known providers, or widely recognized accreditation programs. Individual software manufacturers do offer certification as trainers for their products, but this certification is yet to be standardized, and such certification is not always a key issue for consumers.

The key to success in the industry is to develop a regionally recognized brand in conjunction with online services, as is currently the case with other business services, such as accounting or human resources. Regionally dominant training companies are able to earn revenues and build market share sufficient both to sustain continued development of online courses and to support the high overhead cost of equipment, skilled trainers, subject matter experts, and materials.

Open Competitive Environment

Shows market opportunity.

Currently, the level of service is broadly uneven, and providers enter and leave the field rapidly. Some in-person training is marketed through direct mail and email newsletters by national companies generally offering one- or two-day sessions by traveling trainers in physical locations. Online training companies market online, through email, and through the purchase of keywords from search engine companies. Training companies do not maintain an ongoing local profile or relationship with customers. Other software training is offered by individual consultants.

Generally, these competing training companies are not presented or marketed in any continuing, professional manner. They are not perceived in the marketplace as "businesses," and quality and pricing are widely uneven.

Long-Term Opportunities

Thus, the long-term outlook for the industry is to develop regionally or nationally known companies, as is currently the case with other business services, such as accounting or employment services. These companies will be able to develop revenues and market share sufficient to sustain the high overhead. National franchises or affiliations will make it possible to share training materials and other resources.

ComputerEase Can Develop Strong Position in Region

The current lack of industry leaders represents an exceptional opportunity for ComputerEase to develop a dominant presence in the software training field both in the Greater Vespucci area and online. The company will then be well-situated to take advantage of national affiliations, with franchisors, national associations, or software providers.

CHAPTER 7

Target Market

> *It's easier to get a piece of an existing market than it is to create a new one.*

Know Your Customers

Essential to business success is a thorough understanding of your customers. After all, if you don't know who your customers are, how will you be able to assess whether you are meeting their needs? Since success depends on your being able to meet customers' needs and desires, you must know who your customers are, what they want, how they behave, and what they can afford.

Is Your Company Market Driven?

Moreover, if you are using your business plan to secure financing, defining the nature and size of your market is critical. Many investors look for companies aimed at substantial-sized markets and that are market driven. In other words, they seek to fund companies whose orientation is shaped by the demands and trends of the marketplace rather than the inherent characteristics of a particular product or service.

Being attuned to your market may lead you to make changes in your advertising, packaging, location, sales structure, and even the features and character of the product or service itself. In the long run, a market analysis will save you money. When deciding which marketing vehicles to use (advertising, trade shows, or other), you can then choose approaches based on whether they reach your specific target market.

A market analysis differs from a marketing plan. An analysis enables you to identify and understand your customers; a marketing plan tells how you are going to reach your customers. Laying out a marketing plan is covered in Chapter 10.

If you do not sell your product or service directly to the end-user but rather to retail outlets, distributors, or manufacturers, you have two markets, and you should define the characteristics of both of them—the ultimate consumer and the intermediary who is your actual customer. These target markets may have very different habits and concerns, and you need to understand both of them, as they each affect your sales. For instance, you may sell software you develop to a computer manufacturer that then bundles it with the computers they sell to consumers. The computer manufacturer's biggest concern may be cost; the consumer's may be ease-of-use.

To gather information for this chapter, use the methods discussed in Chapter 2.

Defining Your Target Market

You may be tempted to describe your market in the broadest possible terms, choosing to include all those who might potentially use your product or service. Doing so gives you the comforting sense that you have a huge market to exploit. Unfortunately, this gives you little genuine information on which to base your business decisions. You could end up defining the market for furniture as everyone who lives indoors—hardly helpful if you're trying to come up with a marketing plan for your furniture store.

Instead you need to identify the particular market segments you wish to reach. These segments describe distinct, meaningful components of the overall market and give you a set of specific characteristics by which to identify your target market.

Let's say you are considering opening a discount dry cleaning establishment. You plan your service to be less expensive and faster, but, as a result, it may also be of slightly lesser quality than the dry cleaner now serving the area.

Thus, you might define your target market in these terms: "Employed women in white-collar jobs, price and time sensitive, commute by car, ages 25 to 50, household incomes of $40,000–$80,000 per year, children living at home, reside in the Laurelwood neighborhood." You then need to determine whether the neighborhood has enough consumers who fit this profile to support your business.

To be a useful planning tool, the definition of your target market must meet these criteria:

- **Definable.** It should have specific characteristics identifying what the potential customers have in common.
- **Meaningful.** The characteristics must meaningfully relate to the decision to purchase.
- **Sizable.** It must be large enough to profitably sustain your business.
- **Reachable.** Both the definition and the size must lead to affordable and effective ways to market to your potential customers.

Once you have defined your market, you should then assess its size and trends, evaluate your competitors for that particular market, and probe the market for strategic opportunities.

Demographic Description

Begin describing your market by the most basic, objective aspects of the customer base. These details are the specific and observable traits that define your target market.

Demographic information is particularly useful when devising your marketing plan. Many marketing vehicles, such as publications, mailing lists, radio, and TV, accumulate this kind of data about the market they reach. Thus, you are better able to judge whether such vehicles are appropriate for your company.

Remember, you want to define those characteristics of your target market that meaningfully relate to the interest, need, and ability of the customer to purchase your product or service.

In the previous definition of the target market for the Laurelwood dry cleaner, for instance, the definition "white-collar jobs" directly relates to the need for regular dry cleaning; "women" relates to the fact that most dry

> "Customers can be categorized in several ways, by income level or by lifestyle issues. The income levels can fall into one or more of the following categories: luxury, upscale, upper moderate, moderate, and budget. Lifestyle issues are more subjective. The target customer is less dependent on income level and more on her attitude about how she spends her disposable income."
>
> **Nancy Glaser**
> **Business Strategies Consultant**

> "It's very difficult to create a new market, even if there's a need. Developing a new market takes years, even if you're 100% right about the need and the product. The best market to look for is a market that already exists, that is already being served, but being served in a marginal fashion."
>
> **Eugene Kleiner**
> **Venture Capitalist**

cleaning nationally is purchased by women; "commute by car" is important because the location is not near public transportation; and "$40,000–$80,000" relates to the customer's ability to pay for dry cleaning while being less likely to afford the more-expensive cleaners.

On the Demographic Description worksheet on page 107, describe the demographic details of your target market, whether you are marketing to consumers or to businesses.

Geographic Description

Next, define the primary geographic area(s) you intend to serve. This definition should be as concrete as possible, indicating whether your business serves a particular neighborhood, city, state, region, nation, or portion of the international market.

Also, look at the density of the area—whether urban, suburban, or rural—and, if customers will be coming to your place of business, indicate whether the location is in a mall, strip center, business district, or industrial area, or will be a stand-alone facility. Some businesses define their geographic market by climate, serving only cold-weather or hot-weather locations.

If you are making your product or service available globally—especially online—you may be tempted to view the entire world as your geographic target market. However, even online, there are limitations to which geographic areas are your primary target markets. These limits may be due to issues of fulfillment (e.g., shipping goods), language, licensing, or legal issues, and there are certainly limits of realistic market demand from different areas.

Using the worksheet below and the one on page 108, describe the geographic details of your target customers, whether domestic or international.

> **The decision to locate in Napa was a marketing decision. We could have made our product anywhere, but 'Napa' is associated with premium wines. We wanted Napa on the label."**
>
> *Eugene Kleiner*
> *Venture Capitalist*

Domestic Geographic Description

Area Served (city, region, nation, etc.): _____

_____

_____

Density (urban, rural, suburban, etc.): _____

_____

_____

Nature of Location (mall, strip center, business district, etc.):_____

_____

_____

Climate Conditions: _____

_____

_____

Demographic Description

CONSUMER

Age Range: _____

_____

_____

Income Range: _____

_____

_____

Gender: _____

_____

_____

Occupation: _____

_____

_____

Marital Status: _____

_____

_____

Family Size: _____

_____

_____

Ethnic Group: _____

_____

_____

Level of Education: _____

_____

_____

Home Ownership: _____

_____

_____

Other: _____

_____

_____

_____

_____

BUSINESS

Industries: _____

_____

_____

Sector: _____

_____

_____

Years in Business: _____

_____

_____

Company Revenues: _____

_____

_____

Number of Employees: _____

_____

_____

Number of Branches: _____

_____

_____

Square Footage: _____

_____

_____

Company Ownership: _____

_____

_____

Other: _____

_____

_____

_____

_____

Globalization: International Target Market

Countries Served: _____

Population: _____

Targeted Areas within Country (cities, rural, suburban): _____

Level of Development (developed, emerging): _____

Climate Conditions: _____

Languages Spoken: _____

Quality of Infrastructure (e.g., roads, telecommunications, utilities): _____

Lifestyle/Business-Style Description

In the Target Market section of your plan, convey a sense of the concerns and interests of your customers. How do they spend their time? What issues are they facing in their lives or businesses? With whom do they associate? How do they relate to their employees and community?

Your natural instincts and experience with customers gives you some sense of what your customers are interested in. It's logical, for instance, to assume that receptive targets for your expensive specialty food product are fairly likely to subscribe to *Gourmet* or other food magazines and might belong to local food and wine organizations. Or, if the market for your business service is law firms, you would naturally assume they belong to the local Bar Association.

A little research can help you identify other aspects of your target market's lifestyle or business style. Observe customers in places where they shop or live. What other products or services do they buy? What kinds of cars do they drive? What kinds of clothes do they wear?

Review the publications you think target customers subscribe to. What other companies are advertising? What are the articles about? Survey your customers, whether in person, by mail, or on the phone, and ask them about some of their activities.

What kinds of people or businesses need or want your product or service? Do they go to the movies, watch TV, or stream videos? Do they entertain at home? If so, for whom? What other kinds of products or services would be used in the same setting with yours?

Develop a mental picture of your customer's entire week. Be creative, but logical and realistic. You want to relate to your customer as a whole, which makes you more responsive to their needs and gives you ideas for marketing vehicles and approaches. The worksheet on page 110 helps you achieve this.

Psychographic Description

In addition to the observable, objective characteristics of your market, less tangible but equally important psychological factors also influence your targeted customer's purchasing decisions. These are aspects of self-image: how customers see, or want to see, themselves. Some of these are fairly self-conscious attributes—for example, a homemaker priding himself or herself on being a smart shopper. Some are less conscious, perhaps being status-seeking or gadget-happy. Marketing experts segment consumers into different psychographic and lifestyle groups. Some of these segments become well-known—for instance, the term "early adopters" is widely used for those consumers who are eager to be among the first to try new technologies.

Business customers as well as consumers can be described in psychographic terms. Some companies view themselves as being on the cutting edge of technology, others as fiscally responsible, and still others as socially responsible. These distinctions can help you determine marketing efforts and positioning of your product or service.

On the checklist below, check off the psychographic traits that characterize your target customer.

Psychographic Description	
CONSUMER	**BUSINESS**
☐ Technically Adept	☐ Technically Advanced
☐ Status Seeking	☐ Industry Leader
☐ Trend-Setting	☐ Innovative
☐ Conservative/Responsible	☐ Conservative/Responsible
☐ Socially Responsible	☐ Socially Responsible
☐ Environmentally Conscious	☐ Environmentally Conscious
☐ Smart Shopper	☐ Smart Business Operator
☐ Family-Oriented	☐ Fiscally Prudent
☐ Fun-Seeking	☐ Good Manager of Employees
☐ Good Housekeeper	☐ Influenced by Leading Companies
☐ Other:_____	☐ Other:_____

Lifestyle/Business-Style Description

CONSUMER

Family Stage: _____

_____

_____

Vacation Choices: _____

_____

_____

Television Shows Watched: _____

_____

_____

Favorite Websites: _____

_____

_____

Hobbies/Sports/Other Forms of Entertainment: ____

_____

_____

Publication Subscriptions: _____

_____

_____

Organizations/Affiliations: _____

_____

_____

Political Affiliation: _____

_____

_____

Type of Car Owned: _____

_____

_____

Other: _____

_____

_____

_____

_____

BUSINESS

Business Stage: _____

_____

_____

Employee Relations: _____

_____

_____

Trade Association Memberships: _____

_____

_____

Business Products and Services Used: _____

_____

_____

Workforce Type: _____

_____

_____

Publication Subscriptions: _____

_____

_____

Community Activities: _____

_____

_____

Management Style: _____

_____

_____

Other: _____

_____

_____

_____

_____

Purchasing Patterns Description

In planning, it's particularly important to understand the buying patterns of your customers. For instance, if Fortune 500 companies are your target market, you must recognize that these large companies have slow decision-making processes and, due to their size, resist change even when presented with compelling facts. You must keep these realistic constraints in mind when forecasting your sales to this market.

Complete the worksheet below to describe the likely purchasing patterns of your target customers, whether consumers or businesses.

Purchasing Patterns Description
Reason/occasion for first purchase: _____
Number of times they'll purchase:_____
Interval between purchases:_____
Amount of product/service purchased:_____
Motivation for continued use: _____
How long to make decision to purchase: _____
Where customer first learned about product/service: _____
Place where customer purchases product/service: _____
Where customer uses product:_____
How customer uses product: _____
Method of payment: _____
Special needs:_____
Other: _____

Buying Sensitivities Description

What factors are most important to your customer when deciding to buy? Of course, all customers would say that they want the highest quality, best service, and greatest convenience, at the lowest price. But in reality, customers know they have to make trade-offs: paying a little more for extra features, driving farther to get a lower price. What aspects are your customers least willing to give up? What are the areas of their greatest sensitivity?

The checklist on page 112 helps you indicate how sensitive your customers (consumers or businesses) are to various factors.

Buying Sensitivity Description	High	Medium	Low	Not at All
Price	☐	☐	☐	☐
Quality	☐	☐	☐	☐
Brand Name	☐	☐	☐	☐
Product Features	☐	☐	☐	☐
Salesperson	☐	☐	☐	☐
Sales/Special Offers	☐	☐	☐	☐
Advertising	☐	☐	☐	☐
Packaging	☐	☐	☐	☐
Convenience of Use	☐	☐	☐	☐
Convenience of Purchase	☐	☐	☐	☐
Location	☐	☐	☐	☐
Store Decor/Environment	☐	☐	☐	☐
Customer Service	☐	☐	☐	☐
Return Policy	☐	☐	☐	☐
Credit Availability	☐	☐	☐	☐
Maintenance Program	☐	☐	☐	☐
Warranty	☐	☐	☐	☐
Nature of Existing Customers	☐	☐	☐	☐
Other:_____	☐	☐	☐	☐

> " We received more than our share of rejections from distributors and retail buyers who didn't think we were peddling what the public wanted."
>
> *Seth Goldman*
> *Cofounder, Honest Tea*

Market Size and Trends

Once you have defined the characteristics of your target market, you must then assess the size of this market and evaluate the trends likely to influence both market size and customer behavior in the near future.

Size

You want to make sure your customer base is large enough to sustain your business and, if seeking funding, to convince potential investors that your company can grow to a size that will make their investment profitable.

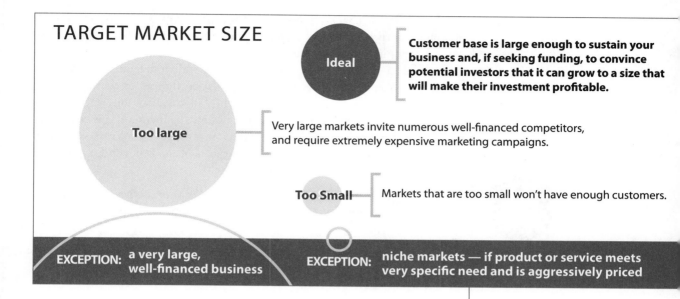

TARGET MARKET SIZE

Ideal — Customer base is large enough to sustain your business and, if seeking funding, to convince potential investors that it can grow to a size that will make their investment profitable.

Too large — Very large markets invite numerous well-financed competitors, and require extremely expensive marketing campaigns.

Too Small — Markets that are too small won't have enough customers.

EXCEPTION: a very large, well-financed business

EXCEPTION: niche markets — if product or service meets very specific need and is aggressively priced

Surprisingly, you generally don't want your target market to be either too small or too large. Markets that are too small are obviously in trouble from the start, as you won't have enough customers. (The exception: Niche markets may be quite small, serving a limited number of customers with a very specific need, but can still be lucrative and able to support a well-defined business if the product or service meets a very specific need and is aggressively priced.) Very large markets, however, invite numerous well-financed competitors, and require extremely expensive marketing campaigns. (The exception: if you are developing a very large, well-financed business.)

For some businesses, particularly smaller retail operations, determining whether your market is sufficiently sizable will be mostly a matter of intuition and observation. You needn't do a scientific study. But if you are unsure about your market, or need to convince investors, you must gather data to support your plan.

When assessing the size of the market, you will find demographic and geographic information easiest to locate. Much of this data is available from U.S. Census Bureau reports, local governmental agencies, real estate brokerages, Chambers of Commerce, and business directories.

Information about other characteristics of your market can be gleaned from existing market research studies about the general population or from trade associations. For more information on how to research market size, refer to Chapter 2.

Trends

Equally important as estimating the size of your current market is evaluating the trends that may affect the market in the coming years. Doing so will give you a sense of your company's continuing viability, the strategic opportunities the market presents, and how the company must plan to respond to changing behavior of customers.

> "We like to fund companies for which there is a real need for their product — a need that's there right now. We're conservative that way."
>
> *Damon Doe*
> *Managing Partner*
> *Montage Capital*

Preparing for change is not so much a matter of predicting the future as analyzing the recent past. Much of your analysis can be based on observable changes in demographics and customer behavior. For instance, let's say your product is designed to appeal to retired individuals in the American Southwest. You can analyze increased population figures for that age group in particular states and membership trends in organizations such as the AARP. This will provide you with a sense of how the market size is changing. Studies of new hobbies, of disposable income growth, and of altered buying habits for the age group will give you indicators of the issues and opportunities facing your company in the near future.

Use the worksheets on page 115 to describe your market size and the trends likely to affect customer behavior in the next few years.

Preparing the Target Market Section of Your Business Plan

Based on what you have learned by analyzing your potential market, you are now ready to prepare the Target Market section of your written business plan.

Using the Target Market Plan Preparation Form on page 116 as a guide, focus primarily on these three areas:

- Description
- Size and Trends
- Strategic Opportunities

This section of your plan particularly lends itself to the use of bullet points, which makes writing easier.

Chapter Summary

A concise description and thorough understanding of your target market will give you focus when developing your product or service, designing your marketing plan, and forecasting sales and expenses. Potential investors want reassurance that your market is sizable and that you comprehend the opportunities and limitations of the market. You need to make certain both that your target market is definable and reachable.

> "Before they'll fund a company, a venture capitalist will always do due diligence; test out the market; call potential customers."
>
> **Mark Gorenberg**
> **Venture Capitalist**

Domestic Market Size and Trends

What is the current approximate size of your target market? _____

_____

What is the rate of growth of the target market?_____

_____

What changes are occurring in the makeup of the market? _____

_____

What changes are affecting the ability to afford the product/service? _____

_____

What changes are affecting the need for the product/service? _____

_____

How are customers changing the use of the product/service?_____

_____

What changes in social values and concerns are affecting the product/service? _____

_____

Globalization: Market Size and Trends

Answer the following questions for each of the countries or regions you are targeting.

What is the current approximate size of your target market? _____

_____

What is the rate of growth of the target market?_____

_____

What changes are occurring in the makeup of the market? _____

_____

What changes are affecting the ability to afford the product/service? _____

_____

What changes are affecting the need for the product/service? _____

_____

How are customers changing the use of the product/service?_____

_____

What changes in social values and concerns are affecting the product/service? _____

_____

Target Market Plan Preparation Form

Outline the Target Market portion of your plan on this form. More-detailed descriptions of your market and results of market research can be included in your plan's Appendix.

Market Description: _____

_____

_____

_____

_____

_____

_____

_____

_____

_____

Market Size and Trends: _____

_____

_____

_____

_____

_____

_____

_____

_____

_____

Strategic Opportunities: _____

_____

_____

_____

_____

_____

_____

_____

_____

_____

Use this information as the basis of your plan's Target Market section.

SAMPLE PLAN: TARGET MARKET

TARGET MARKET

Market Description

ComputerEase operates in the Greater Vespucci, Indiana, area. Online, the target geographic market location includes English-speaking countries with high levels of business automation. In person, the geographic area includes the incorporated cities of:

- Vespucci
- Whitten Park
- Smithfield

And the suburban communities (with business centers) of:

- Karen's Springs
- Gaspar
- Lake Bonneau

Indicates specific geographic market.

Market Size and Trends

The online market for computer training is large and growing exponentially as people have increasingly become accustomed to using—and relying upon—Web-based applications for more and more aspects of their lives, including education and training. Also, as companies automate more of their business processes, they require quick and efficient ways to get their employees up to speed on new or updated business software—both off-the-shelf and specifically designed for their organizations. Vespucci and its surrounding communities make up a large and economically healthy area. According to census figures, the city of Vespucci has a population of approximately 775,000, making it the 16th-largest city in the U.S. The Vespucci Metropolitan Statistical Area (MSA) has an overall population approaching 1,500,000.

The business climate has been consistently strong due to Vespucci's diverse economic base. The Vespucci MSA includes three county seats and is the home to numerous government offices. The Vespucci Chamber of Commerce estimates that, of the more than 2,000 companies and institutions with more than 50 employees in the Greater Vespucci area, at least 1,500 are in the primary industries targeted by ComputerEase.

Relates health and diversity of target market.

Also located in the Greater Vespucci area are:

- An international airport
- The regional processing centers for three national insurance companies
- The data processing center for the state's highway patrol
- A state university and six other colleges and universities
- A major medical center

SAMPLE PLAN: TARGET MARKET (continued)

The economic base has been expanding, and recently a national research institute with 280 employees announced its intention to relocate to Vespucci. A survey for the local newspaper, *The Vespucci Explorer*, showed that 43% of larger companies intended to add employees in the next 24 months.

The breakdown of employment by industry is approximately:

- 25% retail and wholesale sales
- 25% government
- 25% manufacturing
- 25% education, health, and services

Target Customers

Clearly identifies characteristics of target customers.

ComputerEase primarily targets large- and medium-size businesses with high computer use. They have:

- More than 50 employees
- High employee turnover
- An expanding number of employees
- A high dependence on computers

They are in the following industries:

- Government
- Insurance
- Financial/Banking
- Accounting
- Colleges and universities
- Engineering
- Hospitals and other medical facilities
- Airlines

Indicates self-image and sensitivities of potential customers.

Management personnel in these industries generally view themselves as responsible and professional. They prefer to deal with service companies that present a stable, conservative image. They are generally more sensitive to quality than price, and can be considerably influenced by the fact that similar companies already use the service provider.

Market Readiness

ComputerEase's Vice President for Marketing conducted a market research survey with a selection of targeted companies. This survey indicated the particular patterns of these companies in relation to computer training need:

Shows real market exists.

- 97% indicated a need for employees trained in computer use.

- 83% indicated some need for company-provided computer training.

- 67% indicated a need for occasional or specialized training.

- 41% indicated a need for continuing training programs.

The survey also revealed how such companies do or would spend funds on computer training. Specific data indicates:

- 42% of these companies have a "training" amount allotted in their current year's budget.

- 18% specifically have "computer or software training" budgeted for the current year.

- 34% have purchased software training services in the last year.

- 66% indicated they would purchase more training than at present if better-quality, more-reliable training were available.

- 72% said they wanted to minimize the amount of time employees spent out of the office for training, and that they would pay a premium for online training that workers could complete without leaving their desks.

Fully 74% of those using computer training said they were either highly unsatisfied or somewhat unsatisfied with their current training arrangements. This level of dissatisfaction is substantially higher than the satisfaction level with other business services (27% average dissatisfaction level with services such as accounting and legal).

Strategic Opportunities

Computer training services in these companies are overwhelmingly purchased, recommended, or approved by the Human Resources/Personnel Director (83%), providing a clear target for marketing efforts. Clearly, there is a real need for ComputerEase's services in the Vespucci area as well as online. An expanding and healthy market, a highly dissatisfied market, and an identifiable way to reach the market all provide a substantial opportunity for ComputerEase to fill a void in the provision of software training services.

CHAPTER 8

The Competition

It is not enough just to build a better mousetrap;
you have to build a better mousetrap company.

Know What You're Up Against

Famed baseball player Satchel Paige used to say, "Don't look back; someone may be gaining on you." But in business it is imperative to see who's gaining on you. It is far better to know what you're up against than to be surprised when your sales suddenly disappear to an unexpected competitor.

Every business has competition. Those currently operating a company are all too aware of the many competitors for a customer's dollar. Yet many people new to business—excited about their concept and motivated by a perceived opening in the market—tend to underestimate the actual extent of competition and fail to properly assess the impact of that competition on their business.

One of the very worst statements you can make in a business plan is, "We have no competition." A knowledgeable investor will immediately disregard a plan with such a statement because it indicates that either: 1) you have not fully examined the realities of your business; or 2) there is no market for your concept.

You can see this by looking at the example of the photocopier. When the first one was invented, no competition existed from other makers of photocopiers, of course. But competition still came from many sources, including suppliers of carbon paper and mimeograph machines. And if the copier worked and the market was receptive, future competition could realistically be projected. If no competition truly existed at the time it was invented—if people weren't duplicating documents by some means—it would have meant no market for photocopiers existed.

Honestly evaluating your competition will help you better understand your own product or service and give investors a reassuring sense of your company's strengths. It enables you to know how best to distinguish your company in the customer's eyes, and it points to opportunities in the market.

Learn from your competition. The basic concept of competition is responsiveness to customers, and watching your competitors can help you understand what customers want.

As you begin your competitive assessment, keep in mind that you need to evaluate only those competitors aiming for the same target market. If you own a fine French restaurant in midtown Manhattan, you don't have to include the McDonald's next door in your competitive evaluation: You're not aiming for the same customer at the same time. On the other hand, if you are thinking of opening the first sports memorabilia shop in Alaska, you have to look far afield, at any such retail stores in Seattle or Vancouver, mail-order dealers from all over the country, and online dealers from around the world, as that is where your potential customers shop now.

ASSESS THE COMPETITION

When preparing the competitive analysis portion of your business plan, focus on identifying:

Who	**What**	**How**	**Future**	**Barriers**
Who are your major competitors?	On what basis do you compete?	How do you compare to the competition?	Who are your potential future competitors?	What are the barriers to entry for new competitors?

Competitive Position

It is tempting to want to judge your competition solely on the basis of whether your product or service is better than theirs. If you have invented a clearly superior widget, it is comforting to imagine that widget customers will naturally buy your product instead of the competitors' and the money will roll in.

Unfortunately, many other factors will determine your success in comparison to other manufacturers of widgets. Perhaps their brand name is already well-known. Perhaps their widgets are much cheaper. Perhaps their distribution system makes it easier for them to get placement in stores. Or maybe customers just like the color of your competitors' packages better.

The objective features of your product or service may be a relatively small part of the competitive picture. In fact, all the components of customer preference, including price, service, and location, make up only half of the competitive analysis.

The other half of the equation consists of examining the internal strength of your competitors' companies. In the long run, companies with significant financial resources, highly motivated or creative personnel, and other operational assets will prove to be tough, enduring competition.

> You can't be 5% or 10% better than the competition. You have to be 10 times better. There's a huge lethargy factor — you don't get people to change their bank account, or whatever you're trying to get them to change, if you're 10% better; you've got to be 10 times better."
>
> *Andrew Anker*
> *Venture Capitalist*

Thoroughly Evaluate Your Competition

Two Competitive Analysis worksheets on pages 124–125 help you evaluate your competitive position in terms of both customer preference and internal operational strengths.

The worksheets enable you to give greater or lesser importance to each competitive factor, depending on the significance of those particular aspects. To complete each worksheet, give each factor listed a maximum possible number of points, ranging from 1 to 10, with 1 being least important to your overall target market and 10 being the most important. Place the maximum number for each factor in the Maximum Points column.

Competitive Analysis: Customer Perception Factors

Following the directions on pages 123 and 126, allocate points for each of the factors listed below for both your company and your competitors.

Factor	Maximum Points (1–10)	Your Company	Competitor _____	Competitor _____	Competitor _____	Competitor _____
Product/Service Features						
Purchase Price						
Indirect/Peripheral Costs						
Quality						
Durability/Maintenance						
Image/Style/Design						
Perceived Value						
Brand Recognition						
Customer Relationships						
Location						
Delivery Time						
Convenience of Use						
Credit Policies						
Customer Service						
Social Consciousness						
Other:						
Other:						
Total Points						
Comments:						

Competitive Analysis: Internal Operational Factors

Following the directions on pages 123 and 126, allocate points for each of the factors listed below for both your company and your competitors.

Factor	Maximum Points (1–10)	Your Company	Competitor ___	Competitor ___	Competitor ___	Competitor ___
Financial Resources						
Marketing Budget/Program						
Technological Competence						
Access to Distribution						
Access to Suppliers						
Economies of Scale						
Operational Efficiencies						
Sales Structure/ Competence						
Product Line Breadth						
Strategic Partnerships						
Company Morale/Personnel						
Certification/Regulation						
Patents/Trademarks						
Ability to Innovate						
Other:						
Other:						
Other:						
Total Points						
Comments:						

For instance, on the Competitive Analysis: Customer Perception Factors worksheet, let's say your target market is extremely price sensitive but willing to travel a long way to get a bargain. The purchase price factor might be given a maximum of 10 points and the location factor a maximum of 2.

Once you have finished numbering the factors for your company and competitors, you will see how this weighting system gives you a better picture of the actual strength of your competitors as opposed to your own.

Keep in mind that you can also allot negative numbers. If, for example, your target market is interested only in items perceived as luxuries, having too low a price may be a liability. If your market is particularly socially conscious, the fact that your competitor conducts tests on animals may be a negative for the social image factor in their evaluation, giving you a competitive edge.

In your analyses, look both at specific competitors—particular companies you compete against—and at the overall type of competition. In the example of the Alaskan sports memorabilia store, for instance, the Competitive Analysis might have four competitors listed: each of the two specific retail stores in Seattle and Vancouver, mail-order dealers, and online dealers as categories.

If desired, you can include these completed worksheets in the Appendix of your plan, as well as use them for internal planning purposes.

Customer Perception Factors

When doing your analysis, consider these customer perception factors:

- **Product/Service Features.** Specific inherent attributes of the product or service itself; if key features are particularly important, list separately.

- **Indirect/Peripheral Costs.** Costs other than the actual purchase price, such as installation or additional equipment required.

- **Quality.** Inherent merit of the product or service at the time it is provided.

- **Durability/Maintenance.** Quality of the product/service over time; ease of maintenance and service.

- **Image/Style/Perceived Value.** Added values derived from design features, attractive packaging or presentation, and other intangibles.

- **Customer Relationships.** Established customer base and customer loyalty; relationships of sales personnel to customers.

- **Social Consciousness.** Perception of the company, product, or service relative to issues such as environment, civic involvement, and the like.

Internal Operational Factors

Internal operational factors that increase competitiveness include:

- **Financial Resources.** Ability of the company to withstand financial setbacks, and to fund product development and improvements.

- **Marketing Budget/Program.** Amount and effectiveness of advertising and other promotional activities.

- **Economies of Scale.** Ability to reduce per-unit costs due to large volume.

- **Operational Efficiencies.** Production or delivery methods that reduce costs and time.

- **Product Line Breadth.** Ability to increase revenues by selling related products; ability for customers to purchase needed items from one provider.

- **Strategic Partnerships.** Relationships with other companies for purposes of development, promotion, or add-on sales.

- **Company Morale/Personnel.** Motivation, commitment, and productivity of the employees.

Other Factors Affecting Your Ability to Compete

First-Mover Advantage

In new industries or new market segments, the first company to gain a reasonable foothold in the market can often leverage being early into a significant competitive advantage. Having a market to itself for even a brief period may enable a company to define the product, set standards, establish key strategic partnerships, capture customer attention, and in other ways gain dominance. This rush to market, however, does not guarantee success, and many industries have instances of early market leaders being overtaken by later-stage competitors.

Installed User Base

If a sizable portion of the market currently uses a product that performs a similar function or is incompatible with your new product or service, customers may resist the cost and inconvenience of making the transition. This is particularly true for products involving technology or electronics.

Often even superior products have a difficult time getting a foothold in such markets. One of the most cited examples is the familiar "QWERTY" keyboard. Keys on early typewriters were arranged to intentionally slow down typing to prevent the mechanical keys from sticking. Although later keyboards improved on this arrangement, typists were already comfortable with the "QWERTY" keyboard, and it remains to this day.

The Web

Using the Web substantially lowers barriers to entry in many industries, and in some cases it allows competitors to operate at extremely narrow profit margins. The Internet also arms customers with substantially more purchase information, sometimes even wholesale prices. Companies that previously may have been able to compete effectively in a particular geographic area may now face worldwide competition.

> " We have to view our product through the eyes of a consumer and see what we look like to them in comparison to our competitors. It's easy to get involved in the manufacturing process and lose sight of what the consumer sees on the shelf. But if you do, the rest of the process is immaterial."
>
> *Larry Leigon*
> *Founder, Ariel Vineyards*

> " No competition is a red flag for an investor. If you say, 'there is no competition,' then there's either no market or you just don't understand the competition."
>
> *Lauren Flanagan*
> *Cofounder and Managing Director, BELLE Capital USA*

Globalization: Competition

Are there many international competitors currently offering your product/service to your target market? _____

_____
_____
_____
_____

How difficult is it for international competitors to enter your market? What barriers to entry, if any, exist? _____

_____
_____
_____
_____

If known, what are the specific international companies competing with you? _____

_____
_____
_____
_____

Is the amount of international competition increasing, decreasing, or remaining the same? _____

_____
_____
_____
_____

What makes your international competition attractive to your customers (price, quality, selection, convenience, etc.)?

_____
_____
_____
_____

What advantages do you have over your international competitors (price, quality, selection, convenience, etc.)? _____

_____
_____
_____
_____
_____
_____
_____

Inertia

Customers don't do what they should do; they do what they have to or want to do. In almost every case, customers have the option not to buy at all. It's not enough for you to know the customer needs your product or service; the customer must truly believe they need or want to buy from you.

Global Competition

Your competition may not just come from across town or even across your country, it may now come from around the world. If you sell a common product, even something as mundane as hardware, you'll find many international companies selling the same product to your potential customers online. If you're offering a unique product, you may still face worldwide competition. These international competitors can often sell at prices below yours, even when shipping and fulfillment is added to the final price. This can be a difficult challenge, and you must be aware of this global competition so that you can find ways to distinguish yourself from them and compete successfully.

Not only are products sold internationally, but services are as well. It is typical for many service providers to find themselves competing online with sources from other countries where labor costs are far lower. Once again, your challenge is to find ways to make your competitive advantages clear so your value to your customers is apparent even when your price may be substantially higher.

In the worksheet on page 128, identify your global competitive threats.

Market Share Distribution

Some competitors are more important than others, due entirely to the fact that they command a large percentage of the market sales. Although these companies may not necessarily provide the best product or service at the best price, they nevertheless represent a crucial component in evaluating your competitive position.

Companies that generate a significant portion of all sales to the target market must be carefully considered because they:

■ Generally define the standard features of the product or service;

■ Substantially influence the perception of the product or service by customers; and

■ Usually devote considerable resources to maintaining their market share.

Take time to understand the companies that dominate the market, if only to better distinguish yourself from them. Of course, if your company is fortunate enough to control a major share of the market, then you gain the advantage of defining the product or service in the marketplace; you are the proverbial "800-pound gorilla." Even so, you cannot be complacent but must plan on committing the resources necessary to preserve or expand your share.

> " When it comes to competition for a technology-based company, in the early stages, I'm more worried about the small operator than the large company. With the large well-known companies, you generally know what they're working on. Also, they have large overhead. But the small competitor can come in and compete against you head on, especially if the technology is low enough to allow easy entry to the market."
>
> *Eugene Kleiner*
> *Venture Capitalist*

How Will You Obtain Sufficient Market Share?

If yours is a new business, it will generally be easier and less expensive to enter a market with many diverse competitors than one dominated by a few major players. If you are preparing a business plan for financing purposes, you will have to demonstrate to potential funding sources through your marketing plan how your company will gain and maintain a reasonable market share.

Complete the Market Share Distribution worksheet on page 131 to outline how sales are distributed among the competition, both by total sales revenues and by unit volume. (Some companies make fewer but higher-priced sales by targeting the most lucrative customers; others sell greater volume at lower per-unit prices.) Once again, look at competitors both by individual companies and by categories of competition, as they apply to your situation.

You will probably have to estimate the figures required by the worksheet, based on information gleaned from trade associations, annual reports, business publications, and independent industry research firms. Definitive information on sales is notoriously difficult to locate.

Future Competition

Finally, in your competitive analysis you have to do a little fortune-telling. You must make a few reasonable predictions of what the competition will look like in the future. New competitors enter markets all the time, and sometimes current competitors drop out. Don't take comfort in the fact that other companies have overlooked a particular product or service. Once you show you can be successful, someone will want to take a piece of that market from you. Who are your new competitors likely to be? How long will you have the field to yourself before other competitors jump in?

Forecasting the competitive situation over the next five years or so, based on logical conclusions from concrete evidence such as current product lines, gives you as well as potential investors a better sense of the long-term viability of your business.

One of the most important factors to examine is barriers to entry: those conditions that make it difficult or impossible for new competitors to enter the market. Every company can gain a sense of how best to prepare for future competition by examining the barriers to entry.

If your company's competitive position depends on new technology, new manufacturing techniques, or access to new markets, outlining the barriers to entry is essential. This will be one of the first areas judged by potential funding sources.

Barriers to Entry

Few barriers to entry last very long, particularly in newer industries. Even patents do not provide nearly as much protection as is generally assumed. Thus, you need to realistically project the period of time by which new competitors will breach these barriers.

> "As a barrier to entry, it should take significant money and significant skill to enter the business. Patents, while desirable, are not sufficient to protect against new competition, although they help the entrepreneur in raising money because they show the product is unique. Service businesses have a harder time securing venture capital funds because competitors can enter the field easily, and investors are wary. You need barriers to entry to protect your market."
>
> **Eugene Kleiner**
> **Venture Capitalist**

Market Share Distribution

List below the current market leaders and the approximate percentage of the market each one commands.

Competitor	% of Total Revenues	% of Total Units Sold	Trend of Market Share (increasing or decreasing?)
1.			
2.			
3.			
4.			
5.			

Which competitor(s), if any, have historically been the market leader(s)? _____

_____

_____

Which competitors have increased market share substantially in the last three years? _____

_____

_____

Is overall competition increasing, stable, or decreasing? _____

Briefly describe the most important characteristics of the market leader(s):

Competitor #1: _____

Competitor #2: _____

Competitor #3: _____

Divide the pie charts below to indicate market distribution.
(These charts can be included in your written plan for visual interest.)

Market Share by Revenues
(estimate)

Market Share by Volume
(estimate)

BARRIERS TO ENTRY

Some common barriers to entry for new competition are:

Patents

Provide a measure of protection for new products or processes.

High Start-up Costs

Help prevent small competitors from entering the field.

Substantial Expertise

Less likely that competitors have the manufacturing and engineering knowledge necessary to compete.

Market Saturation

Reduces the possibility of competitors gaining a meaningful foothold.

Complete the worksheet on page 133 indicating Future Competition and Barriers to Entry.

Preparing the Competition Section of Your Business Plan

To prepare the Competition portion of your business plan document, synthesize the information from the worksheets in this chapter into a brief synopsis. In particular, you want to provide:

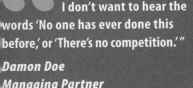

- Description of Competition
- Market Share Distribution
- Competitive Positions
- Barriers to Entry
- Strategic Opportunities

Use the Competition Plan Preparation Form on page 134 to outline the Competition section of your business plan. Don't be afraid to use bullet-point lists and charts (see Chapter 3 for suggestions) in this section. Also, include pertinent information from market research, particularly customer surveys.

"I don't want to hear the words 'No one has ever done this before,' or 'There's no competition.'"

Damon Doe
Managing Partner
Montage Capital

Chapter Summary

You have to understand your competition if you're going to be an effective competitor yourself. Develop a strong sense of your competitive position—your strengths and weaknesses in terms of customer perception and your internal company resources; this will be vital when preparing your marketing strategy. Always assume competition will get more intense, and be prepared for new competitors to enter the market.

Future Competition and Barriers to Entry

Potential future competitors include: _____

_____

_____

_____

_____

Current competitors likely to expand efforts: _____

_____

_____

_____

_____

Current competitors potentially leaving the field: _____

_____

_____

_____

_____

Indicate below how strong the following barriers to entry are and how much time (check the How Long Effective column) it will take before new competition overcomes each barrier.

Type of Barrier to Entry	Extent of Effectiveness Factor				How Long Effective?
	High	Medium	Low	None	
Patents					
High Start-up Costs					
Substantial Expertise Required					
Engineering, Manufacturing Problems					
Lack of Suppliers or Distributors					
Restrictive Licensing, Regulation					
Market Saturation					
Trademarks					
Other:					

Competition Plan Preparation Form

Using this form as a guide, summarize the main points you wish to make in the Competition section of your business plan.

Description of Competition: _____

_____

_____

_____

_____

_____

Market Share Distribution: _____

_____

_____

_____

_____

_____

Competitive Positions: _____

_____

_____

_____

_____

_____

Barriers to Entry: _____

_____

_____

_____

_____

Strategic Opportunities: _____

_____

_____

_____

_____

_____

Use this information as the basis of your plan's Competition section.

SAMPLE PLAN: THE COMPETITION

THE COMPETITION

Competing with ComputerEase to supply software training services to the target market (businesses making substantial use of computers and having more than 50 employees) are these categories of software training providers:

- Online training/distance learning programs
- Individual independent training consultants
- Local software training companies
- National training companies
- Software developers
- Community college classes
- Trainers from within the targeted companies themselves

ComputerEase hopes to build its business of developing custom training for corporations that have developed their own software applications for in-house use, as this represents a very high-margin business. Community college classes are generally not suitable for the corporate market, since classes are typically held in the evenings for at least 10 weeks — conditions that do not meet business customers' needs.

Online Competitors

The number of online computer software training firms has exploded in recent years. A Google search on "online software training" returned more than 100 million results. Yet this is a heavily fragmented market, with many small players and no single vendor dominating. The most-serious single competitor is a major online university, but it primarily targets individuals rather than corporate clients.

Local Competitors

Eight local businesses and four individuals in the Vespucci area actively market their software training services. An unknown number of additional individual consultants provide such training on a less-visible level.

Only one local company has developed a substantial presence with the target market: JMT Training. JMT has operated for more than six years and is the largest local software training company.

The individual independent consultants in this market generally provide training for just one or two software programs.

Other Competition

Three major national software training companies periodically conduct classes in the Vespucci area. Lesser-known national companies also occasionally provide such services, generally targeting recent purchasers of particular software. The current fast growth of online training has opened markets — including our local market — to international and local competition. The three national software training companies all have fairly

Lists categories of competitors.

Indicates specific competitors.

SAMPLE PLAN: THE COMPETITION (continued)

robust online training programs. Since our target market is principally English-speaking countries, we view our international competition as coming mostly from other English-speaking countries. Presently, there are two international companies—one based in the U.K. and one based in Australia—that are potential future competitors.

In-house training by employees of the targeted companies varies widely in content, form, and quality. Very few companies have "trainers"; most training is provided on an ad hoc basis by supervisors and fellow workers. A conservative interpretation of a survey conducted by ComputerEase indicates that at least 20% of such training would be contracted out if satisfactory training could be obtained.

Market Share Distribution

The responses to the ComputerEase survey indicate that target companies currently conducting software training use providers as follows:

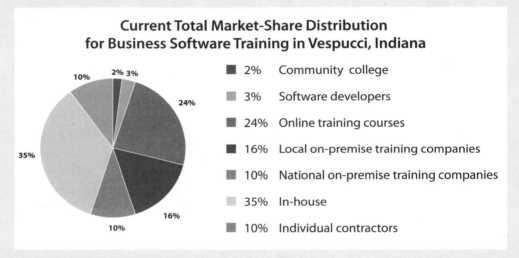

Current Total Market-Share Distribution for Business Software Training in Vespucci, Indiana

- 2% Community college
- 3% Software developers
- 24% Online training courses
- 16% Local on-premise training companies
- 10% National on-premise training companies
- 35% In-house
- 10% Individual contractors

Advantages Over Competition

A chart outlining ComputerEase's competitive position is included in the Appendix. Generally, the advantages ComputerEase has in relation to its competitors are:

- Its status as an "Authorized Training Center" for major software publishers gives it credibility through joint programs, plus the availability of pre-release and steeply discounted software.

- Its management team is business-oriented, rather than computer-oriented, and is entirely focused on the needs of corporate trainers.

- Its course developers are certified in the software for which they are developing courseware.

- It has a proven instructional design methodology for creating, testing, and supporting high-quality courseware.

- It is a local, rather than national, provider of on-premise training.

- It has a sterling reputation for delivering high-quality service.

- It offers ongoing technical support for corporate clients at low cost.

Competitive Positions

This is how ComputerEase ranks the strengths of its competitors:

1. In-house trainers

2. Online training courses

3. JMT Training

4. National training companies

5. Other local companies

6. Independent contractors

By far the biggest competitor for the dollars spent on business software training is the in-house training department. After that, other online competitors are the highest hurdle to winning business, as there are other, cheaper alternatives to the Computer-Ease products on the market. However, ComputerEase is garnering a growing reputation for delivering high-quality and highly effective training in this crowded field.

JMT is considered the strongest competitor due to its current client base, the personality and sales skills of its owner, Janice Tuffrey, and its potential to associate with national franchise training operations. However, JMT's current training staff and materials are of inconsistent quality, and current clients have expressed dissatisfaction with the lack of quality control. Moreover, JMT lacks skilled management of its financial affairs, resulting in insufficient capital for marketing and updating equipment. No other local companies have either the financial or the personnel resources to adequately respond to a well-organized, sufficiently funded competitor.

National training companies market their services through direct mail or telemarketers and have no local sales force. Their customer base is neither loyal nor particularly satisfied with the service.

The quality of in-house trainers varies widely. However, since these trainers are already on staff, there is little or no additional cost to the customer for using them.

Independent contractors lack a substantial client base and adequate resources to respond to new competition.

Barriers to Entry

It is not easy for new competitors to enter the on-premises training market, which requires a substantial overhead due to rent/leasing expenses, equipment, trainers, and printed materials. Moreover, software providers are becoming increasingly selective about which companies they will allow to serve as "Authorized Training Companies." These relationships are crucial in terms of receiving pre-release, below-retail-cost copies of software to prepare new courses, and for cosponsoring product introduction events, as well as bolstering customer perception.

Ranks competitors and describes strengths and weaknesses.

Indicates limits to new competition.

SAMPLE PLAN: THE COMPETITION (continued)

The barriers to entry of online training are much lower, however. All it takes is a single individual designing interactive courseware for the Web using one of the many authoring programs that exist. Even if the content developer is not technically inclined, he or she can easily find someone to do the coding that makes the content accessible via a standard browser. There are no printing costs, as all the documentation and course materials exist online for the student to download. Of course, there are marketing expenses — to address the challenge of getting noticed in such a crowded field — as well as credibility issues, but simply getting a product to market is relatively cheap and easy to do. Although online competitors can come from anywhere, they will need to understand domestic markets.

Strategic Opportunities

The market for computer training services is highly dissatisfied at present as shown by a survey of human resource directors of target companies. Their levels of satisfaction with current training arrangements are shown below:

Highly satisfied — 8%

Somewhat satisfied — 18%

Somewhat unsatisfied — 43%

Highly unsatisfied — 31%

This unusually high dissatisfaction level with current providers represents a unique opportunity for ComputerEase in a rapidly expanding market.

CHAPTER 9

Strategic Position & Risk Assessment

Strategy is destiny.

Why Should Customers Buy from *You*?

In today's highly competitive and constantly changing business environment, it's no longer enough just to know HOW to run a business; you also have to know WHAT business you're really running. While you must, of course, attend to the basics of operating your business, you also have to see exactly where you stand in the marketplace, what makes you compelling to customers, and what advantages you have over the competition. You need a clearly defined strategic position.

Defining a strategic position is as important for the proverbial "mom and pop" family business as for a high-technology company. The old neighborhood hardware store now competes not merely with another hardware store down the street, but also with Home Depot and other "big box" home repair retailers. And the owners of that local hardware store can no longer fall back on the comforting belief that "we're more convenient"—not when they also compete with online hardware suppliers that deliver directly to customers' doors.

Today's business reality is that customers have easy, convenient access to many of your competitors, some of whom may sell the same or similar products or services for lower prices. In this environment, you have to develop a distinct impetus for your customer to keep doing business with you.

A Strategic Position Defines What You Do

One of the great advantages of outlining a strategic position is it gives you a touchstone when making business decisions. Just as a well-written mission statement guides your company's values and long-term vision, a well-delineated strategic position influences almost every aspect of your business, such as the development of your products or services, marketing, operations, and choice of location.

You can differentiate your company from its competitors in many ways. You have probably started a company with a sense of vision or purpose. You may have felt a lack in the market or wanted to pursue a particular passion. The key is to find the strategy that best aligns your strengths and interests to real opportunities in the competitive environment. Your strategic position should be where you find the following coming together:

- Your strengths and interests
- Industry trends and developments
- Market changes and opportunities

- Competitive changes and opportunities
- Changes and opportunities brought through new technologies

If you're now in business, you may have already evolved a strategic position, whether or not you realized it. You may have innately understood that you needed to carve out a distinct identity for your business to separate you from the competition and to help focus your activities.

Take the example of a flower shop in a large city. Two partners opened their store in a middle-class neighborhood, beginning as just a "bucket shop"—a place where people picked up a dozen flowers on their way home from work or sent a birthday bouquet. Over time, however, their talents and interests led them to start designing floral decorations for high-society events and weddings. While that market was being served by others, demand for high-end florists was growing in their city. Because of their talents, they were able to compete effectively for this business.

To reinforce their new position, the two partners changed their operations and marketing. To gain visibility with their target market, they donated floral arrangements to charity benefits, created new brochures, and worked with different, more exotic and expensive flowers. Eventually, only a small percent of their income and profits came from the local neighborhood. As a result, when the nearby supermarket began selling cut flowers, it had little impact on this florist's business.

Instead of pursuing the obvious business strategy—serving their neighborhood—they instead found an opening in the overall competitive market that fit their abilities. They found their strategic position.

A Strategic Position Also Defines What You *Don't* Do

Defining a strategic position is particularly important for new companies that must quickly distinguish themselves from the competition. Since your resources are always limited (especially in younger companies), having a clear strategic position assists you in figuring out how to allocate those resources.

As important as helping you determine what to do, a well-defined strategic position is a boon in helping you decide what *not* to do. This not only saves you a lot of time and money, but also makes you more confident of your business decisions, some of which may not be understood by others.

In the case of the florist, for instance, on any given day, a shopper might have walked into their store and not been able to find so much as a dozen roses or daisies. The partners stopped advertising in local media outlets. When their lease was up, they moved to a less-convenient, second-story location, which could hardly be seen from the street.

These all seem like foolish moves if you think of this florist as a typical retail flower shop, but they were all decisions consistent with the partners' strategy: to target the upscale event market. With minimal desire for walk-in traffic, location was less critical, and they had little need to keep flowers on hand. They had carefully chosen their position, which helped them understand what activities were of lower priority. They didn't try to be all things to all people.

Success ke
term

Business Model
Describes what a company does and the structure it puts into place to make money. Examples of business models include designing and manufacturing a product that is sold to other businesses (B2B); or providing access to a software application online and selling it on a subscription basis.

Mind Share
A relative sense of the awareness level a company has achieved in its target market versus the recognition and awareness of its competition.

Minimal Viable Product
A product that has been created quickly in order to get it to market as soon as possible. Over time, and based on the experience of actual customers, the product is improved on and refined.

> "With the consolidation of department stores, we knew our margins were going to be squeezed. They're doing a lot of their own products, putting their products in the best display spaces. We knew we had to change our strategic direction."
>
> *Kay Koplovitz*
> *Chair, Kate Spade*

Strategic Position Is More than Advertising

Don't be confused: A true strategic position is not the same as an advertising campaign or slogan. Advertising and marketing are means to achieving your strategic position—they help you create the image consistent with your position and get your message to potential customers. Defining a strategic position is about creating a meaningful place for yourself—a position—in the market.

How does Coca-Cola differentiate itself from Pepsi? Very little of the difference is based on the qualities of the products or the market segment they are targeting. The two companies may have incorporated some operational differences, but they differentiate themselves primarily on the basis of advertising—not strategic positioning. When Snapple came along, it created a totally different position for itself in the market. Snapple didn't try to compete head-to-head with Coke and Pepsi; instead, it looked for a different segment of the soft drink market: the non-cola, non-carbonated soft drink.

If a luxury car company that has sold primarily to older consumers decides to market to younger drivers, it won't be enough to take the same kind of car they've been making and devise a clever advertising campaign. The product itself—in this case a car—has to be redesigned to fit the tastes of their target market. It may have to be smaller, sportier, faster, with more electronic gadgets. Not only will the marketing materials need to be geared toward a younger audience, but the salespeople will have to be trained to learn that the 20-something kid in the rock band T-shirt may not be just killing time with a test drive but may actually be a techie millionaire ready to buy.

What Kinds of Strategic Positions Are There?

What makes a company different? Is it the nature of its products or services? The quality or cost? The geographic area or type of customers served? Perhaps the company has proprietary products customers can't find elsewhere.

There are many ways to distinguish yourself from your competitors, including:

- Customer Perception Factors
- Market Segment
- Market Share
- Operational and/or Technological Advantages
- Proprietary Products, Technology, Abilities, or Relationships
- Sales Channels
- **Business Model**
- First-Mover Advantage

- Lean Start-Up
- Branding

Each of these strategic approaches offers opportunities but also poses pitfalls. And they may be related: If you are positioning your company on the basis of low price, you'll also need operational efficiencies to reduce costs or else you won't be able to survive against competitors with higher profit margins.

Customer Perception Factors

This is the "better, faster, cheaper" approach, based on how customers distinguish your company and its products and services from the competition. Some key customer perception factors are below:

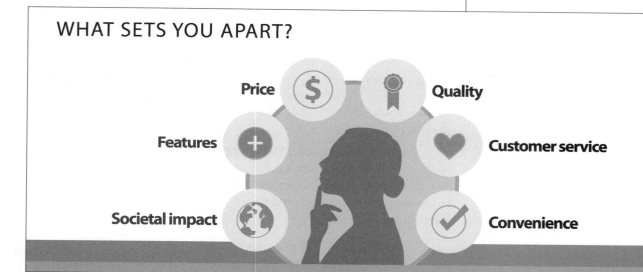

WHAT SETS YOU APART?

Price — Quality — Features — Customer service — Societal impact — Convenience

Concentrating on customer perception factors is the most typical method of attempting to differentiate yourself from the competition. They seem the simplest, most straightforward way to compete. Surprisingly, they may be the most difficult to achieve and maintain. For instance, competing on the basis of price is often perilous. While it is easy—in the short run—to attract customers on the basis of low price, highly price-sensitive customers are the most fickle, quickly tempted away by the next company offering a lower price. Once you appear to be attracting a significant portion of the market, well-funded established competitors can lower prices (even if they have to take a loss) to compete temporarily until you are no longer able to sustain your losses.

Other perception factors may be harder to "prove" to the market. You may have to spend a lot of money on marketing and advertising to get customers to realize that you offer additional features, more convenience, or higher quality. Once you do, however, you may be able to build a loyal and committed customer base that appreciates the differences between you and your competition.

> You have to understand the consumers' need. What's their pain? Why do they need to change? Solve that pain, and then get that message out."
>
> *Andrew Anker*
> *Venture Capitalist*

Market Segment

This strategy is based on targeting a specific portion of the total market.

Some possible ways of segmenting the market are:

- Geographic location
- Age, income, interests, family size, and so on, of consumer served (in business-to-consumer companies)
- Age, size, and/or industry of business served (in business-to-business companies)
- Customers' specialized need

Deciding to aim at a particular market segment or "niche" offers many competitive advantages, especially for newer or smaller companies. While you trade having a larger total market from which to attract customers, you can more easily (and often less expensively) gain visibility and credibility with a smaller, more focused market. Targeting a small market also gives you the opportunity to develop special expertise and experience, giving you an edge when competing head-to-head with others. For instance, a human resources consultant who specializes in serving hospitals will have a far easier time attracting additional hospitals as clients than a general human resources consultant.

The pitfalls in targeting a market segment are that the market size may not be big enough to sustain or grow your company, the target market may already be saturated with specialists, or, once you've proven that the target market is big enough and rich enough, larger companies will come in and compete with you.

Thinking globally, you may want to target a specific region, perhaps one that is underserved, and in which you can become a market leader. For instance, you may be in a highly competitive environment in the United States, but even though Australia and New Zealand are far smaller markets, there may be far fewer competitors and greater potential to be a market share leader, at far lower cost.

Market Share

This strategy is based on establishing and commanding such a dominant portion of the total customer base that it becomes difficult for others to compete. The goal is to become the "800-pound gorilla" of a market.

It's almost impossible—and very expensive—to displace entrenched market leaders in established market segments. In the soft drink market, for instance, it's forbidding to try to compete against Coke and Pepsi. Even well-funded competitors have difficulty gaining a few percentage points of market share. Newcomers in mature markets typically must pursue niche market strategies (or even create new market categories, such as Red Bull did with energy drinks, or VitaminWater did with flavored and fortified water products).

But when factors allow new markets to open—as has happened with the Internet or with falling trade barriers that let foreign competitors enter a nation's market—tremendous opportunities become available. Then, there's a rush to capture customers' awareness—or **mind share** by companies hoping to translate that to market share. In such instances, entrepreneurs try to get their companies, products, or services established before the competition. In technology, there's typically a particular urgency to gain a "first-mover advantage" (see below).

Operational and/or Technological Advantages

Another strategy is to gain significant competitive advantages through instituting better internal procedures, operations, or technology, giving you substantial benefits—such as higher profit margins—over the competition. Because these advantages are often unseen (directly) by customers, their significance is often unrealized. However, many companies have succeeded not by clever market strategies but by running their business better than the competition. For instance, See's Candies' inventory management system results in very fresh candy at its stores with minimal waste; this results in better-tasting candy and higher profit margins.

Proprietary Products, Technology, Abilities, or Relationships

Yet another strategic position is to develop or secure exclusive assets that will be difficult or impossible for competitors to replicate. For manufacturing and technology companies, these may be patents, processes, or copyrights. For others, proprietary assets might include distribution agreements, licenses, strategic partnerships, even hiring certain employees with exceptional talents. The key to this being an effective strategy is that you have to identify those aspects of your business where proprietary assets make a real difference, and then you must secure those assets in such a way that your competitors can't easily replicate or circumvent them.

Sales Channels

In some instances, you may be able to differentiate your company by the manner in which you reach and sell to customers. For instance, some computer companies, such as Dell, distinguished themselves early on by selling directly to consumers rather than through retail computer outlets. Later, the Internet opened up the opportunity for many other companies to circumvent existing sales channels and sell directly to customers. But using various sales channels as a key strategy doesn't necessarily require a high-tech approach—Tupperware successfully uses house parties instead of retail outlets to compete against Rubbermaid.

Business Model

The term "business model" describes what your company does and the structure you put into place to make money. For example, you may design a product, outsource its manufacture, and then sell it to wholesalers. Or you may sell a service for a flat fee or on an hourly basis.

> " The fact that we were first meant that we had to fight the least to get attention. That gave us a period of five or six months of being one of the very few games in town, and that enabled us to build the customers' sense of habit that you need. By the time we had to market ourselves against the competition, we had built customers' habits."
>
> *Andrew Anker*
> *Venture Capitalist*

There are many types of business models to choose from, and picking the right one can give you a strategic advantage. For example, some cloud-based software companies use a "freemium" business model, offering a "free" version and a "premium" version of their applications. The free version typically has fewer features than the full-scale, premium version, making it attractive to new or small companies that don't want to invest a large amount of cash for software. It also attracts customers willing to test drive a product for free. Once the customer's software needs grow, they can then move up to the premium version, usually sold at a recurring, monthly subscription price. They are less likely to make the time-consuming and costly switch to the competition after they have grown accustomed to the product.

First-Mover Advantage?

"No one's ever done anything like this before." Many entrepreneurs believe their key strategic position is that they've developed a new concept—product, service, technology, Internet business, app—before anyone else. They recognize that there's a big advantage in being first; the fear of others beating them to market keeps many entrepreneurs working around the clock.

If you can get your company, product, service, or website established before the competition, you gain what is called the "first-mover advantage." Being first potentially enables you to capture so many customers that it becomes difficult for a significant portion of the market (in technology terms, the "installed user base") to change.

As the graphic below illlustrates, being first to market brings many benefits.

THE ADVANTAGES OF BEING FIRST

Capture significant market share before competitors enter the market

Secure key strategic partners, making fewer opportunities available to later competitors

Attract outstanding employees and management

Capture media attention

Lock in financing sources, such as venture capitalists

Going after a "first-mover advantage" carries its own risks as well as rewards. In most businesses, there are few truly effective barriers-to-entry. Will you end up merely serving as the research-and-development arm of copy-cat companies? There's also the very real risk that if you're doing something truly new, the market (and financing sources) may not be ready for you. In fact, many second- or third-to-market companies benefit from avoiding the costs of educating the market, conducting extensive research and development, and hiring highly creative people.

If gaining the first-mover advantage is part of your key business strategy, ask yourself, "How defensible is this position? What will I need to make it defensible?" Remember, patents, copyrights, and other proprietary information only go so far. Can you develop strategic alliances or lock in customers, distributors, and financing sources to make it difficult for future competitors to take you on?

With a first-mover strategy, there is also the risk of doing something fast but not well, allowing your inevitable competition to honestly tout itself as a much-improved version. So continually work on improving your products, services, marketing, and operations. Look for ways to leverage being first into being best.

Lean Start-Up

Like the process of gaining a first-mover advantage, the lean start-up method, advocated by Eric Ries in his best-selling book, *The Lean Startup: How Today's Entrepreneurs Use Continuous Innovation to Create Radically Successful Businesses* (Crown Business, 2011), advocates launching a product or service as quickly as possible. Companies then see how real customers use the product or service and continually revise it. Ries calls this technique "build–measure–learn." Nimble companies that can quickly create, evaluate, and respond gain a significant competitive advantage.

The key tenets of a lean start-up include the following:

- **Create a minimally viable product.** You don't need to go to market with a fully developed product or service. Indeed, it's not even advisable. Build only to a level that enables you to go out and get your first customers.

- **Test and measure.** Continually learn from customers. Analyze exactly how they are dealing with your product or service.

- **Pivot.** Be able to swivel away from your original vision to adapt to new realities, but stay grounded in what you've learned.

This approach has been particularly popular in the technology world, especially for mobile apps and cloud-based software. It is also well suited to an industry with lots of competition and quickly changing technology, in which users have a relatively high tolerance for glitches.

The lean start-up method applies to more than just technology companies and start-ups. Many businesses can succeed by getting their **minimal viable products** and services to market quickly. Other critical business tasks—launching a website, exhibiting at a trade show, developing another channel—also benefit from the lean start-up approach. You don't have to do everything in your business perfectly right out of the gate.

Branding

One increasingly important strategy that many companies pursue is intentionally trying to build a brand. When you become a brand name, customers can develop such a strong relationship with your company that it is difficult for others to compete.

> "It's all about brand — being in front of the customer. On the Net or in media in general, everything is about brand and creating habits."
>
> *Andrew Anker*
> *Venture Capitalist*

There are, obviously, many advantages to being a brand name, but it is not easy to achieve. First, it is usually expensive. You must spend a great deal of money on marketing and advertising simply to get your name well-known. And, although it seems like some brand names develop overnight, building a brand is hard to achieve quickly.

Building a truly strong brand is more than just a matter of name recognition. A real brand gives customers trust in your products and services because you are consistent in quality, price, service, or convenience—over time. This doesn't mean you have to promise the highest quality or the lowest price—it only means being consistent, so the customer can depend on what they'll get from that brand. McDonald's doesn't have to promise gourmet food to be a reliable brand. It built its brand by giving customers the same experience, the same type and quality of food, the same cleanliness, at every one of its restaurants.

If your goal is to build a brand name, you have to look at those factors that you are able to offer and deliver to your customers consistently and repeatedly over time, making certain you put sufficient company resources into supporting those factors.

Risk

Every business involves risk. Only the most naive and inexperienced entrepreneurs believe their business "just can't fail." Use this section to sit down and think through the various risks facing your new endeavor.

This task might seem daunting. So why shake your enthusiasm? Because risk assessment helps you prepare for and prevent threats to your success. If, for instance, you identify a major risk as the possibility that a well-funded competitor will enter the market, you will want to take steps to quickly secure key customer contracts or line up significant funding yourself.

Evaluating your risks isn't meant to be an exercise in fear (although if you are intimidated by the risks involved, then perhaps you are not yet ready to start your business). Many entrepreneurs think that if they describe the risks they're likely to encounter, they'll scare off potential investors. Quite the contrary is true. For all but the least sophisticated investors, an evaluation of risks shows them you're willing to take a cool, hard look at the situation facing you, and you understand the scope of the threats to your success. It reassures investors that, because you understand the risks involved, you're more likely to take steps to counter those threats.

What Kinds of Risk?

It's not just a matter of high risk or low risk. It's also what kinds of risk. Some risks are more tolerable or more important to different investors—and to you. The key types of risk facing companies include:

■ **Market Risk:** that the market will not respond to your products or services, because either there is no real market need or the market isn't yet ready. Market risks are very difficult to overcome.

> "When I started out, there were only three broadcast networks, and I thought, that can't be all. I thought, I'll start my own network! I have to figure out how to do this. I like being on the edge; I'm a risk taker."
>
> **Kay Koplovitz**
> **Chair, Kate Spade**

■ **Competitive Risk:** that the competitive situation will change dramatically, and new competitors will enter the market and/or established competitors will reposition their products or services to more effectively take you on. You should carefully think through how other competitors might respond to your entering the market and not assume that the competitive environment will remain the same.

■ **Technology Risk:** that the technology or product design and engineering won't work, or won't work as well as you envision. This may be critically important to your company's success, or it may be totally unimportant, depending on the nature of your company, its products/services, customers, and the like. If your business faces substantial technology risks, what is your ability to quickly and effectively improve the technology?

■ **Product Risk:** that the product won't materialize, won't be finished in time, or won't work as promised. This is very similar to the above, only with nontechnology products or services.

■ **Execution Risk:** that you won't be able to effectively manage the rollout and growth of the company because management isn't sufficiently capable, the time allowed isn't adequate, operations aren't in place, and other reasons. You should be able to demonstrate specific steps you are taking to reduce or eliminate such risks.

■ **Capitalization Risk:** that you've badly underestimated costs or overestimated income, and you will run out of money. The best way to avoid this risk is to budget realistically and get enough funding so you do not run out of cash prematurely. Look for investors who have the ability and inclination to offer additional funds as your company progresses.

■ **Global Risk:** that, when doing business internationally, you may encounter unanticipated situations that will interrupt or stop your ability to do business, reach your market, or receive supplies.

Use the Risk Evaluation worksheets on pages 151–152 to assess the risks your business faces domestically and internationally.

Balancing Risks & Opportunities

Once you've outlined your risks, you may feel overwhelmed. But while there are many risks, there are also substantial rewards—otherwise why are you bothering to start this endeavor?

A typical method to illustrate the balance between risks and opportunities is to develop a "SWOT" chart, delineating your company's strengths, weaknesses, opportunities, and threats (thus "S.W.O.T.") This is a good exercise for quickly sizing up your company's position.

Complete the "SWOT" grid on page 153. Be sure to include both internal and external factors as well as current and potential ones.

> " The apparel business is a tough operational business. Manufacturing, shipping, delivering, making sure everything's on time. There's a tremendous amount of competition, and things get hot and then get cool."
>
> *Kay Koplovitz*
> *Chair, Kate Spade*

Preparing the Strategic Position & Risk Assessment Section of Your Business Plan

In preparing the Strategic Position segment of your plan, focus on the following:

■ Strategies that align with your strengths, your interests, and the opportunities available

■ The factors that differentiate you from the competition

■ Risks facing your company

■ Your SWOT analysis

Use the Plan Preparation Form on page 154 to help you develop the Strategic Position & Risk Assessment section of your business plan.

Chapter Summary

A well-delineated strategic position influences almost every aspect of your business, such as the development of your products or services, marketing, operations, and choice of location. In today's business environment, it is critical for every company to understand the ways it is meaningfully different from its competitors. Defining your strategic position enables you to more clearly and thoroughly answer the question, "What business are you in?" Answering this question is especially important for new companies. When you find excellent opportunities in the market that fit with your strengths and interests, you can carve out a strategic position to distinguish your company from others. There is no one "correct" strategy, and your strategic position will evolve over time. Honestly assessing your risks enables you to better reduce potential threats to your success. It also reassures potential investors that you have a clear-eyed view of what you're getting into.

Risk Evaluation

Specify the major risk(s) facing your company in each area, rate the approximate extent of that risk (high-, medium-, or low-risk), and note steps you can take, or have taken, to lessen that risk:

Competitor	Risk Probability/ Percentage	Steps to Reduce This Risk
Market Risk		
Competitive Risk		
Technology Risk		
Product Risk		
Execution Risk		
Capitalization Risk		

Globalization: Global Risks

Specify the major risk(s) facing your company in each area, rate the approximate extent of that risk (high-, medium-, or low-risk), and note steps you can take, or have taken, to lessen that risk:

Type of Risk	Risk Probability/ Percentage	Steps to Reduce This Risk
Supply Chain Interruptions		
Currency Fluctuations		
Labor/Workforce Problems		
Inadequate/Inconsistent Quality Control		
Political/Climate Risks		
Changes in International Trade Laws		
Other:		

SWOT: Strengths/Weaknesses/Opportunities/Threats

In each appropriate box below, list your company's strengths or weaknesses, and the opportunities or threats facing it.

Strengths	Weaknesses

Opportunities	Threats

Strategic Position Plan Preparation Form

The information you provide on this form can be used as the basis for the Strategic Position & Risk Assessment section of your business plan.

Industry Trends: _____
_____
_____
_____
_____
_____

Target Market: _____
_____
_____
_____
_____
_____

Competitive Environment: _____
_____
_____
_____
_____
_____

Your Strengths Relative to the Competition: _____
_____
_____
_____
_____
_____

Risks: _____
_____
_____
_____
_____
_____

Use this information as the basis of your plan's Strategic Position section.

SAMPLE PLAN: STRATEGIC POSITION & RISK ASSESSMENT

STRATEGIC POSITION & RISK ANALYSIS

ComputerEase's objective is to be the premier software training company in the Greater Vespucci, Indiana, area and a major competitor in the online training field for the English-speaking market. To achieve that goal, we have developed a strategic position that emphasizes:

Outlines the company's strategic position.

- Highly effective online training, using the latest interactive instructional technology

- In-person, hands-on training

- Customized training developed for customers' proprietary software or specific needs

- Training that emphasizes productivity as much as skills

ComputerEase's Strategic Position is based on evaluating the following factors:

A. Industry Trends

B. Our Target Market

C. The Competitive Environment

D. Our Strengths

E. Risks

Industry Trends

The software training industry is trending toward development of regional or national providers rather than small training companies or individual consultants. Online, distance learning is a major, cost-effective delivery system for training programs, and the number and quality of such programs keeps increasing. Online applications delivered as software-as-a-service (SaaS), as opposed to downloadable software, continue to grow in popularity. Certification from national software developers also continues to be a critical requirement for doing business.

Describes major developments in the industry.

Target Market

Our target is the corporate training market (rather than consumer). This market is strong and growing and is less price-sensitive than the consumer market. Our target customers often develop customized software for their specific needs as well as use "off-the-shelf" products.

Specifies who the target customers are.

Competitive Environment

There is no other national or regional software training provider yet in the Vespucci area. This affords us the opportunity to build substantial relationships with our target market—corporations and government entities—before an effective competitor enters the area. However, there are several, extremely well-funded online training companies, and we anticipate substantial competitive pressure from them.

SAMPLE PLAN: STRATEGIC POSITION & RISK ASSESSMENT (cont.)

Our Strengths

We excel at in-person training, and select our instructors not only on their computer knowledge but on their ability to translate complex technology issues into understandable language, their patience, and their teaching effectiveness. Another of our strengths is our ability to quickly and effectively develop customized training programs, built around the customers' proprietary software, or to meet other specific customer needs. Our ability to understand the online instructional technology is another major strength.

Risks

One major potential threat is the growth in the consolidation of online software training companies. A number of these companies already offer training at lower fees than ComputerEase can offer, and consolidation may drive prices down further, while increasing the amount and effectiveness of these competitors' marketing efforts. A continuing risk is always the health of the economy: Economic downturns lead to fewer new employees being hired, and thus trained, by our target market. A final risk, one that appears minor at this point, is that software developers will make software that is easier to use, thus reducing the need for training.

Strategic Position

Evaluating the above factors has led us to conclude that our major threat comes from other online training companies. However, although we generate significant revenues from online training, we are confident there will be a continuing need for outstanding live, in-person training. A significant percentage of customers require or prefer an instructor present to answer questions and demonstrate techniques, often on a one-to-one basis. Customers will also need to have customized training programs developed to meet their particular needs. Further, we believe our target market will be willing to pay more to receive customized and/or in-person training.

Devising our training programs to achieve increased productivity as well as to train in basic software skills enables us to continue to offer valuable training programs to customers even if they reduce the number of their new hires. Productivity programs are less vulnerable to economic downturns.

To achieve this strategic position, we place particular emphasis on the skills, attitudes, and personalities of our instructors. We recognize that the quality of their instruction, their patience, and their effectiveness must be substantially superior to that of online teachers. We must also retain effective training program developers capable of devising effective training programs, including customized ones.

Describes various sources of risk.

Lists aspects that distinguish the company from the competition.

Shows how company strengths align with opportunities in the market.

Tell them what they get, not what you do.

Reaching and Capturing Customers

You must have customers to stay in business: It's the most basic business truth. That's why an effective marketing plan to communicate with, motivate, and secure customers is vital for your company's success. Since reaching customers costs money, and money is always limited, your marketing strategy must be carefully and thoughtfully designed. If you are developing a business plan to seek outside funding, remember that many investors read the marketing plan portion closely. They want to know you have a realistic and price-conscious strategy to get your product or service into the hands of customers. In your marketing plan you define:

- How you make customers aware of your product or service;

- What message you are trying to convey to customers about your product, service, or company;

- Specific methods you use to deliver and reinforce that message; and

- How you secure actual sales.

Note that marketing and sales, although closely related, are two different activities. Marketing is designed to increase customer awareness and deliver a message; sales is the direct action taken to solicit and procure customer orders. Thus, marketing includes activities such as advertising, creating brochures, social media marketing, networking, and public relations; sales encompasses telemarketing, sales calls, and **ecommerce** sales.

In devising and implementing your marketing strategy, you may wish to use the services of specialists such as marketing consultants, advertising agencies, and public relations advisors. While these professionals can increase the focus and effectiveness of your efforts, you must never relinquish the marketing program entirely to outsiders—it is far too crucial to the definition and success of your business.

This chapter provides the basic tools you need when outlining a marketing strategy to be included in a business plan document.

Your Company's Message

Every business sends a message in its marketing. This message, based on the strategic position the company stakes out for itself, emphasizes particular attributes, such as "low-price leader" or "one-day service." Or perhaps the message exploits a market niche: "specialists in estate planning" or "software for architects." Maybe the message is less direct and aimed more at the customer's self-image: "the choice of a new generation" or "I'm lovin' it."

The Four Ps of Marketing

What messages do you give customers to motivate them to purchase your product or service? Traditional marketing experts emphasize the elements in the graphic below, known as "the Four Ps," in influencing customers to buy.

WHY CUSTOMERS BUY: THE FOUR Ps

Product	Price	Place	Promotion

The tangible aspects of the product or service itself	The cost advantage	The location's convenience and decor	The amount and nature of the marketing activities

These elements leave a lot out of the marketing picture, however, especially as customers have become more discriminating over the years and look for products or services not just to fill an immediate need but to enhance their overall sense of well-being.

Most marketing strategists agree that people buy benefits, not features. In other words, customers are more concerned about how a purchase will affect their lives than about how the company achieves those results. So your marketing message must tell customers what they get, such as security or an enhanced self-image, rather than merely the detailed specifics of what your product or service does.

What Customers Want: The Five Fs

"The Five Fs," described below, are a convenient way to sum up what customers want.

1. **Functions.** How does the product or service meet their concrete needs?

2. **Finances.** How will the purchase affect their overall financial situation—not just the price of the product or service, but other savings and increased productivity?

3. **Freedom.** How convenient is it to purchase and use the product or service? How will they gain more time and less worry in other aspects of their lives?

4. **Feelings.** How does the product or service make customers feel about themselves, and how does it affect and relate to their self-image? Do they like and respect the salesperson and the company?

Success key terms

Ecommerce
Conducting sales and transactions on the Internet.

Search Engine Marketing (SEM)
The practice of purchasing ads to increase your website's ranking and visibility on relevant search engine results pages—often called paid search.

Search Engine Optimization (SEO)
Optimizing your website by planning content and design that leads to high rankings on search engine results pages when a user searches for relevant keywords.

Social Media
Content created by individuals and disseminated online through networking sites such as blogs, YouTube, and Facebook. Used for awareness, marketing, and customer communication and retention.

The Five Fs

Keeping the Five Fs in mind, describe the message you want to convey to customers about your product or service.

Functions: _____

Finances: _____

Freedom: _____

Feelings: _____

Future: _____

Which of these messages is the most important in motivating your target market to purchase? _____

_____

How will you express this message to your customers in the areas listed below?

Business Name: _____

Slogan: _____

Key Words in Marketing Material: _____

_____

Product Design: _____

Logo: _____

Website Design: _____

_____

Blog Language and Design: _____

_____

Choice of Social Media Sites: _____

_____

Other Graphic Images/Design: _____

_____

Packaging: _____

_____

Decor: _____

Style of Clothing Worn by Employees: _____

Merchandising/Displays/Presentation Materials: _____

_____

Other: _____

_____

_____

5. **Future.** How will they deal with the product or service and company over time? Will support and service be available? How will the product or service affect their lives in the coming years, and will they have an increased sense of security about the future?

Customers, of course, want to receive benefits in all these areas, and you should be aware of how your product or service fulfills the entire range of their needs. However, your primary message must concentrate on one or two of these benefits that most effectively motivate your customers and that stake out a competitive position for your company.

You communicate these benefits through every interaction you have with your customers, not simply through your advertising. Naturally, your company slogan and any words you use in advertisements deliver an overt statement to the potential customer. Perhaps the name of the business itself is a direct message, for example, "Toys 'R Us" or "Cheap Tickets."

Power of the Indirect Message

Indirect messages can leave an even stronger impression with customers. If brochures are cleanly designed and sales representatives conservatively dressed, it conveys the impression that the company is professional and responsible. If the decor features trendy colors and rock music plays in the background, the implication is that the company is youthful and contemporary.

Sometimes, unfortunately, a company sends out mixed messages—for example, having nicely dressed salespeople but poorly printed sales material. How will you convey an image to your customer that reinforces your direct message? How will you add value to your product or service through design, packaging, and presentation?

The Five Fs worksheet on page 160 helps you organize your answers to these questions; the information then can be incorporated into the Marketing section of your business plan. This worksheet helps you summarize how you reinforce your company's image and what you are trying to tell customers about your product or service. Use the information for internal planning as well as in your business plan.

Marketing Strategy

Once you have clarified what you want to tell customers about your company, you must describe how you disseminate that information.

How do you reach potential customers? Do you advertise? If so, where?

Do you send an email newsletter? If so, to what mailing lists? Do you optimize your website for search engines? Do you participate in trade shows? If so, which ones and how frequently?

Since every marketing vehicle costs money, carefully plan how you intend to spend your marketing dollars. In devising your overall marketing program, be sure you look for:

- **Fit.** Your marketing vehicles must reach your actual target customer and be appropriate to your image.

> " Everything supports the vision. That's the key in retailing. Everything must reinforce the central concept you are trying to convey to your target market, including your product lines, the customer service you offer, architectural design, the hours you're open, even the type of bags you use."
>
> *Nancy Glaser*
> *Business Strategies Consultant*

Marketing Vehicles

$ ➤ $$ ➤ $$$

Use this worksheet to outline your marketing schedule, listing each type of marketing vehicle, the frequency with which you use it, and what it costs you annually. This is the basis of your marketing budget and will be used in the Financials section of your business plan.

VEHICLE	SPECIFICS	FREQUENCY	COST PER YEAR
Professional Assistance			
Marketing/PR Consultants			
Advertising Agencies			
Social Media Specialists			
SEO Specialist			
Graphic/Web Design			
Brochures/Leaflets/Flyers			
Signs/Billboards			
Merchandising Displays			
Sampling/Premiums			
Media Advertising			
Print (newspaper, etc.)			
Television and Radio			
Online			
Other Media			
Phone Directories			
Advertising Specialties			
Direct Mail			
Website			
Development/Programming			
Maintenance and Hosting			
Trade Shows			
Fees and Setup			
Travel/Shipping			
Exhibits/Signs			
Public Relations Activities/Materials			
Informal Marketing/Networking			
Memberships/Meetings			
Entertainment			
Other:			
Total			$

■ **Mix.** Use more than one method so customers get exposure to you from a number of sources.

■ **Repetition.** It takes many exposures before a customer becomes aware of a message.

■ **Affordability.**

Use the Marketing Vehicles worksheet on page 162 to document how you employ various marketing vehicles in your business.

Be Resourceful

Often the best marketing vehicles are not the most obvious or the most expensive. A large ad in a specialty publication may prove far more effective and less expensive than a small one in a general newspaper. Building a presence on a **social media** site targeted to a specific audience can bring better results than being on the most popular social media sites.

You may want to consult the *Standard Rate and Data Service* to find names and advertising rates of specialty and general publications. To find information on trade shows, look online for trade organizations in your industry.

You can also find an extensive listing of trade shows online at:

TSNN.COM

www.tsnn.com

SUCCESSFUL MEETINGS

www.successfulmeetings.com

Or refer to the book *Trade Shows Worldwide: An International Directory of Events, Facilities, and Suppliers,* published by Gale Research.

If you are marketing to businesses, identify potential customers for direct mail or telemarketing efforts on ThomasNet at www.thomasnet.com.

Some of the marketing vehicles to choose from are:

■ **Brochures.** Leaflets, flyers, or other marketing collateral; these are particularly useful for service businesses.

■ **Company Website.** Every business must have a website. It may be robust—where you sell products directly to customers, or answer customer service inquiries—or it may be quite simple.

■ **Print Media.** Newspapers, magazines, and specialty publications.

■ **Broadcast Media.** Radio and cable television can likewise target specific markets; network TV stations can be very expensive, however.

■ **Social Networking.** Social media sites, microblogging sites, and blogs that help you build relationships with customers and influencers in your market.

■ **Online Advertising.** Paying for visibility on other websites; these can be banner ads, sponsorship of other sites, purchasing of keywords in search engines, and participating in online portals.

- ■ **Advertising Specialties.** Items imprinted with the company name given to customers, such as calendars, caps, desk sets, and other gifts.
- ■ **Direct Mail.** Flyers, catalogues, brochures, and coupons.
- ■ **Email Mailings.** Regular or infrequent mailings to email mail lists; these can be direct advertisements or online newsletters.
- ■ **Public Relations.** Free feature and news articles in the media and other publicity, usually secured by public relations specialists.
- ■ **Sampling.** Distribution of free product samples, or coupons entitling recipients to free or discounted samples of your product or service.
- ■ **Informal Marketing/Networking.** Activities such as joining organizations, public speaking, or attending conferences.

Traditional Marketing Tactics

In addition to direct marketing methods, you can employ a number of creative strategies to promote your company. These tactics often involve little or no extra cost and can be the source of substantial increased revenues. *Complete the Traditional Marketing Tactics worksheet on page 165 to indicate marketing tactics you use to increase sales.*

Various industries have particular marketing tactics, and enterprising entrepreneurs devise unique methods to reach customers. A few important strategies to consider in your marketing approach are described below.

Media Advertising

Advertising works. Customers expect to learn about products and services from ads in newspapers and magazines, on the radio or television, or online. Advertising gets your company's name and message to a large number of people with relatively little work on your part. But it costs money. Don't buy ads based merely on the number of people reached; make sure the ad is reaching the right people: your target market. A badly designed and poorly written ad may be worse than no ad at all, so spend the time and money to develop a good one. Run ads repetitively; professionals estimate it takes nine exposures to an ad before someone even notices it.

Customer-Based Marketing

Often neglected, this is one of the most fruitful types of marketing. Two particularly effective approaches are to emphasize repeat sales by positioning your product or service to be consumed or replaced, and to offer add-on sales, whereby you increase the total revenues per customer through the sale of extra products or services.

Another approach is point-of-purchase promotion: merchandising displays or other offers presented to customers at time of sale to encourage impulse purchases.

Traditional Marketing Tactics

$\blacktriangleright$ $$ $\blacktriangleright$ $$$

Customer-Based Marketing: How do you increase sales to current customers? _____

_____

_____

_____

_____

_____

Strategic Partnerships: What relationships do you have with other companies to help promote, sell, or distribute your product or service? _____

_____

_____

_____

_____

_____

Special Offers/Promotions: What reduced-priced values do you offer to encourage sales? _____

_____

_____

_____

_____

_____

Premiums: What gifts or prizes do you offer to build goodwill and sales?_____

_____

_____

_____

_____

_____

_____

Other Tactics: _____

_____

_____

_____

_____

_____

_____

Strategic Partnerships

Identify a related company with which to associate for promotion, sales, or distribution. Ways in which you might use such a partnership include:

- **Cooperative Advertising.** This type of advertising occurs when two companies are mentioned in an advertisement and each company pays part of the costs. This is a frequent practice in many industries.

- **Licensing.** One company may grant permission to another to use its product, name, or trademark. For instance, instead of selling your computer software program directly, you might license it to another software publisher to incorporate in its program.

- **Distribution Agreement.** This is an agreement whereby one company carries another's product line and distributes another company's products or services.

- **Bundling.** This is a relationship between two companies in which one company includes another company's product or services as part of a total package.

Special Offers/Promotions

Special offers and promotions enable you to increase sales revenue and build market share by offering customers special values. The tendency is to consider this primarily a retail tactic, yet service companies and business-to-business marketing can also incorporate the practice.

Strategies include leader pricing—products or services on which you make little or no profit—to entice first-time customers and increase patronage, and introductory or limited time offers to build cash flow at critical points.

Premiums

The use of premiums in marketing includes encouraging sales and creating goodwill through gifts, sweepstakes, discounts, and other perceived added value. These "extras" can be packaged with products or services (such as free wine glasses with a two-bottle box of wine), given as gifts with a purchase, or offered as discounts, often in conjunction with other companies (such as travel discounts), for established customers. Many websites use sweepstakes with prizes to attract visitors to their sites.

Online Marketing Tactics

The online universe offers an enormous range of marketing opportunities. New ones are developed as fresh technologies emerge and entrepreneurs create innovative ways to communicate. Add to this the fact that people are now connected to the Web virtually all the time via smartphones and other mobile devices. ***Complete the Online Marketing Tactics worksheet on page 171 to describe which online tactics you'll use.***

Social Media Sites

These sites are based on the concept of user-generated content combined with continuous interactivity and connectedness. The result is a huge number of people constantly attached to the Web, their electronic devices, and each other.

Are you trying to reach consumers or businesses? Does a mass-market site (e.g., Facebook, Twitter, Pinterest), a special interest site (e.g., Chowhound for food), or a professional networking site (e.g., LinkedIn) better suit your offering? Once you've picked the right site (or sites), provide relevant and interesting content to raise your company's visibility in the community.

HOW TO USE SOCIAL MEDIA

Spread the Word	**Advertise**	**Form a Community**	**Network**	**Enhance Credibility**
Create buzz about your products or services.	Use campaigns designed to target your specific audience.	Create your own group to get feedback from customers.	Build referral sources and networking connections.	Contribute meaningful content to sites or positive recommendations or reviews.

Blogs

Blogs—short for Web logs—are frequently updated online journals that can contain text, audio, video, graphics, and photos. From a marketing perspective, blogs work well for businesses in which expertise is valued—for consultants, technology service providers, professional service businesses, and so on.

Whether you create your own blog or regularly contribute to a popular blog in your field, your blogging efforts can greatly enhance your visibility and credibility. If you offer readers something of value (beyond a sales message), it's likely you'll attract people looking for your services or products.

Effective use of blogs can:

■ Build name and brand recognition.

■ Establish you as an expert.

■ Attract customers and clients.

■ Create links to your website.

■ Generate buzz around a new product.

■ Let you tap into a committed market.

Other Social Media Tactics

Creating your own podcast—a radio or TV program that gets downloaded to computers and mobile devices—might be a good option if you have compelling content on the most popular podcast topics: technology, politics, and business.

What about a video? While YouTube is the best known of the video-sharing sites, there are many others out there, and some of them are focused on "how to" videos, possibly providing a perfect opportunity to showcase your expertise.

Review sites and community sites give users the opportunity to rate and post comments about the products, services, and companies they use. These sites include Yelp.com, Angie's List, TripAdvisor, Zagat, and Epinions.com. Their comments and reviews can be powerful marketing tools for your business—or they can result in disaster.

As with every other aspect of your marketing plan, you should carefully evaluate the return on investment you can expect from blogs, social networks, and other online marketing tactics. Although many of these activities don't appear to cost much money, all of them take time. Be sure to factor in the time—yours, your staff's, and any consultants'—that goes into social media marketing.

Mobile Marketing

Mobile devices have transformed the way customers deal with local businesses. How long has it been since you used your smartphone to find a business? To reserve a table at a restaurant? To get directions? Likely, not long. You don't have to develop a gee-whiz app or use every mobile method available in order to reach the increasing number of people searching for businesses like yours on their mobile devices. You do, however, at least need a mobile version of your website.

Daily Deals

The prospect of getting a bargain has driven the phenomenal success of daily deal sites such as Groupon, Living Social, and hundreds of others. For some companies, these offers are invaluable business builders. Other companies, which have lost money and attracted only bargain-hunting customers, have rued the day they ever signed up.

A deal site sends an email daily to those who've registered. People interested in your discounted product or service purchase your deal. You typically pay nothing to be included, but the deal site gets a hefty piece of the sale: 30% to 50%. And typically, you must offer at least a 50% discount. So if your business creates custom photo books, here's what a money breakdown might look like: You offer your $40 leather-bound photo book for $20. With each sale, you get $10; the site gets $10. Those who never redeem the coupon add to your profit margin: Businesses report 5% to 40% nonredemption rates.

Deals are best offered to launch a new business or get your name out there, for slow periods to drive new traffic, and to move excess inventory.

SEO and SEM

With **search engine optimization (SEO)**, you design a website that is optimized for search engines to find you quickly and easily. The goal: your website listed high on the "results" page when a user searches for relevant keywords. With **search engine marketing (SEM)**, you buy keywords so that your advertisement appears every time a user searches the Internet using them.

- **SEO.** First, you need to figure out which words your target customers are most likely to use when searching for the types of products or services (or content) you offer. You'll need to repeat your keywords throughout your site so that search engine crawlers are likely to associate your website (or certain pages within it) with those keywords. As you develop and update your site, keep these keywords in mind.

  Be aware, however, that SEO is as much art as science. Since search engines frequently change their search algorithms, the optimization rules that kept a company in the top spot one month might not apply the following month.

- **SEM.** This broad term could apply to any type of marketing activity aimed at associating your company's name and website with search engine results; however, to distinguish it from search engine optimization, the term SEM has come to mean those activities in which you pay to have your site appear high within search results. SEM can also be called search engine advertising.

  SEM is very popular for two reasons. Searchers are often highly qualified prospects—especially for the most narrowly defined terms. And advertisers are charged only when a searcher clicks on their ads (called a click-through). They do not pay just for the ad being displayed.

Email Newsletters

Like their print counterparts, email newsletters offer an extremely effective way to build your business and stay in front of your customers and prospects. They also have the advantage of being fast, easy, and inexpensive to produce.

In an email newsletter, you can include information and tips your customers can use, short articles, business updates, special announcements, or coupons and special offers. Avoid filling your newsletter with sales information about your products and services—instead, provide recipients with some benefit for opening your email. That way, they're more likely to open the next one you send.

But a word of caution about all email marketing: Be careful not to abuse it. Send email only to those who've signed up to receive email from you or have had some dealings with you (including giving you their business card), otherwise you may be breaking the law. Limit the frequency of your messages; generally once or twice a month is enough for an email newsletter. Try to use a compelling "Subject" line to increase the chance that people will open and read your mail. And make sure your mailings are meaningful, are valuable, and don't contain offensive content or language. If not, recipients will soon block your email as spam, and if enough people do that, email filters will block your messages to many larger servers.

Online Advertising

Even if you find most online ads bothersome, it's a good bet that there are others you're happy to see. For instance, if you're looking for environmentally sensitive products—solar-powered heating, energy-efficient lights, recycled building materials, and so on—and come across a website listing and describing suppliers of such products, you'll be thrilled. You won't care that these companies paid to be listed; you'll just be glad to find all of these resources in one location.

What's important is that you design your own online ads to attract (not annoy) your target customers and then place them where potential customers are most likely to see them.

Some major types of online website advertising opportunities are:

■ **Portal Sites/Directories.** Portals and directories serve as online hubs—usually grouped around a common theme, topic, product, or location—where users come to look for information, products, and services. As such, portals can provide effective (and affordable) places to advertise your product or service.

■ **Website Ads.** Banner ads typically include graphics or photos as well as text, and are placed adjacent to the content of the webpage itself. Interested viewers can then click through to the advertiser's website.

Another form of website advertising is interstitial ads—that is, ads that appear between (or before) other content and websites. With this type of ad, viewers become a captive audience. After they type in a website address, an ad appears before the actual site they want to visit opens.

■ **Sponsorships.** With a sponsorship, an advertiser pays to support a website, portion of a website, content within a website, or the organization behind the website. In return, the website gives the advertiser visibility and recognition. Often, this visibility takes the form of a static banner ad; however, it can also mean displaying the sponsor's name, logo, or tagline in immediate proximity to content.

■ **Online Classifieds.** Some of the most effective ads are pure text (or, perhaps, text augmented with a few pictures)—the equivalent of online "classified" ads.

The best known is Craigslist (www.craigslist.org). While most people look for jobs or used goods on Craigslist, many businesses also use the site to advertise their products or services. Advertising on Craigslist takes time (you have to continually update your ad to stay visible), but, in most cases, it's free.

■ **Affiliate Auction.** Online auction sites, such as eBay, are more than just places for individuals to auction off used goods to the highest bidders. Representing huge online marketplaces, such sites have created myriad marketing opportunities for entrepreneurs. Since you can set up "stores" on these sites or list products as "Buy It Now" without conducting an

Online Marketing Tactics

$ ➤ $$ ➤ $$$

Website: How will your website promote your products or services or add credibility to your business? What are the primary objectives of your website in marketing and selling your products and services? _____

_____

_____

_____

SEO/SEM: Will you drive traffic to your website using either unpaid or paid search engine marketing? If so, how? ____

_____

_____

_____

Email Newsletters: Will you create an email newsletter to connect with your customers and prospects? What type of content will you include? How often will you send the newsletter out? How will you build your mailing list? _____

_____

_____

_____

Blogs: Will you write a blog? What blogs will you actively participate in to increase your visibility? _____

_____

_____

_____

Social Media: Will you use social media such as Facebook, Twitter, YouTube, LinkedIn, Pinterest, and the like, to spread the word about your products and services, and to engage customers and prospects? _____

_____

_____

_____

Other Online Advertising: Will you use paid advertising on other websites or portals? If so, which ones? _____

_____

_____

_____

Other Online Tactics: Will you use other online vehicles such as podcasts, video, daily deals, or review sites? If so, how will you use them? _____

_____

_____

_____

_____

_____

_____

auction, you can use auction sites as an advertising medium—just as you would online classified sites.

■ **Affiliate Programs.** You can advertise your products or services on other people's websites by setting up an affiliate program (which can also be thought of as pay-per-sale advertisements, since the hosting website only gets paid if the ad results in a sale).

Affiliate advertising offers incentives for others to place your ads on their sites in exchange for a piece of the action. For instance, if one of their site visitors clicks your ad, goes to your site, and makes a purchase, the originating site gets a commission on the final sale.

Marketing Globally

In today's connected world, it's far easier to find and serve customers worldwide than ever before. While your domestic market may seem like a large enough target market to pursue, especially if yours is a young company, you should also at least consider expanding your potential customer base internationally.

Even if you don't directly target global customers, it's likely that you'll have customers throughout the world, especially if you have an online presence. International customers may find you even if you are not actively seeking them.

Before you decide to market your products or services internationally, you must determine whether there's likely to be market demand from other countries, and if you can affordably and effectively fulfill orders should you receive them. After all, there's no point in marketing a product if it's going to be impossible or unaffordable to ship. So begin your global marketing evaluation by determining which—if any—of your products or services are appropriate for global sales. Are there customers in other countries who are likely to want or need your products or services? If so, in which countries?

Keep in mind that you do not necessarily need to have a physical presence in another country to be able to market to customers. You might, for instance, find a locally based company with which to partner that can import and market your products or that can license your products or intellectual property, adapt your offerings to meet the needs of the local market, and market them under either your name or its company name.

For most businesses, however, their online presence—particularly through their website or their sales through other websites—is going to be their major global marketing vehicle. So as you build or redesign your website, keep international prospects in mind, with considerations such as:

■ Making your website friendly for international customers (for example, the use of multiple languages, prices in other currencies, use of the metric system for measurements, customer support for different time zones).

■ Creating special websites or landing pages for each country or region you're marketing to.

Globalization: Marketing

Complete this worksheet if you intend to market your products or services and make sales internationally.

1. Which of your products or services are particularly well suited for international sales? _____

_____

_____

_____

_____

_____

_____

2. Which countries are your best prospects? _____

_____

_____

_____

_____

_____

_____

_____

3. Which steps will you take to market your products or services internationally?

☐ a. Create or adapt globally friendly website(s)

☐ b. Support multiple languages in product info

☐ c. Use social media

☐ d. Buy adwords targeted to specific countries

☐ e. Partner with international marketing firms

☐ f. Participate in international trade shows

☐ g. Open international locations

☐ h. Other: _____

4. How will you adapt your website to accommodate international customers?

☐ a. Support multiple languages

☐ b. Indicate prices in other currencies

☐ c. Provide customer service in different time zones

☐ d. Provide measurements in metrics

☐ e. Adjust website content to be sensitive to cultural norms

☐ f. Use visuals (e.g., photos) that reflect international orientation

☐ g. Other: _____

- Making an attempt to understand cultural norms. For instance, in some countries, comparison advertising (e.g., taste tests of Coke versus Pepsi) is not done. In many Asian countries, red is a symbol of good luck.

- Using social media. Participating in social media—blogs, and social networking sites—where many or most users are from your target countries.

- Buying ad words to appear when searchers are from a specific country. Some search engines allow you to target particular countries. Keep in mind that in some countries, other search engines may be dominant—such as Baidu in China.

Of course, you can also create a local presence if the opportunity in a specific country is large enough to warrant it. In such a case, you will certainly want to learn about that country's customs when it comes to marketing and sales. You may wish to engage locals on your marketing team or hire local marketing companies (public relations or advertising firms, for example) that better understand the local market. You'll also need marketing collateral materials (such as brochures) appropriate for that country.

Use the worksheet on page 173 to sketch out your global marketing efforts.

Your Sales Structure

Directly related to your marketing strategy is your sales structure—how you achieve actual customer orders. In this section of your plan, describe the two main components of your sales system: the sales force and the sales process.

If your business plan document is being used for external funding requests, you don't need to go into great detail; it is enough to provide a general outline, giving a sense of your understanding of what is necessary to produce sales. For internal planning, however, you should flesh out these concepts more thoroughly.

The Heartbeat of Your Sales Force

At the center of your company's income-producing activities are those members of your staff with specific sales responsibilities. These are the people who come in direct contact with your potential customers and who most immediately determine whether your product or service is actually purchased. These key staff members are your sales team, and you must carefully plan how you make the best use of their skills and time.

What responsibilities do you give your sales team? What commissions and incentives do you provide? How do you train and supervise the people responsible for bringing in your revenues?

Of course, every employee actually has a part in attracting and retaining customers: If the janitor does a poor job and the store looks dirty, customers may not want to buy from you. Thus, many companies incorporate some form of sales-related training for all personnel. But certain staff members (and nonemployees, as well) have particular responsibilities for securing sales, and these individuals are at the center of your sales team.

> "With public relations, you need to keep your best foot forward at all times. You should be scrupulously honest, as direct as possible; at the same time, you want to protect your long-term goals and the reputation and dignity of any individuals involved. It's important to maintain a certain public perception of your organization, so you can't go into all the details of each decision. The public has a hard time handling negatives. You must have standard, acceptable methods and forms of response to critical questions and inquiries."
>
> **Bill Walsh**
> **Former Coach and President**
> **San Francisco 49ers**

Sales Force

List below the type of sales force you use, and how many salespeople you have in each category.

Inside Sales Force: _____

Outside Sales Force (employee): _____

Outside Sales Representatives, Agents (nonemployee): _____

Ecommerce Sales and Support: _____

Telemarketing Services: _____

Other: _____

_____

_____

How do you divide responsibilities, e.g., by product line, territory, customer type, and so on? _____

_____

_____

Do sales personnel have additional responsibilities as well as sales? _____

_____

What commissions do you pay sales personnel? _____

_____

Do commissions vary by product line or goals achieved? _____

_____

What other incentives or bonuses do you provide? _____

_____

For which expenses do you reimburse sales personnel, e.g., travel, entertainment? _____

_____

_____

What expenses must sales personnel pay for themselves? _____

_____

_____

Who supervises sales personnel? _____

Do they receive any commissions or bonuses based on performances of people they supervise? ☐ Yes ☐ No

Who trains sales personnel? _____

How often is training provided? _____

What kind of training is provided? _____

Which other employees are involved in generating sales? _____

_____

_____

Sales Activities

Sales activities can be conducted either on your business' premises or by calling on customers at their homes or places of business. And your sales force can consist of either inside or outside salespeople.

- **Inside Sales Personnel.** Employees who remain on the company's premises to secure sales; includes floor salespeople in retail stores, personnel who take phone orders, and telemarketing.

- **Outside Sales Personnel.** Salespeople who go to customers' locations to solicit orders; these can be company employees working on salary alone, salary plus commission, or straight commission; or they can be independent contractors—sales representatives and manufacturer's agents, either representing many product lines or handling one company's products exclusively, usually on a commission-only basis.

- **Online Sales.** Online sales can include websites that sell products directly to customers through either an ecommerce site or an auction site such as eBay. Lead generation sites generate sales indirectly by collecting leads for salespeople. Lead sites often require that visitors provide contact information if they want to access the sites' content, videos, and/or downloads. Salespeople then use this contact information to follow up with users.

You can also hire independent telemarketing services to conduct your telephone sales from their place of business, using their employees.

Once you determine the nature of your sales team, delineate how you divide responsibilities among personnel—for example, assigning sales representatives by territories, product lines, or customer types.

Employee Compensation and Training

How do you pay your sales force? Some form of commission is common in most selling situations. What commission percentage do you provide?

Do you give bonuses for reaching certain goals?

Do you use other incentives, such as awards, gifts, or vacations? Do district managers or other supervisors receive commissions on their staff's sales?

You also need to consider how you continue to train, motivate, and supervise your sales force. Selling is a difficult, often dispiriting, task, and salespeople need frequent encouragement and support. Who will be responsible for this? ***The Sales Force worksheet on page 175 helps you outline the structure of your sales team.***

Sales Process

Finally, you need to identify the procedures you use in making sales calls and presentations, and to project the level of results you expect from your sales force. Although this information is not necessary to include in a business plan prepared for external financing purposes, the data on sales productivity is important in developing realistic sales forecasts.

Sales Process and Productivity

On this worksheet, outline the procedures and productivity levels you expect in your sales efforts.

CUSTOMER IDENTIFICATION

How do you identify potential customers? _____

Do you use "cold-calling"? _____

What prospect lists, if any, do you purchase? _____

What other methods do you use to determine customer interest? _____

Do you capture the contact information of your website visitors? _____

CUSTOMER CONTACT

How do you contact customers? Email? Phone calls? _____

Who contacts potential customers? _____

How many times is a potential customer contacted before he or she is discarded from the list? _____

When are potential customers contacted? _____

How long does each contact take? _____

How frequently are current customers contacted for additional follow-on sales? _____

Who contacts current customers? _____

SALES PRODUCTIVITY

What are your sales goals? Delineate volume and revenues expected within a certain time frame. _____

_____

What percentage of your revenues will come from online sales? _____

What percentage of your website visitors do you project will convert to purchasing customers? _____

How many times, on average, must a potential customer be contacted before securing:

   An appointment? _____ A sale? _____

What percentage of potential customers agree to an appointment or demonstration? _____

What percentage of those agreeing to an appointment or demonstration subsequently purchase? _____

How many calls will each salesperson be expected to make, and in what time period? _____

Who handles phone, mail, email, and online orders? _____

Who ensures orders are filled promptly and properly? _____

Does this information get reported to the salesperson? ☐ Yes ☐ No

How? _____

Who checks credit? _____

OTHER SALES PROCEDURES

_____

_____

_____

How will actual sales be achieved? You will likely use more than one of the methods shown in the graphic below. Set goals for each method you employ.

SALES METHODS

| On-site sales | Mail order sales | Telephone sales | Online sales | Off-site sales | Third-party sales |

Aspects you should consider in evaluating your sales process include:

- **Cold-Calling.** Contacting targeted customers before they have indicated any interest in purchasing your product or service; this can be done in person or on the phone.

- **Leads.** Developing or purchasing names of potential customers who have expressed at least some level of interest in your product or service.

- **Productivity.** Estimating the amount of time it takes to secure sales, and the level of sales realistically expected from each salesperson.

- **Order-Fulfillment.** Ensuring that orders are completed promptly and accurately, an essential completion of the sales process.

- **Goals.** Establishing specific, measurable objectives for each salesperson and the total sales force; realistically assessing the number of sales possible for each sales representative given the nature of his or her assigned territory/product line/customer base; setting sales quotas based on these assessments.

- **Follow-up Efforts.** Making sure that the sales representative maintains ongoing contact with the customer after the sale and seeks out repeat sales opportunities.

- **Optimize Your Website.** Adding keywords to your site and/or buying keywords to help boost your rankings in search engines and direct more traffic to your site.

Use the Sales Process and Productivity worksheet on page 177 to outline the procedures and productivity levels you expect in your sales efforts.

International Sales

Once you have determined that there is likely to be demand from customers in other parts of the world for your products or services, you need to evaluate how you will make and fulfill sales.

One of the biggest challenges in serving international customers is fulfilling orders. If you have a physical product, it may be difficult and expensive to ship, and you may face tariff or custom considerations. You need to examine those issues before you spend time or money marketing and building a sales operation.

If, however, what you are providing is a downloadable product (such as software, an app, or content) or an online hosted service, there's almost no problem in fulfilling orders—assuming, of course, that the product or service has some international appeal. If that is the case, you should certainly give consideration to how to improve your online presence to attract global customers.

Recognize that sales conditions and terms may be different in other countries. For instance, in some countries, many consumers will not have credit cards, or you may have limits on the interest rates you can charge even your commercial customers. As you make your sales plans and projections, you'll need to understand those differences.

A typical way for companies to develop international sales is to partner with another company/corporation or a sales company or distributor in that country. Or, you may license your product or intellectual property (for example, software, designs, content) for them to sell under either your brand name or theirs. Contact your industry trade associations to see what's typical in your industry and how other companies currently license similar products in other countries.

One excellent way to test the waters for global markets is by participating in international trade shows. These expositions bring many parties in an industry together to show their products to potential customers. Trade shows are an excellent, efficient way to reach a large number of international customers and partners. They can be a method of finding local distributors or licensors in other countries. ***Use the worksheet on page 181 to outline any plans you have for international sales.***

Preparing the Marketing Section of Your Business Plan

You need to distill the highlights of your marketing and sales planning into a concise and compelling statement of how you reach customers and convince them to purchase from your company. The Marketing section of your business plan should include:

- The message you attempt to send customers; how you position your company in the market.

- The marketing methods and vehicles you use.

- The sales force and sales procedures you use.

The Marketing Budget and Sales Projections worksheets and the Plan Preparation Form on pages 182–186 help you organize information for completion of your business plan's Marketing section.

Refer to the previous worksheets in this chapter when completing your marketing budget estimates for the Marketing Budget worksheet. Some of this information will also be used in the Financials section of your business plan. To complete the Sales Projections worksheet, estimate income by each product line, then total the income from all product lines and transfer this information to the appropriate financial forms in Chapter 16.

Chapter Summary

Your marketing plan and sales strategy are at the heart of your company's business. To stay in business you have to reach customers and secure sales. That is why this section of your plan is likely to be closely reviewed by prospective investors. When studying your marketing plan, these investors want to see that you have a realistic, cost-effective approach to positioning your products or services in the market and to motivating customers to purchase.

In your sales strategy section, potential funders want to see that your sales methods are appropriate for your business and that your sales force is both large enough and trained well enough to be able to secure the sales levels necessary to sustain your business.

Globalization: International Sales

1. Do you intend to make sales internationally? _____

2. What is the nature of the products you're selling (downloadable apps, content, products, services)? _____
_____
_____
_____
_____

3. Have you researched which concerns, if any, there are with fulfillment (shipping, customs, tariffs, etc.)? _____
_____
_____
_____
_____

4. Which specific products or services in your line are most appropriate for international sales? _____
_____
_____
_____
_____

5. When selling internationally, will you be selling through a third party or with direct sales? _____

6. Do you intend to open a sales office in other countries? _____

7. Do you plan on hiring sales reps in other countries? _____

8. What are the typical commissions in the countries where you'll be selling? _____
_____
_____
_____
_____

9. What are the typical terms of sale in the countries where you'll be selling? _____
_____
_____
_____
_____

10. What other concerns with selling internationally have you identified? _____
_____
_____
_____
_____

MARKETING BUDGET

	JAN	FEB	MARCH	APRIL	MAY
Professional Assistance					
Marketing/PR consultants					
Advertising agencies					
Social media specialists					
SEO specialist					
Graphic/Web design					
Brochures/Leaflets/Flyers					
Signs/Billboards					
Merchandising Displays					
Sampling/Premiums					
Media Advertising					
Print (newspaper, etc.)					
Television and radio					
Online					
Other media					
Phone Directories					
Advertising Specialties					
Direct Mail					
Website					
Development/programming					
Maintenance and hosting					
Trade Shows					
Fees and setup					
Travel/shipping					
Exhibits/signs					
Public Relations/Materials					
Informal Marketing/Networking					
Memberships/meetings					
Entertainment					
Other:					
GRAND TOTAL COSTS					

NOTE: A Microsoft Excel version of this worksheet is available as part of PlanningShop's Business Plan Financials package, available from **www.PlanningShop.com**.

$➤ $$➤ $$

JUNE	JULY	AUG	SEPT	OCT	NOV	DEC	TOTAL

SALES PROJECTIONS

	JAN	FEB	MARCH	APRIL	MAY
Product Line #1					
Unit volume					
Unit price					
Gross sales					
(Commissions)					
(Returns and allowances)					
Net Sales					
(Cost of Goods Sold)					
GROSS PROFIT					
Product Line #2					
Unit volume					
Unit price					
Gross sales					
(Commissions)					
(Returns and allowances)					
Net Sales					
(Cost of Goods Sold)					
GROSS PROFIT					
Product Line #3					
Unit volume					
Unit price					
Gross sales					
(Commissions)					
(Returns and allowances)					
Net Sales					
(Cost of Goods Sold)					
GROSS PROFIT					
Product Line #4					
Unit volume					
Unit price					
Gross sales					
(Commissions)					
(Returns and allowances)					
Net Sales					
(Cost of Goods Sold)					
GROSS PROFIT					
Totals for All Product Lines					
Total unit volume					
Total gross sales					
(Total commissions)					
(Total returns and allowances)					
TOTAL NET SALES					
(Total Cost of Goods Sold)					
TOTAL GROSS PROFIT					

NOTE: A Microsoft Excel version of this worksheet is available as part of PlanningShop's Business Plan Financials package, available from **www.PlanningShop.com**.

JUNE	JULY	AUG	SEPT	OCT	NOV	DEC	TOTAL

$ ▶ $$ ▶ $$

Marketing and Sales Strategy Plan Preparation Form

Use the information recorded on this form to summarize the points you will cover in the marketing portion of your business plan.

Describe the message you are attempting to send customers:_____

_____

_____

_____

_____

_____

Describe how you are positioning your company in the market:_____

_____

_____

_____

_____

_____

_____

Describe the traditional and online strategies you use: _____

_____

_____

_____

_____

_____

_____

_____

Describe your sales force and procedures: _____

_____

_____

_____

_____

_____

_____

Use this information as the basis of your plan's Marketing section.

SAMPLE PLAN: MARKETING PLAN

MARKETING PLAN

ComputerEase distinguishes itself from its competitors by better understanding the needs of its customers. Other computer software training companies, both in the Vespucci area and online, market their services as if their customer were the individual student taking the class. ComputerEase, on the other hand, knows that the customer is actually the student's employer—the business that has contracted with ComputerEase.

ComputerEase Meets Customers' Needs

Employers have slightly different motivations than the students themselves. Although the companies, as well as the students, want high-quality, easy-to-understand training, the businesses also want:

- Increased overall productivity.

- One company to deal with for all computer training needs.

- Ongoing support for their employees.

- The convenience of not having to disrupt the workplace for computer training sessions.

These business customers want to deal with a training company with which they can have an ongoing relationship.

ComputerEase's slogan, "We speak your language," is designed to reassure its primary market: large corporate customers. The slogan implies both that the software training itself will be comprehensible and that ComputerEase understands the needs of the business customer.

Describes the company's message.

As a play on the word "computerese," the name is designed to be memorable, with the added implication that the company makes dealing with computers easy. Computer-Ease prominently features its slogan, "We speak your language," on all its marketing materials, on its company website, and at the bottom of email messages.

ComputerEase Emphasizes Training

ComputerEase emphasizes high-productivity training. This is accomplished by selling not only training at the introductory, basic user-level, but also additional, advanced training to substantially increase the benefits to the corporate client. This additional training expands the number of services ComputerEase can sell each customer, and increases the revenues produced from each sale.

Organization of Sales Team

Since ComputerEase's primary target market is mid- to large-size companies, it has to carefully tailor its sales pitch to the buyers of corporate training—either in-house training managers or human resource professionals. It does this through a small tele-sales team of three contractors who are each paid $20 per hour plus commissions. Their primary job: to get past the primary "gatekeeper" and then pass the lead on to Vice President of Marketing Susan Alexander or President and CEO Scott Connors.

Tells sales mechanism.

SAMPLE PLAN: MARKETING PLAN (continued)

All queries coming in through the website are first screened by the receptionist, who doubles as the customer service representative, and who responds to each one immediately and personally, and passes the lead onto Alexander or Connors. Each website inquiry is called back within 24 hours. A part-time channel administrator is in charge of handling all requests for information or orders that come in through software or hardware resellers or consultants.

Indicates sales training for staff.

Additionally, all company personnel are considered members of the sales team. Even the software trainers themselves participate in monthly sales training meetings, and all employees receive financial bonuses if the company reaches overall sales goals.

Marketing Vehicles

Most of ComputerEase's marketing for its online products is done—appropriately enough—online. The firm buys keywords from the major search engines so that its ads show up anytime a user performs a search using those words, directing traffic to the company website. Additionally, the firm has bought a sponsorship on the premier corporate training website, and makes sure it is listed on every major business directory under "corporate training/software." (Sometimes it has to pay for these listings; sometimes they are free.) ComputerEase has also been sending out a highly regarded email newsletter every month to a growing list of corporate trainers that explores best practices in technology training. The firm will also use social media as a mechanism for marketing services and for providing customer support.

Gives specifics of marketing plan.

The firm has also sponsored ads in *Corporate Trainer* magazine, and is one of the sponsors of the largest software training conference in North America.

For its on-premise marketing, ComputerEase focuses on face-to-face solicitation of human resource and training directors of large local corporations with the goal of generating regularly repeated sessions.

Additionally, the company maintains an ongoing direct mail program. A schedule of ComputerEase's downtown classes is sent out every two months to the target audience. Currently 3,500 pieces are sent. ComputerEase purchases lists of human resource directors and another list of local subscribers to a leading computer magazine. All prior students are also included in the direct mail program.

Cooperative Marketing Plans

ComputerEase partners with leading software publishers on many collaborative marketing activities. These include sharing the cost of cooperative advertisements placed in regional computer publications, sponsoring special events to introduce corporate clients to the publishers' new software, and sponsoring a trade show booth at the regional human resource directors' annual convention.

As one of the key sponsors of the corporate training world's largest conference on software training, ComputerEase has earned a good deal of credibility through its presentations and executive speeches by Vice President of Marketing Susan Alexander and President Scott Connors. Additionally, ComputerEase has agreements with three of the top national software distributors and the largest hardware reseller chain as well as a growing network of computer consultants to "bundle" its training courses with new hardware and software sales for a discounted fee.

CHAPTER

11 Operations

Ninety percent of success comes from properly executing the fundamentals.

Describing How You Run Your Business

How are you actually going to run your business? The Operations section of your business plan is where you begin to explain the day-to-day functions of your company. This is where you translate your theories into practice.

Much of the information in this chapter appears mundane—for instance, how you keep track of inventory, or what equipment you need and when it must be replaced. These seem like the kinds of details that take care of themselves. But there's a far greater chance that a business will fail because fundamentals aren't handled properly than because the basic business concept is faulty.

Examining your basic operation is particularly important for internal planning. A capable manager does not take any activity in the business process for granted. Each step is worthy of evaluation and improvement. A little bit of extra planning in operational areas can mean marked improvements in profit margin. Assessing and developing the underlying mechanisms of your business will certainly pay off.

To do a thorough job planning your internal operations, you may want to develop a separate operations or procedures manual. Such a manual should describe the specific details of the processes by which you produce, distribute, or maintain your products and services.

For the purpose of preparing a business plan, however, your operations section does not need to be thoroughly detailed. Be brief. Describing your operations too specifically in a business plan is not only unnecessary, it may even be counterproductive, especially if you are seeking outside funding. Focusing on very small details may make it appear that you are not seeing the big picture in your business.

A section follows to help you plan your technology needs. However, if you are seeking financing, you do not need to include a separate Technology section in your written business plan unless yours is a technology-based business. You can instead incorporate key technology issues in your Operations section.

What Your Operations Section Should Cover

This chapter describes most of the subjects commonly included in an Operations section of a business plan. In your own plan, you do not necessarily need to address each of these topics. Rather, limit your Operations section to those issues that:

- Are essential to the nature and success of your company;
- Provide you with a distinct competitive edge; and
- Overcome a frequent problem in businesses of your type.

> "The biggest part of becoming a winner is developing standards of performance. Know how you go about doing things; know your process. Constantly develop the application of your knowledge and skills. Having standards means many, many people function within a framework. That framework includes more than just how you do the job at hand. For instance, it might include punctuality and how people dress. Sometimes almost symbolic, ritualistic matters become important; on the 49ers, everyone's shirt had to be tucked in at all times. It reinforced the sense of professionalism and being part of a team."
>
> *Bill Walsh*
> *Former Coach and President*
> *San Francisco 49ers*

Thus, if yours is a manufacturing business in which distribution is often a major difficulty, you may want to include one or two paragraphs clarifying your company's improved approach to distribution. However, if yours is a retail business, distribution may not be an issue at all, and you needn't discuss it.

Of course, if your business is an enterprise that develops or relies heavily on new technology, you need to explain those aspects fairly thoroughly. Likewise, if you are counting on a new manufacturing or merchandising method to significantly improve your competitive position, you must describe the mechanisms and importance of those techniques.

Many sources of information exist if you need to locate resources to prepare your Operations section. Commercial real estate agents can easily describe the advantages, disadvantages, and resources available in your location. Trade associations can assist in helping you find consultants for plant and manufacturing design and direct you to sources of equipment. ThomasNet (www.ThomasNet.com) is an invaluable source of suppliers, distributors, and equipment manufacturers.

Operations, naturally, have many financial implications. You should note these in the Flow-Through Financial worksheets in this chapter and transfer the numbers to your financial statements in Chapter 16. If yours is a new business, you should include the Start-Up Costs worksheet in your business plan. For both new and existing businesses, the Equipment Schedule worksheet, which you need for internal financial projections, can also be included in the Appendix of your business plan.

Facilities

In real estate the old saying is that the three most important factors are location, location, location. In business, as well, location can prove the critical factor for success. For example, with retail operations, a bad location can mean you just don't attract enough customers to your store. Likewise, in manufacturing and distribution companies, a location lacking adequate access to transportation or suppliers may prevent you from manufacturing or distributing your product in a timely or cost-effective manner.

The physical aspects of the facilities themselves can be extremely important for a company's continued growth. Are your facilities large enough to accommodate expansion in the coming years? Are the necessary utilities available and energy efficient? Are you near an airport or rail terminal? Or, are you locked into an inadequate facility that reduces your overall production and distribution **capacity**?

Occasionally, the length and terms of a lease may be a particularly attractive (or problematic) aspect of a business. Having a long-term, low-rent lease in a desirable area may be, in and of itself, a significant business asset. A lease that needs to be renegotiated in the near future may spell trouble for your company, as you may be facing substantially increased rents. In a new lease, look to negotiate certain concessions, such as **leasehold improvements** or a few months' free rent (particularly while construction is occurring).

Success **ke term**

Capacity
The amount of goods or work that can be produced by a company given its level of equipment, labor, and facilities.

Leasehold Improvements
The changes made to a rented store, office, or plant, to suit the tenant and make the location more appropriate for the conduct of the tenant's business.

Offshoring
Using outside vendors located in another country or transferring your own company's operations to another country, usually to reduce costs. Offshoring also includes setting up an independent subsidiary in another country to both lower costs and reduce taxes.

Outsourcing
To have certain tasks, jobs, manufacturing, and so on, produced by another company on a contract basis rather than having the work done by one's own company "in-house."

When evaluating your facilities, examine those aspects most important for your particular business. Do you need a prestigious address in a downtown office building for your law firm? Do you need to be close to key suppliers for your manufacturing plant? Do you need access to environmentally approved disposal sites for your chemical company?

In the Facilities worksheet on page 193, describe all the facilities in which your company operates, emphasizing any competitive and cost-saving advantages they may have. Specific points to mention are listed below.

FACILITIES CONSIDERATIONS

Location **Lease** **Improvements** **Utilities/ Maintenance** **Key Factors**

Location

Include company headquarters, retail store(s), branch offices, additional plants, distribution centers, and the like. Describe any mobile facilities. List square footage, and how the square footage is allocated (office space, retail, production, shipping, etc.). Describe access to parking and transportation; air, rail, and surface shipping access; and loading docks, warehouse, and other necessary facilities.

Lease

What are the terms and length of the lease? Do you pay straight rent or rent plus a percentage of gross or net profits? Can you sublet? Did you receive concessions in the lease? What restrictions are in the lease (for instance, hours of operation or promotional activities that are often mandated in mall leases)?

Improvements

What additions, such as walls, signage, or utility hookups, have been made to the property, or remain to be made? Who pays for such improvements—you or your landlord?

Utilities/Maintenance

Include the costs of gas, water, and electricity. Note seasonal or production level variation. List the cost of janitorial, trash-removal, and other ongoing facility maintenance expenses. Emphasize energy-efficient measures. Is the facility wired for high-speed data transmission, or for Ethernet connections, or otherwise fitted out for technology uses?

> "People have no idea you're there if they can't see you. Get a good location; it's money well spent. As a start-up, it's hard to advertise; so, instead of a big advertising budget, spend the money on a better location. Find a good real estate broker with retail experience. Have them identify successful businesses serving your target customer and then locate near them. Capture their customers."
>
> *Nancy Glaser*
> *Business Strategies Consultant*

Facilities

$ ➤ $$ ➤ $$$

Describe the attributes of your facilities.

PRINCIPAL LOCATION(S)

Location: _____

Square Footage: _____

Description of Use: _____

Parking/Transportation: _____

Shipping Access/Facilities: _____

Warehouse Facilities: _____

Other: _____

_____

_____

BRANCH OFFICES/ADDITIONAL PLANTS/DISTRIBUTION CENTERS/OTHER FACILITIES

Number: _____

Locations: _____

Square Footage: _____

Description of Use: _____

Other Aspects: _____

_____

LEASE(S)

Length of Lease: _____

Rent/Terms of Rent:_____ Other Terms:_____

Restrictions: _____

Concessions:_____

IMPROVEMENTS

Existing:_____

To be made: _____

Paid by landlord:_____ Paid by company:_____

UTILITIES/MAINTENANCE

Average monthly utility costs?_____ How do costs vary seasonally? _____

How do costs vary due to production levels? _____ Are there energy-efficient methods in use? _____

Average maintenance costs? _____ Do any maintenance costs vary? _____

Other: _____

_____

_____

Key Factors

What aspects of your facilities are most likely to affect your company's success? Are you near your target market? Are you in a prestigious or convenient location? Does your lease have particularly favorable terms? Will you be able to grow in these facilities without moving?

Production

Every manufacturing business has a production process—the way it goes about fabricating a raw or component material and creating an item with greater usefulness or desirability. But even if yours is a service or retail business, you have a method of "producing" something of value for your customers, although you may not have given this process much thought.

Take time to evaluate and assess your production plan to see if you can enhance efficiencies, improve the quality of the finished "product," and, in the long run, increase your profit margin. Look at the various stages involved in creating your product or service: Can these stages be shortened? If so, you will be able to produce and sell more in less time.

One concept that has taken hold in the development of certain products is the minimal viable product. The idea is to quickly get a product to market, and later make improvements based on the experience of actual customers. Google's product development mantra, for instance, is "Experiment, Expedite, Iterate." In other words, the company tries a lot of new things, moves quickly, and refines and improves along the way.

Clearly, you don't want a minimally viable product for a medical device or automobile. But in some categories, such as online services, mobile apps, and personal electronics, consumers are willing—even eager—to pay for version 1.0.

Examine how you organize and deploy your workforce. Do you use a team approach—with one group of workers responsible for a job from start to finish? Or, do you use a production-line approach, with a worker doing the same portion of each job and then passing it along to someone else? Do you have clear-cut lines of authority, or do workers often not know who is responsible for making decisions?

Increasingly, companies are using variable labor in addition to permanent employees, as an integral part of their workforce. Variable labor—employees hired to perform a specific task for a specific period of time—is particularly useful for seasonal work or unusually large or special orders. Many companies even use variable labor, in the form of consultants, for professional positions. Using variable labor gives you more control over ongoing expenses, since you can add these employees in good times but don't have them on the payroll when business is slow. Maintaining high quality in a variable labor force is frequently difficult, however, and employee motivation is often low.

Another way to increase flexibility in fixed costs is to subcontract—or outsource—various aspects of production to other companies. These companies then have the responsibility for maintaining the workforce, facilities, and equipment necessary to produce their component piece. While the per-piece cost to you includes a profit to these companies, and thus your per-piece cost is probably greater than if you had all the necessary means of production in-house, the advantages of not having your money tied up in overhead may be well worth the additional cost. Even service businesses can consider ways to subcontract portions of their contracts.

You should also pay particular attention to the issue of quality in your production process. Poor quality can be costly—it can not only cost you in the form of goods you have to discard as being faulty, but it can cost you customers. If you intend to sell your goods internationally, you will likely want to follow procedures to get your products or processes certified as meeting international quality standards, such as ISO 9000. These measures are set by the International Organization for Standardization and have been adopted by more than 90 countries worldwide. To find out more about such procedures, check the ISO website at www.iso.org.

Assessing Your Production Plan

Two worksheets on pages 196–198 help you evaluate your production process. The Production worksheet covers the major aspects other than equipment, which is handled on a separate form, the Equipment Schedule worksheet. You may wish to include the Equipment Schedule in the Appendix of your business plan. If yours is a manufacturing business, you might also wish to include a flow chart of your production process in the Appendix.

The aspects covered in the Production worksheet are:

- **Labor/Variable Labor.** What kinds of and how many employees do you require to produce your product or service? How do you use them? How are decisions reached in the workforce? Do you use variable labor, employ subcontractors, or outsource portions of the production process?

- **Productivity.** Productivity measures how long and how many people it requires to produce your product or service. This can have a major impact on your profit margin.

If you can produce more goods in less time, you increase the amount of profit earned from every dollar spent on salaries, equipment, and rent. What methods can you use to increase productivity without reducing quality?

- **Capacity.** Capacity is the measure of how much work your current facilities, labor force, and equipment can handle. If you have excess capacity, you have the ability to produce more than you are currently selling using your current workforce, equipment, and plant.

Excess capacity represents a waste of already paid-for earning potential.

Can you find ways to use or reduce excess capacity? If you are operating at close to full capacity, what plans do you have for expansion, to handle growth?

- **Quality Control.** All the various measures you take to ensure that you maintain the same standards with each product or service come under the category of Quality Control.

> The apparel business is fun — a combination of creative and business. But it's hard to execute because of the manufacturing. You're not just shipping little digital files."
>
> *Kay Koplovitz*
> *Chair, Kate Spade*

Production

Describe the key factors (other than equipment) involved in producing your product or service.

PROCESSES

What are the stages of production? _____

_____

How does the product/work get transferred from one stage to another? _____

_____

How does the process use new technologies? _____

_____

What are the advantages of your production process? _____

_____

What are the drawbacks of your production process? _____

_____

What components are contracted for others to produce? _____

_____

What are the costs of these outside services/components? _____

_____

Briefly describe the subcontracting company(s): _____

_____

What other costs are directly associated with the production process? _____

_____

LABOR

Total number of employees: ___   permanent: full-time: ___ part-time: ___   variable: full-time: ___ part-time: ___

When do you use variable labor? _____

How many shifts do you operate? _____ How long are the shifts? _____ What are the hours of operation? _____

What are the basic qualifications required of employees? _____

_____

How are employees organized: ☐ team approach? ☐ production line? ☐ other?_____

Who supervises employees? _____

_____

Other labor issues: _____

_____

Other labor costs: _____

_____

_____

$> $$> $$$

PRODUCTIVITY

For each product or service, list how many minutes, hours, days, weeks, and workers it takes to produce one unit.

_____

_____

_____

_____

How many units can each worker produce in a minute, hour, day, and week? _____

What methods could reduce the amount of production time required without reducing quality? _____

_____

What other methods can you use to increase productivity? _____

_____

CAPACITY

How many units of goods or services can be produced in your current facility in a day _____ week _____ month _____?

How many units of goods or services can your workforce handle in a day _____ week _____ month _____?

At what percentage of capacity are you now operating in terms of workforce _____ equipment _____ facilities _____?

How is excess capacity currently used? _____

_____

What are other ways to use excess capacity? _____

_____

How can you provide for increased capacity, if needed for growth? _____

_____

QUALITY CONTROL

Who is responsible for overall quality control issues? _____

What steps are taken to inspect finished goods or services? _____

_____

What intermediate steps are taken to ensure quality in the process? _____

_____

Are products and services tested for quality? _____

How are employees motivated to ensure quality? _____

How do you solicit customer comments? _____

What other steps are taken for quality control? _____

_____

_____

_____

Equipment Schedule $ ➤ $ $ ➤ $ $ $

List your company's existing and anticipated equipment.

CURRENTLY OWNED EQUIPMENT

Description (Name/Model #)	Status	Date Purchased	Cost	Payments

EQUIPMENT TO BE PURCHASED

Description	Purchase Date	Cost	Terms	Payments

Such activities include regular inspection throughout the production process, occasional testing or sampling of randomly selected goods, employee-involvement training, reward programs for quality assurance, and solicitation of customer comments.

■ **Equipment and Furniture.** (*List separately on the Equipment Schedule worksheet on page 198.*) Include manufacturing equipment, transportation vehicles, store fixtures and office equipment, and furniture. List any payment obligations or leases. Under "Status" describe the state of the equipment in terms of future use potential, technological development, and substantial maintenance required. Also indicate date to be replaced, if known.

Inventory Control

Many businesses overlook the vital contribution that careful inventory management makes to the profitability of a company. How much money you have tied up in supplies or finished product sitting in your warehouse makes a direct impact on your bottom line. Every box of raw material is not just taking up space; it's money sitting around, losing value.

Of course, if you don't have sufficient inventory, you occasionally can't make sales. Every business dreads the possibility of receiving lucrative orders it can't fill due to inadequate supplies. And sometimes you don't just lose sales; you lose a customer. This is the risk in maintaining too low an inventory.

The answer is to develop inventory management systems that substantially increase the flow of information from the sales point to the production and purchasing teams. Information can reduce the amount of guesswork that goes into maintaining inventory. Know how sales are going, even on a daily basis.

> We are changing the way our suppliers think about organic, fair trade. In 2008, we bought 800,000 pounds of organic ingredients. In 2013, we bought five million. That changes the way our suppliers interact with the environment."
>
> *Seth Goldman*
> *Cofounder, Honest Tea*

Suppliers can help. Work with them to see how to reduce the amount of time necessary to receive goods and to explore the potential of lowering the number of minimum orders. Large businesses often have significant clout with suppliers, but even smaller companies should look for suppliers who are willing to increase flexibility in their orders and deliveries.

Methods of Inventory Management

One of the approaches to inventory management is "just-in-time" inventory control. This concept emphasizes keeping inventory stocked only to the levels needed to produce goods just in time for delivery, usually in response to orders in-hand. Such a system is highly dependent on adequate communication systems and good supplier relationships.

In devising your inventory control and communication procedures, you will want to devise a management information system (MIS). Usually such a system centers on the computerized maintenance and communication of information, such as order and stock levels, reorder dates, historical tracking of sales, and so forth. Computer professionals can help you select and adapt an MIS for your company.

You will also need to discuss how you want to value and record your inventory. Two commonly used methods are LIFO (last in, first out) and

FIFO (first in, first out). These are basic methods of valuing your remaining stock, and they can have significantly disparate tax implications, so this decision should be reached in consultation with your accountant. ***Complete the Inventory Control worksheet on page 201 to assess your procedures.***

Supply and Distribution

Almost every business has goods or materials coming in to the company and finished products or services going out. The companies you rely on to provide you with incoming goods, and the methods you use to sell and distribute your product, are both essential to the continuing well-being of your business.

Most businesses will experience difficulties with their suppliers or distributors at some point. So it can serve you well to explore the abilities, flexibility, and alternatives of your current suppliers and distributors.

Try not to be dependent on just one supplier or distributor; your financial future will be too vulnerable if they fail you. Work to develop excellent relationships with your suppliers and distributors; you want them to feel that you are in a partnership together so that they will try to do everything possible to meet your needs. Be responsive to their needs as well; work out payment plans and communication methods to reduce pressures on them.

Select Suppliers that Understand Your Needs

Usually, competitive supply sources exist, giving you a number of choices and enabling you to negotiate better prices. But don't make your decisions based on price alone, for you may find the price right but the delivery time and quality problematic. Select suppliers with whom you can communicate well; make certain they understand your specifications and can consistently meet your standards.

Reliable Distribution Is a Must

Reliable distribution often presents a far more difficult problem. If your product is distributed through a wholesaler or "middleman," you need to carefully examine your choice of such distributor(s). Your selection of distributor(s) may be one of the single most important decisions you make, especially if they are responsible for most of your sales.

Once again, try not to put all your eggs in one basket. If you can ethically use more than one distributor, do so. Ask retailers or consumers about the reputation of distributors who sell to them so that you can be certain you are dealing with a reliable company and one that is well-regarded.

Complete the Supply and Distribution worksheet on page 202 to assess your sources of supply and distribution.

Order Fulfillment and Customer Service

Remember, your work is not finished when you produce a product or secure an order from a customer. You still need to make sure your customer receives the product he or she wanted, in good condition, and in a timely fashion. You need to know that you have satisfied your customer.

> **Marketing came naturally to me, but I didn't get the importance of distribution. Distribution was a bear. We had to realize that the distributor was our customer. It's a sharp-elbow, rough business."**
>
> *Seth Goldman*
> *Cofounder, Honest Tea*

Inventory Control

This worksheet helps you get a clear picture of your inventory control procedures.

Who is responsible for inventory control?_____

_____

What is the minimum level of inventory necessary to be maintained at all time? _____

_____

_____

What is the minimum amount of time necessary to get materials from suppliers? _____

_____

_____

_____

What is the minimum amount of time necessary to produce goods to order?_____

_____

_____

_____

What is the minimum amount of time necessary to ship goods?_____

_____

_____

_____

How is information about sales translated to the production and purchasing departments? _____

_____

_____

_____

What management information systems does your company use? _____

_____

_____

_____

_____

What steps do you take to reduce theft of inventory?_____

_____

_____

_____

What other inventory control steps does your company take? _____

_____

_____

Supply and Distribution

$ ➤ $$ ➤ $$$

These questions help you evaluate your current supply and distribution needs.

SUPPLIERS

Who is responsible for your purchasing decisions? _____

What are the key goods or materials necessary? _____

What are the average costs of these goods? _____

List your sources of key goods or materials: _____

_____

List any alternative sources of these supplies: _____

_____

Are any goods available from only one or two suppliers? ☐ Yes ☐ No

If so, how reliable or secure are these suppliers?_____

Can your suppliers provide you with "on demand" or short-notice goods? ☐ Yes ☐ No

If so, what additional costs do you incur? _____

Will your suppliers negotiate no- or low-minimum order contracts? ☐ Yes ☐ No

What kinds of credit terms will your suppliers offer? _____

What are your average credit costs? _____

Which key factors will determine your choice of suppliers?_____

Other supplier issues: _____

DISTRIBUTION

How is your product or service distributed to the consumer?_____

_____

Is there a wholesaler or distributor between you and the consumer? ☐ Yes ☐ No

If so, how many such companies do you use? _____

What are the key qualifications and advantages of such companies? _____

_____

What are the drawbacks of such companies? _____

If you use only one or two distributors, how secure are these companies? _____

What is their reputation among consumers? _____

What kinds of payments or commissions do these distributors receive? _____

Describe any alternative distribution methods available: _____

_____

_____

_____

Surprisingly, many companies pay relatively little attention to order fulfillment and customer service since they do not seem like pressing concerns or sources of increased profit margin. However, order fulfillment is part of any current sale, and customer service is part of any future sale.

Customers are constantly demanding better and better service. They expect to get what they want, when they want it, and to be treated graciously and fairly in the process. Many companies are renowned for their customer service and have built entire marketing strategies around it.

Some companies assume they are doing just fine in the way of customer service because they don't receive many complaints. But you can't judge how well you are serving your customers solely by the number of complaints you receive; the unhappy customer who doesn't complain is almost certainly a lost customer. At least a customer who tells you the problem gives you a chance to make it right.

So, it is your job to make certain that customers have little reason for complaints. Training all employees—from the shipping clerk to the sales representative—in customer service can pay off for you in customer retention and referrals. Build sufficient flexibility into your policies so that you can easily handle unusual or difficult requests. Empower employees to make certain decisions on the spot (such as accepting returns) instead of requiring each customer request to be approved by a manager. Make it easy for your customers to let you know what they want by soliciting customer suggestions and feedback.

Examine your order fulfillment processes. Often, orders are not communicated clearly or quickly to the processing department, and valuable time is lost due to inadequate internal communication. Assess the methods by which you prepare goods for shipping and deliver goods to customers. If you hire outside companies to ship or deliver your product directly to the customer, make certain they can deliver on emergency or rush-time schedules, or line up other shippers for such deliveries.

Look at the kinds of services you provide customers after sale. Good customer service emphasizes developing an ongoing relationship with your customers, so you need repair, service, warranty, and return policies that reassure customers that you continue to be interested in them even after you have their money.

Complete the worksheet on page 204 to evaluate your order fulfillment and customer service practices.

Global Operational Issues

Virtually any aspect of your operations can have a global component today, regardless of the size of your business. For example, a in Sioux Falls, South Dakota, has its website built by a company in India. A wholesaler in Virginia imports handmade purses from Vietnam. An electronics company has its video games manufactured in China. A San Jose, California, travel agency's call center is staffed in the Philippines.

> "One method of ensuring quality-control is to put guest comment sheets in each room. The comment sheets are read, assessed, and charted. Every month, we do detailed assessments of cleanliness, friendliness, ground maintenance, telephone service, and so forth, for each managed property."
>
> *Andre Tatibouet*
> *Founder, Aston Hotels*

Order Fulfillment and Customer Service

$ ➤ $$ ➤ $$$

Describe your company's order fulfillment and customer service practices.

Who processes orders? _____

How are orders communicated from the salesperson to the order fulfillment department? _____
_____

How are online orders transmitted to the order fulfillment department?_____
_____

How are orders checked to be certain they are filled promptly and accurately? _____
_____

What percentage of orders are prepared incorrectly? _____

How are goods prepared for shipping? _____
_____

How do you ship products? _____
_____

What is the shipping cost of your average order?_____

Are your shippers able to ship on short or emergency notice? ☐ Yes ☐ No

If so, are extra expenses incurred? ☐ Yes ☐ No

Who pays these: ☐ you or ☐ the customer?

What alternative methods exist to ship products? _____
_____
_____

What service programs do you offer?_____
_____

What maintenance or repair programs do you offer? _____
_____
_____

What percentage of your orders require repairs?_____

What is the average cost of the repair to your company?_____

What is your return policy? _____

What is your average rate of returns?_____

What is the cost of the average return? _____

Do you have a complaint or customer service department? ☐ Yes ☐ No

How do you solicit the opinions of customers? _____
_____
_____

Another example is PlanningShop, the publisher of this book. Although a small company, it does business globally. The content is created in the United States. Mobile applications are developed in Australia. Other publishers in more than 30 countries license the content and translate it for their nations. And books are sold to business schools and consumers throughout the world.

With the Internet, VoIP (Voice over IP), and other technologies, it's both easy and inexpensive to do business internationally, even to have staff members or critical subcontractors or vendors located halfway around the world.

You, too, can take advantage of a more connected global business world to source supplies, inventory, or raw materials; to have your products manufactured; or to have services provided. Perhaps you may choose to have actual facilities or production in other countries.

As you begin to consider your international operations, it is useful to understand two terms that are widely used:

- **Outsourcing:** Having another company or vendor provide a business service or component product. For example, a company may outsource the manufacturing of its products to another company or may outsource its technical support service to a separate company. Technically, using an independent contractor to accomplish a key business function, such as managing your company's public relations or human resource functions, is also outsourcing. You can outsource to companies in your own country or internationally.

- **Offshoring:** Having some of your company's operations or functions performed in another country. This typically means using outside vendors located in another country, but it could technically mean transferring your own company's operations to another country, usually to reduce costs. It can also mean setting up an independent subsidiary in another country to both lower costs and reduce taxes.

POSSIBLE HIDDEN OFFSHORING COSTS

Additional time describing project requirements

Additional time managing offshore staff/ vendors

Lower productivity levels

Lower quality levels

Time and expense of occasional face-to-face meetings

Currency fluctuations or exchange costs

Globalization: Operations

Complete the worksheet on global operations if you plan to handle any of your company's operations internationally.

Do you plan on having any international locations or facilities? ☐ Yes ☐ No

If so, where will they be located? _____

_____

Have you identified the specific facilities? _____

_____

ORDER FULFILLMENT

Will you sell any tangible products internationally? ☐ Yes ☐ No

If so, how will you fulfill those orders? _____

_____

Are there custom, tariff, shipping, or other problems? _____

_____

SUPPLIERS AND VENDORS

Which products can be provided by international vendors? _____

_____

Which parts/supplies/inventory can be provided by international vendors? _____

_____

Are there any import/custom/tariff considerations? _____

_____

What is the potential for disruption of your supply chain (due to political, climate, or other factors)? _____

_____

Which services can be provided by global vendors? _____

_____

MANUFACTURING/PRODUCTION

Customer service/tech support/call centers: _____

Design/creative: _____

Business infrastructure services (e.g., marketing, HR, and so on): _____

Other technology services: _____

OTHER GLOBAL OPERATIONAL ISSUES

_____

_____

While offshoring is chosen typically to reduce costs, hidden expenses may reduce the anticipated savings. Many companies that offshore key services—such as software development—have found that they must spend significantly more of their onshore staff time developing clear project descriptions and requirements and that projects are not completed as quickly. ***In the worksheet on page 206, identify any global operations issues you may have.***

One solution many smaller companies use when dealing with international suppliers is to go through brokers in their home countries who find and manage global suppliers. Your industry association may help you identify brokers who deal with international vendors.

Research and Development

A business that stands still is one that is almost certainly going to fail. You must keep on top of new developments that are going to affect your business. Your target market is always changing: growing older, developing new tastes, using new products. Your competitors understand this, so you need to stay aware of what they are doing if you wish to increase your ability to compete effectively.

All Companies Need Ongoing Product Development

Some companies need relatively large research and development components because they deal with constantly evolving technology or rapidly changing consumer preferences. But even companies that sell old-fashioned products (chocolate chip cookies, for instance) need to be developing new products based on changing customer values and concerns (such as low-fat cookies).

Your research and development activities may range from running a complete department staffed with researchers experimenting with new products and new equipment, to merely subscribing to certain publications and attending conferences. Regardless of the extent of such activities, research and development must be a priority in any business.

Examine the ways you plan to stay aware of developments likely to change your company's products, services, and practices. Make certain that key employees are likewise involved in research and development activities.

Complete the Research and Development worksheet on page 208 to evaluate research and development in your company.

Financial Control

Amazingly, some businesses give relatively little attention to how they handle money. Businesses may have serious cash flow problems just because they don't send out invoices in a timely manner. Or, they may incur substantial credit charges because they don't process their bills when due. Even very large companies are often guilty of inadequate financial control systems.

Set up procedures to ensure that your financial information is handled promptly and accurately. Invoices should be sent out quickly, and a system of regular follow-ups should be established for delinquent accounts.

Research and Development

$ ➤ $$ ➤ $$$

This worksheet helps you assess your ongoing research and development efforts and costs.

Describe any new products currently in development: _____

_____

_____

_____

Describe any new services currently in development: _____

_____

_____

_____

Which staff members have research and development responsibilities? _____

_____

How are staff members used for research and development? _____

_____

What percentage of your staff's time is devoted to research and development? _____

_____

Costs: _____

What equipment is needed for research and development?_____

_____

Costs: _____

What supplies are needed for research and development? _____

_____

Costs: _____

What publications are needed? _____

_____

Costs: _____

What conferences will your employees attend for research and development purposes? _____

_____

Costs: _____

List any other research and development activities your company is involved in: _____

_____

_____

_____

Costs: _____

_____

Accounts payable records should be thorough and easily retrieved, and sent regularly to appropriate decision makers within the company. Make certain your accounting practices and data retrieval systems are such that you can receive ongoing information on sales and expenses. Don't depend on monthly reports.

One particularly difficult problem is how to make certain that employees do not have the opportunity to embezzle or pilfer. Work with your accountant to set up practices that ensure there are adequate safeguards against theft in your financial procedures. Bring in a computer consultant to design safeguards in your data processing programs as well.

Design your financial systems to be a source of regular information and constant feedback. Avoid cumbersome systems that bury your employees in paperwork; this increases your costs and reduces efficiency. Streamline the process as much as possible.

Complete the Financial Control worksheet on page 210 to examine your financial control systems.

Contingency Planning

Bad things happen even to good companies. Sooner or later, your company will face an emergency. It could be a natural disaster—flood, fire, earthquake—or it could be something more mundane—a burglary, power interruption, slowdown from a supplier, product failure. As you develop your internal operational procedures, include contingency planning to help you anticipate and prepare for the unexpected. These contingency plans do not need to be included in any written plan for funding, but they may prove to be a substantial benefit to your company's future.

Develop procedures to safeguard your records and data in case of emergency. These procedures should include regular backup and storage of data offsite. Next, look at those things that are absolutely critical for your specific business and find ways to make certain they are protected or able to continue even in the event of an emergency. Devise a disaster plan to ensure the safety and well-being of employees and a method for you to communicate with employees during emergencies. Examine your business insurance. In addition to insurance to cover loss of physical equipment, records, and inventory, you can also get business interruption insurance to cover the costs of lost income and other costs incurred if an emergency closes your business.

Emergencies also come in the form of personal disasters—illnesses and accidents—so examine your procedures to get bills paid, checks deposited, and payroll out if key personnel are unavailable.

Other Operational Issues

A variety of other operational concerns will face your company, depending on the size and nature of your business. Some of these topics might include protecting the safety of your workers, protecting the environment, dealing with governmental regulations, or exporting goods. Other resources for some

> We probably waited too long to hire professional operations staff. We could have saved ourselves lots of money and sleepless nights if we had gotten some knowledgeable folks in earlier."
>
> *Seth Goldman*
> *Cofounder, Honest Tea*

Financial Control

This worksheet helps you evaluate your company's financial control methods.

Who is primarily responsible for designing financial control procedures in your company? _____

_____

_____

Which other employees are involved in financial control processes? _____

_____

_____

Who is responsible for invoicing? _____

What is the average amount of time that elapses before an invoice is sent after an order?_____

How are delinquent accounts handled? _____

_____

_____

Who is responsible for handling your accounts payable?_____

_____

What is your company's policy on paying outstanding bills?_____

☐ Pay when due

☐ Pay when received

☐ Pay on 30 days

☐ Other

Who makes decisions on variations in payment or billing procedures? _____

_____

What protections have been designed to reduce theft? _____

_____

_____

_____

What systems have been designed to produce ongoing reports of financial status? _____

_____

_____

_____

What other financial control systems have been devised?_____

_____

_____

_____

_____

of these topics are listed in the References & Resources chapters in the back of this book.

To briefly look at some of these concerns, complete the Other Operational Issues worksheet on page 212.

Preparing the Operations Section of Your Business Plan

In preparing the Operations section of your business plan, emphasize these aspects of your operations:

- Key characteristics
- Competitive advantages
- Cost and time efficiencies
- Problems addressed and overcome

The aim of this section is to show that you have a firm grasp on the operational necessities of carrying out your business, that you understand how those operations relate to your overall business success, and that you have taken steps to achieve maximum efficiency at the least cost. You do not want to give a step-by-step explanation of how your company functions or go into the specific details of your activities. Save that information for your internal procedures manual.

The Start-Up Costs worksheet on page 213 can be used by new businesses to tally the initial investment necessary to begin their operations. The Operations Plan Preparation Form on page 214 lays out the basic areas you should cover in your written document.

Chapter Summary

While the Operations section of your written business plan should not be overly detailed, careful planning in this area brings you meaningful rewards. Analyzing the day-to-day operations of your business will pay off in the form of increased profits as you find ways to reduce costs and improve productivity. You can find ways to make your money work harder and go farther, at the same time improving the quality of the product or service you produce and enhancing the work environment for your employees.

Other Operational Issues

$ ➤ $$ ➤ $$$

The questions below elicit your company's concerns and plans involving other operational issues.

SAFETY AND HEALTH

What procedures do you take to protect the safety and health of your workforce? _____

_____

What safety programs do you have in place to encourage your workers to maintain safety precautions? _____

_____

Other safety issues:_____

_____

INSURANCE AND LEGAL

What types of insurance do you need for your business? (include fire, accident/liability, malpractice, auto, etc.)_____

_____

_____

What amounts of coverage do you require to be adequately protected? _____

_____

What kinds of legal problems do you face in your business? _____

_____

Does your company need ongoing legal advice and assistance?

Other insurance and legal issues: _____

_____

REGULATIONS AND ENVIRONMENTAL

What licenses or permits are you required to have by law? _____

_____

What kinds of regulations cover your type of business?_____

_____

What kinds of environmental regulations affect your business?_____

_____

What precautions can your company take voluntarily to protect the environment?_____

_____

How can your company use products or processes that don't cause harm to animals?_____

_____

Other regulatory or environmental issues: _____

_____

Other operational issues: _____

_____

Start-Up Costs

$ ➤ $$ ➤ $$$

List the specific details of your start-up cash requirements. Remember, these are expenses you plan to incur before you launch your business. Post-launch expenditures should be entered in your Income Statement.

		Cost
Facilities	Land Purchase	
	Building Purchase	
	Initial Rent	
	Deposits (Security/Utilities/etc.)	
	Improvements/Remodeling	
	Other:	
	Other:	
Equipment	Furniture	
	Production Machines/Equipment	
	Computers/Software	
	Cash Registers	
	Telephones/Telecommunications	
	Vehicles	
	Other:	
	Other:	
Materials/Supplies	Office Supplies	
	Stationery/Business Cards	
	Brochures/Pamphlets/Other Descriptive Material	
	Other:	
	Other:	
Fees and Other Costs	Licenses/Permits	
	Trade or Professional Memberships	
	Attorneys	
	Accountants	
	Insurance	
	Marketing/Management Consultants	
	Design/Technical Consultants	
	Advertising/Promotional Activities	
	Other:	
TOTAL		

Operations Plan Preparation Form

On this form record specific information relating to your company's operational processes.

Key Aspects of Operations (possibilities include facilities, production process, equipment, labor force utilization): _____

_____

_____

_____

_____

_____

_____

Cost and Time Efficiencies: _____

_____

_____

_____

_____

_____

_____

Competitive Advantages: _____

_____

_____

_____

_____

_____

_____

Problems Addressed and Overcome: _____

_____

_____

_____

_____

_____

_____

_____

_____

Use this information as the basis of your plan's Operations section.

SAMPLE PLAN: OPERATIONS

OPERATIONS

A key element of ComputerEase's operations is its Corporate Training Center, located at 987 South Main Street in Vespucci. The Center currently consists of 20 student computer stations, equipped with all the major business software programs, an instructor's computer station and projection equipment, and state-of-the-art technology enabling the instructor to monitor exactly what each student is doing.

Describes a key aspect of operations.

The Corporate Training Center is vital because most of ComputerEase's corporate customers have limited, if any, extra computer facilities on their premises appropriate for conducting on-site corporate classes. Thus, ComputerEase can only grow its in-person training courses to an adequate level of income by having well-equipped training facilities of its own to offer.

For its online training courses, ComputerEase decided not to buy and manage its own servers and build its own data center, but to outsource that to a managed hosting vendor who provides a turnkey solution for all hardware/software needs and maintenance, backups, and upgrades.

Corporate Training Centers

On August 1, 2014, ComputerEase opened its first Corporate Training Center, along with its company's headquarters. This Training Center is equipped with 20 personal computer stations. Prior to the opening of the Training Center, ComputerEase was limited to conducting training programs at the clients' place of business (referred to as on-site programs).

Cost- and Time-Effective Programs

These on-site programs produce lower profit margins than Training Center classes or online classes. Generally, fewer students attend each on-site training session; instructors spend additional time for travel and setup, and costs arise from the transportation of equipment and materials and subsequent wear and tear. While ComputerEase charges higher fees per student in these on-site classes, the market will not bear prices that truly absorb the increased costs.

Shows method of increasing profitability.

Moreover, the potential customer base for Training Center classes is substantially larger than that for on-site programs. More businesses can afford to send employees to scheduled classes at ComputerEase's Corporate Training Center—or have a class developed for them at the Center—than can incur the costs and disruption of an on-site program. Online programs offer even greater flexibility.

With the funds now being sought, the company will open a second Corporate Training Center in the city of Whitten Park, where many of its corporate customers are located.

Competitive Advantages

In addition to an offshore technical support center, ComputerEase outsources its data center operations. These centers created several key advantages for ComputerEase. First, these strategic operations decisions allow ComputerEase to focus on what it does

SAMPLE PLAN: OPERATIONS (continued)

Indicates how excess capacity is used profitably.

best—design classes to efficiently and effectively teach computer software—rather than worry about the nuts and bolts of the underlying supporting technology. ComputerEase doesn't have to worry about finding and retaining qualified technical staff, or expend large capital investments in hardware and software. Instead, it pays predictable monthly wages and fees to its offshore team and outsourcer respectively, which it can write off on its taxes as an operating expense. The outsourced data center especially gives ComputerEase the flexibility to grow as needed: Rather than having to constantly buy more hardware and software as the business grows, it merely contracts for additional capacity from the outsourcing firm.

Regarding ComputerEase's in-person training, having its own training classroom enables the company to enjoy higher profit margins than its competitors who merely train corporate customers at their place of business.

While maintaining a classroom does incur the additional costs of rent and equipment, training classes held at ComputerEase's Corporate Training Center produce higher profit margins than classes conducted at customers' facilities ("on-site classes") or online.

ComputerEase management chose to lease rather than purchase its Corporate Training Center equipment and negotiated favorable lease terms with Wait's Electronics Emporium, enabling the company to upgrade its computers every 12 months. This not only significantly reduced the initial capital outlay, which would have exceeded $100,000, but ensures that ComputerEase always has the latest technology for its students—a useful marketing, as well as educational, advantage.

Problems Addressed

Details ways to minimize inventory and cost of goods.

A major part of the cost of high-quality corporate training is the teaching materials provided to each student. Although ComputerEase leverages all the development, writing, and updating work that goes into these materials for both its online and on-premises courses, that's still one of the biggest expense the company incurs. Materials are revised for each new software upgrade, so their average lifespan is less than 12 months.

To reduce materials costs, we develop all of our training materials, such as course manuals, for online publication only. Instead of receiving printed materials, each student receives a password to access training materials. This also helps the company be more green, by reducing paper use and waste. Although ComputerEase pays more in technical support than it would if course materials were printed, the net result is substantially increased profit margins.

A major operational challenge is staying on the cutting edge of instructional techniques, as technology evolves quickly and users demand richer experiences. This includes adopting updated online courseware platforms and incorporating into the training materials more-costly features such as audio and video.

ComputerEase emphasizes high-quality, productivity-oriented training. To help ensure quality, the company conducts interviews with each corporate client approximately one week after the training session to ascertain that the customer is satisfied. In the case of problems, the company offers free remedial training, preferably at the Training Center. To date, only two students have required remedial training.

The choice of location for the Training Center was key. It had to be within walking distance of a large number of Vespucci target customers (located in a five-block radius in the central downtown business district). It needed to be close to transportation and parking facilities and had to present a professional image. And, of course, rents had to be affordable. For this reason, South Main Street stood out as the best choice. It is downtown, immediately available to the prime office locations, but it offers significantly lower rents than offices on the north side of Main.

Explains choice of location.

> *Computers are useless.*
> *They can only give you answers.*
>
> —*Pablo Picasso*

Technology Is the Backbone of Your Business

Every business needs technology. Even if your company makes old-fashioned chocolate chip cookies, you'll rely on technology to handle many, if not most, routine business operations, from maintaining financial records, to processing orders, to staying in contact with suppliers and customers. Because technology is so central to running a business today, you need to plan what technology you will use and how you will use it.

This section helps you outline your technology needs. If yours is a technology-intensive company, your technology needs may be far more complicated than indicated in this chapter.

Why a Technology Plan?

Sometimes even the simplest technology issues prove to be difficult and time-consuming. For example, options for today's telephone systems can be surprisingly confusing, even for relatively small companies. Few of us have the technical expertise to understand the wide range of technology choices available to us. Often, we don't even know the right terms to use or questions to ask.

Many decisions you make about your technology, such as the choice of your database program, may be costly or cumbersome to change later. When outlining your technology plan, keep in mind how your company might grow or change; try to choose technology that is flexible enough to grow and change with you. As much as possible, choose technology that, while meeting your needs, is simpler rather than overly complex. All those extra "features" may just make your technology, whether it be a software program or a telephone, harder to use.

You may benefit greatly by using the services of a technology consultant to help you figure out the best products and systems for your company. There are consultants who can help you design a total system—hardware, software, telecommunications, and so on—and there are also specialists in specific areas.

Some industries have vendors who produce specialized software or hardware to meet industry-specific demands. Your trade association can help you identify vendors of such industry-specific technology, and you can typically find many sources exhibiting at industry trade shows. Although these products may be more expensive than general "off-the-shelf" software, they may better suit your company's specific needs, and they're less expensive than having software created specifically for you. Check, however, to see how compatible these industry-specific items are with common software or hardware; you'll probably want to be able to use some "off-the-shelf" products.

If you are just starting your business, you may not need to figure out each of these technology issues in detail, but you should have a realistic sense of costs as you put your financial statements together.

Planning for Technology Businesses

If you are preparing a business plan for a company that is heavily dependent on technology, expect some potential funders, especially venture capitalists, to scrutinize your technology plan in great detail. They will want to see both that you understand the nature and scope of your technology needs and that you have planned adequately for your hardware/software needs and your need for specialized personnel.

Of course, some companies are specifically in the business of developing or exploiting new technology, not just using technology to achieve other business goals. In these companies, technology is essentially the core business, so potential investors want detailed information about the nature of your technology. This description can be included as part of the section on "Products and Services" or it can be a separate section of your plan. It should describe the basic concept and features of your technology with a level of detail geared to the expertise of the potential reader.

Be careful, however, about how you provide the necessary data. You'll need to show the viability of your concept without revealing extremely sensitive company secrets (which should not be put in a written business plan). If, on the other hand, you are seeking **conventional financing** (e.g., bank loans) or investment from less knowledgeable sources, then the description of your new technology should be fairly general. If your plan is for internal use only, your technology section may be very detailed and include sensitive information about product development. In this case, be extremely cautious as to how the plan is distributed; you don't want it to fall into the wrong hands.

What Do You Use Technology For?

If you walk into a computer store and say, "I need a computer," the first question the salesperson will ask is, "What do you need it for?" Base your technology choices on your actual and projected business needs.

When you examine your business operations, look at which functions require or could benefit from technology. The graphic on page 222 features common business needs that use technology.

Many of these functions are offered online, "in the cloud." At its most basic level, **cloud computing** enables you to access your data anywhere you have Internet access and to pay a monthly fee for the service instead of purchasing costly software outright. Cloud service providers maintain,

Success key terms

Cloud Computing
A way of delivering computing power and applications over the Internet as a service rather than a product that the end-user purchases and maintains in-house. Software, memory, and storage space are all shared and provided to computers and devices as a utility (much like the way electricity is provided).

Conventional Financing
Financing from established lenders, such as banks, rather than from investors; debt financing.

upgrade, manage, and sometimes even integrate your computing needs and business applications.

One of your first decisions when planning for technology is whether to install and manage software on your own premises or in the cloud. Once you've committed your business to a particular software program or application, it's often difficult to change, either because you can't export your data easily or because the time and effort needed to learn a new program is a barrier to making a switch.

TECHNOLOGY USES

Accounting, taxes, finances · Order taking and tracking · Order fulfillment/ shipping · Inventory management · Database management · Mailing lists · Communication with customers

Internal communication · Presentations · Graphics · Personnel management · Production · Internet marketing · Internet sales

Choosing Technology

Key issues when choosing technology include:

- Functions
- Ease-of-use
- Cost
- Security
- Ability to be upgraded and expanded
- Integration with existing data, technology, systems, and the like

  As a guideline, ask yourself the following questions:

- What features do you absolutely need? Make certain the technology can handle your most important functions. If you can't do the things you have to do, you'll waste your money.

- What features would be helpful, although they are not absolutely essential? In addition to meeting your essential needs, some technology products or features can save you time or money in the long term. Look for those solutions that can improve your business, and review them in light of the extra cost and complexity they present.

■ Does your new technology have to be compatible with other technology? We live in an increasingly interconnected world where everything has to work with everything else. So be careful buying an unknown brand of hardware or software unless you've checked out that it will work with the other technology you purchase.

One of the many terrific advantages of cloud-based applications is that a number of them can "talk" both to one another and to on-premise software programs, by sharing data. For example, if you use Web-based Salesforce CRM, you can share customer data with an on-premise QuickBooks financial program. When you add new customers to your CRM, all of their information automatically flows into QuickBooks. Not only will you enter data only once, saving time and reducing errors, you'll have access to richer data, and you'll be able to share information more efficiently with your team.

■ Are your needs basic or complex? If your needs are fairly basic, you can start very inexpensively, using low-cost online applications that only require fairly low-powered computing devices. For instance, you can find simple, cloud-based software applications—often for free—to handle tasks such as word processing, bookkeeping, and customer relationship management (CRM). Because you access this software over the Internet, rather than running it on your own machines, you need only the most inexpensive computers.

Generally, identify the processes you will need for your specific business, then determine how much computing power those processes will actually require. But whenever possible, look to the cloud for solutions. Cloud-based versions enable you to scale up or down as you add or subtract employees or as your needs change (as they often do in a new business), and you can access cloud applications anytime, anywhere, from any device that has an Internet connection.

It's always a good idea to first decide what kind of software you'll run—on-premise or in the cloud—and from that choose hardware that will support it properly.

■ With equipment that uses "consumables," such as ink cartridges for printers, find out if replacement supplies are readily available. Office and discount stores usually carry only the most well-known brands. Take into account the availability and costs of supplies before making your final selection.

■ Do you perform tasks like design, desktop publishing, or presentations? If so, go for the latest equipment. Those types of software programs eat up lots of memory and processing speed.

■ How cool do you want to be? Some people and some companies want to be seen as on the cutting edge of technology.

> "At HotWired, we tried to build a company where the process, the flexibility, was more important than the product. We knew that the product was going to change a thousand times before we were done with it, but the process had to work."
>
> *Andrew Anker*
> *Venture Capitalist*

Global Technology Concerns

It's easier than ever to operate internationally, due primarily to technology. The Internet, mobile communication, and VoIP (Voice over IP) all make it possible to connect with virtually anyone throughout the globe.

Technology is generally well suited to being used internationally. Most technology has been developed for international standards. In a few, rare instances, however, you may find conflicts between technology systems. Some issues may arise from things such as electrical currents or telecommunications standards. Some mobile phones will not work in other countries, for example. Occasionally some governments may place limits on the use or access of technology. For instance, certain countries limit their citizens' access to particular search engines or social networking websites. Other countries put limits on what can be advertised on auction sites.

Complete the Globalization: Technology Concerns worksheet on page 225 to address any technology conflicts or problems you may face when operating internationally.

Preparing the Technology Section of Your Business Plan

Whether your company produces technology or merely uses it, in this section of you plan, show how your technology choices benefit your business.

Use the Technology Budget worksheet on page 226 to determine how much money you will spend on technology and how you will spend it. Fill out the Technology Plan Preparation Form on page 227 and use it as a basis for the Technology section of your plan.

Chapter Summary

Technology is a critical aspect of all businesses today, used in most areas of business operations and marketing. Because technology decisions can be confusing and costly, you may want to seek the help of outside experts who can assist you in making your technology choices. Developing an overall technology plan gives you a framework to understand the scope of your technology needs and create a more realistic technology budget.

Globalization: Technology Concerns

What kinds of conflicts could there be in your software, hardware, or other technology solutions?

Compatibility:_____
_____
_____
_____

Time zone: _____
_____
_____
_____

Currency conversion: _____
_____
_____
_____

Paper source: _____
_____
_____
_____

Measurement standards (e.g., metric versus Imperial, pounds vs. stones): _____
_____
_____
_____

Language and terminology:_____
_____
_____
_____

Steps you will take to mitigate these potential issues: _____
_____
_____
_____

Technology Budget $ ➤ $$ ➤ $$$

Use this worksheet to specify the costs of your ongoing technology needs.

	Year 1	Year 2	Year 3	Year 4	Year 5
Software					
Accounting					
Customer relationship mgmt.					
Human resource mgmt.					
Inventory mgmt.					
Office suite					
Custom software					
Other:					
Other:					
Hardware					
Desktop and laptop computers					
Tablets and mobile devices					
Servers					
Backup systems					
Printers					
Networking					
Peripherals					
Other:					
Other:					
Telecommunications					
Telephone system					
Mobile phones					
Fax machines					
Internet access					
Other:					
Other:					
Consulting Personnel					
Systems design/maintenance					
Tech support/help desk					
Other:					
Total					

Technology Plan Preparation Form

Using this form as a guide, summarize the key technology concerns and technology needs of your business, which you can then include in your business plan, either in a separate Technology section, or in the Operations section.

Software Needs (specify on-premise and "in the cloud"): _____

_____

_____

_____

_____

_____

Hardware Needs: _____

_____

_____

_____

_____

_____

Telecommunications Needs: _____

_____

_____

_____

_____

_____

_____

_____

Personnel Needs (specify in-house or outsourced): _____

_____

_____

_____

_____

_____

_____

_____

Use this information as the basis of your plan's Technology section.

SAMPLE PLAN: TECHNOLOGY PLAN

TECHNOLOGY

ComputerEase is in the technology business. As such, we must always stay on top of new developments and continually upgrade not only our equipment, but also our skills.

The most critical component of our technology plan is making certain our course developers and instructors are fully capable of using new software in the most productive ways possible, so that they, in turn, develop appropriate training materials and train our students. To that end, our course developers and instructors receive prerelease copies of software programs and pre-release training from major software manufacturers.

Key to success is staying on the cutting edge of instructional design technology. We are partnering with experts in the field to stay abreast of new developments in interactive online courseware and anticipate adding enhancements as they are developed.

ComputerEase offers online classes. National competitors currently offer such training, and we want to be prepared to be able to take on such competition. Additionally, we believe our online programs will enable us to expedite our geographic reach into other areas not only in the Midwest and other parts of the U.S., but also into any English-speaking country.

Our Training Centers are also critical. One Training Center is already in operation, and we anticipate opening a second center by January 2015. This center will have 20 to 30 of the most up-to-date personal computers, 3 or 4 printers, overhead projection equipment, and other audiovisual equipment. We lease our computers for the Training Centers rather than purchase them; this enables us to always offer students the latest equipment.

Our company website contains background information on the company and lists the schedule and descriptions of training classes for both online and in-person training sessions. Students of corporate training classes taking place in our center can register for sessions online and access password-protected areas to receive additional assistance after completing their training sessions. This will enable us to provide more continual support for our corporate clients. Online students enjoy these same capabilities, in addition to access to their training sessions through the website.

ComputerEase has developed training materials and applications that can be accessed online not only via desktops, but also through smartphones and tablets. We recognize that users tend to rely on their phones and tables as their primary electronic devices. We have also made our online classes accessible via mobile devices.

Demonstrates how a technology-based company stays up to date.

Details necessary hardware.

Describes website and its capabilities.

CHAPTER

13 Management & Organization

No matter what you sell, you're selling your people.

> "There are lots of companies to be created, lots of technologies to be built. There's an excess of money to fund those companies. The limiting asset is still people."
>
> *Andrew Anker*
> *Venture Capitalist*

> "Lots of entrepreneurs let ego get in the way. You've got to be the conductor. You can't play all the instruments yourself. You have to get others to work together."
>
> *Bill Rancic*
> *Serial Entrepreneur*

Your People Determine Your Success

People are the heart of every business. Overwhelmingly, the quality of the people determines the success of the business. Many investors base their investment choices almost entirely on the strength of the people involved in the enterprise. They know that the experience, skills, and personalities of the management team have a greater impact on the long-term fortunes of a company than the product or service provided.

For this reason, investors and lenders are likely to review the management portion of a business plan before they read many other sections. They read this section thoroughly, carefully scrutinizing the qualifications of the people behind a business. They look to see not only if the management team has the expertise necessary to run the business, but also if the internal structure makes maximum use of the talents of team members.

So, if you are preparing your business plan for financing purposes, you need to take particular care in crafting your Management section. Even if you are developing your business plan solely for internal use, an honest evaluation of your key employees' strengths and weaknesses will help you make the best use of your management team.

Most entrepreneurs give serious thought to choosing people for key positions. They may undertake extensive recruitment efforts, often using professional executive search firms, to find just the right person. But what do they do with that man or woman once on board?

All too often, no one gives careful consideration to creating clear lines of organizational responsibility and developing a management style that motivates employees. This is particularly true in newer companies. Even outstanding people will only do their best work in a system that encourages, recognizes, and rewards achievement. If you can create such an atmosphere, you can give yourself a true competitive edge.

Thus, in developing your Management plan, focus on two main areas: 1) the people who run your business; and 2) your management structure and style. Together, these two thrusts represent the core of your management system.

The Management Team

Who are the people most important to your company's future? Who are the people determining the strategies you will pursue? Who makes final decisions? Which members of your management decide on the products or services you will sell and the prices you will charge? Who is in charge of your sales efforts?

In all but the smallest businesses, these tasks are assigned to or shared by many people. So when you evaluate your management team, include the roles listed in the graphic below.

EVALUATE YOUR MANAGEMENT TEAM

Key Employees/ Principals

Board of Directors

Advisory Committee

Consultants and Other Specialists

Key Management Personnel to Be Added

Key Employees/Principals

Usually, the most important person in a business is the founder or founders, especially if the company is a start-up. In start-ups, the founders usually serve as the top managers and exercise day-to-day control over affairs. For this reason, the first person to evaluate in your management assessment is the founder, even if it is yourself.

Occasionally, either the founders themselves or major investors will bring in others to serve in top positions, such as president and chief executive officer. But if the founders remain active in the business in any way, serving on the Board of Directors, remaining as a company consultant, or taking a secondary management position, their skills and qualifications must be described in your plan. Other managers to evaluate in your business plan include:

- Top decision-makers: president, chief executive officer, division presidents.

- Key production personnel: chief operating officer, plant manager, technical director.

- Key technology personnel: chief technology officer, MIS director, systems administrator.

- Principal marketing staff: director of marketing, director of sales.

- Primary human resources staff: personnel director, training director.

- Head of research and development.

In looking at these key players, ask yourself:

- Do they possess the skills necessary for their specific jobs?

- Do they have a record of success?

- Have their business setbacks given them insights that will help them in their current roles?

- Do their personalities make them effective members of the team?

Success ke
term

Equity
Shares of stock in company; ownership interest in a company.

Options
The right to buy stock in a company at a later date, usually at a preset price; if the stock rises higher than the original price, an option holder is likely to exercise these options.

Key Employees Evaluation

Describe the attributes of your top managers.

PRESIDENT/CEO: _____

Experience: _____

_____

Successes: _____

Education: _____

Strengths: _____

Areas Lacking Strength: _____

CHIEF OPERATING OFFICER: _____

Experience: _____

_____

Successes: _____

Education: _____

Strengths: _____

Areas Lacking Strength: _____

CHIEF FINANCIAL OFFICER: _____

Experience: _____

_____

Successes: _____

Education: _____

Strengths: _____

Areas Lacking Strength: _____

MARKETING/SALES DIRECTOR: _____

Experience: _____

_____

Successes: _____

Education: _____

Strengths: _____

Areas Lacking Strength: _____

PRODUCTION MANAGER: _____

Experience: _____

Successes: _____

Education: _____

Strengths: _____

Areas Lacking Strength: _____

HUMAN RESOURCES DIRECTOR: _____

Experience: _____

Successes: _____

Education: _____

Strengths: _____

Areas Lacking Strength: _____

CHIEF TECHNOLOGY OFFICER/TECHNICAL DIRECTOR: _____

Experience: _____

Successes: _____

Education: _____

Strengths: _____

Areas Lacking Strength: _____

OTHER KEY PERSONNEL: _____

Experience: _____

Successes: _____

Education: _____

Strengths: _____

Areas Lacking Strength: _____

OTHER KEY PERSONNEL: _____

Experience: _____

Successes: _____

Education: _____

Strengths: _____

Areas Lacking Strength: _____

■ If they have supervisory responsibility, are they able to direct and moti-vate employees effectively?

■ Taken as a whole, does your team incorporate the full range of expertise and management skills you require?

If you are preparing your business plan solely to seek outside financing, you should limit the number of key employees discussed in this section to no more than five or six. Focus only on those who are most responsible for the company's long-term success.

Some companies are fortunate enough to have enlisted the services of "stars," individuals with particularly outstanding track records. If you have such a star associated with your company, highlight the role that he or she plays in your enterprise. You will want to feature them prominently in your Executive Summary as well. If key personnel have been associated with well-known, successful companies, indicate those associations too. If you choose, you can include the resumes of key personnel in your plan's Appendix.

Complete the Key Employees Evaluation worksheet on pages 232–233 to outline the attributes of your top managers. Assess their:

■ **Experience.** State the specific positions held and job responsibilities that directly relate to the current position. This is not a resume, so do not list every previous job, only those that indicate a skill or talent transferable to the job at hand.

■ **Successes.** Describe noteworthy successes, particularly those that can be quantified. Include accomplishments that indicate the ability to plan, manage, overcome obstacles, and reach a goal.

■ **Education.** Include education in the written plan only if the person is new to business or the education is directly related to or necessary for the task at hand.

■ **Strengths.** Describe the individual's best attributes in a business setting, including traits such as the ability to motivate others, industry knowl-edge, and financial capabilities.

■ **Areas Lacking Strength.** Describe the attributes the individual must enhance to become a more effective manager; such traits might include specific skills or knowledge, better communication techniques, or ability to handle additional tasks. While you might not include this in your written plan, this information can help you develop more-successful leaders.

Management Compensation and Incentives

Next, you need to discuss the compensation and incentives you offer your key employees as a way of retaining and motivating them. Will they receive a salary, commission, **equity**, stock **options**, or a combination of incentives? Most incentives have monetary implications, and investors often want to know the financial stake that top management has in the company.

In the Compensation and Incentives worksheet on page 235, list the financial incentives given key employees.

Compensation and Incentives

$ ➤ $$ ➤ $$$

Describe the compensation package for each of your key employees.

PRESIDENT/CEO

Salary:_____ Bonuses:_____

Other Incentives:_____

CHIEF OPERATING OFFICER

Salary:_____ Bonuses:_____

Other Incentives:_____

CHIEF FINANCIAL OFFICER

Salary:_____ Bonuses:_____

Other Incentives:_____

MARKETING/SALES DIRECTOR

Salary:_____ Bonuses:_____

Other Incentives:_____

PRODUCTION MANAGER

Salary:_____ Bonuses:_____

Other Incentives:_____

HUMAN RESOURCES DIRECTOR

Salary:_____ Bonuses:_____

Other Incentives:_____

CHIEF TECHNOLOGY OFFICER/TECHNICAL DIRECTOR

Salary:_____ Bonuses:_____

Other Incentives:_____

OTHER KEY PERSONNEL

Salary:_____ Bonuses:_____

Other Incentives:_____

Salary:_____ Bonuses:_____

Other Incentives:_____

TYPES OF COMPENSATION

Salary: Amount of money paid annually, regardless of company or personal performance.

Bonuses: Additional money given, usually at the end of the year, based on company or personal performance.

Commissions: Money given based on a percentage of sales made; rarely given to top management.

Profit Sharing: Money distributed to all eligible employees, based on the company's annual profit.

Equity: Stock in the company, which gives employees a direct financial stake in the overall performance of the business.

Stock Options: Ability to buy stock at a future date, but for a current set price; if the stock price increases, employees can exercise these options for a financial gain.

> "It's easy enough to acknowledge success. The tough part is finding the time and the right way to reinforce the person who made the effort but didn't quite succeed or the one who made sacrifices for the good of the team."
>
> *Bill Walsh*
> *Former Coach and President*
> *San Francisco 49ers*

Board of Directors

Every business that is incorporated must have a Board of Directors. In very small corporations, the directors are usually just the principals running the company. The board then serves little more than a legal function.

In larger companies, however, the board often includes members outside of management. Most frequently, these board members are people who have invested large sums in the company. Venture capitalists often require board seats as a condition of their investment.

Obviously, investors serve on boards to protect their money; they want to exercise some control over the management and direction of the company. But management should not view these investor–directors only as "Big Brothers," watching their every move. They often bring valuable insight and judgment to the company and contribute to its overall viability and success.

In forming your Board of Directors, you might also want to include members who bring you specific business expertise, such as financial acumen or industry knowledge. Such directors typically receive compensation for their service on the board.

Remember, however, that the Board of Directors has legal responsibility and authority for the corporation. Thus, outsiders should be chosen very carefully.

Advisory Committee

You may identify a number of individuals whose ongoing judgment and advice you want for your company, but whom, for legal considerations, you don't want on your Board of Directors.

One way of using their services, other than hiring them, is to institute an informal Advisory Committee. Such a committee would have little or no legal responsibility but could still render great assistance in your company's development.

Board of Directors/Advisory Committee

List the members of your Board of Directors, their financial stake in the company, and their professional expertise:

_____
_____
_____
_____
_____
_____

Describe how often the Board of Directors meets and its responsibilities:_____

_____
_____
_____
_____
_____
_____

If you have an Advisory Committee, state its functions and responsibilities and how often it meets: _____

_____
_____
_____
_____
_____
_____

List the members of your Advisory Committee, their professional expertise, and their compensation, if any: _____

_____
_____
_____
_____
_____
_____
_____

An Advisory Committee can also be helpful to a proprietorship or partnership that does not have a Board of Directors.

Complete the Board of Directors/Advisory Committee worksheet on page 237 to describe the members of your Board of Directors and Advisory Committee, if applicable.

Consultants and Other Specialists

Smaller businesses often think that consultants and specialists are only for large corporations. But hiring consultants can bring you the specific expertise of highly qualified individuals without the expense of a full-time employee. Both large and small businesses benefit from the services of outside consultants and specialists.

The use of consultants can also enhance the image you present in your business plan. Being represented by one of the leading law firms in town, or having your accounts prepared by one of the major accounting firms, adds credibility to your company.

Consultants with particular skills can help fill in the gaps in your management team. For instance, you might not yet be able to hire a full-time marketing director, but you could use the assistance of a marketing consultant.

Every business, no matter how small, should use an attorney and accountant, at least to set up the initial books and review contracts and leases. If you can't afford their services, you can't afford to go into business. It is a foolish economy to forego their advice for the sake of a few hundred dollars. Consultants and specialists you might use, other than attorneys and accountants, include:

- **Management Consultants.** To help you plan your business, develop strategies, solve particular problems, and improve management techniques.

- **Marketing Consultants.** To design ways to position your company in the market, oversee the creation of advertising and promotional materials, and structure your sales strategy.

- **Designers.** To add perceived value and improve your company's image through the talents of graphic design, product design, packaging design, website design, or interior design.

- **Industry Specialists.** Every industry has areas requiring special knowledge or specific technical skills, and "experts" offer consultation in these areas; examples might be kitchen design for restaurants, production line design for manufacturing companies, or merchandising specialists for retail stores.

- **Technology Specialists.** To help you identify your technology needs and solutions, set up your database, website, communications systems, etc.

Complete the Professional Services worksheet on page 239 to describe the consultants and specialists used by your company.

> " Our management consultant was extremely helpful in developing an overall strategy and helping us understand financial implications. Our accounting firm was helpful in setting up internal controls and helping us to know what is going on."
>
> *Larry Leigon*
> *Founder, Ariel Vineyards*

> " Who you know is important. It makes a lot of sense to have first-class consultants. Find out who are the good small business attorneys and accountants in town and hook up with them. Then you can believably say, 'I've found the best law firm, the best accountant, and now I'm looking for the best bank to complete my team.'"
>
> *Robert Mahoney*
> *Corporate Banker*

Professional Services

Profile your key consultants below.

ATTORNEY

Firm name: _____   Lawyer's name: _____

Qualifications: _____

Ways used by the company: _____

Annual compensation: _____

ACCOUNTANT

Firm name: _____   Accountant's name: _____

Qualifications: _____

Ways used by the company: _____

Annual compensation: _____

MANAGEMENT/MARKETING CONSULTANT

Firm name: _____   Consultant's name: _____

Qualifications: _____

Ways used by the company: _____

Annual compensation: _____

INDUSTRY SPECIALIST

Firm name: _____   Specialist's name: _____

Qualifications: _____

Ways used by the company: _____

Annual compensation: _____

TECHNOLOGY CONSULTANT

Firm name: _____   Specialist's name: _____

Qualifications: _____

Ways used by the company: _____

Annual compensation: _____

OTHER

Firm name: _____   Specialist's name: _____

Qualifications: _____

Ways used by the company: _____

Annual compensation: _____

Key Management Personnel to Be Added $ ➤ $ $ ➤ $ $ $

Describe the factors concerning management personnel you intend to add to your staff.

POSITION:_____

Qualifications Sought: _____

_____

_____

Approximate Date to Be Added: _____

Approximate Level of Compensation: _____

Other Incentives to Be Offered:_____

POSITION:_____

Qualifications Sought: _____

_____

_____

Approximate Date to Be Added: _____

Approximate Level of Compensation: _____

Other Incentives to Be Offered:_____

POSITION:_____

Qualifications Sought: _____

_____

_____

Approximate Date to Be Added: _____

Approximate Level of Compensation: _____

Other Incentives to Be Offered:_____

POSITION:_____

Qualifications Sought: _____

_____

_____

Approximate Date to Be Added: _____

Approximate Level of Compensation: _____

Other Incentives to Be Offered:_____

Key Management Personnel to Be Added

Don't worry if your management team is not fully complete, especially if your company is a start-up. Investors and bankers are accustomed to seeing plans for companies that have key positions vacant.

You must, however, indicate the positions you intend to add in the future and the qualifications of the individuals you will seek to fill the positions. This gives a more complete picture of your overall management team and indicates that you understand the gaps in your organization.

When thinking about what you are lacking, consider not only the specific functional responsibilities that have yet to be covered, but also how you can create a sense of "balance" in your total team.

If most of your current management has strong technical experience in your industry, but less in business management, business experience should be a primary requirement of your new managers.

Sometimes your top manager is a good "inside" person, able to run production, supervise employees, and manage accounts, yet you still need a strong "outside" person, able to secure sales, entertain clients, and conduct promotional activities.

Complete the Key Management Personnel to Be Added worksheet on page 240 to describe the key employees you intend to add to management.

Management Structure and Style

How will you actually run your company? How will decisions be made? What are the lines of authority? How do you want employees to feel about the company? What voice do employees have when company policies and goals are set?

A company's organization and management style act as powerful invisible forces shaping both the daily working atmosphere and the future of the company. But all too often managers, especially new managers, pay only cursory attention to the development of their structure and style. In looking at your company's structure, examine both the formal lines of authority that exist and the informal ways in which decisions are made and employees are treated.

Lines of Authority

When examining their organization, managers usually begin with the formal structure—the official lines of authority. They decide how employees will be supervised and how job functions will be allocated. While clear lines of authority are vital in large organizations, they are equally important in small companies. A frequent source of tension in partnerships is the failure to plainly delineate areas of responsibility and decision-making.

Increasingly, companies use "horizontal" management structures rather than strict hierarchical, "top-down" lines of authority. In such organizations, employees have greater authority for decision-making in their own areas of responsibility. This enables those closest to the customer or to the production

"Building a sense of the 'team' must be planned and orchestrated. You must continually note that the team is all-important. The only bottom line, the only true satisfaction, is when the team does well. Team-building is an ongoing process. In your training, use every conceivable example from other fields to bring home the importance of the concept of the team. Look to develop an atmosphere where players expect and demand a lot of each other, where they feel that individually they are an extension of their teammates. This doesn't just happen, it must be planned."

Bill Walsh
Former Coach and President
San Francisco 49ers

KAMPLE: FLOW CHARTS

AREAS OF RESPONSIBILITY

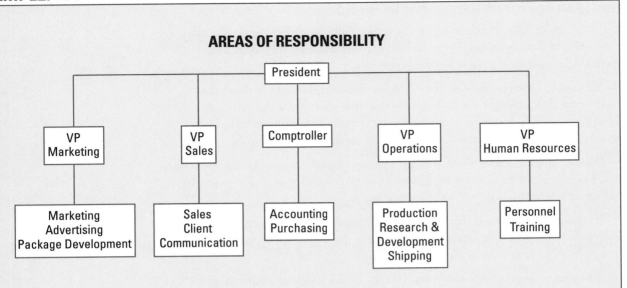

REPORTING RELATIONSHIPS

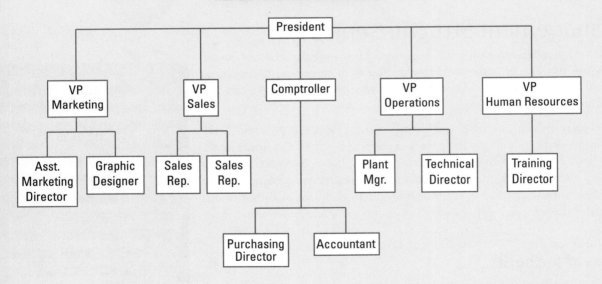

process to make decisions quickly and respond to change faster than in more centrally controlled organizations.

Some questions to ask when examining your company's structure are:

- Should responsibilities be allocated by functional area, product line, or geographic divisions? For example, should all your marketing efforts be assigned to a marketing department, or should each division handle all aspects of a product or service, including marketing?

- Which employees will each manager supervise, and over what functions will each manager have responsibility?

- Will you use a production line or team approach in producing your product or service? Thus, will each worker be responsible for one particular task, or will a group be responsible for many tasks?

Perhaps the quickest and clearest way to communicate your management structure is through a graphic organizational flow chart. You can use two kinds of charts: one describing areas of responsibility, and the other outlining reporting or supervisory relationships. Examples of each are shown on page 242. You should also provide a short narrative description explaining the relationships shown on the charts. If you do not wish to use a chart in your business plan, you need not do so. Just expand the verbal narrative to encompass the same material.

Informal Relationships

Flow charts describe your formal organizational structure, but every business also has an informal structure that can have at least as much impact on the company. Although you should not discuss these informal relationships in a business plan prepared for outside funding, you should look at less-formal relationships within your company when undertaking internal planning.

Questions to ask when evaluating your informal organization include:

- Which managers have the most impact on decisions?

- Which managers have ready access to the president or members of the Board of Directors?

- Do decisions at the top get effectively translated into action by others?

- Which subordinates have substantial influence on their superiors?

- Which divisions or groups of employees have the greatest morale problems? To whom do they report?

- How do you communicate and share values throughout the company?

- How do you create an atmosphere of tolerance for differences and diversity?

Generally, you want to evaluate how authority is distributed and how decisions are made in reality, not just on paper.

> "The team is very critical for us, and for all angel investors. We're investing in a group of people and their ability to work together."
>
> **Lauren Flanagan**
> **Cofounder and Managing Director, BELLE Capital USA**

> "The pedigree of the entrepreneurs, and their experience, are both very important. It's not so much that they have been successful at everything they touch, but they should have experience in the industry they are in."
>
> **Damon Doe**
> **Managing Partner**
> **Montage Capital**

Management Style

Describe the nature and functions of your company's management.

How does your company's management style fit with your corporate culture? _____
_____
_____
_____

How do the personalities of your key employees complement or contrast with the company's management style? ____
_____
_____

How do you develop a sense of teamwork among your employees? _____
_____
_____

Do you have a clear set of company policies, covering items such as benefits, termination, and promotion? _____
_____
_____
_____

How do you ensure ongoing communication with your employees? Do you hold meetings, have informal conferences,
or print newsletters? _____
_____
_____
_____

How do you recognize and acknowledge employees' achievements? What financial rewards do you give? _____
_____
_____

What nonmonetary recognition do you provide? _____
_____
_____

How do you solicit and act on employee suggestions? How can employees affect the development of company products, services, or policies? _____
_____
_____

Are policies enforced evenly? Are rewards and acknowledgments given fairly? Does management play "favorites"? __
_____
_____

Management Style

All managers have management styles, even if they've never thought about their approach to management. Most managers define their jobs in terms of the tasks to be done rather than the methods to be used. They see their role as making widgets, rather than motivating and aiding the widget makers. Their management styles are usually just extensions of their personal styles.

Managing people is far too important to be left to chance. Your employees are one of your most valuable resources. Just as you need to take care of other resources in your company, such as equipment and materials, you must make certain you are not wasting your human resources.

Developing your managers' capabilities in such skills as communication, leadership, motivation, team-building, and the like, affects your company's productivity, employee retention, and customer loyalty.

Moreover, you want to develop an overall company management and communication style that is independent of the personalities of your key managers and that fits your corporate culture. As discussed in Chapter 1, your corporate culture should permeate every aspect of your business and should reflect how you want your employees and customers to see you.

For most companies, especially smaller ones, building a sense of teamwork is essential. Help your employees feel that they are an important part of the organization and that their contribution matters. Communication is a vital ingredient in team building; if employees know what's going on in the company, they feel a part of the whole picture.

Regardless of your management style, remember that everyone, whether mailroom clerk or company president, wants to feel important. Recognize achievement, both privately and publicly. Reward initiative with both monetary and nonmonetary awards. Acknowledge jobs well done. Solicit suggestions, and be responsive to concerns.

The five most important elements of your management style are:

1. Clear Policies

2. Communication

3. Employee Recognition

4. Employee's Ability to Affect Change

5. Fairness

Complete the Management Style worksheet on page 244 to evaluate your company's management style.

Globalization: Management

Unless you have significant international operations, you may not need international management, but the more you operate in other countries, the more challenging it will be to manage that solely domestically. It can be very hard to manage customers, employees, or substantial outsourced operations from a far distance, especially when there are barriers due to language or culture, or even significant time zone problems.

> **The best management is management by walking around. Employees know the boss is accessible and a real person they can identify with, not an anonymous entity. It gives management a personal quality. I shake hands with every employee; everybody calls me by my first name, from the mailroom clerk on up. I'm listed in the telephone book; any employee or any guest can call me. With 1,500 employees and over one million guests, this could be a problem if we didn't have an effective operation."**
>
> *Andre Tatibouet*
> *Founder, Aston Hotels*

> **I had the good fortune to find the right people who had a compatible idea of what we could do."**
>
> *Kay Koplovitz*
> *Chair, Kate Spade*

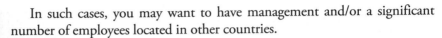

In such cases, you may want to have management and/or a significant number of employees located in other countries.

Typically, some of the management responsibilities that are most likely to be located abroad include:

■ Supervision of technical staff

■ Sales

■ Marketing

■ Customer service

■ Call center management

Even if you do not actually locate management abroad, you may need locally based management to supervise your internationally based contractors or employees. Complete the Globalization worksheet on page 247.

Preparing the Management Section of Your Business Plan

How you prepare the Management section of your business plan depends a great deal on whether it is being written for internal use only or whether it will be submitted to outside investors.

If your plan is for internal use, emphasize the management aspects centering on structure, style, and gaps in personnel. However, if you are preparing the plan for financing purposes, you should focus primarily on the relevant backgrounds of your management team members. These summaries should be brief and written in an objective style. Even if your vice president for marketing truly is "highly motivated, results-oriented, and exceptionally creative," those types of judgments appear naive when read in a business plan.

The Management Plan Preparation Form on page 248 enables you to outline the Management section of your business plan.

Chapter Summary

People are the key to success for every business. It takes capable people, with appropriate experience and abilities, to develop both a management structure and a style that make full use of the personnel and financial resources of the business and that keep the company focused on its mission. Thus, potential investors will thoroughly examine the backgrounds of the management team that will be running your company.

Globalization: Management

Fill in the worksheet to identify the types of management you need to locate internationally or deploy in-house to manage your international activities.

What tasks will you have handled by management or employees in foreign countries where you do business?

Operations, including Manufacturing _____

_____

Logistics/Shipping/Order Fulfillment _____

_____

Customer Service _____

_____

Marketing _____

_____

Sales _____

_____

Software/Technology Development _____

_____

Call Centers_____

_____

Other Back-Office Functions _____

_____

_____

Other Administrative Functions (legal, accounting, administrative) _____

_____

_____

What management personnel will you have located internationally?

Position	Country

What management personnel will you use in your own country to manage international activities? _____

_____

_____

_____

Management Plan Preparation Form

List the key members of your management team, with a brief description of each person's relevant business background, responsibilities they have in your company, and the compensation they receive.

Key Management and Employees: _____

_____
_____
_____
_____
_____
_____
_____
_____
_____
_____
_____

Board Members and Advisors: _____

_____
_____
_____
_____
_____
_____
_____
_____
_____
_____
_____

Management Structure and Style: _____

_____
_____
_____
_____
_____
_____
_____
_____
_____
_____
_____
_____

Use this information as the basis of your plan's Management section.

SAMPLE PLAN: MANAGEMENT & ORGANIZATION

MANAGEMENT

Key Employees

SCOTT E. CONNORS, PRESIDENT. Prior to founding ComputerEase, Scott E. Connors was the regional vice president for Wait's Electronics Emporium, a computer and electronics retailer with 23 stores in the Midwest. Before that, he was a sales representative with IBM for five years.

Connors began his association with Wait's Electronics Emporium as manager of the downtown Vespucci, Indiana, store. In his first year, he increased sales by over 42%, in his second year by 39%. He was named "Manager of the Year" for the Wait's chain in both years.

Connors assumed the role of regional vice president of the Wait's chain three years ago. He was responsible for the company's strategic development for Indiana, Ohio, and Illinois. In that position, Connors conducted an evaluation of the potential of adding software training to augment the chain's computer hardware sales. This evaluation led Connors to believe that a substantial need for corporate software training existed but could not be met by an electronics retailer. Instead, a stand-alone operation should be formed. This was the concept behind ComputerEase.

Connors' association with Wait's Electronics Emporium, coupled with his years at IBM, has given him an extensive background selling technology services and products to large corporations.

Connors owns 60% of the stock in ComputerEase and serves as Chairman and Treasurer of the Board of Directors.

SUSAN ALEXANDER, VICE PRESIDENT, MARKETING. Susan Alexander joined ComputerEase with primary responsibility for the company's marketing and sales activities.

Prior to joining ComputerEase, Alexander served as assistant marketing director for AlwaysHere Health Care Plan. Her responsibilities included making direct sales to human resource directors, developing marketing materials and campaigns, and supervising sales personnel. She held that position for seven years prior to joining ComputerEase. Alexander's experience marketing to the human resources community gives her the ideal background for ComputerEase, which sells its services primarily through human resources and training directors.

In previous relevant positions, Alexander was a sales representative for SpeakUp Office Equipment, where she sold technological equipment to corporations, and a copy editor for the Catchem Advertising Agency.

Alexander owns 10% of the stock in ComputerEase.

Gives examples of achievements.

Shows relevant experience.

Specifies ownership interest in company.

Shows directly applicable experience.

SAMPLE PLAN: MANAGEMENT & ORGANIZATION (continued)

Lists management to be added at a later date.

VICE PRESIDENT OF INSTRUCTIONAL DESIGN (TO BE SELECTED).

In the next year, ComputerEase will add a third key management position, Vice President of Instructional Design. The individual selected will have substantial experience designing courseware and running a training organization in a mid-size to large organization composed of instructional designers, writers, editors, videographers, and instructors. This future vice president will possess outstanding training skills and have experience developing interactive computer-based training programs. Ideally, he or she will have training experience specifically related to software applications as used in the corporate environment. This person will be tasked with staying abreast of evolving technology and customer demands in the instruction arena, especially in the online environment.

Board of Directors

Scott E. Connors is the Chairman of the Board and Treasurer. Cathy J. Dobbs, the company's attorney (and founder of the firm Dobbs, Kaye, and Babbitt), serves as Secretary. The position of Vice Chairman has been reserved for an outside investor.

Advisory Committee

An informal Advisory Committee provides guidance to the officers and staff of ComputerEase. The committee meets quarterly, and members of the committee are available as resources to the company on an ongoing basis. The members represent professionals from industries directly related to ComputerEase's mission and target market.

Members of the committee are:

Advisory Committee reflects business leaders and potential customers.

— Charlotte Travis, Director of Human Resources, RockSolid Insurance Company

— Justin Glen, Director of Training, Vespucci National Bank

— Michael Wheaton, Marketing Director, SANE Software

— Dr. A. A. Arnold, Professor of Instructional Media, Vespucci State University

Consultant

Dr. A. A. Arnold, Ph.D., Professor of Instructional Media at Vespucci State University (VSU), serves the company as a consultant in the conception and development of training manuals. A specialist in the design of instructional materials, Dr. Arnold received his Ph.D. in Education with an emphasis on interactive computer-aided training. Currently, Dr. Arnold designs training programs for industry in addition to holding his position at VSU.

Management Structure

President Scott Connors is involved in the day-to-day operations of all aspects of the company. He directs the administrative and financial aspects of the company and works closely with the vice presidents to help guide and support activities over which they have specific responsibility. However, each vice president is given a wide degree of decision-making authority in his or her assigned areas.

Management responsibilities in ComputerEase are divided as shown on the flow chart below.

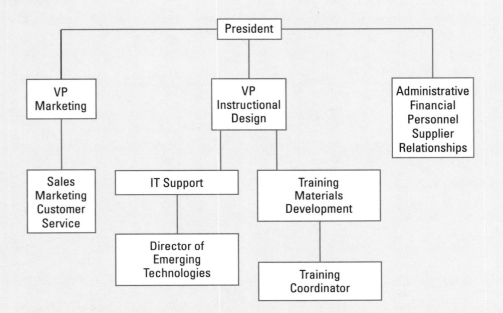

Outlines the company's management structure.

Because the company's emphasis is on building relationships with its customers and constantly improving quality, ComputerEase has instituted an incentive program in which all employees receive awards for providing outstanding customer service and making accepted suggestions for improvement.

CHAPTER

14 Social Responsibility & Sustainability

> *At the point in life where your talents meet the needs of the world is where God wants you to be.*
> — *Albert Schweitzer*

Do Well by Doing Good

As you start your business, you have many goals. You're focused on developing your business concept, getting funded, making money. What does social responsibility have to do with these?

Just as individuals have responsibilities to their communities, companies likewise have responsibilities and obligations to society at large. "Corporations" are unique entities with many rights and privileges. Society, through its laws, grants "corporations" special and favorable benefits, such as the limits on personal liability of a corporation's shareholders. Imagine, if you can, that every shareholder in a company had personal liability for that company's actions: There certainly wouldn't be much of a stock market. Every business, whether it realizes it or not, relies on the continuing support of society.

Moreover, being socially responsible is part of the overall health of your company. First, it establishes your company's values and fosters your corporate culture. Businesses that act with integrity and honesty are more likely to have their employees act with integrity and honesty toward the company and their fellow workers. Being a good corporate citizen makes it less likely that your company will get in trouble with regulatory agencies, arouse the ire of taxing authorities, or face law suits or fines.

Additionally, employees themselves get value from being part of an organization that is committed to enhancing the social good. Programs that allow employees to be involved in community causes as part of their company activities are viewed as a valuable benefit, much like other employee benefits. Prospective employees often look at a company's values and social commitment when comparing job offers. Being able to attract and retain the kind of people you want is critical to the success and growth of your business, so your social commitment helps the long-term value of your company.

Corporate social responsibility benefits

■ The business

■ The community

■ The economy

Being socially responsible is the right thing to do, and there's always strength in doing the right thing.

What's in It for You?

Your business derives a number of benefits by being committed to social responsibility and involved in community activities and causes.

DIRECT BENEFITS

 Visibility: Community activities can be a particularly effective way for small, new companies to increase visibility in their community and industry, at less cost than other marketing methods.

 Positive Corporate Image: Being seen as a good corporate citizen helps foster positive feelings about your company in the community and by potential customers, employees, and others.

 Recruitment Tool: Helps your company attract employees; job applicants often seek out companies whose values and social commitment they respect.

 Stronger Team: Shared values and shared activities help develop cohesiveness and commitment among employees and management.

 More Satisfied Employees: Enhances the experience of employees, not only by allowing them to be involved with community/social afairs, but also by letting them know they work for a company that acts with integrity in its dealings; employees never have to lie for an employer.

 Contacts with Other Companies: By participating in community activities, you and your employees will meet people from other companies, giving you valuable contacts with potential strategic partners, customers, and suppliers.

Being a Good "Corporate Citizen"

The most basic component of social responsibility is being a good "corporate citizen." Good corporate citizenship begins with a company's own internal practices and policies. It starts with corporate integrity.

Aspects of being a good corporate citizen include:

■ Obeying the law, acting ethically, and being honest and responsible in all your dealings;

■ Treating employees fairly and with respect; compensating employees fairly, and considering the well-being of employees as part of decision-making;

■ Being honest and fair to your customers and suppliers, and in your advertising and marketing;

■ Being cognizant of the impact your actions have on the environment; and

■ Being involved in your community and concerned about the well-being of others.

Ethics

Most companies, especially large ones, now develop clear ethics guidelines and policies. Because employees are faced with many situations that have ethical implications, it is extremely useful to have a set of clear, consistent policies that are firmly and fairly enforced throughout the company on matters such as accepting or giving bribes, and the nature of gifts, gratuities, or special favors that will be given or accepted.

For a new or small company, an ethics policy doesn't have to be complex, but laying out clear guidelines on certain issues, such as expense reimbursement policies and adhering to all laws, can help avoid conflict or legal trouble.

Describe your ethics policy as part of the Social Responsibility Plan Preparation Form on pages 261–262.

Social Activities

The term "social responsibility" can encompass or describe many of a company's activities and attitudes. Often it is used to describe companies with very active social or charitable programs. Some companies, including many new entrepreneurial ventures, are developing creative ways to act on their social commitment and contribute to their community. For example, the online auction site eBay, before its IPO (**Initial Public Offering**) of stock to the public, set aside a fair amount of company stock to establish a philanthropic foundation. As eBay's stock rose dramatically, the value of its foundation also rose.

There are many ways your company can be involved in social responsibility activities. The first, of course, is to be a good corporate citizen. Beyond that, many companies want to take a more active role in their communities, often donating time or money to various causes and organizations. They may look farther—working to help address global concerns, for instance.

You have many options for choosing how your company can incorporate social responsibility. One of the best ways to decide on your social responsibility activities is to involve employees themselves in choosing the projects and policies and to discuss how your company's values intersect with your programs.

While a company is young and/or small, you may want to limit your social activities to simple things: After all, you do have a company to build. You might only select one-time activities that could involve all members of your company as a team, such as participating in a walk for a community charity or volunteering one day to work on building a house for Habitat for Humanity. These can help promote team spirit, but the time commitment is clear and limited. You can also choose an ongoing project that is not too demanding; one new company gives one hour a week to help out at a local school. As your company grows, you may choose more ambitious projects.

> "Create a culture of community involvement. Start early. Start easy. Some of the kinds of things you can do are goodwill drives for clothing, food, toys, blood, etc.; volunteering in a local elementary school; working on a park cleanup day or a Habitat for Humanity day."
>
> *Gib Myers*
> *Venture Capitalist*

Social Responsibility

Triple Bottom Line

Increasingly, companies judge their performance not merely on profits, but on the concept of the "Triple Bottom Line"—or People, Planet, Profit.

TRIPLE BOTTOM LINE

People	**Planet**	**Profit**
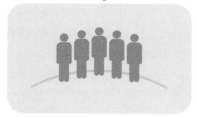		
How do you affect other people, whether your employees, your community, a specific group of disadvantaged people, or society as a whole?	How do your actions affect the environment, not just now but in the future?	How do you achieve financial sustainability since you must be profitable to remain in business? Without focusing on profits, no company can long meet any of its other goals.

As you build your business and your business plan, consider your triple bottom line and not just a financial bottom line.

Social Ventures

Many entrepreneurs want to achieve more than merely profits with their companies. They want to do something positive for humanity—improve the world, or make the planet a cleaner, greener place. These companies make social goals an integral part of their company mission.

There are different approaches to being socially responsible in business:

1. **Social ventures (or social entrepreneurship):** creating a business with a *primary* purpose of achieving a social or environmental goal but that embraces a profit motive and utilizes the best business practices. For example, you may have a company that wants to build affordable housing for low-income families but still make a profit for yourself.

2. **Socially responsible companies:** running a business whose products or services are specifically oriented not toward a social mission but toward using business practices that achieve positive social goals. For example, you may have a construction company building market-rate homes but primarily utilizing recycled and environmentally sensitive materials.

> " If the plan is well thought out and the social responsibility component is an added benefit, then it has the impact of making everybody feel good. But if the social good detracts from the competitiveness of the company, then it's not considered a positive. For instance, a company building software and arbitrarily deciding it wouldn't sell to the military, confining its market, would be considered a negative."
>
> *Mark Gorenberg*
> *Venture Capitalist*

If you do want to create a **social venture** or social enterprise, you have a number of strategies for achieving social goals. Consider the following five major strategies for social entrepreneurs:

- **Invent something.** Create something new, which has not yet been developed, to meet a social goal.

- **Bring something to market.** Take a new product that has been developed by someone else and create a distribution, retail, or sales company to market that product.

- **Create new services.** To meet a social goal, develop new services that haven't been offered before.

- **Provide services.** Offer established services that meet a social goal.

- **Adapt an existing product.** Take an existing product but slightly change its properties or use so it can achieve social goals.

Of course, any and all businesses can incorporate social and environmental responsibility into their goals and operations, regardless of the product or services they sell. For example, you might be manufacturing soap, and you can look for ways to reduce the environmental impact of your manufacturing process—lowering waste and energy consumption, using environmentally sensitive raw materials, and the like.

Remember, one of the most important social goals you can achieve is to create good jobs. If you build a company that pays employees a living wage and treats them with respect and dignity—especially if you are able to sustain those jobs over time—you have made an immeasurable contribution to society. You can always be proud of achieving that social goal.

Socially Responsible Certifications

If you are positioning your company and/or its products as socially responsible, many of your customers will want to know that you truly practice what you're promoting. To that end, there are a number of organizations and governmental or quasi-governmental entities that can certify you in specific areas of social responsibility. You may need to or want to get the benefit of getting certified by one of these trustworthy groups. Many consumers look for such certification before deciding which companies to do business with or which products to purchase.

Investigate the types of certifications available in your industry and for the social goals you are attempting to achieve.

A few of the types of certifications you can get are:

- **Organic:** for food products and produce.

- **LEED:** green building certification (stands for Leadership in Energy and Environmental Design).

- **Fair trade:** to ensure fair labor treatment, especially in international agriculture.

■ **Humane certified:** to ensure that farm-raised animals are treated in a humane and decent manner.

■ **Energy Star:** for lower-energy-consumption electronics and appliances.

Globalization: Social Responsibility

If you are doing business internationally, you may encounter a number of issues relating to what type of corporate—and world—citizen you are or want to be. You may particularly face social and ethical issues in developing countries. For instance, in countries where economies are less developed, there may not be very strict labor laws, pay scales may be below a living wage, working conditions may typically be unhealthful, children may work in factories, production practices may be environmentally harmful, censorship may be prevalent, and bribery and corruption may be a frequent aspect of business life.

Responsible businesspeople facing issues such as these must ask themselves how they are going to deal with these situations from both a business and a moral perspective. Do you want to be part of improving the lives and conditions of those who work for or with you? Or do you want to just accept the status quo?

Keep in mind that going along with socially irresponsible practices—even if they are the current standard in the countries where you operate—may put you and your company at risk. You may find your company the focus of bad publicity in your home country, the target of strikes or political unrest in the countries where you're located, or the cause of low morale and disgruntlement from your own employees who find such practices hurt their pride in their country and lower their motivation and productivity.

By contrast, promoting positive socially responsible business practices helps make you a force for improving working and environmental conditions worldwide. When you operate in the global business community, your actions—no matter how small—matter and make a difference.

Social responsibility activities frequently encompass global goals or are directed toward global concerns.

Fill out the Global Social Responsibility worksheet on page 260 if you plan on conducting any business outside of your own country. The Social Responsibility Plan Preparation Form on pages 261–262 can assist you in outlining your company's social responsibility activities.

> " We are looking to contributing to building a 'virtuous supply channel.' Fair Trade tea gardens are raising the bar. In addition to providing working conditions that meet International Labour Organization standards, Fair Trade gardens allocate an additional royalty paid by brand owners (like Honest Tea) that puts the children of tea pluckers on a path away from the tea garden."
>
> *Seth Goldman*
> *Cofounder, Honest Tea*

Chapter Summary

While a new business should not be overly focused on social issues to the extent that it takes attention away from more fundamental business concerns, being socially responsible brings many benefits to your company. It aids in building a corporate culture, attracting employees, and gaining visibility for the company. Every company should be a good corporate citizen, acting with integrity in all its dealings.

Globalization: Global Social Responsibility

How will you respond to some of the social dilemmas your company may face when doing business internationally, such as below-living-wage pay scales, lack of labor protections, bribery, or lack of gender equality in the workplace?

If you are developing an international social venture, identify the social issues you plan to address:

ENVIRONMENTAL GOALS

☐ Energy reduction

☐ New energy sources

☐ Waste reduction

☐ Water purification and access

☐ Food purification and access

☐ Improved production and agricultural processes

☐ Other: _____

LABOR GOALS

☐ Living-wage pay scales

☐ Gender equality

☐ Ethnic, religious, or other equality

☐ Eliminating child labor

☐ Healthy working conditions

☐ Ensuring fair trade practices

OTHER INTERNATIONAL SOCIAL GOALS

☐ Improving human rights

☐ Improving the treatment of animals

☐ Reducing censorship

☐ Eliminating bribery and corruption

Social Responsibility Plan Preparation Form

Describe the attributes of your social responsibility plan in the space below.

CORPORATE CITIZENSHIP

Describe the ways you will ensure that your company:

Obeys the laws: _____
_____

Treats employees fairly/with respect: _____
_____

Deals honestly with customers, suppliers: _____
_____

Is honest in its advertising and marketing: _____
_____

Considers the impact of its actions on the community: _____
_____

Acts with integrity in all its dealings: _____
Other: _____

ETHICS

How will your company handle issues such as:

Gifts from or to suppliers/potential suppliers/vendors: _____
_____

Special favors, recreational outings, meals from or to suppliers/vendors/customers: _____
_____

Conflicts between laws in different countries where your company operates: _____
_____

Selecting suppliers based on their ethics: _____
_____

Ensuring that subcontractors act ethically: _____
_____

Personal use of company property (e.g., company cars, phone, email): _____
_____

Expense accounts: _____
_____

Social Responsibility Plan Preparation Form (continued)

SOCIAL RESPONSIBILITY ACTIVITIES/PROJECTS

What are your business goals?

☐ Visibility in community

☐ Visibility in industry

☐ Aid in recruiting employees

☐ Enhancing employee morale/employee involvement

☐ Developing contacts with other companies

☐ Other:_____

In what ways will you participate?

☐ Donate money from operating budget

☐ Participate as a company in community events

☐ Donate a set percentage of profits/sales

☐ Donate in-kind products or services

☐ Allow employees to be active in projects on paid time

☐ Formulate socially responsible operations practices (e.g., waste disposal management)

☐ Encourage employees to be active on a volunteer basis/after-hours

☐ Encourage company personnel/management to serve on agency boards

☐ Donate company facilities for use by community

☐ Formulate socially responsible purchasing groups practices (e.g., environmental-friendly-only products or type of vendor)

☐ Donate product overruns

☐ Other: _____

What period of time are you willing to commit for? (e.g., day, week, year):_____

What types of concerns do you want to be involved with?

☐ Animal Welfare

☐ The Arts

☐ Children

☐ Community Enhancement and Improvement

☐ Economic Empowerment

☐ Education

☐ Environment

☐ Gender Equality/Issues

☐ Health Issues

☐ Recreation/Athletics

☐ Safety

☐ Other:_____

Use this information as the basis of your plan's Social Responsibility & Sustainability section.

SAMPLE PLAN: SOCIAL RESPONSIBILITY & SUSTAINABILITY

SOCIAL RESPONSIBILITY & SUSTAINABILITY

ComputerEase is committed to making a positive contribution to our community, to being a good corporate citizen in all our actions, and to implementing environmentally responsible practices into every aspect of our operations.

Recognizing our responsibilities, ComputerEase has adopted a number of operational policies and developed a community involvement program. This program and these policies reflect the reality that we are still a new, small company and our primary efforts are directed toward building and growing a healthy business.

Company Philosophy

Reflecting our desire to be a good corporate citizen, ComputerEase has adopted the following "Company Philosophy":

— We will, as a company and as individuals, take responsibility for our actions;

— We will, as a company and as individuals, deal fairly and honestly with our customers, students, suppliers, the public, and each other;

— When making decisions, we will, as a company and as individuals, consider the impact of our decisions on others and on the environment;

— We will consistently try to give the highest level of performance to each customer and each student;

— We recognize that without profits our company cannot survive, so we will make our best efforts to increase the profitability of our company within an ethical and honest framework;

— We will give back to our community and society and make a positive commitment to its health and well-being;

— We will respect our coworkers and recognize their needs as employees and as human beings; and

— We will listen to each other.

Shows how the company behaves as a good "corporate citizen."

Community Involvement

In developing our community involvement program, the staff of ComputerEase first looked to identify those ways in which we could use our corporate strengths (given our limited time and financial resources) to make a meaningful contribution to our community. We recognized that our unique strength is our ability to teach computer programs in an understandable manner, along with our Computer Training Center facility located in the heart of downtown Vespucci.

ComputerEase has entered into a partnership with the Downtown Vespucci Community Center to provide free computer training programs for inner-city youth, low-income residents, and "welfare-to-work" program participants. These training programs are held once a month at ComputerEase's downtown Computer Training Center on days or times when the Center would otherwise not be in use (Sundays/

Specifies community activities.

SAMPLE PLAN: SOCIAL RESPONSIBILITY & SUSTAINABILITY (Cont.)

some evenings, etc.). ComputerEase management and instructors have volunteered their time to conduct these sessions, and the company, in turn, is contributing meals, transportation expenses for volunteer instructors, and an imprinted T-shirt for all program participants. ComputerEase will also donate all its older computers to the Community Center. ComputerEase will use up to 5% of its capacity on a pro bono basis to support these programs.

In addition to the project with the Downtown Vespucci Community Center, ComputerEase staff determined they would like to do a one-day community project each year to make a contribution together. The staff chose to participate in the annual Vespucci Friends of the Trees Arbor Day Planting & Picnic. As a team, we will work with other members of the corporate and civic community to plant trees in public parks, on boulevards, and in other locales.

Sustainability

Describes current and future activities to improve sustainability.

In assessing the impact of ComputerEase's operations on the environment, we realized that our biggest opportunity for improving sustainability comes from curbing our energy consumption. For this reason, we will invest in the installation of solar panels on the roof of our new Training Center, which will generate 50% of our electricity. We will receive a government rebate for these panels and in 10 years, they will have paid for themselves. In addition, we will lease the most energy-efficient computers and other electronics to reduce the number of solar panels necessary to power our new building.

Employees and students commuting to and from our Training Centers also consume a great deal of energy. ComputerEase provides subsidies to employees who use public transportation. We also allow employees, depending on their roles in the company, to telecommute and work from home. As we move to more online training sessions, the number of commuter miles logged by both students and instructors will drop sharply.

In addition to reducing commutes, online training sessions also lend themselves well to our goal of becoming paperless. We develop all of our training materials, such as course manuals, for online publication only. This not only reduces our paper use and waste but saves a substantial amount of money. We also use online applications for billing, payroll, and our newsletters. When we do purchase office supplies, we choose only products made of post-consumer recycled materials, when available.

Beyond energy consumption and waste reduction, we recognized other areas of our operations that could be made more "green." We worked with the city of Vespucci to establish an environmentally conscious e-waste program for electronic equipment. We send our old electronics to this recycling center if they are unsuitable for the Community Center.

CHAPTER

15 Development, Milestones & Exit Plan

You can't reach a goal you haven't set.

Where Do You Want to Go?

If a business plan serves as a road map for your company, then to use it properly you need a sense of your ultimate destination. What do you want your business to look like in three, five, or seven years? You can't hope to just stumble across success; you have to figure out how to get there. One of the most important aspects of the business planning process, therefore, is the examination of your long-term goals.

Moreover, in the course of your planning process you will find it useful to establish markers — milestones — to keep you on track. By developing specific objectives, you have signposts to measure progress along the way.

Investors are greatly interested in this section of your business plan. When they invest capital in your company, they want to see what they are getting in return. They know how much money they can lose — the **downside risk**. But they also want to gauge what they might gain, how big the company might become — the upside reward. Lenders, by contrast, are somewhat less interested in long-term growth than investors. They already know their upside potential; it's defined in the terms of the loan.

In this section you will spell out the specific ways whereby your company can be judged and the risks involved. You may find this prospect a bit unsettling; perhaps you even fear that it will scare off financing sources. Don't be intimidated. Sophisticated investors and lenders give greater credence to entrepreneurs who acknowledge risk and are willing to be measured against clear-cut objectives. They understand that progress takes time and that risks are an inherent part of doing business.

In developing your company's long-term plans, you must evaluate your goals, milestones, risks, and exit plan, each of which is discussed in this chapter.

Goals

What do you want in the future, both for yourself and for your company? In founder-led and small companies, the personal goals of the entrepreneur(s) and the goals for the business should reasonably relate to one another. Otherwise, the inherent tensions will undermine the success of the business. There's no use envisioning running a $50 million company, when what you really want is to take long vacations and be home every afternoon by 3:00 p.m. That's just not a realistic fit. *(Refer to the worksheet "Four Cs," in Chapter 1.)*

You probably have a vision of what your company may be. The vision may not be well-formed, perhaps something like "One day I want this company to be known for making the very best product of its type." Or the vision may be very specific, set by you or investors; it might be a goal such as "Sales of $10 million within five years."

BUSINESS VISION

 Steady Provider: Maintain a stable level of profit; earn a good, reliable income while owning your own business.

 Innovator: Produce new and different products or services; change the way the market views the product or service; act on your creativity.

 Market or Industry Leader: Dominate the market in terms of sales and products; have a well-known name and run a large operation.

 Worldwide Market Seller: Sell or distribute products or services to a global audience or to a specific country or region.

 Niche Leader: Carve out a narrow place in the market that your company dominates; do only one thing, but do it extremely well.

 Exploiter: Take advantage of the trends of the moment or copy the successes of others; take risks for quick rewards.

 Quality Leader: Produce the product or service everyone would buy if price were no object; develop a reputation for excellence; take pride in creating the best.

The vision that you and the other decision-makers hold for your company shapes the nature of your day-to-day activities and should determine the priorities for the expenditure of your resources. You want to emphasize those actions that support your eventual aims. Grow toward your vision.

Use the Company Vision worksheet on page 268 to focus your thoughts about the future. In assessing your business concept, consider which of the visions in the above graphic you have for your company and yourself.

These goals are not necessarily mutually exclusive, and you can choose more than one, if they aren't contradictory. Or, perhaps you have another vision for your company.

Although these concepts are relatively intangible, they have tangible consequences. If you see your company as an innovator, you may have to sacrifice short-term profits for the ability to experiment. If you want a company that is a market leader, you must position your company to grow to a substantial size.

To give substance to your vision, express your goals in concrete terms.

This process will help you understand and articulate your goals; it is meant for internal planning rather than for inclusion in a written business plan, especially one prepared for outside funding.

Success key terms

Downside Risk
The maximum amount that can be lost in an investment.

Event
Investors or others may speak of an "event" taking place, usually a time at which value can be liquidated from the company. Commonly, it's a funding round, an acquisition, or an IPO.

Go Public
To issue an initial public offering (IPO).

Company Vision

Describe the vision you hold of your company for the next decade.

Overall Long-Term Development: _____

_____

_____

_____

SPECIFIC GOALS	One Year	Five Years	Ten Years
Number of Employees			
Number of Locations			
Annual Sales			
Profits or Profit Margin			
Number of Products or Services			
Awards or Recognition Received			
Ownership Allocation			
Other:			

_____

_____

BUSINESS STRATEGIES

One year:_____

_____

_____

_____

_____

Five years:_____

_____

_____

_____

Ten years:_____

_____

_____

_____

_____

Priorities

Rate each area's priority for the expenditure of funds, in hierarchical order (1-2-3, with 1 being the highest priority). Describe the specific priorities or amounts in each area.

Priorities	Specifics	Rating
Add Employees		
Add New Lines		
Increase Marketing		
Add Locations		
Add Capacity		
Increase Salaries		
Increase Inventory		
Increase Profits		
Retire Debts		
Increase Reserve		
Acquire Other Companies		
Other: _____		

Strategies

You now must consider which business strategy will take your company from its present situation toward your long-term goals. Developing an overall strategy gives you the basis for deciding on the priorities for specific actions and expenditures of funds.

Consider these business strategies when assessing the long-term development of your company.

BUSINESS STRATEGIES

Market Penetration: Gain a foothold in the market as you introduce either the company or a new product or service and attempt to develop sufficient sales to sustain your initial development.

Promotion and Support: Intensify the marketing and development of your current product or service lines to increase sales and gain market share.

Expansion: Add products or services in existing lines, additional locations, production capacity, or distribution systems in an effort to increase sales.

Increase Focus: Eliminate some products or services and marshal your resources on your remaining line(s) to increase profit margin.

Diversify: Add product or service lines (or buy other companies) to broaden the nature of the company. Such an expansion of the company's size and sales reduces your dependency on current products or services for survival.

Go Global: Find and exploit a foreign market instead of, or in addition to, your own. If you don't plan on being a global company at launch, consider the long-term international opportunities.

Refocus: Modify the essential nature of the company in terms of market, products, or services to respond to changing conditions or substantial business reverses.

Priorities

To implement those strategies, you must undertake specific actions. For instance, if your strategy is to promote and support, you will want to use any additional resources, either of money or of time, on your marketing efforts. If, on the other hand, your strategy is to diversify, you want to accumulate resources to expend on the introduction of new product lines or the purchase of new companies.

To clarify the significance of particular activities relative to your long-term goals, develop a set of priorities for the expenditure of your resources. A list of priorities is a critical tool for every business. Although this list does not need to be included in a business plan for outside financing sources, it would be wise to refer to it whenever making major business decisions.

On the Priorities worksheet on page 269, specify the relative importance of each activity when it comes to the expenditure of funds.

Milestones Achieved to Date

State the specific objectives you have achieved and when you achieved each one.

Event	Specifics	Date Completed
Incorporation		
Lease Signed		
Key Employees Hired:		
Initial Financing Secured		
Product Design Completed		
Market Testing Completed		
Trademarks/Patents Secured		
Strategic Partnerships Secured		
First Product Shipped		
Level of Sales Reached ($)		
Level of Sales Reached (units)		
Level of Employees Reached		
Profit Level Reached		
Second Product Line Developed		
Second Product Line Tested		
Second Product Line Shipped		
Additional Financing Secured		
Debts Retired		
Additional Location Opened		
Other: _____		

Future Milestones

State your specific future objectives and when you plan to achieve each one.

Event	Specifics	Goal Date
Incorporation		
Lease Signed		
Key Employees Hired:		
_____		
_____		
_____		
_____		
Initial Financing Secured		
Product Design Completed		
Market Testing Completed		
Trademarks/Patents Secured		
Strategic Partnerships Secured		
First Product Shipped		
Level of Sales Reached ($)		
Level of Sales Reached (units)		
Level of Employees Reached		
Profit Level Reached		
Second Product Line Developed		
Second Product Line Tested		
Second Product Line Shipped		
Additional Financing Secured		
Debts Retired		
Additional Location Opened		
Other: _____		

Milestones Achieved to Date

You may describe your company as a start-up. Your potential investor may think of you as a start-up. But many new companies already have histories, sometimes impressive ones, before they have a written business plan. You can inspire confidence in your company by indicating this past history in your plan. You also demonstrate your ability to set and meet goals.

Delineating the milestones you've achieved to date likewise shows the level of commitment you've made to your new business. A potential investor can get a sense of the financial and time expenditures that you've had to invest to reach the achievements to date.

The worksheet Milestones Achieved to Date on page 271 helps you record your accomplishments. A list of such Milestones can be included in the front of your written plan, directly after your Executive Summary, especially if your progress has been particularly impressive. If yours is an annual plan for an existing company, you can indicate the milestones achieved since your last plan.

Future Milestones

How will you and your investors know that you are making sufficient progress toward your goals? If your long-term goal is to reach sales of $3 million in year five, how much do you need in sales by year two and year three?

In the daily press of business, it can often seem that you're making no progress at all. At any given time, you'll have a stack of bills to pay, troublesome customers, and problems with your staff. So you need a reminder that you have, in fact, been going forward.

A milestone list allows you and your financing sources to see what you specifically plan to accomplish, and it clearly sets out delineated objectives. These objectives are part of your business plan and are included with the written document.

A milestone list focuses on the specific objectives you intend to achieve and the dates by which you expect to accomplish them. These must be defined in concrete terms and a number assigned to any measurable activity. Thus, omit goals expressed in ways such as: "developing a substantial customer base." Instead, specify: "reaching annual sales level of 50,000 units by the end of the third fiscal year."

A milestone list also shows how you intend to build your company, roll out products, add new locations, secure strategic relationships, and so forth. This list creates a very detailed picture of your company's future, and gives readers of your plan a clear idea of the size and scope of the company you envision.

When assigning dates to your milestones, remember that everything takes longer than planned; problems always arise. One of the frustrations of all entrepreneurs, but especially new ones, is realizing how long everything takes to get done. Progress comes slowly. So allow yourself plenty of time when you are establishing chronological goals.

"Long-term planning must be a part of everything you do. You must continually work to stay contemporary. Be inquisitive and open-minded. Don't make comments like 'We've always done it this way,' or 'We've tried it before.' Look for reasons to respond to new ideas and evaluate how they can improve your performance."

Bill Walsh
Former Coach and President
San Francisco 49ers

Globalization: Future Development

Complete this worksheet to identify potential international opportunities and approximately when you hope to enter other countries.

Which countries, if any, would be good candidates for your products/services in the future? _____

_____

_____

_____

_____

_____

_____

_____

_____

_____

Which countries would be good for you to locate operations in (manufacturing, administrative, customer service, call

centers, etc.) in the future? _____

_____

_____

_____

_____

_____

_____

_____

_____

_____

List the specific countries you intend to expand into and the approximate years when you plan on entering those

countries:

Country	Business Function	Year

Complete the Future Milestones worksheet on page 272 to outline your objectives. This list should be included with your business plan, whether used for internal planning or for raising funds.

Risk Evaluation

Investors make financing decisions based on an evaluation of the potential risks versus potential rewards. They will naturally consider what risks your company faces, whether or not you outline such risks in your plan. Showing that you have already assessed the potential risks in your business reassures investors that you are not just naively optimistic in your planning.

On the Risk Evaluation worksheet in Chapter 9 (page 151), you assessed the nature of the risks facing your company in each area and described the steps you can take, or have already taken, to lessen that risk. Include this risk assessment in either the Strategic Positioning section or the Development and Milestones section of your plan.

Globalization: Future Development

Having a global vision expands your company's long-term growth potential. You may not be planning on being a worldwide company when you first launch your business, but going global may be part of your long-term development plans. You should certainly at least think about your international sales opportunities even if merely reaching your local or national market seems daunting at this early stage. Of course, you do not want to dilute your limited resources while just getting established but, as part of your business plan, looking beyond your borders can help you recognize the larger opportunities available to you.

Looking internationally, you may find markets that are far more underserved than your home market. As you grow your business, you may find that competing in your home country is more expensive, less profitable, and more challenging than exploiting global opportunities. And, as you become successful in your home market, other countries present you with new market opportunities, allowing you to leverage your investment in products, services, personnel, and infrastructure across a broader geographic area.

You'll also want to look ahead to your global operations options. For example, in your first years in business, you may only want or need to hire local staff or to do your manufacturing in your home country. As you grow, you may look internationally to save costs or to handle growing demand.

As part of your long-term development planning, consider your global options. Complete the Globalization: Future Development worksheet on page 274.

Exit Plan

When banks or individuals lend you money, it's clear how they expect to get their money back and make a profit: You are to pay them out of income, with interest. They evaluate your business on the basis of whether they think there's enough profit in your operating budget to pay back the loan.

> **A plan should tell us how, as funders, we will know you're making progress, that you're on the road to success. Spel out what challenges you face in getting to market, what specific accomplishments you must achiev to build your company. We want five or six milestones to measure as we go along. For us, these are 'risk-reduction points' — they let us know you're on the right track."**
>
> **Ann Winblad**
> *Venture Capitalist*

But how *do* investors get their money back? Since investors become owners of the company (through their stock holdings), their profit is earned in a different manner than that of banks and lenders. Some investors may be putting money in for the long run, expecting to take an active part in the development and operation of the company and getting their reward through the distribution of profits.

Other investors, however, especially venture capitalists, eventually plan to liquidate their investment—to convert their holdings to cash or easily traded stock. Ideally, these investors want to know at the outset how they will get a substantial profit out of their investment. They want to see your exit plan.

Developing an Exit Plan

Considering your potential exit plan benefits you as well as investors. After all, you've devoted substantial time and money of your own to this company, and you should have an idea of the way in which you'll reap rewards. Annual income is the major motivation for many entrepreneurs, but ideally your company will have worth beyond its annual profits, and you should eventually benefit from that worth.

If there is more than one partner or principal in the business, creating a clear exit strategy can reduce the friction that comes from having unspoken exit assumptions. One founder may dream of building a company worth millions with the aim of selling it in the next few years, while the other founder may hope to build a modest business to run for many years to come.

A number of options exist for exiting from a company, although venture capitalists may be interested in only two or three of them. Generally, sophisticated investors look for companies that can **go public** (sell stock that will be traded to the general public on stock exchanges or "over the counter") or that are candidates for acquisition by larger companies. Investors prefer these exit strategies because they get out of the company cleanly, usually with substantial rewards, based on just one **event**: either an IPO—an initial public offering (when the stock is first publicly traded)—or the sale of the company.

These two strategies, though, often result in the top management, including the founder(s), either having to leave or ending up with far less control over the company. This may be an acceptable option given the nature of the financial rewards involved.

Novice entrepreneurs often imagine being able to buy out their investors, but this is not usually a realistic option. In companies that are very successful, the investor has little motivation to sell and the amount of money needed to purchase their stock could be prohibitive. In less successful companies, the investors may want to get out, but the entrepreneur is unlikely to have the extra cash necessary to buy them out.

Exit plan options are briefly outlined on page 278, describing the major exit strategies and their advantages and disadvantages. The disadvantages assume that the current management would like to have a continuing role in the company, which may or may not be true in your situation.

Preparing the Development, Milestones, and Exit Strategy Section of Your Business Plan

In preparing a business plan for outside investors, the two most important aspects of your Development section are your milestones lists and the description of your exit plan. Through these, investors get a clear idea of how the company has grown, will continue to grow, and how they will realize their financial rewards.

For a plan to be used for internal purposes, more details can be included about the specific priorities for expenditures of resources, making your plan a useful tool that you can refer to frequently when making major expenditure decisions.

A Development Plan Preparation Form on page 279 is provided for you to outline the Development section of your business plan.

Chapter Summary

The Development section of your business plan shows that you have given careful consideration to how your company will grow over time. By including a Future Milestones chart, you provide a clear timetable of your company's development and allow yourself to be judged by objective measurements. And by describing the potential risks your company faces, you display confidence in your ability to overcome such risks. Investors will be interested in how they can recoup the money they have devoted to your company, and they will appreciate that you have considered a realistic exit plan.

> " It's easy to get into an investment, but investors want to know 'how do we get out?' It's not good enough to just say that there will be a public offering, because selling to the public may not be realistic at times. Instead, you have to show you have an attractive business that other businesses will want to own, either because it complements an existing product line or on its own."
>
> *Eugene Kleiner*
> *Venture Capitalist*

Exit Plan Options

Option	Description	Advantages	Disadvantages
Go Public	Sell shares in the company to the public, traded on a stock exchange "over the counter."	Stock easily convertible to cash, liquidity; current management stays.	Must be large company: approx. $25 to $50 million; or highly regulated; management can be replaced by stockholders.
Acquisition	Bought by another existing company.	Receive cash and/or stock; current management may have continuing role.	Must be appropriate fit for existing co.; management leaves or has new boss.
Sale	Bought by individuals.	Receive cash.	Must find willing buyer; management goes.
Merger	Join with existing company.	Combined resources; current management may stay; may receive stock or some cash.	New partners or bosses; usually little or no cash; less control.
Buyout	One or more stockholders buy out the interests of another.	Seller gets cash; others stay in control of company.	Must have sufficient cash; seller must be willing.
Franchise	Sell concept to others to replicate.	Receive cash; current management stays; future potential.	Concept must be appropriate; legally complicated.
Hand Down	Give company to next generation.	Stays in family; current management may continue.	Family tensions; no cash; tax implications.
Close	End operations.	Relatively easy; feeling of being finished.	No financial reward; feeling of loss.

Development Plan Preparation Form

Describe your company's goals for the next five years, in terms of position in the market, sales, number of employees, etc.:

_____
_____
_____
_____
_____
_____

Describe the basic strategy you will use to reach those goals, and the priority for the expenditure of funds: _____

_____
_____
_____
_____
_____
_____
_____

Describe the major risks facing your company: _____

_____
_____
_____
_____
_____
_____
_____

Describe the exit plan for your investors: _____

_____
_____
_____
_____
_____
_____
_____

Use this information as the basis of your plan's Development section.

SAMPLE PLAN: DEVELOPMENT AND EXIT PLAN

States vision of company.

Gives priority for expenditure of funds.

DEVELOPMENT AND EXIT PLAN

Long-Term Goals

ComputerEase plans to grow steadily over the next five years, becoming a known and respected brand providing software training to large- and medium-size businesses in person and in the online sphere. In its on-premise business, it will capture a market share of at least 50% of all corporate software training (in terms of revenues) in the Greater Vespucci area. The company will also bring in $5 million annually in online sales. The company also plans to have expanded its physical presence throughout the Midwest, with offices in five locations, with revenues of $3 million annually. In total, within five years the company hopes to reap $8 million annually in sales.

Strategy for Achieving Goals

To reach the long-term goal of becoming one of the major players in corporate software training in the online world as well as the dominant training provider in the Midwest, ComputerEase will continue to add new courses to its product line and add training classrooms and locations each year.

The first priority is to double the number of products in the company's online course portfolio within the year, and to continually expand it every year. A second priority in that same time frame is to open the company's second Corporate Training Center in the city of Whitten Park. That location will serve both as an additional training classroom and as a base of additional marketing activities.

In each of the following two years, ComputerEase plans to win at least 10 major new corporate accounts to deliver custom online training on enterprise applications as well as off-the-shelf software. ComputerEase also plans on opening at least one additional company-run Corporate Training Center per year, concentrating on cities within a three-hour drive of Vespucci that have a substantial number of large- and medium-size corporations.

By year three, ComputerEase management will assess future options for growth. Likely scenarios include the addition of more company-run Corporate Training Centers, the possibility of franchising the operation, or the possibility of merging with or being acquired by another online training company.

Greater Expansion Plans

In addition to expanding online operations, ComputerEase will continue to develop in-person training programs as well, by increasing the number of company-run locations. ComputerEase will choose major metropolitan areas based on an assessment of sales potential and the intensity of the competition in each market at the time of expansion. It is estimated that at least one metropolitan area would be added each year. To fund such expansion, the company will require additional capital, which would ideally be secured from bank financing. In the event that conventional financing is not secured, funds will be sought from investors.

The ComputerEase concept for in-person training also lends itself well to franchising. Since corporations with offices throughout the United States often prefer to have all their computer training provided by the same company, a franchise operation gives the company greater marketing clout. Moreover, the franchising concept produces additional revenue streams to the company from the franchisees, both from franchise fees and through the purchase of materials and staff training. If the decision is made to franchise, venture capital investment will be sought. Current investors could choose to liquidate their holdings in ComputerEase at that time or to convert their holdings to stock in the franchise operation.

Describes potential exit opportunity for investor.

In addition to increasing its number of physical locations, ComputerEase plans to develop into a leading online provider of software training in English-speaking countries where businesses are automated. We also plan to support additional languages in the future, beginning with Spanish, due to the proportion of Spanish-speakers in North and Latin America.

Risks Associated with Expansion

ComputerEase faces risks on two fronts. The first is that increased competition in the online training market will become so intense that margins collapse, making it difficult to be profitable, given the cost of developing and supporting high-quality courseware. The second is that new on-premises competitors will enter the market from outside the Greater Vespucci area. It is highly likely that existing franchised software training companies from other parts of the country will open franchises in this region. Since these national companies offer financing to their franchisees, the major barrier to entry—the cost of establishing a Training Center — can be overcome. If the franchisee is highly capable, this represents the greatest risk to ComputerEase.

To prepare for both these eventualities, it is critical that ComputerEase quickly and aggressively increase its market share—both in its geographic market and online—and begin building strong brand awareness for its products. Corporate customers are slow to change established vendors, and ComputerEase anticipates that it will be able to retain a high percentage of existing customers, even in the face of new competitors. Moreover, ComputerEase management remains open to the possibility of a merger or other agreement with a national company if that appears to be a better financial option.

Recognizes and acknowledges potential risks.

Another risk is that market conditions will deteriorate. ComputerEase is highly dependent on the business economy. Companies reducing their training budgets will have a direct negative impact on ComputerEase revenues.

To counteract that, the company is rapidly increasing its marketing to individual consumers—on the Web, in print publications, and in offering Saturday and evening classes. In the face of an economic downturn or layoffs, individuals need to take classes to improve their marketable skills, and this provides some balance to fluctuations in the corporate market.

The Exit Plan

In establishing itself as a market leader, ComputerEase will become a likely target for acquisition by or merger with a national software training company or other national for-profit educational institution. For-profit education companies are among the fastest growing firms in the United States, and they regularly acquire existing training schools as a method of achieving their growth targets.

Moreover, as other software training companies have demonstrated, the ComputerEase concept lends itself well to franchising. Franchising would produce additional revenue streams to the company from the franchisees, both from franchise fees and through the purchase of materials and staff training. If the decision is made to franchise, venture capital investment will be sought. Current investors could choose to liquidate their holdings in ComputerEase at that time or convert their holdings to stock in the franchise operation.

CHAPTER

16 The Financials

> *Numbers are merely the reflection of decisions you make.*

How to Painlessly Deal with Numbers and Financial Forms

People in business usually fall into one of two categories: those who are fascinated with numbers, or those who are frightened by them. If you're in the first category, you are probably delighted to finally reach this section. You may have even skipped previous sections to do this one. If you are one of those in the second category, however, you're probably intimidated by the very prospect of having to fill in the forms encountered in this chapter.

Numbers Represent Your Decisions

Take heart: Numbers are neither magical, mysterious, nor menacing. They merely reflect other decisions you have made previously in your business planning. If you decided to advertise each week in your local newspaper, there's a number attached to that decision. If you projected sales at a certain level, there's a number attached to that decision as well.

Every business decision leads to a number, and, taken together, these numbers form the basis of your financial forms. But numbers themselves are not decisions. You cannot pull a number out of thin air, because the financial forms you are completing call for a specific figure on a specific line. Rather, your numbers should always be the result of careful planning.

Getting Control of Your Finances

Even if you are not responsible for preparing ongoing financial reports, you should have a working understanding of financial statements so that you can better control your company.

Financial statements provide you with the information you need to make decisions. Many managers mistakenly believe that they are in charge of the big picture, while bookkeepers and bean counters get caught up with mere details. Numbers are *not* just details: They are the vital signs of any business; you must understand your company's numbers to realistically assess the condition of your business.

Read Your Financial Statements

Get in the habit of reading your financial statements at least monthly, and make sure you understand what you read. Track items such as sales receipts on a daily or weekly basis. Don't wait for reports to come back from the accountants before knowing your cash position. You will find you have more confidence in your decisions if you comprehend the financial implications of each of your choices.

Try to view your financial statements in a relatively dispassionate manner. True, it is difficult, especially when you own your business, to keep emotions from clouding your ability to properly examine your financial reports. If you know it has been a bad month, you may be tempted just to ignore that month's cash flow or income statements. Don't.

Set Policies and Stick with Them

Set financial policies in place and stick with them, in good times and bad. Many businesses, even big companies, get in trouble through inadequate billing and collection procedures. Stay on top of your finances.

If you are establishing accounts for the first time, get professional assistance from an accountant or bookkeeper. A professional can set up your initial books, assist you in understanding financial terms, and give you valuable advice on billing, payment, and payroll procedures.

Cash-Basis Accounting

One aspect of your business an accountant will help you decide is whether to set up your books on an accrual basis or a cash basis. Most smaller businesses are generally advised to use the **cash-basis accounting** method, meaning that income and expenses are entered in the books at the time money actually changes hands.

Thus, if you receive a $5,000 order in January, but you don't receive payment until March, the $5,000 credit appears as income only on your March statements. This gives a truer picture of your company's ability to meet its financial obligations than does accrual accounting.

Success key terms

Accrual-Basis Accounting
An accounting method whereby income and expenses are entered on the books at the time of contract or agreement rather than at the time of payment or receipt of funds.

Cash-Basis Accounting
An accounting method whereby income and expenses are entered on the books at the time of actual payment or receipt of funds.

Collateral
Assets pledged in return for loans.

Convertible Debt
Loans made to a company that can be repaid with stock ownership (or a combination of stock and cash), usually at the lender's option.

Debt Financing
Raising funds for a business by borrowing, often in the form of bank loans.

Debt Service
Money being paid on a loan; the amount necessary to keep a loan from going into default.

Disbursements
Money paid out.

Funding Rounds
The number of times a company goes to the investment community to seek financing; each funding round is used to reach new stages of company development.

Net Worth
The total ownership interest in a company, represented by the excess of the total amount of assets minus the total amount of liabilities.

Working Capital
The cash available to the company for the ongoing operations of the business.

Accrual-Basis Accounting

With **accrual-basis accounting**, income and expenses are counted at the time they are originally transacted; thus, the $5,000 order would show as income in January. If payment is never made, additional accounting entries would later be made to write off the loss. Larger businesses choose this accounting form to have a better sense of overall profitability.

Globalization: Financial Considerations

Whenever you cross a country border, you cross financial borders as well. If you do business internationally, you will encounter a number of financially related issues, which are shown in the graphic below. You must keep these in mind and plan for them.

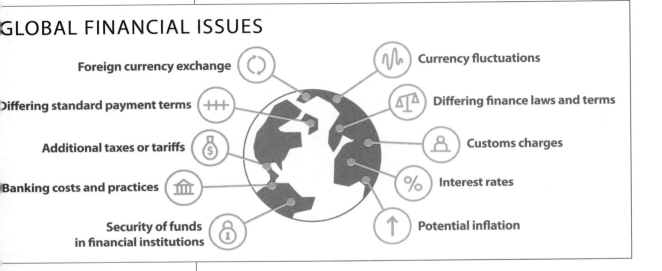

GLOBAL FINANCIAL ISSUES

- Foreign currency exchange
- Differing standard payment terms
- Additional taxes or tariffs
- Banking costs and practices
- Security of funds in financial institutions
- Currency fluctuations
- Differing finance laws and terms
- Customs charges
- Interest rates
- Potential inflation

You need to understand the financial situation of the specific countries where you'll be doing business and plan for how it differs from the financial practices of your home country. For instance, in the United States, it is typical for business-to-business customers to extend credit with "30 day net" payment terms and for consumers to frequently pay with credit cards. Those terms may be very different in the countries where you are doing business, or, in some countries, consumers may not typically use credit cards.

As much as possible, you must also plan for the various factors that can affect or disrupt your financial situation when doing business offshore. For instance, some currencies are historically very stable, while others fluctuate greatly. Some countries regularly face rampant inflation. You should also look at the practices and laws related to keeping your funds in foreign financial institutions—how safe are they, what kinds of interest rates do they pay, are the funds insured? Political unrest or climate emergencies can also affect the value and security of your funds.

Consider all these factors when pricing your products or services internationally, establishing credit policies and charges, and determining where to keep funds and how much to keep overseas.

You'll want to confer with an accountant knowledgeable in foreign business operations to help you plan your financials if you're doing considerable business internationally. Be certain to ask about the tax ramifications, as tax issues when dealing with international operations and sales can be complicated.

Use the Globalization: Financial Considerations worksheet on page 290 to think through some of the financial issues facing you when doing business internationally.

Using the Abrams Method of Flow-Through Financials

One of the most difficult questions, especially for new businesses, is "Where do I get the figures for my financial forms?"

If you have been filling out the Flow-Through Financial worksheets throughout the previous chapters, you have already compiled many of the figures you need to complete the worksheets in this chapter. For instance, you have already computed your marketing budget in Chapter 10. Likewise, on other worksheets, you have detailed costs of salaries, equipment, and other aspects of your business.

Now just transfer the figures from each of your Flow-Through Financial worksheets (marked with the dollar-sign logo) to their appropriate line(s) on the Financials forms that follow. Refer to the chart on pages 288–289 to see on which form and line each specific figure should be placed.

Business Plan Financials

To make this process even easier, an Excel-based Business Plan Financials package is available for purchase as a supplement to this book. The worksheets are identical to the financial worksheets found in the book and embrace the Flow-Through Financials methodology used here. In addition, the Business Plan Financials perform all calculations for you, generate charts, and allow you to "tweak" your numbers to obtain the most accurate financial picture. Once you are satisfied with your numbers, you can print out all the financial forms necessary to include with your business plan. Visit www.PlanningShop.com to purchase the Business Plan Financials package.

Types of Financial Forms

For the financial portion of your business plan, the three most important forms are:

- **Income Statement.** Shows whether your company is making a profit.
- **Cash Flow Projection.** Shows whether the company has the cash to pay its bills.
- **Balance Sheet.** Shows how much the company is worth overall.

> " In financials, we look for professionalism. Use standard formats. Hire an accountant, not so much as to come up with your numbers but for your forms. We want to see a cash flow analysis as well as everything else in a standard annual report (balance sheet, income statement). You or an accountant should compare your numbers with those of existing companies. If they are very different from those of well-managed companies, they may be unrealistic."
>
> *Eugene Kleiner*
> *Venture Capitalist*

Abrams Method of Flow-Through Financials

All of the Flow-Through Financial Worksheets throughout this book are recognizable by the dollar-sign icon ($ ➤ $ $ ➤ $ $ $) in the top right-hand corner.

WORKSHEET	CHAPTER	TRANSFER TO	USE ON LINES
Financial Patterns	6, page 98	Income Statement	Sales, Returns, Cost of Goods, Commissions, Utilities, Salaries
		Cash Flow Projection	Sales, Cost of Goods, Operating Expenses
		Break-Even Analysis	
Marketing Vehicles	10, page 162	Marketing Budget (Chapter 10, p. 182–183)	
		Income Statement	Marketing
		Cash Flow Projection	Operating Expenses
Traditional Marketing Tactics	10, page 165	Marketing Budget (Chapter 10, p. 182–183)	
		Income Statement	Profit Margin, Marketing
		Cash Flow Projection	Operating Expenses
Marketing Budget	10, pages 182–183	Income Statement	Marketing, Travel/Entertainment, Professional Services
		Cash Flow Projection	Operating Expenses
Sales Projections	10, pages 184–185	Income Statement	Sales, Commissions
Facilities	11, page 193	Income Statement	Rent, Utilities, Maintenance
		Cash Flow Projection	Operating Expenses, Other Expenses
		Balance Sheet	Fixed Assets, Depreciation
Production	11, page 196–197	Income Statement	Cost of Goods, Salaries, Employee Benefits, Payroll Taxes
		Cash Flow Projection	Operating Expenses
Equipment Schedule	11, page 198	Income Statement	Depreciation, Equipment Rental, Furniture and Equipment
		Cash Flow Projection	Operating Expenses, Equip. Purchase
		Balance Sheet	Fixed Assets, Depreciation
Supply and Distribution	11, page 202	Income Statement	Cost of Goods, Commissions
		Cash Flow Projection	Cost of Goods, Operating Expenses

WORSHEET	CHAPTER	TRANSFER TO	USE ON LINES
Order Fulfillment	11, page 204	Income Statement	Postage and Shipping, Returns and Allowances, Salaries (Customer Service Personnel)
		Cash Flow Projection	Operating Expenses
Research and Development	11, page 208	Income Statement	Allot costs to appropriate lines (e.g., salaries, equipment) or create separate R & D line
		Cash Flow Projection	Operating Expenses
Other Operational Issues	11, page 212	Income Statement	Insurance, Professional Services, Other (for permits, licenses)
		Cash Flow Projection	Operating Expenses
Start-Up Costs	11, page 213	Income Statement	First month's operating expenses on appropriate lines
		Cash Flow Projection	First month's operating expenses (and months for term payments)
		Balance Sheet	Current and Fixed Assets, Current and Long-Term Liabilities (for loans secured to pay costs), or Equity
Technology Budget	12, page 226	Income Statement	Depreciation, Equipment Rental, Furniture and Equipment
		Cash Flow Projection	Operating Expenses, Equip. Purchase
		Balance Sheet	Fixed Assets, Depreciation
Compensation and Incentives	13, page 235	Income Statement	Salaries, Employee Benefits, Payroll Taxes
		Cash Flow Projection	Operating Expenses
Professional Services	13, page 239	Income Statement	Professional Services
		Cash Flow Projection	Operating Expenses
Key Management Personnel to Be Added	13, page 240	Income Statement and Cash Flow Projection	Salaries (projections for future months and years)
Staffing Budget	16, pages 296–297	Income Statement	Salaries, Benefits, Payroll Taxes
Monthly Cash Income Projections	16, pages 298–299	Income Statement	Gross Sales (unless your business is accrual-based)

Globalization: Financial Considerations

Answer the following questions if you will be dealing with foreign currencies, conducting international operations, or selling your products or services internationally.

Have you accounted for the way exchange rates will affect your financial analysis and projections? _____

_____

_____

How stable are the foreign currencies you will be dealing with? Are they historically consistently stable or do rates fluctuate greatly? Is there political or social unrest that could affect the value of the currency in the areas where you plan to operate? _____

_____

_____

_____

Are there any unique start-up costs associated with doing business in some regions? _____

_____

_____

_____

Are there unique tax or tariff considerations you should be aware of in the countries where you plan to operate? _____

_____

_____

_____

What seasonal factors will affect financial projections or cause revenue fluctuations in the regions in which you plan to operate? _____

_____

_____

_____

Will you be paying any staff in a foreign currency? If so, what are the average pay rates for the positions you plan to fill? Are there expected region-specific benefits you need to be aware of? _____

_____

_____

_____

What are the average costs of supplies, goods, or services that you may purchase locally if working internationally? Would it be more economical in some cases to purchase goods in the United States and ship them to international locations? _____

_____

_____

Other forms include:

- **Sources and Use of Funds.** Shows where you will get financing for your business and how you will spend the money invested or lent. A potential investor or loan officer will want to see this.

- **Break-even Analysis.** Shows the point at which sales exceed costs and you begin to make a profit. Advisable for internal planning.

- **Start-up Costs.** For a new business shows the initial investment necessary to begin operations. *A Start-Up Costs form can be found in Chapter 11, on page 213, and should be included in your completed business plan.*

- **Assumption Sheet.** Shows those reading your financial statements how you determined the figures used. A good adjunct to other forms.

Time Frames Your Forms Should Cover

Generally, investors want to see financial projections for three to five years in the future, plus historical records of the past three to five years for currently operating businesses. If possible, find out what periods your lending institution or potential investor wants to see and prepare your forms accordingly. Otherwise, prepare forms to cover the time frames cited below.

- **Income Statements.** First year: monthly projections. Years two and three: quarterly projections. Years four and five: annual projections. Existing businesses: actual annual income statements for the last three years.

- **Cash Flow Projections.** First year: monthly projections. Years two through three: quarterly projections.

- **Balance Sheet.** First year: quarterly projections. Years two through five: annual projections. Existing businesses: current balance sheet and actual balance sheets for the last two years.

General Financial Terms

The terms that follow are frequently used in financial forms. If you are in business, you should have a working knowledge of these terms.

Even if you're familiar with financial statements, take a few minutes to update your understanding of these key words; and if you've never produced (or reviewed) a financial statement before, study these terms until you feel comfortable with them.

- **Accounts Payable.** Obligations owed to others; list of outstanding bills.

- **Accounts Receivable.** Obligations owed to your company by others; a list of outstanding invoices.

- **Accumulated Depreciation.** The amount of depreciation a company has already taken in the form of tax deductions; such accumulated depreciation must be accounted for when selling fixed assets.

- **Assets.** Anything the company owns having a positive monetary value.

- **Cash.** Immediately available money in the form of currency, checks, or bank deposits.

- **Cost of Goods.** Expenses directly associated with producing and making a specific product. Companies differ as to which expenses they attribute to cost of goods, but generally items such as source materials, direct labor, and freight are included.

- **Cost of Sales.** Expenses directly associated with selling a product or service. This typically includes items such as sales commissions, distributors' fees, and so on, but does not generally include more indirect costs such as marketing.

- **Current Assets.** Assets that can be converted quickly, with relative ease, to cash; these assets are designed to be turned over in the normal course of doing business, such as bank deposits, inventory, and accounts receivable.

- **Current Liabilities.** Any bills, debts, or obligations occurring in the ongoing course of business; any debt due within the next year. Includes accounts payable, accrued payroll expenses, and loans and credit lines with less than one year's maturity date.

- **Debt.** An ongoing obligation of the company, such as a bank loan.

- **Depreciation.** The wear and tear on fixed assets—not a cash expenditure, but an ongoing expense of the business as equipment wears down. A tax deduction.

- **Equity.** Ownership of a company, usually distributed by means of shares of stock. A person who owns part of a company is said to have an equity interest in the company.

- **Exchange rate.** The price at which one currency is converted to be received in another currency. For example, if 100 US dollars are worth 120 Australian dollars, the exchange rate is 1.2, and if 100 US dollars are worth 80 Euros, the exchange rate is 0.8.

- **Fixed Assets (or Property, Plant, and Equipment).** Assets that are the ongoing means of doing business; such assets are generally cumbersome to turn into cash; includes buildings, land, and equipment.

- **Fixed Costs.** Ongoing expenses or overhead of a business that occur regardless of the amount of sales. These expenses usually include items such as rent, utilities, and salaries.

- **Gross Profit.** Percentage of income your company realizes on each sale before administrative expenses.

- **Liabilities.** Any outstanding obligation or debt of the company.

- **Long-Term Liabilities.** Loans and other debts that come due in more than a year's time. This year's interest payments on such loans, or **debt service**, are included in Current Liabilities.

- **Net Profit.** Amount of income after deducting all costs of doing business, including administrative overhead and other fixed costs.

- **Net Worth.** Value of a company after deducting liabilities from assets.

- **Other or Intangible Assets.** Aspects of your company that have value not easily interpreted in specific monetary terms or directly convertible to cash; assets such as a popular trademarked name and the goodwill a company has built up over time.

- ■ **Profit.** Amount a company earns after expenses.
- ■ **Pro Forma.** Financial statements based on projected future performance rather than actual historical data.
- ■ **Retained Earnings.** Net worth amount the company keeps internally for ongoing development of the business rather than distributing to shareholders.

Financial Symbols

The symbols below commonly appear on financial forms:

( )   Numbers appearing in parentheses are negative numbers; they represent losses.

------   Single lines represent subtotals.

===   Double lines represent totals.

000's   This indicates that numbers are expressed in thousands.

Guidelines for Preparing Your Financial Forms

In preparing your financial forms, you will almost certainly have questions as to how to attribute certain expenses for your business. You might wonder whether you should ascribe sales commissions to cost of goods sold or to operating expenses. Accounting practices differ, so follow these guidelines:

1. **Be conservative.** Avoid the tendency to paint the rosiest picture possible; doing so reduces your credibility.

2. **Be honest.** Experienced financing sources will sense dishonest or manipulated figures; expect to be asked to justify your numbers.

3. **Don't be creative.** Use standard formats and financial terms; otherwise you look inexperienced to financing sources.

4. **Get your accountant's advice.**

5. **Follow the practices used in your industry.**

6. **Choose the appropriate accounting method.**

7. **Be consistent.** Make a decision and stick with it for all your accounts, otherwise you can't compare one year's figures to another.

Staffing Budget

In many companies, the costs associated with employees are often the largest expenses of the business. In any company, labor costs are a critical issue. When planning a business, it's easy to underestimate or overlook labor costs.

> " It was years before we were profitable, but we had good cash flow that we managed well. We paid back the initial investment before we were even profitable."
>
> *Kay Koplovitz*
> *Chair, Kate Spade*

Number and Timing

You must first figure out how many employees you will need and exactly when you will need them. It is easy to underestimate this number, anticipating that you will only hire outstanding employees, all of whom will work to maximum capacity. But remember, employees will probably not work as hard or as long as you do, so don't plan your expenses based solely on your own level of productivity.

Some industries, such as those in the service sector, are particularly labor intensive. And in a small business, customers often expect very high levels of personal service, which can mean higher staffing levels. Even if yours is a sole proprietorship, you may occasionally need to hire some assistance, and you should plan accordingly.

If yours is a new business, you may want to talk with entrepreneurs in existing businesses about the level and timing of their personnel, to help you devise your own projections. If you are changing the direction of an existing business, how will your new needs affect your staffing levels and deployment? Will current employees be able to be trained for new tasks, or will new staff need to be hired?

Not all employees will be hired at once, and not all employees will be permanent. The staffing budget allows you to change the number of workers in each category, depending on the actual month(s) they work. You may have seasonal work that requires additional staff for some portions of the year. Timing your hiring can be very important in making certain you are adequately prepared for your workloads. Most people, even those who have been in business for a long time, underestimate the time it will take to hire and train new staff. Allow yourself realistic lead-time for staff recruitment, and don't forget to account for the costs of any temporary help you may need until permanent staff is in place.

Also, it's almost inevitable that you will at some point hire people who do not perform well. There will be costs associated with dismissing employees. These costs may include temporary help to fill their slots while you seek replacement and any severance pay that is required by their contract.

Benefits and Taxes

One of the first things you will need to do is to figure out the benefits that you will need and want to attract and retain qualified staff. These benefits may include health, life, dental, or disability insurance; pension benefits; and paid vacation.

Some employee costs are required by law. Check with your state's department of labor to find out about mandatory benefits, such as workers' compensation. There will also be payroll taxes, which can add a substantial amount to your total employee costs. You may want to talk with an accountant or lawyer to learn what costs to anticipate with regard to benefits and taxes.

The Staffing Budget worksheet on pages 296–297 will help you plot out all the labor costs associated with your business. The worksheet is presented in a monthly format to enable you to reflect the changes in your staffing, depending on when you hire new employees, add new divisions, or use seasonal or variable labor.

The information in the Staffing Budget transfers to the Salaries and Wages, Employee Benefits, and Payroll Taxes lines on your Income Statement, pages 300–303. The supplemental Business Plan Financials package available from www.PlanningShop.com includes the Staffing Budget and will automatically handle these calculations and transfers for you.

Cash Projections

An important fact to remember when preparing your financial projections is that you will often not receive full payment at the time of an actual sale or transaction. Projecting cash flow solely on the sales made, rather than cash actually received, will leave you seriously short on money.

Some industries have particularly long lag times between orders and payment. This can be especially true in manufacturing companies. A clothing manufacturer, for instance, may make sales many months before payment is due. Even in retail, you may find that you establish some credit accounts for very large or repeat customers and these customers take longer to pay.

Your business may allow payment terms over a number of months, or the type of work you do may make payment over time a necessity. In almost any company, some customers will be slow payers. While most customers may pay within 30 days, some may take as much as 120 days, and some will never pay at all. For instance, if you make a $10,000 sale in the month of February, you may only receive a deposit of $2,500 in February, with the rest paid as partial payments through June. Of course, you can try to reduce the amount of slow or nonpayers by requiring larger percentages of payment at the time of sale or delivery or by charging interest on unpaid balances, but it is still necessary to anticipate actual payment patterns in your cash flow projections.

It's also a good idea to differentiate between the income of each product or service line. While it may seem like a bit more work to keep track of each product line's or service line's income separately, this information will help you make decisions about the long-term direction of your company and better understand exactly where your profits come from.

Complete the Monthly Cash Income Projections worksheet on page 298. The information from this worksheet can then be transferred to your "Cash Flow Projection" forms and to your "Income Statement" forms if you operate your business on a cash, rather than accrual, accounting basis. If yours is an existing business, review your past records to determine the average payment pattern to use in this form. If you are new to business, check with others in your industry to see what are typical payment patterns. Be conservative in your projections. It's always better to find out that you have more cash than you anticipated rather than less.

Income Statements

The Income Statement is also frequently called either a Profit and Loss statement—P&L—or an Income and Expense statement. This form shows

> " Projections are actually far less important than the assumptions to projections. Generally, poor financials tend to be negative indicators rather than good financials being positive indicators. Are you assuming you'll get an 80% market share when there's no way you'll get 10%? Do you think that way?"
>
> *Andrew Anker*
> *Venture Capitalist*

STAFFING BUDGET

For Year: _____	JAN	FEB	MARCH	APRIL	MAY
Management #Employees					
Salary/wages					
Benefits					
Payroll taxes					
Total Costs					
Administrative/Support #Employees					
Salary/wages					
Benefits					
Payroll taxes					
Total Costs					
Sales/Marketing #Employees					
Salary/wages					
Benefits					
Payroll taxes					
Total Costs					
Operations/Production #Employees					
Salary/wages					
Benefits					
Payroll taxes					
Total Costs					
Other #Employees					
Salary/wages					
Benefits					
Payroll taxes					
Total Costs					
TOTAL #Employees					
Salary/wages					
Benefits					
Payroll taxes					
TOTAL COSTS					

NOTE: A Microsoft Excel version of this worksheet is available as part of PlanningShop's Business Plan Financials package, available from **www.PlanningShop.com**.

| | | | | | | | $ ➤ $$ ➤ $$ |
JUNE	JULY	AUG	SEPT	OCT	NOV	DEC	TOTAL

MONTHLY CASH INCOME PROJECTIONS

For Year:_____	JAN	FEB	MARCH	APRIL	MAY
PRODUCT LINE #1 SALES **Cash Received**					
Current month sales					
30 days prior sales					
60 days prior sales					
90 days prior sales					
120 days prior sales					
Total Product #1 Cash Income					
PRODUCT LINE #2 SALES **Cash Received**					
Current month sales					
30 days prior sales					
60 days prior sales					
90 days prior sales					
120 days prior sales					
Total Product #2 Cash Income					
PRODUCT LINE #3 SALES **Cash Received**					
Current month sales					
30 days prior sales					
60 days prior sales					
90 days prior sales					
120 days prior sales					
Total Product #3 Cash Income					
PRODUCT LINE #4 SALES **Cash Received**					
Current month sales					
30 days prior sales					
60 days prior sales					
90 days prior sales					
120 days prior sales					
Total Product #4 Cash Income					
TOTAL CASH INCOME					

							$ ➤ $$ ➤ $$$
JUNE	JULY	AUG	SEPT	OCT	NOV	DEC	TOTAL

INCOME STATEMENT: ANNUAL BY MONTH

For Year: _____	JAN	FEB	MARCH	APRIL	MAY
INCOME					
Gross Sales					
(Commissions)					
(Returns and allowances)					
Net Sales					
(Cost of Goods)					
GROSS PROFIT					
EXPENSES - General and Administrative					
Salaries and wages					
Employee benefits					
Payroll taxes					
Professional services					
Marketing and advertising					
Rent					
Equipment rental					
Maintenance					
Depreciation					
Insurance					
Telecommunications					
Utilities					
Office supplies					
Postage and shipping					
Travel					
Entertainment					
Interest on loans					
Other:					
Other:					
TOTAL EXPENSES					
Net income before taxes					
Provision for taxes on income					
NET PROFIT					

NOTE: A Microsoft Excel version of this worksheet is available as part of PlanningShop's Business Plan Financials package, available from **www.PlanningShop.com**.

JUNE	JULY	AUG	SEPT	OCT	NOV	DEC	TOTAL

$ ➤ $$ ➤ $$$

INCOME STATEMENT: ANNUAL BY QUARTER $ ➤ $$ ➤ $$

For Year: _____	1st Quarter	2nd Quarter	3rd Quarter	4th Quarter	TOTAL
INCOME					
Gross Sales					
(Commissions)					
(Returns and allowances)					
Net Sales					
(Cost of Goods)					
GROSS PROFIT					
EXPENSES - General and Administrative					
Salaries and wages					
Employee benefits					
Payroll taxes					
Professional services					
Marketing and advertising					
Rent					
Equipment rental					
Maintenance					
Depreciation					
Insurance					
Telecommunications					
Utilities					
Office supplies					
Postage and shipping					
Travel					
Entertainment					
Interest on loans					
Other:					
Other:					
TOTAL EXPENSES					
Net income before taxes					
Provision for taxes on income					
NET PROFIT					

INCOME STATEMENT: ANNUAL FOR FIVE YEARS $ ➤ $$ ➤ $$

	YR. _____	YR. _____	YR. _____	YR. _____	YR. _____
INCOME					
Gross Sales					
(Commissions)					
(Returns and allowances)					
Net Sales					
(Cost of Goods)					
GROSS PROFIT					
EXPENSES - General and Administrative					
Salaries and wages					
Employee benefits					
Payroll taxes					
Professional services					
Marketing and advertising					
Rent					
Equipment rental					
Maintenance					
Depreciation					
Insurance					
Telecommunications					
Utilities					
Office supplies					
Postage and shipping					
Travel					
Entertainment					
Interest on loans					
Other:					
Other:					
TOTAL EXPENSES					
Net income before taxes					
Provision for taxes on income					
NET PROFIT					

how profitable your company is—how much money it will make after all expenses are accounted for. It does not give a total picture of what your company is worth overall, or its cash position.

A company can be losing money but still be worth a great deal because it owns valuable property, or it can be profitable but still not have enough cash to pay its bills due to cash flow problems. An income statement does not reveal either of these "hidden" situations.

You read an income statement from top to bottom. The first line accounts for sales. Each subsequent line represents deductions from income. The result is the company's profit (or, possibly, loss).

To prepare an income statement, accumulate detailed information about your sales and expenses. Specific lines on the form should mirror the categories by which you maintain your ongoing accounts. When completing the income statement, refer to the previous list of financial terms.

Additionally, note these references:

- **Gross Sales.** Total sales from all product line categories.

- **Employee Benefits.** Items such as health and dental insurance; any other benefits with specific costs associated.

- **Professional Services.** Attorney's, accountant's, designers', technology specialists', and consultant's fees.

- **Marketing.** Advertising and marketing expenses other than Travel, Entertainment/Meals, which may have different tax treatments; transfer this figure from your Marketing Budget worksheet in Chapter 10.

- **Maintenance.** Janitorial or cleaning services, regular maintenance programs or service contracts, and repairs.

- **Depreciation and Amortization.** The value of either fixed assets (depreciation) or intangible assets (amortization) that is allocated as a yearly expense or deemed to be lost each year through use or obsolescence.

- **Insurance.** Insurance premiums such as those for liability, malpractice, auto, or equipment insurance. Excludes insurance included in Employee Benefits line.

- **Telephone/Telecommunications.** Costs of telephone and telecommunications services. Costs of Internet access can go in this line or in Utilities.

- **Office Supplies.** Usual office or business supplies, rather than the materials necessary to produce the item for sale.

- **Travel.** Costs of necessary business travel, including airfare, hotels, taxis, and so on; auto expenses (which may have different tax treatment) can go here or on a separate line.

- **Entertainment/Meals.** Costs of entertaining customers, potential customers, and employees; including events, parties, meals, and the like. These expenses typically are only partially tax deductible.

Complete the income statements on pages 300–303. Document income on a monthly (first year), quarterly (first two to three years), and

> " What kind of numbers do we like to see? The more mature a business is, the more we rely on numbers. For a newer business, the numbers matter less and the words matter more."
> *Robert Mahoney*
> *Corporate Banker*

annual basis (years four and five). If necessary, adjust the form to meet the needs of your company.

The supplemental Business Plan Financials package available from www. PlanningShop.com includes the Income Statement worksheets and will automatically handle calculations and transfers from other worksheets for you.

Cash Flow Projections

For almost every business, cash flow analysis is the single most important financial assessment. After all, if you can't pay your employees, your bills, or yourself, you're not going to stay in business long, and you're certainly not going to sleep very well at night.

The cash flow projection is not about profit—it's about how much money you have in the bank. It doesn't tell you whether your company will show an overall profit at the end of the year or how many orders you are placing, but instead gives a real-life picture of the money going in and out of your business on a monthly basis.

Cash flow analysis is particularly important for seasonal businesses, those with large inventories, or those that sell much of their merchandise on credit. You must plan for the slow months and for the long time lag between paying for materials and actually realizing cash receipts.

Maintaining historical cash flow records gives you an idea of what to expect in certain months of the year and helps you plan future cash management. Get in the habit of keeping monthly cash flow accounts.

In preparing these forms, separate out cash you receive from doing business (sales) and the cash you get from taking out loans or receiving investments (financing). This will give you a better sense of where your money is coming from and how much you are relying on credit. Note these items used in your cash flow analysis:

- **Cash Sales.** Sales made for immediate payment or prepayments.
- **Collections.** Income collected from sales made in a previous period.
- **Interest Income.** Income paid from bank and other interest-bearing accounts.
- **Loan Proceeds.** Income from bank loans and other credit lines.
- **Cost of Goods.** Actual payments made on items in this category. Cash and accrual accounting methods treat this line differently; consult your accountant.
- **Operating Expenses.** Actual payments made on items in this category, minus depreciation (as depreciation is not an actual cash payment). Since cash and accrual accounting methods treat this line differently, consult your accountant.
- **Reserve.** Money put into accounts for future, unanticipated expenses.
- **Owner's Draw.** Money paid to owner in lieu of salary in a proprietorship, or money otherwise distributed to owners (except for expense reimbursement). In a corporation it is called a dividend and paid from

> " Spreadsheets lie… fail to take into account all the unexpected and unpleasant surprises that inevitably happen… Once you've developed your annual projection, cut your sales by 40% and raise your expenses by 50% and make sure you've got cash to weather that scenario."
>
> *Seth Goldman*
> *Cofounder, Honest Tea*

CASH FLOW PROJECTION: ANNUAL BY MONTH

For Year: _____	JAN	FEB	MARCH	APRIL	MAY
CASH RECEIPTS **Income from Sales**					
Cash sales					
Collections					
Total Cash from Sales					
Income from Financing					
Interest income					
Loan proceeds					
Total Cash from Financing					
Other cash receipts					
TOTAL CASH RECEIPTS					
CASH DISBURSEMENTS **Expenses**					
Inventory					
Operating expenses					
Commissions/returns & allowances					
Capital purchases					
Loan payments					
Income tax payments					
Investor dividend payments					
Owner's draw					
TOTAL CASH DISBURSEMENTS					
NET CASH FLOW					
Opening cash balance					
Cash receipts					
Cash disbursements					
ENDING CASH BALANCE					

NOTE: A Microsoft Excel version of this worksheet is available as part of PlanningShop's Business Plan Financials package, available from **www.PlanningShop.com**.

| | | | | | | | $➤ $$➤ $$$ |
JUNE	JULY	AUG	SEPT	OCT	NOV	DEC	TOTAL

CASH FLOW PROJECTION: ANNUAL BY QUARTER $ ➤ $$ ➤ $$$

For Year: _____	1st Quarter	2nd Quarter	3rd Quarter	4th Quarter	TOTAL
CASH RECEIPTS **Income from Sales**					
Cash sales					
Collections					
Total Cash from Sales					
Income from Financing					
Interest income					
Loan proceeds					
Total Cash from Financing					
Other cash receipts					
TOTAL CASH RECEIPTS					
CASH DISBURSEMENTS **Expenses**					
Inventory					
Operating expenses					
Commissions/returns & allowances					
Capital purchases					
Loan payments					
Income tax payments					
Investor dividend payments					
Owner's draw					
TOTAL CASH DISBURSEMENTS					
NET CASH FLOW					
Opening cash balance					
Cash receipts					
Cash disbursements					
ENDING CASH BALANCE					

Balance Sheet

$ ➤ $$ ➤ $$$

Balance Sheet

For Company: _____

For Period: _____ **Ending:** _____ , 20_____

ASSETS

Current Assets
Cash   _____
Accounts receivable   _____
Inventory   _____
Other current assets   _____
Total Current Assets   _____

Fixed Assets
Land   _____
Facilities   _____
Equipment   _____
Computers & telecommunications   _____
(Less accumulated depreciation)   _____
Total Fixed Assets   _____

Other Assets   _____

TOTAL ASSETS   ==================

LIABILITIES

Current Liabilities
Short-term notes payable   _____
Income taxes due   _____
Other current liabilities   _____
Total Current Liabilities   _____

Long-Term Liabilities
Long-term notes payable   _____
Other long-term liabilities   _____
Total Long-Term Liabilities   _____

Net Worth
Paid-in capital   _____
Retained earnings   _____
Total Net Worth   _____

TOTAL LIABILITIES AND NET WORTH   ==================

Include in the Financial section of your business plan.

NOTE: A Microsoft Excel version of this worksheet is available as part of PlanningShop's Business Plan Financials package, available from **www.PlanningShop.com**.

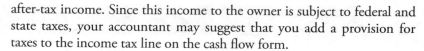

after-tax income. Since this income to the owner is subject to federal and state taxes, your accountant may suggest that you add a provision for taxes to the income tax line on the cash flow form.

- **Net Cash Flow.** Money left over after all **disbursements** have been deducted from all cash received.

- **Opening Cash Balance.** Amount of money in the bank at the beginning of the month being evaluated; should be the same as the previous month's ending cash balance.

Complete the cash flow analysis, on a monthly basis for the first year (or two) and quarterly for the next year. The supplemental Business Plan Financials package available from www.PlanningShop.com includes the Cash Flow worksheet and will automatically handle calculations and transfers from other worksheets for you.

Balance Sheet

For those who are new to business, the balance sheet is probably the least understood of the financial forms. In essence, the balance sheet gives a snapshot of the overall financial worth of the company—the value of all its various components and the extent of all its obligations.

The balance sheet accounts for all the company's assets minus all the company's liabilities. The remaining amount (if any) is figured to be the net worth of the company. The net worth is then distributed either as belonging to the owners of the company—equity—or as retained earnings for the company to use. These allotments are listed in the Liabilities category. Once you do this, the amounts in the Assets and Liabilities categories are equal: They balance.

While entrepreneurs rarely view the balance sheet as a planning tool, bankers and investors rely on the balance sheet to give them a fuller picture of the company's value. Only on the balance sheet can one see the worth of existing property and equipment. Some companies own valuable land or buildings that far exceed the income of the actual business; other businesses own expensive machinery. Yet others may be profitable but heavily in debt.

See the Balance Sheet worksheet on page 309.

Refer to the General Financial Terms section at the beginning of this chapter for an explanation of the items listed on the balance sheet.

Additionally, note that the balance sheet uses these terms:

- **Land.** Often broken out separately on a balance sheet, because, unlike other property—such as buildings—land is subject to different tax treatment and often retains higher value.

- **Facilities.** The value of all buildings, warehouses, or physical property owned by the business, excluding land and equipment.

- **Short-term notes payable.** Debts that are typically due to be paid off within a year. This includes lines-of-credit and other operating credit other than accounts payable.

- **Other current liabilities.** Other debts owed, including accounts payable.

Sources and Use of Funds

Complete the following form to describe how much money you are seeking and how you will use the funds raised. Be as specific as possible: If you know what equipment you are going to buy, list it; if you have a loan from the First State Bank, for example, state the name of the lending institution, amount, and terms.

Number of funding rounds expected for full financing: _____

Total dollar amount being sought in this round: _____

Sources of Funds

Equity Financing:

Preferred Stock: _____

Common Stock: _____

Debt Financing:

Mortgage Loans: _____

Other Long-Term Loans: _____

Short-Term Loans: _____

Convertible Debt: _____

Investment from Principals: _____

Uses of Funds

Capital Expenditures:

Purchase of Property: _____

Leasehold Improvements: _____

Purchase of Equipment/Furniture: _____

Other: _____

Working Capital:

Purchase of Inventory: _____

Staff Expansion: _____

New Product Line Introduction: _____

Additional Marketing Activities: _____

Other Business Expansion Activities: _____

Other: _____

Debt Retirement: _____

Cash Reserve: _____

When completing the balance sheet, you may find you need more help with this form than with any other, especially when trying to figure accumulated depreciation or the worth of inventory. Get help from your accountant or have your accountant prepare the form. But you must still understand it.

Since much of the information on balance sheets does not change very quickly, you can prepare balance sheets primarily on a quarterly or annual basis (unless, of course, your potential funding sources want monthly projections).

The supplemental Business Plan Financials package available from www.PlanningShop.com includes the Balance Sheet worksheets and will automatically handle calculations and transfers from other worksheets for you.

Sources and Use of Funds

If you are seeking outside financing, either through loans or investors, those contemplating giving you money will naturally want to know what you're going to do with the money you raise. They will also want to see what other sources of money you have, if any, and whether you have contributed any of your own funds.

To provide such information, devise a one-page description of the sources and use of funds. This can go in the business plan itself or can be sent with the cover letter to potential financing sources. It should tell a potential investor that you have specific plans for the money you raise, that you are not taking on debts or giving up equity thoughtlessly, and that you will use funds to make your business grow.

Your Sources and Use of Funds statement on page 311 is particularly helpful to you with investors or lenders if you show you are using your funds to start or expand a business rather than to offset existing debts (a use that investors notoriously dislike), or if you already have some commitment of financing already from respected sources (which shows that other people believe in your company), or if you are committing significant personal funds (which shows you believe in the project enough to take substantial personal risk).

In "Sources of Funds," you should include both funds you have received to date and the amounts you are now seeking, clearly delineating each.

In preparing the "Sources and Use of Funds" statement, consider the following issues and terms:

■ **Funding Rounds.** The number of development stages at which you will seek financing from the investment community.

■ **Total Amount.** Amount of money sought in this round of financing, from all funding sources.

■ **Equity Financing.** Amount you will raise by selling ownership interest in the company.

■ **Preferred Stock.** Outstanding stock for which dividends will be paid, before other dividends can be paid for common stock or before other obligations of the company are paid; investors often want preferred stock.

- **Common Stock.** Stock for which dividends are paid when the company is profitable and has paid preferred stock dividends and other obligations.
- **Debt Financing.** Amount of money you will raise by taking out loans.
- **Long-Term Loans.** Loans to be paid back in more than a year's time.
- **Mortgage Loans.** Loans taken out with property as **collateral**.
- **Short-Term Loans.** Bridge loans, credit lines, and other loans to be paid back in less than a year.
- **Convertible Debt.** Loans that are later convertible to stock at the funder's option, giving both the security of a loan and the potential of stock.
- **Investment from Principals.** Amount of money that you or other key employees are contributing to the company; this can be in the form of cash or property.
- **Capital Expenditures.** Purchase of necessary equipment or property.
- **Working Capital.** Funds to be used for the ongoing operating expenses of the business.
- **Debt Retirement.** Funds used to pay off existing loans or obligations.

Assumption Sheet

Financial forms are merely meaningless numbers unless they are based on decisions and facts. Your potential financing sources want to see how you arrived at your numbers and must be convinced that your assumptions are reasonably accurate. If, for instance, you have indicated your sales at a certain amount, investors want to see what size you are assuming the market to be and what percentage of the market you are assuming you will be able to secure. If those figures seem realistic, you increase your credibility; if those assumptions seem based on inaccurate numbers or overly optimistic projections, investors are going to look at the rest of your plan with greater skepticism.

It is good discipline for you, as well, to learn to develop an assumption sheet whenever you do financial projections. Otherwise, you can be too easily tempted to write down figures that look good on paper but have little to do with reality.

If you have worked through the business planning process, putting together an assumption sheet should be a relatively easy task. You have already asked yourself most of the questions called for on this form and have the answers available to you.

An assumption sheet should list purely straightforward information; it does not require substantial detail or explanation. You do not even need to use sentences; just provide the data in each category. (You can use the first sentence, as written on the worksheet, on your own assumption sheet.) Be familiar with these assumptions so that you are ready to defend your assumptions when meeting with investors.

> " In the financials, I look for a well-prepared, well-annotated balance sheet. And I like an Assumption Sheet with the Income Statement, so I know exactly how those figures got there."
>
> *Ann Winblad*
> *Venture Capitalist*

Complete the Assumption Sheet on pages 316–317 and include a finished Assumption Sheet at the conclusion of your financial forms in your business plan.

Break-Even Analysis

Finally, you want to determine how much income you must earn to pay your expenses—at what point you break even. At the break-even point you are neither making a profit nor losing money; you have just covered the cost of staying in business and making your sales. Most people new to business assume their break-even point is when sales equal the amount of fixed expenses: rent, telephone, insurance, and so forth. Fixed expenses are easy to determine, since they are in place from the time you first open your doors, and they remain relatively stable regardless of the amount of sales.

But because almost all sales have some costs associated with them, you must also figure the variable cost of sales into your break-even analysis; otherwise you do not have a true picture of your cost of doing business.

For instance, if you are a florist and your fixed expenses (rent, utilities, salaries, and so on) are $20,000 a month, it's not just enough to make $20,000 in sales: You would still be losing money. You must pay for flowers, vases, delivery, and commissions to floral wire services before you earn income on a sale. If these costs amount to an average of 30% of the cost of each sale, at $20,000 in income, you're still $6,000 in the hole ($20,000 in fixed expenses plus $6,000 in costs of goods).

The total cost of goods keeps rising as your sales rise; unlike your fixed costs, the figure keeps changing and is harder to pin down. But your gross profit margin—the average percentage you earn on each sale after direct costs are deducted—stays basically the same. (As you sell greater amounts, you may be able to increase your profit margin by receiving volume discounts; for the purpose of this exercise however, you can assume a stable gross profit margin.)

To determine an actual break-even point, you must know your:

■ Fixed expenses

■ Gross profit margin (average percentage of gross income realized after cost of goods)

Then, to figure the amount of total sales needed to break even, you work the equation:

Fixed Expenses = Total Sales x Gross Profit Margin (GPM)

or, saying the same thing:

$$\frac{\text{Fixed Expenses}}{\text{GPM}} = \text{Total Sales}$$

In the above example of the florist, we know:

■ Fixed Expenses = $20,000

■ Gross Profit Margin (GPM) = 70% (since cost of goods is 30%)

So, the numbers would look like:

$$\frac{20{,}000}{.70} = \text{Total Sales to Break Even}$$

Doing the arithmetic, we see that this florist must make $28,571 to reach the break-even point.

A break-even analysis is an important tool for your internal planning. However, it is not necessary for you to include a break-even analysis in a business plan submitted to outside funding sources. (Of course, there is nothing wrong with including it if you wish.)

Break-Even Analysis

Monthly Total Fixed Expenses (FE): $_____

Gross Profit Margin, in percentage terms (GPM):_____%

Divide: FE: $ _____

$\overline{}$ = $ _____

  GPM: _____ %   (Sales to Break Even)

Complete the worksheet above to figure your own break-even point. The supplemental Business Plan Financials package available from www. PlanningShop.com will perform a break-even analysis for you.

Chapter Summary

The financial portion of your business plan will consist mostly of the actual financial projections. You should include the following forms:

- Income Statement
- Cash Flow Analysis
- Balance Sheet
- Sources and Use of Funds
- Assumption Sheet
- Start-up Costs (for a new business)

Additionally, you will want to do a break-even analysis for your internal planning.

It is advisable to get professional help in putting together your financial forms and setting up accounts. Set good financial procedures in place from the beginning of your business and stick to them. If yours is an existing business, review your procedures to make sure you have adequate control of billing and payments.

Get in the habit of reviewing your financial statements regularly and understanding what you read. Don't leave the finances entirely up to others, and don't be intimidated by numbers.

Assumption Sheet

The figures on the previous financial forms are based on the following assumptions:

SALES	Year		Year		Year		Annual Growth
Product Line	$	Units	$	Units	$	Units	Rate %
_____	_____	_____	_____	_____	_____	_____	_____
_____	_____	_____	_____	_____	_____	_____	_____
_____	_____	_____	_____	_____	_____	_____	_____
_____	_____	_____	_____	_____	_____	_____	_____
_____	_____	_____	_____	_____	_____	_____	_____
_____	_____	_____	_____	_____	_____	_____	_____
_____	_____	_____	_____	_____	_____	_____	_____
Total	_____	_____	_____	_____	_____	_____	_____

Describe the projected increase/decrease in selling price of each product line/service. _____
_____
_____

PERSONNEL/MANAGEMENT

Describe the number of employees and assumptions regarding total payroll projected in the financial forms. _____
_____
_____

Describe key management positions to be added, and timing. _____
_____
_____

GROSS PROFIT MARGIN

List the projected gross profit margin for each product line or service. _____
_____
_____

Describe any major changes in cost of goods that are projected to affect gross profit margin. _____
_____
_____
_____

KEY EXPENSES

Describe the timing and costs of key projected expenses.

Plant Expansion or New Branches _____

_____

Major Capital Purchases_____

_____

Major Marketing Expenses_____

_____

Research and Development _____

_____

Other Key Expenses _____

_____

FINANCING

Describe any financing debt (loans) that are projected to be added or retired.

_____

_____

_____

Describe the interest rates assumed to be in effect for these financial projections.

_____

_____

_____

OTHER

Describe any other major developments that are assumed in creating your financial projections (such as strategic partnerships, competitive situation, etc.).

_____

_____

_____

_____

_____

Notes

SAMPLE PLAN: INCOME STATEMENT THREE-YEAR PROJECTION

INCOME STATEMENT

	2014	2015	2016
INCOME			
Gross Sales	**$466,000**	**$987,750**	**$1,637,230**
(Commissions)	19,220	122,720	165,840
(Returns and allowances)	0	0	0
Net Sales	**446,780**	**865,030**	**1,471,390**
(Cost of goods)	77,740	124,266	173,220
GROSS PROFIT	**369,040**	**740,764**	**1,298,170**
EXPENSES — General and Administrative			
Salaries and wages	178,000	353,600	453,200
Employee benefits	13,200	30,000	43,200
Payroll taxes	12,190	30,000	40,000
Professional services	15,100	10,000	12,000
Marketing and advertising	40,100	60,000	90,000
Rent	21,000	78,000	78,000
Equipment rental	23,500	76,000	96,000
Maintenance	1,200	4,800	9,000
Depreciation	4,000	8,000	8,000
Insurance	6,800	8,400	11,000
Telecommunications	3,500	3,600	4,000
Utilities	4,400	10,000	11,000
Office supplies	6,790	10,000	12,000
Postage and shipping	5,010	7,200	10,000
Travel	2,360	5,190	9,140
Entertainment	2,370	3,610	6,860
Interest on loans	2,750	3,000	0
Other: Technology	12,000	20,000	28,000
Other: Furniture	820	1,000	0
TOTAL EXPENSES	**355,090**	**722,400**	**921,400**
Net income before taxes	13,950	18,364	376,770
Provision for taxes on income	2,092	2,754	113,440
NET PROFIT	**11,858**	**15,610**	**263,330**

Shows increasing profit margin.

Includes sales personnel salaries in General & Administrative expenses.

SAMPLE PLAN: INCOME STATEMENT ANNUAL

INCOME STATEMENT

Year: 2014 (Actual through 8/31/14)

	JAN	FEB	MAR	APR	MAY
INCOME					
Gross Sales	$0	$4,000	$4,000	$10,000	$24,000
(Commissions)	0	0	0	0	700
(Returns and allowances)	0	0	0	0	0
Net Sales	0	4,000	4,000	10,000	23,300
(Cost of goods)	0	648	648	1,624	3,892
GROSS PROFIT	0	3,352	3,352	8,376	19,408
EXPENSES — General and Administrative					
Salaries and wages	5,000	7,400	11,400	12,400	15,400
Employee benefits	550	550	1,020	1,020	1,020
Payroll taxes	420	620	1,010	1,010	1,010
Professional services	5,000	500	4,000	400	400
Marketing and advertising	6,400	3,600	8,000	3,000	3,000
Rent	0	0	0	0	0
Equipment rental	500	500	500	500	500
Maintenance	0	0	0	0	0
Depreciation	4,000	0	0	0	0
Insurance	800	0	0	400	0
Telecommunications	200	100	200	200	240
Utilities	500	120	250	420	320
Office supplies	900	250	430	370	250
Postage and shipping	420	160	620	130	900
Travel	110	300	200	300	0
Entertainment	0	0	220	640	390
Interest on loans	0	250	250	250	250
Other: Technology	6,000	0	0	0	0
Other: Furniture	0	0	0	820	0
TOTAL EXPENSES	30,800	14,350	28,100	21,860	23,680
Net income before taxes	(30,800)	(10,998)	(24,748)	(13,484)	(4,272)
Provision for taxes on income	0	0	0	0	0
NET PROFIT	(30,800)	(10,998)	(24,748)	(13,484)	(4,272)

Includes materials and freight in Cost of Goods.

Includes contractors and variable labor in Salaries and Wages.

Purchased $20,000 in Furniture and Equipment and depreciated it over five years; entered on Depreciation line.

JUNE	JULY	AUG	SEP	OCT	NOV	DEC	TOTAL
$32,000	$41,000	$56,000	$68,400	$83,600	$100,000	$43,000	$466,000
1,500	1,550	2,470	3,000	3,700	4,400	1,900	$19,220
0	0	0	0	0	0	0	$0
30,500	39,450	53,530	65,400	79,900	95,600	41,100	$446,780
5,190	6,898	9,482	11,382	13,852	16,800	7,324	$77,740
25,310	32,552	44,048	54,018	66,048	78,800	33,776	$369,040
16,800	12,600	19,800	18,200	20,200	22,200	16,600	$178,000
1,020	1,020	1,400	1,400	1,400	1,400	1,400	$13,200
1,010	1,010	1,220	1,220	1,220	1,220	1,220	$12,190
400	400	2,400	400	400	400	400	$15,100
600	3,000	3,500	4,000	500	4,000	500	$40,100
0	0	4,200	4,200	4,200	4,200	4,200	$21,000
500	500	4,000	4,000	4,000	4,000	4,000	$23,500
0	0	240	240	240	240	240	$1,200
0	0	0	0	0	0	0	$4,000
0	400	2,000	700	1,100	700	700	$6,800
260	200	500	400	400	400	400	$3,500
400	350	520	440	420	360	300	$4,400
170	220	2,200	500	500	500	500	$6,790
170	520	120	820	150	600	400	$5,010
50	200	0	300	300	300	300	$2,360
400	150	170	100	100	100	100	$2,370
250	250	250	250	250	250	250	$2,750
6,000	0	0	0	0	0	0	$12,000
0	0	0	0	0	0	0	$820
28,030	20,820	42,520	37,170	35,380	40,870	31,510	$355,090
(2,720)	11,732	1,528	16,848	30,668	37,930	2,266	$13,950
0	0	0	0	0	0	2,092	$2,092
(2,720)	11,732	1,528	16,848	30,668	37,930	174	$11,858

SAMPLE PLAN: CASH FLOW PROJECTIONS

CASH FLOW PROJECTION

Year: 2014

	JAN	FEB	MAR	APR	MAY
CASH RECEIPTS					
Income from Sales					
Cash sales	$0	$4,000	$4,000	$10,000	$24,000
Collections	0	0	0	0	0
Total Cash from Sales	**0**	**4,000**	**4,000**	**10,000**	**24,000**
Income from Financing					
Interest income	0	0	0	0	0
Loan proceeds	30,000	0	0	12,000	20,000
Equity capital investments	40,000	0	20,000	0	0
Total Cash from Financing	**70,000**	**0**	**20,000**	**12,000**	**20,000**
Other cash receipts	0	0	0	0	0
TOTAL CASH RECEIPTS	**70,000**	**4,000**	**24,000**	**22,000**	**44,000**
CASH DISBURSEMENTS					
Expenses					
Inventory	0	648	648	1,624	3,892
Operating Expenses	30,800	14,350	28,100	21,860	23,680
Commissions/Returns & Allowances	0	0	0	0	700
Capital Purchases	20,000	0	0	0	0
Loan Payments	0	250	250	250	250
Income tax payments	0	0	0	0	0
Investor dividend payments	0	0	0	0	0
Owner's draw	0	0	0	0	0
TOTAL CASH DISBURSEMENTS	**50,800**	**15,248**	**28,998**	**23,734**	**28,522**
NET CASH FLOW	**19,200**	**(11,248)**	**(4,998)**	**(1,734)**	**15,478**
Opening cash balance	0	19,200	7,952	2,954	1,220
Cash receipts	70,000	4,000	24,000	22,000	44,000
Cash disbursements	(50,800)	(15,248)	(28,998)	(23,734)	(28,522)
ENDING CASH BALANCE	**19,200**	**7,952**	**2,954**	**1,220**	**16,698**

Enters investment from S. Connors as Other Cash Receipts.

Operating Expenses is total of General & Administrative Expenses and Sales Expenses minus Depreciation.

Shows $20,000 Equipment and Furniture payment as January cash disbursement.

Cash disbursements deducted from opening cash balance and cash receipts.

JUNE	JULY	AUG	SEP	OCT	NOV	DEC	TOTAL
$24,000	31,000	39,600	40,000	61,600	70,000	31,000	$339,200
8,000	10,000	16,400	28,400	22,000	30,000	12,000	$126,800
32,000	**41,000**	**56,000**	**68,400**	**83,600**	**100,000**	**43,000**	**$466,000**
0	0	0	0	0	0	0	$0
0	0	8,000	0	0	0	0	$70,000
0	0	0	0	0	0	0	$60,000
0	0	8,000	0	0	0	0	$130,000
32,000	**41,000**	**64,000**	**68,400**	**83,600**	**100,000**	**43,000**	**$596,000**
0	0	0	0	0	0	0	0
32,000	**41,000**	**64,000**	**68,400**	**83,600**	**100,000**	**43,000**	**$596,000**
5,190	6,898	9,482	11,382	13,852	16,800	7,324	$77,740
28,030	20,820	42,520	37,170	35,380	40,870	31,510	$355,090
1,500	1,550	2,470	3,000	3,700	4,400	1,900	$19,220
0	0	0	0	0	0	0	$20,000
250	250	250	250	250	10,250	20,250	$32,750
0	0	0	0	0	0	0	$0
0	0	0	0	0	0	0	$0
0	0	0	0	0	5000	5000	$10,000
34,970	**29,518**	**54,722**	**51,802**	**53,182**	**82,320**	**70,984**	**$524,800**
(2,970)	**11,482**	**9,278**	**16,598**	**30,418**	**17,680**	**(27,984)**	**$72,200**
16,698	13,728	25,210	34,488	51,086	81,504	99,184	$0
32,000	41,000	64,000	68,400	83,600	100,000	43,000	$596,000
(34,970)	(29,518)	(54,722)	(51,802)	(53,182)	(82,320)	(70,984)	($524,800)
13,728	**25,210**	**34,488**	**51,086**	**81,504**	**99,184**	**71,200**	

SAMPLE PLAN: BALANCE SHEET

BALANCE SHEET

For ComputerEase, Inc.
For Year Ending: December 31, 2014

ASSETS

Current Assets

Cash	$71,200	
Accounts receivable	34,400	
Inventory	4,200	
Other current assets	1,560	
Total Current Assets		**$111,360**

$20,000 in Furniture and Equipment shows as company asset minus depreciation taken as expenses.

Fixed Assets

Land	0	
Facilities	0	
Equipment	20,000	
Computers & telecommunications	0	
Less accumulated depreciation	(4,000)	
Total Fixed Assets		**$16,000**
Other Assets		**0**
TOTAL ASSETS		**$127,360**

Short-term loan from S. Connors due in less than one year.

LIABILITIES

Current Liabilities

Short-term notes payable	27,350	
Income taxes due	6,100	
Other current liabilities	590	
Total Current Liabilities		**$34,040**

Long-term loan from L. Silver due in more than one year.

Long-Term Liabilities

Long-term notes payable	30,000	
Other long-term liabilities	0	
Total Long-Term Liabilities		**$30,000**

Owners' interest in company is valued at $63,320 at end of year.

Net Worth

Shareholders' equity	63,320	
Retained earnings	0	
Total Net Worth		**$63,320**
TOTAL LIABILITIES AND NET WORTH		**$127,360**

SAMPLE PLAN: SOURCES AND USE OF FUNDS

SOURCES AND USE OF FUNDS

Total Dollar Amount Being Sought: $160,000 in equity financing. The company prefers that this entire amount be secured from only one investor.

Funding Rounds: ComputerEase expects only one funding round for full financing. If the company were to later become a franchise, another funding round would be considered at that time.

USE OF FUNDS

Capital Expenditures

Leasehold Improvements	$10,000
Purchase of Equipment and Furniture	30,000
Total Capital Expenditures	**40,000**

Working Capital

Purchase of Inventory	10,000
Staff Expansion	50,000
Additional Marketing Activities	30,000
Other Business Expansion Activities	30,000
Total Working Capital	**120,000**

TOTAL USE OF FUNDS	**$160,000**

SAMPLE PLAN: ASSUMPTIONS

ASSUMPTIONS

The figures on the previous financial forms are based on these assumptions:

Sales by line ($ expressed in 000's)	2014 $ / Units	2015 $ / Units	2016 $ / Units	Growth Rate 2015–2016
Training Center classes (Corporate)	91 / 11	228 / 25	443 / 45	80%
On-Site (Corporate)	223 / 25	310.5 / 30	440.3 / 39	30%
Center classes (Saturday)	27.7 / 11	207.1 / 40	207.1 / 60	50%
Online classes	125 / 16	242.2 / 28	545.5 / 58	107%

These sales figures reflect price increases of 10% annually for Corporate Training Center classes and online classes; 15% in 2015 and 10% in 2016 for corporate on-site training classes, and 10% in 2015 and 15% in 2016 for Saturday classes.

Personnel

The staff size of the company (two FT professionals and one PT support) will stay constant for the remainder of 2014. In 2015, the payroll increases to four FT professionals, one FT support, and one PT support. In 2016, the payroll is projected at four FT professionals, one PT professional, and two FT support.

Expansion

Figures in these projections assume opening a second Training Center classroom on 1/1/15. Direct costs associated with expansion include leasehold improvements, equipment/furniture, and marketing. Additional operating costs include equipment rental and addition of a staff trainer. This expansion increases capacity in corporate training classes by 100%.

Financing

To date, ComputerEase has been financed by a $60,000 investment from Scott E. Connors; a $30,000, 10% interest-only loan from L. Silver (Mr. Connors' sister-in-law), due 12/31/14; and a $40,000 no-interest loan from Mr. Connors, principal due on or before 3/31/15. Projections call for the retirement of $30,000 of the Connors loan in 2014, with the remainder by 3/31/15, and the remainder of the Silver loan when due. The 2015–16 financial projections assume securing an additional $160,000 of investment income by 1/1/15.

CHAPTER

17

The Plan's Appendix

It's not over till it's over, and even then it's not over.

> **If you have a lot of appendices, put them in a separate binder, so the plan itself stays small."**
>
> *Ann Winblad*
> *Venture Capitalist*

Use an Appendix to Reinforce Your Plan's Content

One of the frustrations of developing a business plan is that you are limited in how much information you can include. You may be excited about your product's new packaging, a contract from a large customer, or positive market research results, but you should not go into great detail about these items in the business plan itself. Such details make the document too long.

Instead, your plan's Appendix is the proper place to provide information that supports, confirms, and reinforces conclusions you reach in the plan. An Appendix is where you give greater details about particular aspects covered in the plan, and you can include very specific details regarding market research, technology, location, and so on.

An Appendix is not the place, however, for any data that is essential to understanding your business. Essential information goes in the plan itself.

Guidelines

If you choose to include an Appendix, follow these guidelines:

1. Your plan must stand on its own; many people do not read appendices, especially on the first examination of a business plan.

2. You don't have to include an Appendix at all; add one only if you believe the additional information is compelling (in the case of a plan for outside financing) or can be used for reference (in the case of internal plans).

3. Do not put totally unrelated information in the Appendix; the material in the Appendix should be directly related to or supportive of information in the plan itself.

4. Keep it short. The Appendix should be no longer than the plan itself. If your plan and Appendix are both fairly long, consider putting the Appendix in a separate binder.

Remember, your plan must not seem overly long or intimidating to the reader, so give the same careful consideration to what you put in your Appendix as you give to what you put in the plan.

Appendix Content Options

The kinds of information described below are appropriate for inclusion in an Appendix. Notice that this material all supports information already in your plan.

Letters of Intent/Key Contracts

One of the very best items that can be included in an Appendix is a copy of a letter of intent to purchase or a contract from a key customer, especially for a new business. This immediately shows that the business has a source of income and that customers are interested in the product or service.

Endorsements

Letters, articles, or other information from credible sources, particularly customers, reinforce the sense that the company is capable and the product or service desirable. Laudatory newspaper or magazine articles about the company are appropriate and convey the message that the company is well-established or able to generate publicity.

Photos

Generally photos do not belong in the body of the business plan; so if photos of your product, location, or display cases are useful, include them in the Appendix. In most cases, avoid photos of management personnel.

List of Locations

If your company has numerous locations—stores, branch offices, plants—a complete list can go in the Appendix rather than in the plan.

Market Research Results

If you conducted extensive market research as part of your business planning process, you may want to include descriptions of your findings in the Appendix. You can also include information from city or county planning departments or other government agencies that give additional details about the nature of your market.

Resumes of Key Managers

If the resumes of your key managers are particularly impressive, consider including them in your Appendix; otherwise, the description in your Management section should suffice.

Technical Information

If your company is using or developing new technology, and the readers of your plan are knowledgeable in those areas, more-detailed descriptions of your technology can be placed in the Appendix rather than in the business plan. You may also want to include technical drawings.

Manufacturing Information

If yours is a manufacturing business, you may want to include a detailed description of the manufacturing process or a flow chart describing the process.

Marketing Material

You can include nonbulky marketing material, such as a brochure or leaflet. For cumbersome marketing materials, such as packaging, use a photograph.

APPENDIX CONTENT OPTIONS

Letters of Intent/ Key Contracts

Endorsements

Technical Information

Manufacturing Information

Photos

List of Locations

Marketing Material

Work Schedule

Market Research Results

Resumes of Key Managers

Floor Plan

Other Information

Work Schedule

You can include a work schedule describing how you utilize employees; such a schedule is useful when the company has more than one shift.

Floor Plan

Especially if yours is a retail or manufacturing business, you may want to include a floor plan showing the layout and use of space.

Other Information

You can also include other information derived from the business planning process, such as:

■ Competitive Analysis (see Chapter 8).

■ Marketing Budget (see Chapter 10).

■ Equipment Schedule (see Chapter 11).

Any other information that you believe supports and reinforces information in your plan can be included in the Appendix.

Chapter Summary

Use an Appendix to provide information that is too extensive to be included in your business plan itself. Remember, if you are submitting your business plan to outside financing sources, the Appendix is likely to be reviewed only by those who have already read the plan and decided that it warrants further examination. If readers lose interest in your plan itself, the Appendix will go untouched. If after reviewing your plan, however, they are still interested in your business, the Appendix becomes a subtle marketing tool. So be certain to use it only for information that reinforces the sense that yours is a well-conceived, well-run business.

> The only kind of market research that impresses me is to see what you've learned from testing your product in the real world and to get a list of those companies already using the product."
>
> *Ann Winblad*
> *Venture Capitalist*

SECTION II

Putting the Plan to Work

CHAPTER

18

Preparing, Presenting & Sending Out Your Plan

It's not just what you've got;
it's what you do with what you've got.

Putting Your Plan to Use

Ideally, this book has helped you work through the process of developing your plan and improved your understanding of the forces that affect your business success. If you now do nothing more than put the written document on the shelf and never look at it again, you will still have already reaped major benefits.

But a business plan is a working document, and you probably have a specific idea of how you intend to use it. Most likely, you want to use your business plan as 1) a tool for raising funds (either investments or loans); 2) an internal reference document to guide your company's development; or 3) a recruitment tool for key personnel—or all of the above. If you're using it for a class or a business plan competition, be certain to look at Chapter 20 for more insight.

Whether intended for internal or external use, your business plan must be made presentable for others. You must consider how you can best distribute the plan for maximum impact and how to make the finished plan an effective instrument for achieving your aims.

You have many different ways available in which to present your plan. Although a banker will probably want a written document, an investor or strategic partner may require something more compelling, such as an electronic presentation.

A Word About Confidentiality— Nondisclosure Agreements

Once you begin to circulate your business plan, you inevitably begin to worry about the confidentiality of your information. Obviously, you don't want your competitors, or potential competitors, to know your strategy or technology.

Most new entrepreneurs are probably overly concerned about issues of confidentiality. Very few business ideas, after all, are truly new—it's the execution rather than the concept that makes a business a success. Generally, bankers, **angel** investors, and venture capitalists respect the confidentiality of plans they receive; they're financiers, not entrepreneurs, and aren't interested in running businesses. Nevertheless, it pays to be careful.

To help ensure confidentiality, you may want to draw up a "nondisclosure agreement," or NDA, for the recipient to sign before receiving your plan. You can use NDAs with less-sophisticated investors, potential employees, suppliers, and the like.

> " If you need complete confidentiality, you should most likely not pursue venture capital as a source of funds. While venture capitalists are experienced in maintaining confidentiality, for a number of justifiable reasons, in general they will not sign confidentiality agreements. Also, if you do not need a lot of money at this stage, don't seek venture capital. You will be able to demand a better price and increase the likelihood of getting funding if the company is further developed."
>
> *Eugene Kleiner*
> *Venture Capitalist*

However, many professional investors—particularly venture capitalists—do not sign NDAs. This is standard policy with venture capitalists, and asking a venture capitalist to sign an NDA is viewed as a sign of inexperience. They see so many plans in so many related industries that they would inevitably have the possibility of a conflict. It is part of their business to respect the confidentiality of entrepreneurs, and they have their reputation at stake.

The best way to protect your information is to be selective about to whom you send your plan. Research your recipients and make certain they are not already funding a competitor. Check their reputations for honesty and discretion. Deal only with reputable people. On top of that, limit the number of copies of your plan in circulation and omit from your plan highly technical, sensitive information. You can provide that information later to only the most serious sources of potential funding.

An attorney can help you draft a nondisclosure agreement; an example is provided on page 336.

Preparing Your Plan for Distribution

Your plan should look as good as the business really is. It is a shame to have an outstanding business overlooked or turned down by investors merely because the plan doesn't represent the company well.

Before you prepare your plan for either internal or external distribution, refer back to Chapter 3. Now is the time to edit and proofread your plan; see how you can make the language more concise and clear. Have someone else edit and proofread the plan as well. You may want to use the services of a professional writer to help make your language clearer, or a graphic designer to help you lay out your plan or to create graphs and charts to enhance its impact.

Whether you prepare the plan yourself or with professional assistance, make certain it is a good representation of you and your company and is visually appealing. Pay attention to details of layout and graphics to make it easier to be read or skimmed quickly. Once you are confident that your plan is both easy to read and to skim, you can apply the final touches to prepare it for distribution.

Cover Sheet

The very first page in your plan should be a simple cover sheet (different from the cover letter). When binding your plan with a clear front cover (which is recommended), your cover sheet then becomes, in effect, your plan's cover. As such, it should make a positive first impression. It must be uncluttered and businesslike. On your cover sheet, include this information:

- The words "Business Plan"
- The name of your company
- The date
- A copy number

Success key term:

Angel
A private individual who invests their own money in new enterprises.

Nondisclosure Agreement

Nondisclosure Agreement

Re: (Company Name)

I agree that any information disclosed to me by _____
Company in connection with my review of the company will be considered proprietary and confidential, including all such information relating to the Company's past, present, or future business activities, research, product design or development, personnel, and business opportunities.

"Confidential Information" means any information disclosed, either directly or indirectly, in writing, orally, or by inspection of tangible objects (including business plans, research, product plans, products, services, customers, markets, software, inventions, processes, designs, drawings, engineering, marketing, or finances).

Confidential information shall not include information previously known to me or the general public or previously recognized as standard practice in the field. It shall also not include information that becomes generally available in the public domain through no action or inaction of myself, my employees, or others associated with me.

I agree not to use any Confidential Information for any purpose except to evaluate and, if applicable, implement a potential business relationship with _____ Company.
I agree not to disclose any Confidential Information to third parties or to anyone except those who are required to have the information in order to evaluate or engage in discussions concerning the contemplated business relationship.

I agree that for a period of five years, I will hold all confidential and proprietary information in confidence and will not use such information except as may be authorized by the Company and will prevent its unauthorized dissemination. I acknowledge that unauthorized disclosure could cause irreparable harm and significant injury to the Company. I agree that, on request, I will return all written or descriptive matter, including the business plan and supporting documents, to the Company.

Accepted and Agreed to:

_____

Signature

_____

Printed Name

_____

Company/Title

_____

Date

- A disclaimer or confidentiality statement

- The name, address, phone number, and email address of the contact person (for external distribution)

- The name of the division or department and contact person (for in-house corporate plans)

- The company logo, if desired

This sounds like a lot, but it's not. You should be able to put all this information on a cover sheet and still leave attractive white space on the page.

If you are using a cover other than a clear front cover with the cover sheet visible, make certain that the name of your company is printed on the cover. Funders often have stacks of business plans on their desks; you want them to be able to easily locate your plan without having to open the cover.

Both you and your readers will find that page numbers make it easy to refer to specific information when discussing your plan. Rather than numbering the pages consecutively from start to finish (page 1, 2, 3, etc.), a better method is to number pages by section and page. Thus your Executive Summary would be numbered 1-1, 1-2, 1-3, etc.; the next section 2-1, 2-2, 2-3, etc.; the next section 3-1, 3-2, 3-3, etc.; and so on. This pagination method enables you to update or make changes in one section without having to reprint the entire plan. Of course, if you change the order of sections to tailor your plan for specific readers, you have to renumber the plan.

Table of Contents

Any plan more than 10 pages long benefits from a table of contents. Place it at the beginning of your plan, immediately after your cover sheet and before the Executive Summary. Title your table of contents simply "Contents," and list the sections and page numbers on which each section starts. If you want to draw attention to particular portions of certain sections, do so by using subheadings for those sections in the table of contents, but don't get carried away. After all, a business plan should be relatively short, so that your readers can find their way around it fairly easily.

Date

Because securing financing can take a long while, be careful about distributing a plan that appears outdated. A reader who in November receives a plan dated "March" can easily assume that you have met with nothing but rejections for many months. Thus, it may be advisable to use only the year on the cover sheet: "Business Plan, 2015." You can also choose to generate a new cover sheet for each recipient, including the month and year: "Business Plan, August 2015." You needn't cite anything more specific than the month and year.

Copy Number

Number each copy of your business plan before distribution, and keep a list of which individual has received which copy. This way you can keep track of how many copies are in circulation, and, if necessary, can ask to have a copy returned. Most important, if a copy is circulated without your permission, it's easier to trace the responsible party.

Further, since you may revise your business plan as your business develops, you may produce different versions of your plan. To keep track of which version a recipient has, you may want to devise a code number or letter along with the copy number. Refrain from writing "Version 16" on your plan; it makes a poor impression. A code could look like "Copy C.4," which might indicate to you that it's the third version, fourth copy. "Copy 3.4" could indicate it's the third version, copy four. Or you could call it "Copy 7.4" to mean the version you completed in July, fourth copy.

Disclaimer

When circulating your business plan to outside funding sources, you want to make certain you don't find yourself in legal hot water. Difficulties can arise when you offer ownership in your company in return for an investment; in actuality, you are selling stock in your company, and federal law regulates the sale of stock.

The best way to protect yourself is to consult an attorney. You can also include a disclaimer on the front cover that indicates your plan is not an offering for sale but rather a document for information purposes only. The same disclaimer can also be used to help protect the confidentiality of your business plan, especially when you are not adding a nondisclosure agreement. Your attorney can provide you with the best language, but a typical disclaimer might look like this:

> *"This document is for information only and is not an offering for sale of any securities of the Company. Information disclosed herein should be considered proprietary and confidential. The document is the property of _____ Company and may not be disclosed, distributed, or reproduced without the express written permission of _____ Company."*

Layout, Design, and Presentation

Because you must limit the total number of pages in your business plan, you may be tempted to fill each page from top to bottom. Resist this urge. A page crammed with too much information intimidates and may annoy the reader.

People make up their minds about how difficult a page is to read before they actually start reading it. Therefore, leave sufficient "white space" (unused, blank space) on the pages of your plan to make the text appear inviting to the reader.

"Frame" your text by leaving a border around it. Generally, leave about a 1" margin on the top and right side, with a little more (such as $1^1/_4$") on the bottom and left side (to allow for binding). Print on only one side of each page.

Single-space your text, but leave double spaces between paragraphs. Keep your paragraphs short. Use either underlined or bold-print headers (such as the one near the top of the next page) to begin each section or show a change of topic.

Use charts and graphs in your business plan. These engage the reader and highlight impressive and important information.

Choosing a Typeface

Software programs provide many choices of serif and sans-serif typefaces. A serif typeface is a more traditional style, having small fine lines or "feet" that make words and lines of type easier to read; this type style is especially effective when a document has a lot of text, as in the case of a business plan.

More modern-looking, sans-serif type has no fine lines. Use it for headings, lists, and other places where there is a limited amount to read.

Shown in the graphic below, in their actual form, are a few of the more commonly used serif and sans-serif typefaces.

TYPEFACE OPTIONS

Serif	Sans-Serif
Garamond	Univers Condensed
Times	**Univers Bold**
Times Roman	Helvetica Condensed
Bembo	**Helvetica Bold**
Palatino	**Arial Black**

When selecting type for your business plan, follow these guidelines:

T

abc — Choose type that is easy to read and businesslike in appearance.

ABC — Use no more than two plain and one italic typeface in your plan.

Abc — Use serif type for the text, and serif or sans-serif type for headlines.

Type size is measured in "points." For text, 10-point type is recommended; smaller than 9 points is a strain to read. Section headings and titles generally can be set in 12- or 14-point type.

The Final Step: Editing Your Plan

Once you finish your plan, go through it again thoroughly. Find ways to make your sentences shorter and easier to understand.

Eliminate unnecessary words. Change passive verbs and jargon to clear, active language. For example, instead of saying "Profitability will have been reached by Teddy's Dog Togs in its third year of operation," be more direct with a sentence like this: "Teddy's Dog Togs will show a profit by year three."

A business plan must inspire trust. Misspellings, typographical errors, and improper grammar undermine trust. Proofread your plan for such mistakes and have at least one other eagle-eyed person proofread it as well.

Preparing an Electronic Presentation

For most sophisticated investors, such as venture capitalists, you will want to—or need to—prepare a computer presentation, outlining the highlights of your business plan. A computer slide presentation is an excellent way of conveying the most important aspects of your business in a short time. (This type of presentation may be referred to as a "slide show," a "deck," or a "preso" since each frame of a computer presentation is called a "slide.")

Some venture capitalists and other investment groups now prefer to see computer presentations instead of written business plans. While they used to ask for your executive summary and financials first, now they ask for your slides and financials. However, you will still need a written plan, either to be reviewed before you are granted a meeting or to leave behind after you meet with potential investors.

In some cases, you won't present your plan in person. Many investors will likely ask for your slides before they will consider looking at your plan. In that case, you will send your computer presentation electronically. For this reason, you must create a presentation that's compelling enough to stand on its own without a presenter.

Take advantage of the electronic medium. Consider embedding video or audio into your slide show. Your content can include a prototype if you have one, a demonstration such as how your service will be performed, a look at your location, or anything else that will make your plan more comprehensible and exciting. You can link to a password-protected YouTube video if you have one. You may also choose to put the slides online on a password-protected site (more on this on page 341).

A computer presentation is an excellent opportunity to tell certain investors the strongest reasons to invest in your business. Since you control the content of your presentation, you get to highlight those aspects of your business that will be most compelling to your financing prospect.

Of course, the computer presentation should contain all the major points of your business plan. You need not present them in the exact order of the written plan, but you may have to explain some elements before other points will be understandable. If you make your presentation in person, the investors will interrupt you to ask questions, challenge your assumptions, and so forth, so make certain you get to your most important points early in your slides. If there's an obvious issue with your plan, such as a large competitor entering your same niche, address it up front before your investors do.

Adjust the content of your slides according to the knowledge base of your audience. You don't want to bore them with information they already know or don't need to know, such as the nitty-gritty details of your day-to-day operations. You can, however, include background information for those recipients who need it. And do your homework. Some quick research on your potential investors can reap big rewards. If you include some of this information in your presentation, your credibility increases dramatically.

When putting together your slides, don't try to overwhelm an investor with too many. Remember, your slides are meant to whet their appetite.

> " The value of a Power-Point presentation is that you (the entrepreneur) get to control the agenda of the meeting. Otherwise we can have an open-ended discussion, but I'm going to control the meeting through my questions rather than you guiding it through your presentation. If you have a computer presentation, you can make sure you make all the points you want to make."
>
> *Mark Gorenberg*
> *Venture Capitalist*

> " Increasingly, we're seeing people delivering Power-Points, but they still have to have the essential information. Having a business plan that is clear and that everyone understands is a sign of a sophisticated management team."
>
> *Lauren Flanagan*
> *Cofounder and Managing Director, BELLE Capital USA*

While there is no exact number that will be right for every business, you should be able to convey all the key details of your company in 12 slides. If you have too many and you are presenting in person, you're going to feel as if you have to rush through your presentation to get to them all.

The text of each slide should be primarily in short, bulleted points. You rarely need whole sentences. Put no more than 3–5 bullet points on each slide. You can use an effect to make bullet points appear one-by-one; this gives you control over the flow of information during your presentation.

If you are presenting your slides in person, practice first. Make certain you are comfortable working with the computer and the software so that you are not distracted during your meeting. *Use the sample slide presentation "12 Critical Slides" on pages 343–346 as a guide when developing your electronic presentation. The sample outlines the different slides you need, and describes what information to include in each one.*

Putting Your Business Plan Online

Some entrepreneurs, especially those involved in Internet-related or technology businesses, may choose to put their business plan on a website. There are many advantages to having your plan online: It is easily available to you or potential investors, you can update it frequently, and investors can access it anywhere they can get online.

Of course, there are also many disadvantages. The biggest one is security. NEVER put a business plan on the Internet without making it password-protected. Even if you think no one will find it because it is at some obscure site, search engines may turn up your pages when looking for keywords. Moreover, investors will be skeptical of any business plan that is essentially out there for the entire world to see.

Another disadvantage of having your plan online is that many people find it difficult to read a long document on a screen (assuming they don't print it out). Readers can't "flip through" your plan to get an overview of your business, colorful graphics might not catch their eye, and if your potential reader, such as someone traveling, is away from online access, they have no way of bringing your plan along to read.

If you do put your business plan online, create a homepage with links to each section and/or subsections of your plan. You want readers to be able to easily get to the information that interests them without having to scroll through pages of text.

Keep in mind that financial forms can be particularly difficult to read online and the formatting may be lost or distorted when printed out. Graphics, however, usually work extremely well online.

For all these reasons, always have printed copies of your business plan as well. Don't let the Internet be your only method of presenting your business to the investment world.

> " Your PowerPoint presentation should be a half hour at most. First and foremost we need to understand what you're selling. That's the name of the game from the first slide to the last slide. You're telling a story: have a beginning, middle, and end. Don't tell the end of the mystery first. Tell us the pieces of the story: the big idea that gets you excited, the execution, the fact that you're the ones to do it. Set it up, then give us the punch line. End with what value you add, so we can really be excited."
>
> *Andrew Anker*
> *Venture Capitalist*

Updating Your Plan

Your quest for financing may take many months, and your plans for your company may change during that time, especially if yours is a new enterprise. You want to make certain that your written plan is always reasonably current with your actual business strategy and position.

So, before sending out a plan to a new financing source, review its contents and update it. Bring your financial information up to the close of the last month or quarter, revise your financial projections to reflect recent developments, and add descriptions of any new members of management.

Chapter Summary

The appearance of your business plan should be of the same high quality as its contents. It should be a good representation of you and your company. Prepare your plan with care, and include active language, graphs and charts, and attractive page layouts and businesslike typefaces. Pay attention to the final touches such as the cover sheet and table of contents. Once you have completed your written plan, review and edit it carefully—and update it as needed. Before you distribute it, you may want to draw up a Nondisclosure Agreement for less sophisticated investors, potential employees, suppliers, and the like to sign.

Consider preparing a slide presentation, as more-sophisticated investors will want to see one before even looking at the written plan. You may also want to put your plan online on a password-protected site.

12 CRITICAL SLIDES

Title slide: **your company's name, a short company description, name of presenter(s) if presenting in person.**

What We Do

- Business software training services for corporate clients
- Classes conducted on-premise or online
- B2B and B2C target markets
- First 9 months: $171K revenue

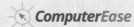

Your elevator pitch: **a succinct description of your products or services, market, and competitive advantages. Use vibrant language, and if possible, embed audio or video to demonstrate your product or service.**

The Opportunity

- Corporate training in No. America = $130 billion industry
- 42% of training outsourced = $54.8 billion
- No market leader
- Huge growth in online training
- Franchise opportunities

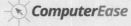

Size of opportunity: **this is what investors — VCs even more so than angels — want to know. To what size can your company potentially grow and what are your plans for future development?**

Your specific target customers: who they are and the customer needs that your product or service will meet.

Target Market

- Corporations with 50+ employees
- Government, insurance, financial, health care, engineering, colleges
- 2,000+ corporations in Vespucci area
- Online market includes U.S. and other English-speaking countries

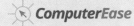

The market size: numbers and dollars, past growth, growth forecasts.

Market Size

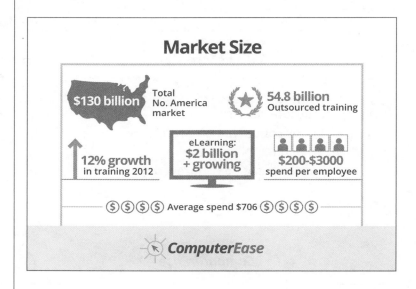

$130 billion — Total No. America market

54.8 billion — Outsourced training

12% growth in training 2012

eLearning: $2 billion + growing

$200-$3000 spend per employee

Average spend $706

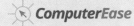

The competition: division of market share, how your product compares to theirs, your value proposition in comparison to the competition's, and barriers to entry.

Competition

Current competition:
- Heavily fragmented, no leader
- 3 national training companies
- Online colleges & universities
- Small companies & individual trainers

Competitive advantages:
- Strong team; experienced trainers
- Outstanding training materials
- Corporate market focus
- Certified training

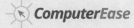

The Team

Founders:

Scott E. Connors: President
• Experience selling tech services

Susan Alexander: VP, Marketing
• Experience selling to target market

Advisory Committee includes:
• Top customer targets
• Dr. A. A. Arnold, Instructional Design

 **ComputerEase**

*Your team: **who they are, their past successes and experience, and why they are qualified to do the job.***

Business Model

• B2B: Top pricing for customized training
• B2C: Top pricing for certification training
• In-house sales team
• Per-seat annual subscription

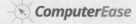 **ComputerEase**

*The business model: **how you will distribute your product, pricing strategies, how you will reach your customers.***

Milestones

• January, 2014 – launched
• August, 2014 – opened first center
• To date
    • $171K revenue
    • 184 training sessions
    • 11 key corporate clients
• 2015 – second center opens
• 5 years
    • $5 million annual online sales
    • 5 locations
    • $8 million total annual sales

 **ComputerEase**

*Milestones: **a time line that outlines when you expect to reach key achievements.***

inancials: a brief summary of key oints from your income statement, alance sheet, and/or cash flow rojections.

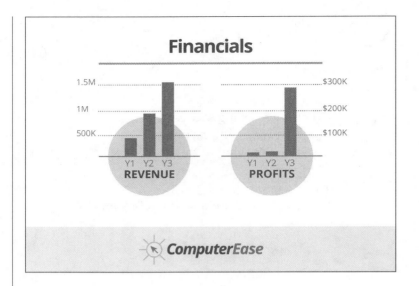

Financials

1.5M $300K
1M $200K
500K $100K

Y1 Y2 Y3   Y1 Y2 Y3
REVENUE   **PROFITS**

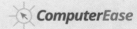
ComputerEase

nding: how much you are asking for this round, how many future rounds e expected, how much you will quest during those rounds, and w the funds will be used.

Funding

- Funds sought: $160,000
  - Training Center, staff, marketing
- Funding to date
  - $60K investment – Connors
  - $70K loans – Connors/family
- No future funding rounds

ComputerEase

he investment opportunity: potential xit strategies and financial return for nvestors.

The Upside

- High projected annual sales & ongoing profitability
- Proven business concept
- Key customers secured: RockSolid Insurance, Vespucci National Bank, Vespucci State University
- No significant local/regional competition
- Strong potential franchise opportunity

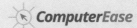
ComputerEase

CHAPTER

19 Looking for Money

> *Money buys you time: When you run out of money, your business runs out of time.*

> "Getting an investor is like getting married. But it's harder to divorce your investors than it is to divorce your spouse."
>
> **Mark Gorenberg**
> **Venture Capitalist**

> "I went to Silicon Valley in 1999, and people in venture funding said they weren't seeing women founders. So we looked for women-led businesses that could scale. We hoped to find 100 companies. We got 350 applications; we were overwhelmed!"
>
> **Kay Koplovitz**
> **Chair, Kate Spade**

Not All Money Is Equal

When you start to look for financing, you imagine that you'll take any money you can find, but you should exercise care. The various sources of money require different types of return on their investments, have varying levels of sophistication and comfort with risk, and provide you with significantly different auxiliary benefits and disadvantages.

Whose money do you want? As you begin your search for financing, stop and ask yourself these questions:

- Are you willing to give up some amount of ownership of your company?
- Are you willing to have debt that you must repay?
- Are you willing to risk property or other assets?
- How much control of the direction and operation of your company are you willing to relinquish?
- What other help do you want from a funder, besides money?
- How fast do you want to grow?
- How big do you want your company to be?
- What do you see as the long-term relationship between you and your funding source?

Keep in mind that you are going to have an ongoing relationship with your money source; make sure it is someone you can live with.

Debt Versus Equity

Everybody who gives you money for your business wants something in return. Funders either want their money paid back with interest or want to participate in the profits your company eventually makes. There are two basic formulations for financing your business: taking on debt, or giving up equity (ownership interest) in return for investment income.

Debt Financing

When you acquire debt financing, you have the advantage of keeping complete ownership of your business. You keep control, and you keep all the eventual profits. You borrow a specific amount, and you have to repay only that amount plus interest, regardless of how profitable your company becomes. The lender does not share in the profits.

Because lenders do not reap the benefits of substantial profits, they have to reduce risk as much as possible. To do so, they may ask you to secure the loan with the collateral of your assets (including your home). Using debt financing may jeopardize these assets if your business income is unable to pay back the loan, and if the business fails, you may still have the debt. This is a major risk, especially for a new entrepreneur. You should be extremely cautious before risking your home, your children's college education, or any other funds on which your lifestyle depends.

Loans from banks and other lending institutions (often referred to as conventional financing) are difficult to secure for new enterprises. Many banks will only finance businesses in operation more than three years, and very small businesses may have difficulty at any time. Credit unions may be somewhat more lenient than banks. And for very short-term financing, some small companies have even used cash advances on credit cards.

Be especially careful of shady lending companies that prey on small business start-ups; these companies make easy loans, requiring significant personal collateral, knowing most of the businesses they fund will fail and the assets will be seized. Or they charge hefty up-front fees to supposedly help find financing they can never truly secure.

Well-established businesses are far better candidates for conventional financing than are start-ups. A healthy, ongoing business needing funds for modest expansion activities should certainly consider bank financing. If the business is incorporated, the company itself can take on the loan debt and shield the owners from personal liability in most cases.

Equity Financing

By contrast, equity financing allows you to avoid the personal risk of taking on debt. Instead of committing to repay a specific amount of money, you give the investor a piece of the eventual profits. This takes the form of stock in the company or a percentage ownership. If your company is very successful, an equity investor may end up receiving many times the amount originally invested. However, if the company fails to produce sufficient profits, these investors may never get their money back.

Thus, equity investors often want to participate in decision-making to ensure that the company operates in a manner that will produce profits. They may take seats on your Board of Directors or even play an active role in management.

In some cases, you may have to give up so much equity that others actually have controlling interest in your company. In this case, the investors might even be able to remove you from management altogether. Still, a capable investor can bring you sound business advice, useful business contacts, and maybe even links to additional future financing.

Equity financing is a usual and practical method of funding start-up companies. Most of the best-known entrepreneurial high-technology firms are financed through equity investors. The popularity of investing in start-ups—and thus the availability of money—goes through cycles. It is far easier to get a new venture funded at a time when the marketplace is rewarding new entrepreneurial endeavors, particularly through growth or increase in the valuation of the company and its stock.

> " If you start from scratch and you want steep growth, you have to have the ability to finance internally due to very large margins, or you'll have to reconcile yourself to either selling out or accepting financing from outside sources and giving up equity."
>
> *Larry Leigon*
> *Founder, Ariel Vineyards*

Success key terms

Corporate Venture Capital (CVC)
Venture capital funds established by corporations.

Crowdfunding
A method of raising money from a large number of people (the "crowd") for a new venture, cause, artistic endeavor, or product. Typically, the funds are raised through online, crowdfunding "platforms."

Elevator Pitch
A concise summary of a company's service, business, or product idea that can be delivered in a very short time.

Because it has proved so successful, equity investing has become institutionalized through venture capital firms, "angel" investors, and other entities, such as small business investment companies. But equity financing need not be sought only from these professional funding sources. Your accountant or attorney may put you in touch with someone who is looking for an investment, or your sister-in-law or college roommate may be willing to underwrite your business.

Sources of Money

Where do you go to find the money you need? And what are the obligations and benefits you receive from each source? Two charts on pages 364–365 outline the various sources of debt and equity financing available for businesses.

When choosing a financing source (and you *do* choose them, just as they choose you), pay particular attention to the personal qualities of the individual and the reputation of the venture financing company you use. Just as not all banks are alike, certainly not all investors are alike.

You want to choose a financing source that:

■ Stands by you during difficult times and works to overcome setbacks.

■ Deals with you in a professional and businesslike manner.

■ Values your contribution to the company.

■ Maintains open and clear communication with you.

■ Is fair, ethical, and honest.

Ideally, your financing source also brings you sound business advice, excellent business connections, and the ability to help secure future financial support. These qualities are particularly important when looking for an angel investor or venture capitalist. Such an investor is likely to play a very active part in your company; make certain that it is someone who offers your enterprise other benefits in addition to money.

Venture Capitalists

As you search for money, you probably will hear the term "venture capitalist" quite often, but those who use the term may be referring to different entities. True venture capital firms are among the most sophisticated investors available, typically providing an entrepreneur with more than money. Their knowledge, experience, and connections may prove to be as important to your company as the dollars they bring.

Venture capital firms invest large sums of money pooled from various sources such as pension funds and institutional investors. These private firms are established expressly for the purpose of investing in developing companies. Their partners and associates generally have a background in business management and/or the industries in which they invest.

Venture capital firms typically invest only in companies they believe can grow to be very large: often in the hundreds of millions or even billions of dollars in eventual value. As such, they generally invest large amounts of

> **There's an unspoken question from entrepreneurs when dealing with investors: 'how soon will they replace me?' The truth is, male or female, not every founder can scale the company, and there comes a time when they need to be replaced."**
>
> *Lauren Flanagan*
> *Cofounder and Managing Director, BELLE Capital USA*

> **An entrepreneur should only go to a venture capitalist if they want the added value a venture capitalist can bring. With a venture capitalist, you're asking them not only to invest money, but to use every leverage point they have, each business and industry contact, leadership and support in subsequent funding rounds, and an honest critique of your business. And it's useful to have the venture capitalist serve as a member of your Board of Directors."**
>
> *Ann Winblad*
> *Venture Capitalist*

money at one time to help these companies grow quickly. They are not appropriate vehicles for companies with more modest goals or financial needs.

Venture capital firms specialize in particular industries or stages of a company's development. If your company is presently in formation, you need to look for a venture capital firm that invests in "seed" or "early-stage" companies.

Expect venture capitalists to take a very active role in the growth and development of your company—sitting on your Board of Directors, selecting key executives, perhaps even determining the nature of your role in the business. Because they will have such influence, if not control, over the fate of you and your company, choose your venture capitalist wisely.

Private or "Angel" Investors

A frequent source of capital for new or smaller entrepreneurial companies is the private, or "angel," investor. Private investors are usually well-to-do individuals, seeking investments that provide more personal satisfaction and the potential of greater financial reward than are offered by conventional investments such as stocks and bonds. Private investors can be an excellent source of financing.

> " Angels are looking for companies that are scalable and capital efficient. We're not in a position to fund businesses that need $25 million—lots of capital—like venture capitalists invest."
>
> *Lauren Flanagan*
> *Cofounder and Managing Director, BELLE Capital USA*

	Angel Investor vs. Venture Capitalist	
Growth company	**Investment criteria**	Extremely high-growth company
Personal assets	**Source of investment dollars**	Other people's money; institutional funds
$25,000–$2,000,000	**Investment range**	$2,000,000+
3–10 times original investment	**Expected return**	5–10 times original investment
Seed, start-up, or early	**Typical stage of investment**	High-growth start-up and expansion
Early funding and hands-on expertise	**What they bring to the deal**	Large amounts of money, team building, industry-specific strengths
Some to significant	**Extent of due diligence**	Significant to huge amount
Less likely	**Replace founder as CEO?**	More likely
1–3 per year	**Number of deals**	15–18 per fund per year

Being an angel investor has become more popular over the years, and there are now organizations or groups of angel investors. These groups help facilitate meetings between entrepreneurs and potential investors. Often, angel investors who are part of an angel network can provide a broader range of assistance (in addition to money) than can a single private investor. Other methods of finding angel investors are through professional financial advisors, accountants, attorneys, and the like, who often know of wealthy individuals seeking investment opportunities.

Of course, the quality and nature of private investors varies widely. Some are entrepreneurs who were successful in business and now want to use their money and expertise to invest in companies related to their area of expertise. These angels may bring outstanding assets to your company.

> " The good thing about talking to a venture capitalist is that they will bring you down to earth. It's not that they're negative, but they'll give you a feel for what it will really take to succeed. With a private investor, a relative or friend, you won't get realistic input. With a venture capitalist, you get more than just money, you get partners who give you valuable help. They can introduce you to others and share the benefit of their experience. But with this help, you also get supervision and someone looking over your shoulder. But if your plan can attract venture capital, you should pursue it."
>
> *Eugene Kleiner*
> *Venture Capitalist*

Other private investors may have little to offer besides money. Less-sophisticated investors often have unrealistic expectations regarding the amount and timing of profits. Frequently, they are unfamiliar and uncomfortable with risk, and they may apply pressure for producing profits far earlier than a business can reasonably manage or than is healthy. If you do pursue private investors, make certain that the investor understands the nature of your business, and be particularly conservative in your projections of how much profit you will produce and when.

Corporate Investors

Other potential source of funding for some start-ups are the venture capital funds established by corporations. **Corporate venture capital (CVC)** funds have been set up by a few very large corporations that see the potential of investing in high-potential, early-stage entrepreneurial ventures—especially in technology and biotech industries. Recognizing the significant innovations introduced by start-ups and early-stage enterprises, CVCs have become active investors.

Corporations invest in start-ups and early-stage companies for many reasons, but in almost all cases, the investment must make strategic sense for the corporation itself. They may see the start-up's product or service as complementary to their current corporate offerings or as a potential competitor that they'd rather own. Corporate venture investing tends to be cyclical—increasing in times of strong economies—so when the economy weakens, corporate venture investing is typically cut back.

Corporate venture funds tend to be more conservative in their choice of investment than traditional VCs or angel investors. CVCs tend to invest in early-stage companies that have already reached significant milestones—have secured substantial revenues, have secured patents, or have in other ways shown a proof of concept. As a result, deals with CVCs tend to be significantly larger than deals with VCs or angel investors—in terms of amount of funds invested and at later stages of a start-up's development.

Securing a corporation as an investment partner is a two-edged sword for a start-up. A corporation may offer more generous terms, higher valuation, and more money. They may be able to help open doors to vendors and customers, help you understand your industry better, and provide infrastructure—enabling you to concentrate on your product or service instead of administrative concerns.

However, CVCs may or may not be sophisticated in dealing with their investment companies—they may not understand the entrepreneurial mind-set and timelines; they may be bureaucratic or overly eager for short-term results. In terms of product development, the corporation may push you to take their needs into greater consideration than your own entrepreneurial concepts.

Ask a final question when considering approaching corporations for investment: Will such an investment help you get customers, or will it scare away your corporate investor's competitors?

Small Business Investment Companies

Some private firms exist to provide both investment financing and long-term loans to small businesses. Examples are Small Business Investment Companies (SBICs) and Specialized Small Business Investment Companies (SSBICs). Some SBICs provide only equity; others rely on debt; and still others provide either. Each SBIC has its own policy.

SBICs are licensed by the U.S. Small Business Administration (SBA) and may receive funds from the government for the purpose of investing in small businesses. SBICs are willing to consider any small business, while SSBICs restrict their investments to companies operated by minority or economically disadvantaged entrepreneurs.

SBICs are good vehicles for financing a small business. However, most of them maintain rigorous evaluation procedures, and you will have to meet some of the same criteria required when applying for conventional financing or funding from venture capitalists. Many of the SBICs now only make loans, and they will seek the same type of collateral and evidence of creditworthiness as banks.

U.S. Small Business Administration

The SBA guarantees loans from other institutions; it does not make loans directly (except for Vietnam-era veterans and disabled persons). If you are seeking financing, the SBA can provide you with a list of lending institutions active in giving loans to small businesses. Remember, these banks and institutions must approve your application, so you must meet bank criteria to qualify. Typically, new businesses do not qualify for SBA-guaranteed loans. The SBA guarantee, however, sets interest limits and may make a difference if the lending institution is "on the fence" about your loan. Expect to provide a personal guarantee for any loan you are granted.

The SBA has created some other loan programs that may be more accessible for new businesses. The "micro-loan" program offers very small amounts of money to young companies. These are administered through nonprofit and community organizations.

Friends and Family Members

Be careful when financing your business through family or friends, with either loans or investments. This money may be the easiest to secure, but may cause you to risk personal relationships; by mixing your personal and business affairs, you may find you make both your business and your personal life more difficult. Unsophisticated investors are nervous about money—they don't understand that it takes time before profits are realized. They view every natural delay or setback with alarm.

If you do take a loan from a personal source, later repay it with the required interest, and subsequently become very successful, the friend or relative may not understand why he or she does not participate in the profits. And, if you are unable to pay back the loan, the relative may never forget and may remind you of your failure at every family occasion for the next 20 years.

> " For a bank, it's more important to have our fallback positions covered than our upside measured. A bank is different than a venture capitalist; we don't get larger profits if the company is very successful. So we spend most of our time assessing the fallbacks in a plan in case of error. The fallbacks we look to are receivables, guarantees [collateral], inventory, and fixed assets."
>
> *Robert Mahoney*
> *Corporate Banker*

> " One of the differences with women investors is we want to make money, but we're doing this to pay back too. In the past, women were philanthropists; they gave money away. We're trying to teach women to be more comfortable with investing."
>
> *Lauren Flanagan*
> *Cofounder and Managing Director, BELLE Capital USA*

Customers—Raising Money through Revenue

Never forget the power of making sales. The very best money comes from customers. With that income stream, you neither have to give up a piece of your company (as with investors) nor do you (necessarily) have to take on debt (as with a loan). In the process of looking for money, don't overlook the potential of finding money through actual sales.

Customers bring you more than money. They show potential investors that you have a company that is meeting real market needs. Having orders, of course, may cost money. If you are fortunate enough to land a big order when your company is still young, you may not have the resources to fill those orders. But this is a better time to approach financing sources. You may find a bank or other lender much more receptive when you have a contract in hand. Some banks are particularly aimed at entrepreneurs. You may also find that investors are much more willing to meet with you when you have customers, especially if any of your customers are companies that demonstrate to them your ability to land important deals.

The fund-raising process can take a long time, so consider the possibility of building your business through income while you look for the capital you need. Sales are good.

Crowdfunding

For many years, if you wanted to secure investors for your new company, product, or creative project, you had to solicit funds either from a small number of friends and family, or from VCs or angels. It was difficult—both logistically and legally—to reach out to a large number of acquaintances and strangers who might believe in your concept and be willing to help fund it.

However, both technological and legal developments have made securing investment money—and/or raising money through early presales—possible through a process broadly referred to as "**crowdfunding**."

When people refer to crowdfunding, they generally mean raising money in return for a small amount of stock or ownership in the new company. However, there are two types of crowdfunding:

- **Nonequity Crowdfunding:** soliciting funds in return for some type of benefit that does not include receiving stock or equity. Benefits might include such rewards as prerelease products, invitations to special events, recognition as a sponsor, T-shirts or other gifts; this kind of crowdfunding has fewer legal restrictions than equity-related crowdfunding.

- **Equity Crowdfunding:** soliciting funds from a large number of individuals in return for small amounts of stock or equity in the new company. The rules and regulations for this type of crowdfunding continue to evolve. In the United States, there are both federal and state laws covering this kind of solicitation.

Historically, to protect unsophisticated people from losing money in high-risk and uncertain ventures, many countries have limited the type of person who could invest in such businesses. In the United States, only "accredited investors"—those who had assets sufficient enough that they could afford to lose their investment, or those who had significant invest-

Crowdfunding Pros and Cons

Pros	Cons
Market feedback: You get real-time feedback from the people you value most—potential customers.	**Your idea is public:** On a crowdfunding platform, anyone can see what you're planning, including potential competitors.
Customer engagement: You can develop highly enthusiastic fans before you even launch a product or company.	**Marketing ability:** To raise sufficient funds, you need to generate a great deal of interest in your idea, requiring significant marketing effort.
More control: Since equity is spread around so many small investors, you don't have to answer to one or two major financial backers.	**Limited fund-raising rounds:** You may not be able to raise more money when needed to grow; start-ups often return to professional investors for second or third rounds of funding.
Raise more money: You may be able to raise money for projects that professional investors are not interested in.	**Unsophisticated investors:** Public supporters do not bring the business knowledge, contacts, and financial acumen of professional investors.
Anyone can do it: You don't need to know or have access to VCs or private investors.	**Time:** You will only succeed if you make the crowdfunding aspect of your company a top priority.
Marketing tool: A very successful campaign can drive traffic to your website and social media outlets, and create awareness about your company.	**Legal concerns:** You'll need to navigate a still-evolving sea of laws at both the federal and state level.

ment experience—could invest in these fledgling ventures. Most new companies could secure funds from no more than 35 nonaccredited investors.

This policy worked well to protect the general public until the "dot-com" era in the late 1990s, when suddenly, many people became extremely rich from investments in early-stage Internet companies. But, due to the accredited investor rule (and other Securities regulations), average small investors were kept from getting in on the ground floor of the few blockbuster investments. Of course, they were also protected from losing money from the many flops. Yet, there seemed to be a basic unfairness. Importantly, such investing restricitons also severely limited the amount of money available to entrepreneurs for new ventures.

By the second decade of the 21st century, "crowdsourcing" on the Internet—engaging with a broad number of people for ideas on new business concepts—became increasingly popular. Through social media and other sites, entrepreneurs, inventors, artists, and others were soliciting ideas and support for bands, creative endeavors, nonprofit organizations, causes, and the like.

This led to entrepreneurs and inventors using crowdsourcing to make early sales of their prerelease products to fund their start-up. In return for a certain "donation," supporters would receive products once they finally became available. In essence, these prerelease "customers" were crowdfunding the new business, instead of professional investors.

To help facilitate such crowdfunding, a number of platforms launched, such as IndieGoGo (www.indiegogo.com) and Kickstarter (www.kickstarter.com). At first, such platforms generally focused on creative or artistic endeavors. Later, some of them evolved to specifically help fund new products and companies. Many crowdfunding sites now serve specific industries or niches, such as CircleUp (www.circleup.com) for consumer and retail products, RallyMe (www.rallyme.com) to raise support for athletes, and Mosaic (www.joinmosaic.com) for solar projects.

One of the great successes that demonstrated the potential for crowdfunding was Pebble, a "smart watch," which raised over $10 million in presales of product on Kickstarter, after the founders failed to raise money through traditional venture capital sources.

Securities rules prohibited these crowdfunding ventures from offering equity, or shares of ownership, to funders. Yet, it was clear that the general public had a large appetite for supporting, and investing in, early-stage ventures. In response, new laws were enacted in the United States to allow crowdfunding in return for equity.

KEYS TO SUCCESS IN CROWDFUNDING:

- **Have the right type of business or product.** For crowdfunding success, your idea must be easily understandable by a large number of people (on that platform). Consumer, food, consumer electronics, and fashion products are particularly well suited to this. Complex concepts and many business-to-business ventures are likely to have a harder time gathering widespread support.

- **Create a compelling video.** A great video helps engage potential funders, as most funders will want to hear your story, see you, and view prototypes of your product (if any).

- **Raise sufficient funds.** On some crowdsourcing platforms, you don't receive any money until your goal amount is raised in total. This means you want to set an achievable fund-raising target. However, on some platforms, you can raise no more than the financial target you originally set. So you want to make sure you are raising enough to execute on your vision. This can be very hard to get right—even for seasoned entrepreneurs.

- **Choose the right crowdfunding platform.** Make sure the platform you choose meets your particular needs—type of product/service, type of rewards/equity you can give, amount of money you can raise and whether you need to raise the full amount before receiving any of it.

- **Have good-quality photos as part of your campaign.** Pics help supporters spread the word through social media.
- **Have a "coolness" factor.** Your idea is more likely to garner support and go viral if it's unique, attractive, or cutting-edge.
- **Plan a marketing campaign.** You must plan your crowdfunding fundraising campaign like you would for launching any new product. It will take time, effort, and creativity.

To search for a crowdfunding platform that meets your needs, check out CrowdsUnite (www.crowdsunite.com).

Improving Your Chances of Getting Funded

When using your plan to raise money, you can increase your chances of getting funded by researching potential funders, their interests, and their areas of expertise. You can further enhance the possibility of success by understanding how the funding process works, how long it takes, and how to stay in touch with potential funders.

Researching Your Recipients

It pays to do a little homework on potential funders so that you understand the nature of the investments or loans they make. It's a waste of everyone's time to send a business plan for your service business to a venture capital firm that funds only manufacturing companies, or to submit a loan for your new business to a bank that only funds companies established for more than three years. You'll end up waiting weeks or months just to hear an inevitable "No."

> " We want to understand how we're going to make money. Angels want to have liquidity within five years, seven years max. Things that take a lot of time and a lot of money aren't appropriate for angels, like finding new drugs or new energy sources."
>
> *Lauren Flanagan*
> *Cofounder and Managing Director, BELLE Capital USA*

FUNDING RESEARCH QUESTIONS

Do they fund businesses in your industry?

Do they fund businesses in your sector?

At what stage of development do they provide funding?

What are the minimum and maximum amounts of funding they consider?

What are the minimum and maximum potential sizes of the businesses they fund?

What other criteria do they use to make their funding decisions?

On what basis do they generally provide funding: equity or debt?

What companies in your industry have they funded previously?

What information do they require you to submit with your plan?

For instance, how many years of financial projections do they want to see?

Instead, a little research can save you a lot of time. Often, this can be accomplished with just a few phone calls, especially if your potential funding targets are established venture capital firms or banks. These institutions are used to answering questions about their funding patterns and have definite procedures and guidelines. Start by visiting their websites. Many venture capital firms outline exactly what types of companies they fund, cite the criteria for their investments, and include a list of companies they have already funded—their "portfolio" companies. If you can't find what you need on the Internet, don't hesitate to contact these professional financing sources for information; they'd much rather answer your questions now than waste their time having to process a business plan in which they have no interest.

With other sources, such as private or angel investors, it may be somewhat harder to get information. If they are a member of an angel investing network, they may list the types of companies they are interested in. They are far less likely to offer specific criteria than venture capitalists. Nevertheless, it is quite businesslike to send a letter of inquiry to ascertain the kinds of investments they are willing to consider before submitting your plan to them.

Once you have this information, you can better determine whether a funding source is appropriate for your business. Make sure your type of business and financial scope fall within the interest areas of your potential recipient. Don't send a plan requesting an investment of $50,000 to a venture capital firm that only funds companies seeking a minimum of $2 million. (Many do.)

If possible, you also want to find out less-tangible information about your funding sources. What is the potential funder really like? When deciding on funding, does the funder tend to place more emphasis on the experience of management, the product or service, or the market potential? Does the funder take a really long time making decisions, or do they respond quickly? Once they've financed a company, how does the funder perform as an ongoing partner? What's the funder's reputation in the industry?

Some of these questions you can ask in a phone call to an associate or member of the funding institution; better yet, you can request an informational interview with the funder (see page 359).

You can also get a great deal of information about funders by joining entrepreneurs' groups in your community or industry. Many larger cities have organizations in which entrepreneurs help one another get started, and members often have first-hand experience with funding sources.

If the funder is prominent, you may find information about them online or through sources such as magazine and newspaper articles. Next, see if you can talk to any others already funded by the same source, particularly those funded in the last few years. They can supply a wealth of information, and if you hit it off with them, perhaps they will even arrange an introduction to the funder for you.

Informational Interview

If you intend to send your plan to a large or well-established funding source, such as a bank or major venture capital firm, consider asking for an informational interview to get a feel for the institution and to better determine exactly what it is looking for in a business.

Request this only after you have finished researching your funding source and your plan is complete. The interview need not be long; 10 to 15 minutes may be sufficient. Your meeting doesn't have to be with a partner or decision-maker: An associate may be more willing to meet with you. Even an administrative assistant can be a source of a great deal of information.

It won't be easy to get such an interview, so treat any interview you are able to secure as an excellent opportunity, even if it's with a secretary. This is the beginning of your relationship with the funder, and you want to make a positive impression. Moreover, you then know a person inside the company, and when you send your plan, you can send it directly to that person.

Don't choose your prime funding target for the first interview you schedule. Get some experience with your second or third choice. That way you'll be less nervous, and you'll learn how to make a better impression when you finally meet with your first choice.

Finding an Intermediary

The best way to distinguish your plan from the many others received by a funding source is to find someone known to the funder to act as an intermediary. Intermediaries can either send or deliver the plan personally or can allow you to use their name when you send or deliver the plan yourself.

The best intermediary is:

- Someone in a related business to the funder.
- Someone who received financing (and whose business was successful) from the funder.
- A friend or relative of the funder.
- Someone highly regarded in the industry or community, even if not known personally by the funder.

Having an intermediary does not guarantee you'll receive funding, but it improves your chances of getting a fair and careful review.

If you are fortunate enough to secure intermediaries, be sure to send them a copy of any cover letters you have sent using their name (and perhaps a copy of your business plan as well). Potential funding sources may very well call an intermediary about your business, and when this happens, you want the intermediary to remember who you are.

Do not use a funder as your intermediary to send your plan to another funder unless there is a specific reason, otherwise it raises the question of why your contact isn't providing the funding. If, for instance, you are trying

> "If you already have one or two successful stores, you have a much better chance of receiving funding from a venture capitalist. Venture capitalists in the retail field are looking for a proven concept with experienced management. They are looking for 'cookie cutter' concepts, businesses that can be repeated almost identically from location to location."
>
> *Nancy Glaser*
> *Business Strategies*
> *Consultant*

> "If I get a phone call from somebody I respect about a plan, then that plan gets more of my attention. Who refers a plan to me can be quite important, but in the end the plan has to stand on its own."
>
> *Eugene Kleiner*
> *Venture Capitalist*

to raise money for a new retail concept and you know someone who funds companies only in the software industry, then it makes sense for her to send your plan to a friend who funds retail companies.

Tailoring the Plan for Your Recipients

Once you have researched your potential funders, you should organize your cover letter and Executive Summary to highlight those aspects of your business most likely to fit the needs and interests of each funder. Is the venture capital firm particularly interested in patentable new technology? Will the bank fund only those companies established for more than three years? Does the division president want to see new market opportunities? If so, discuss these areas in the first paragraph of your cover letter, or place more emphasis on them in your Summary.

Be certain to target your Executive Summary to address the concerns of the company rather than just an individual's preferences. Remember, your plan is most likely to end up in the hands of someone other than the person to whom it was sent originally.

Cover Letter

You must include a cover letter with any plan you send or deliver to a potential funding source. The cover letter will probably be read before the plan, so make certain it entices the reader to give careful consideration to your business.

The best way to start a cover letter is with this sentence:

"_____ (name of intermediary) suggested that I contact you regarding my business, _____ (name of business), a _____ (type of business)."

For example, the first sentence might read:

"Aaron Schneider suggested that I contact you regarding my business, AAA, Inc., a food products and service company."

This immediately draws attention to the person connecting you to the funding source and gives you a measure of credibility (assuming, of course, that your intermediary is credible).

Next, indicate why you (or the intermediary) feel that the recipient is an appropriate funding source. Continuing with the above example, the next sentence might read:

"He knows of your experience in funding food product companies and believes you might find AAA, Inc. of interest."

If you don't have an intermediary, your first sentence should state the name and nature of your company and why you have chosen to send your plan to the recipient. It should read something like:

"Knowing of your interest in funding food product companies, I am enclosing a copy of the business plan for AAA, Inc., an established food products and service company now seeking financing to enable us to expand operations."

> " The best way to get introduced to a bank is through someone who already has a relationship with that bank. Come through a friend who's a customer or a lawyer or accountant. Open an account yourself. References are important in getting an introduction to a bank, but they are irrelevant in the decision to loan itself. Except, of course, if you have references from major customers who show their intention to buy from you."
>
> *Robert Mahoney*
> *Corporate Banker*

Generally, your cover letter should state:

- Why you've chosen the particular funder to receive your plan.
- The nature of your business.
- The developmental stage of your business.
- The amount of funds sought.
- Whether you are looking for an investment or a loan.
- The terms of the deal, if appropriate.

Keep your cover letter brief. It should motivate the recipient to read your plan, not replace the plan itself. A sample cover letter is provided for your review at the end of this chapter.

Following Up

Your job is not done once you have sent out your business plan; you must follow up on its progress to ensure receiving an answer from your funding source. Some investors or banks tell you exactly when you can expect to hear from them. Others are far less diligent in their communication with fund seekers. You must take the initiative.

Don't become a pest, however. Keep your inquiries brief and professional, and don't call or email too frequently. You might call for the first time about a week after sending your plan, just to inquire whether the plan has been received by the funder. During this first phone call it is appropriate to ask when you can expect to hear from the funding source or when you may call back. It's perfectly acceptable to request an appropriate time to follow up again: "May I call back in two weeks to check on my plan's progress?"

Generally, refrain from calling any funding source more frequently than every two weeks. And if they ask you not to call, DON'T.

Email and Voice Mail

Much of your interaction with potential funding sources will be through email and voice mail messages. As such, you want to take some time preparing what you want to say before you pick up the phone or hit the "Send" button.

But be careful: Most funding sources are inundated with emails and phone calls—yours can easily be viewed as another intrusion. Keep all your initial or uninvited emails and voice mails short. You have a better chance of having your message read or listened to if it is not too long. If you've worked on your "**elevator pitch**" (see page 363), you should be able to quickly explain the nature of your business.

If you have the name of an intermediary who suggested you contact the funding source, use that name right away, whether in a voice mail or email. In an email message, you might put the intermediary's name in the "Subject" line to make it more likely the recipient will open your message.

> " In a cover letter, I want to know how you knew who I was. How did you get to me? Who are the other people pulling for you? The first plans I read are those that come to me from a credible source."
>
> *Ann Winblad*
> *Venture Capitalist*

Your "Elevator Pitch"

MY COMPANY...

Named: _____

Does: _____

_____

_____

_____

_____

Serves Which Market: _____

_____

_____

_____

_____

Makes Money By: _____

_____

_____

_____

_____

_____

Is Like Which Other Companies: _____

_____

_____

_____

_____

Will Succeed Because It: _____

_____

_____

_____

_____

Aims to Achieve: _____

_____

_____

_____

_____

For a voice mail message, state the nature of your call and your business up front and then clearly and slowly explain how you can be reached. Describe your company in "big picture" terms: Do not go into too many details; they may misunderstand the nature of your business. Always indicate that you will also phone back—that gives you an opening to call again without seeming too pushy.

Your voice mail message might be something like, "Aaron Schneider suggested I call you about my new food products and service company, AAA, Inc. Aaron thought our approach to growth and our established customer base would interest you. I'd appreciate the chance to speak with you. I can be reached at 650-555-1000 or you can email me at arnie at aaa.com. I will also try you again in a couple of days. Thank you."

Your email message can be very similar to your voice mail. It should be short and direct, and you should provide a way for them to contact you by phone. You can include the address of your website, if you have one up and running, and if you are willing to have the potential funder see it before they've talked to you. Refrain from using any attachments, especially in your first contact. Be careful not to be too vague in your "Subject" line, such as "Great Business Opportunity" or "New Business Venture." You don't want your recipient to think your message is spam and delete it without even opening it.

"The Elevator Pitch"

When considering a prospective investment, venture capitalists and other investors often want to hear what they call the "elevator pitch." This is the concise description of a company—its product or service, market, competitive advantages—that an entrepreneur could give in the time it would take to ride up an elevator (and not to the top floor of a skyscraper!). An "elevator pitch" shows that you understand your business. (If you're unclear on your strategic position, you'd still be mumbling as you pass the fifteenth floor.)

Your "elevator pitch" doesn't have to be made in an actual elevator to be useful. You'll find you'll use it often: in emails to prospective financing sources, to introduce yourself and your company at networking events, and to describe your business to potential customers. ***Take a few moments to write a concise elevator pitch using the worksheet on page 362.***

Chapter Summary

If you are raising money for your company, you can increase the chances of raising the capital you need through preparation, research, and cultivating contacts. Research your recipients and tailor the presentation of your plan to each recipient's interests and concerns. Choose your potential funding sources wisely; remember that your funding source will become an ongoing participant in your business. And be realistic. You must always give something in return for the money you receive.

> " **Emailing a summary is the most common and the best way to convey a plan. Email a summary with the idea of trying to set up a meeting to present a full presentation."**
>
> *Mark Gorenberg*
> *Venture Capitalist*

> " **The classic elevator pitch is very important to us. Angel investors typically co-invest with others. If an entrepreneur can't describe their concept quickly, it's hard for us to raise money from others."**
>
> *Lauren Flanagan*
> *Cofounder and Managing Director, BELLE Capital USA*

Sources of Debt Financing

	WHAT THEY LOOK FOR	ADVANTAGES	DISADVANTAGES
Banks and Lending Institutions	Ability to repay, collateral, steady current income from business.	No profit-sharing; no obligation for ongoing relationship after repayment; definite preset amount to repay. **Best For:** Established companies needing funding for specific activities; short-term cash flow problems.	Difficult to secure for new businesses; must often risk personal assets; same financial obligation regardless of business's income. **Worst For:** Ongoing operational expenses; new companies with relatively inexperienced management.
Loans from Family or Friends	Likelihood of repayment; your personal character; other personal considerations.	Easier to secure than institutional loans; specific amount to repay; no profit-sharing. **Best For:** Companies with no other option; companies with secure future.	Can jeopardize personal relationships; unsophisticated lender often nervous about money; probably no professional expertise; often get unsolicited advice and frequent queries. **Worst For:** Very risky enterprises; entrepreneurs with difficult family circumstances.
Cash Advance on Personal Credit Cards	Ability to repay.	Relatively easy to secure. **Best For:** Businesses requiring small amounts of money for a limited time; short-term cash flow problems.	High interest rates; limited amount of money; ties up and risks personal credit. **Worst For:** Ongoing, long-term financing.

Sources of Equity Financing

	WHAT THEY LOOK FOR	ADVANTAGES	DISADVANTAGES
Venture Capitalists	Businesses in their area of interest; companies that can grow to significant size; experienced management; new technology.	Large sums available; sophisticated investor familiar with industry; can bring expertise, connections, and future funding; understand business setbacks and capital risk. **Best For:** Potentially large companies; sophisticated entrepreneur or industry wizard.	Difficult to secure; must have exit possibilities in three to seven years; take substantial, perhaps controlling, equity in company. **Worst For:** Small and medium-size businesses; inexperienced entrepreneurs.
Private Investors	Good business opportunities with better potential rewards than conventional investments such as the stock market; appealing concept.	May fund small and medium-size businesses; easier to secure than professional venture capital or bank loans. **Best For:** Smaller companies; those able to locate relatively sophisticated or capable investors; those with appealing business concept.	Often unsophisticated, nervous investor; take equity in company; may want involvement in decisions without having necessary expertise; long-term relationship; expect profits soon. **Worst For:** Companies requiring long development time before profitability; companies needing additional business expertise.
Investment from Family and Friends	Interest in you and your business concept; chance to make money.	Easier to secure than other investors; no set amount to repay. **Best For:** Companies with no other options; entrepreneurs having friends or relatives with significant business or industry expertise.	Jeopardizes personal relationships; long-term involvement; unsophisticated nervous investor; makes friend or relative a decision-maker in your business; doesn't understand risk. **Worst For:** Very risky enterprises; companies requiring long development time before profitability.

SAMPLE PLAN: COVER LETTER

Ms. Tamara Pinto
617 North Compton Boulevard
Vespucci, Indiana 98999

Scott@ComputerEase.biz
phone number: 812-555-1234

Dear Ms. Pinto:

Opens with reference to intermediary.

My attorney, Mr. Kenneth Pollock, suggested I write to you regarding my business, ComputerEase. I am currently seeking an investor, and I believe that the company would coincide with your interest in technology-related service businesses.

ComputerEase is positioned to take advantage of the market opportunities presented in the corporate software training field. Through a professional approach to marketing, experienced management, and an emphasis on outstanding customer support and service, ComputerEase can become the premier provider of in-person software training in the Greater Vespucci area. From that base, the company will be able to expand to become a regional force. An even greater potential for growth comes from online training, in which no company has yet dominated the market.

Specifies amount of funds sought.

We are seeking $160,000. We anticipate this will be the sole round of funding. The funds will be used to add one Training Center location, expand staff, and increase marketing activities.

I appreciate your consideration of the enclosed business plan for ComputerEase. I will telephone in approximately 10 days to see if you have any questions or how we may proceed.

Thank you.

Sincerely,

Scott E. Connors
President

CHAPTER

20 Using Your Plan for Classes & Competitions

Once in a while, what you learn in school you can actually use in real life.

> " When we're looking at an entrepreneur in the real world, we definitely judge an entrepreneur on how realistic they are in understanding their financial growth, their business models. In college competitions, we tend to look more at the concepts and the products that they're building and don't put very much weight on the financial sections where they really don't have much experience."
>
> *Mark Gorenberg*
> *Venture Capitalist and*
> *Competition Judge*

Planning to Win

Since this book was first published, it has been adopted for use in over 1,000 universities and business schools throughout the United States as a standard text. (It's even used by Culinary Academies to help future chefs plan restaurants!) It is also regularly employed as a guidebook for teams preparing business plans for competitions, often sponsored by business schools. While the fundamental issues covered in this book are every bit as applicable for entrepreneurs, corporate in-house teams, and students, this section is designed to help address the special needs of those who are preparing a business plan as part of a class project or to enter it in a business plan competition.

"Entrepreneurship"

People are starting new businesses in record numbers. Entrepreneurs get more respect and understanding from the business community at large than they did in years past, and more and more people hope to one day start and run their own company. Over half a million new businesses are started *each month* in the United States. And worldwide, entrepreneurship is flourishing.

Increasingly, people are not merely going out and starting a company, they're preparing for it. There's been an explosion of interest in classes on starting and running new companies, and a new field of study and research has developed. Business schools around the United States and throughout the world have responded by developing classes, even majors, in "entrepreneurship."

Do Class or Competition Plans Differ from the "Real World"?

One significant difference in preparing a business plan for a class or competition is that you're much more likely to be working with a team—as equals—rather than having one entrepreneur with a vision driving the process. In the "real world," it's often clear who the leader and final decision maker is.

This places more importance on managing the process of developing your plan and the process of decision-making. One of your first tasks will be to figure out how you will make decisions, assign tasks, and stay on top of due dates. In fact, in some classes, part of your grade may be determined by how well you manage team dynamics. While this makes the business planning process more complicated than in the "real world," it helps you develop the very much needed "real-world" skills of working with a group to build a business.

Another major difference from the "real world" is the way your plan will be "judged," whether by a professor or a competition judge. When you're out there actually raising money, potential funders have their own set of criteria by which they'll review your plan that may be very different from the criteria in a competition or class. The most important difference is that classes and competitions typically place more emphasis on the quality of the written plan itself. In the "real world," a company with a genuine likelihood of being very successful might get funded even if its plan was somewhat sloppy. Additionally, potential funders base much of their decision on their opinion of the capabilities of the key founders, often more than on the content of the plan or the business concept. You might have a terrific plan—one that would get you an "A" in a course or an award in a competition—that potential funders don't believe you're capable of executing.

Perhaps the biggest difference, however, may be the passion you bring to the process. When you develop a business plan in the "real world" for your own business, you have a vision of the company you want to create; you're driven by a desire to create something new or a lifelong dream of owning your own business. The downside to this passion, though, is that the visionary entrepreneur may not bring as much objectivity to evaluating the business concept and assessing the likelihood of success, since their dreams are at stake. If you can, bring a bit of passion, without losing objectivity, to your class or competition business plan process.

The Team Process

As was said above, one of the major challenges of developing a business plan for a class or competition is working with a team. Mastering the dynamics of working together in a group—how to reach decisions, allocate tasks, communicate, and so forth—will help prepare you for the very real situations you'll be in when developing an actual business.

> " The best teams in university competitions tend to be well rounded. Engineers have reached out to people in the business sector, and business school people have reached out to those in other disciplines. The most successful plans are those that cross-pollinate people between different departments. The teams that are almost all from one discipline tend to have groupthink."
>
> *Mark Gorenberg*
> *Venture Capitalist and*
> *Competition Judge*

KEY STEPS IN MANAGING YOUR PROCESS

Choose Your Team

Devise a Decision-Making Process

Select the Business

Identify Key Issues

Assign Tasks

Reevaluate Assumptions

Integrate the Work
Preparing and Presenting the Plan

Choosing Your Team

Perhaps no decision you make will be as important as whom you choose to be part of your team. Your people determine your success. The same is true when you start an actual business—with one difference. If you start a business and your Vice President of Marketing isn't working out, you can fire that person. You don't always have the option of jettisoning members of your class or competition team. So choose carefully. (In some class situations, team members are assigned, and you don't have a choice.)

When choosing team members, you may be tempted to simply put together a group of your buddies. Resist this temptation! While it is absolutely an advantage to have a group of people who work together well, you want to put together the best team possible. Your buddies may not have the range of knowledge or skills to help you form a well-balanced team, and, if you're honest, some of them may not be as responsible as you need them to be.

When putting together your team, look for a balance among the functional areas you'll address in your plan. Think of this as putting together the founding group for your new business: Having three great marketers may be overkill, leaving you without sufficient depth in operations, technology, or finance. If you're planning a technology company, definitely try to balance your technology strength with management capability. It's certainly possible to form a business solely around the work of one technology genius, but you'll need capable managers to actually make the business work.

The traits to look for when choosing members of your team are:

- Capability, even excellence, in a functional area;
- Responsibility in carrying out assigned tasks, follow-through;
- Intelligence, ability to evaluate data and think creatively;
- Communication and interpersonal skills;
- Ability to work together in and with a group; and
- Willingness to work hard and long to get the job done.

Before finalizing your team, you may want to interview potential team members to see what skills and capabilities they have as individuals and whether you'd work well together as a group.

Making Decisions

The first decision any group must make is to decide how they're going to make decisions. Devising a clear and fair decision-making process makes every other decision easier and the group interaction more pleasant. The important thing in devising a decision-making process is that all team members "buy in" to the process. This doesn't necessarily mean you have to make all decisions by consensus or by a vote—the team may be willing to have one person always have the final say—it only means all members of the team must agree to the process. If you get too far along in the process without determining how you make decisions, you may find yourself at the end of the project still fighting over issues.

One basic area of concern is which decisions members of the group can make individually—will team members have complete say-so over their areas of responsibility?—and which decisions have to be made by the whole team. You may want to operate by consensus, by taking a vote, or by requiring unanimous decisions. If you choose to make decisions by consensus—by having the group discuss an issue until a decision emerges—you need a sense of whether the group is capable of doing so in a reasonable amount of time, whether all members of the team will participate in discussions, and whether team members each respect the opinions of other group members. You may also want to discuss what happens if you can't reach consensus. If you require unanimous decisions, you are, in effect, giving each member of the team a veto.

If you have a strong team leader—perhaps the person who has pulled others in to work on their "vision"—that person may expect to make most of the decisions. Discuss how well this will work with the other team members.

Choosing Your Project

How do you decide which business you're going to plan? Some classes or competitions may limit the kinds of businesses you can select as a project, but more often you have a universe of options from which to choose. Since the quality of your business plan necessarily rests on the nature of the business you're planning, choose carefully.

You may have a team member with a very clear vision of the business they want to plan. Perhaps they've even formed the team around their business concept. If so, you're ahead of the game, but it's still useful to submit their idea to the same kind of scrutiny you would give to all other suggestions. This will help you identify possible obstacles and challenges to their business idea.

If you don't have a particular business idea chosen, you'll probably start your selection process with a brainstorming session of team members to come up with a list of possibilities. In fact, some professors require you to submit a number of potential business plan projects. ***Refer back to the section and worksheet on the Business Concept in Chapter 1 to help you focus your selection process.***

You'll probably narrow down your choices to a few that innately seem reasonable to you and your team members. To start to choose between them, ask these additional questions:

- How do team members' backgrounds, skills, and knowledge relate to each business—that is, do we have sufficient expertise to understand each business?

- What is of interest to the members of the group?

- Do members of the team have unique talents or knowledge that could give us a clear competitive advantage in a particular business?

- How possible is it for us to gather the information we need about each business in the time allotted?

> " Secrets to winning? Showing a propensity that you're writing the plan to start a real business rather than just writing it as an exercise. Having a well-rounded initial team. Really doing your homework counts even more in a competition because financials aren't typically well thought-out; having a realistic set of financials that mirrors a real business tends to be much more novel in a competition and shows a level of sophistication. Having a plan that looks at the market first rather than the products — that's extremely positive and tends to characterize most of the winning plans. Businesses that have unique technology tend to be viewed more highly than in the real world where market size is typically viewed as more critical than uniqueness of product."
>
> *Mark Gorenberg*
> *Venture Capitalist and*
> *Competition Judge*

■ How do these businesses fit the values and social concerns of team members?

■ What other factors affect our ability to prepare a plan for each of these businesses? And most importantly,

■ What business do we believe has the best chance of success?

Identifying Key Issues

Once you've decided which business you're going to plan, you need to identify the key issues you'll have to address in developing that plan.

This is the time to discuss the business concept in greater detail. ***Get the group together to go over the Business Concept worksheet in Chapter 1.*** Be critical: Don't be afraid to tear your business idea apart. Ask yourself all the tough questions that a reader—whether a professor, judge, or potential funder—is inevitably going to ask. The best method to identify key issues is by asking yourself questions (see Chapter 2), so have a brainstorming session to come up with those questions.

Once you have a list of questions, you then have a list of issues to examine. ***Use the worksheet Research Questions in Chapter 2 to organize and clarify those issues.***

Assigning Tasks

In assigning tasks, the first decision you'll probably want to make is to choose a group leader. It's often far easier to work in a group if there is one person designated as the "leader." The group can decide the nature and extent of the responsibilities of the leader, but it's generally helpful to have one key person act as the focal point for reporting in, setting meetings, and so on.

You can choose to either divide up tasks based on functional areas or share all tasks among team members. Some teachers may require you to rotate tasks among team members so that each member gets experience in all the areas.

Functional Division: This more resembles the "real world," where each person would prepare the portion of the plan related to their job responsibilities. For example, the VP of Marketing would do the marketing section, the COO would prepare the operations section, and so forth. The advantage to dividing tasks along functional lines is that it makes the best use of the skills and talents of the team members and the best use of time. The disadvantage is that team members may end up with little or no understanding of areas other than their own, the quality and content of information may be inconsistent, and if one member doesn't perform well, that entire area of the plan suffers.

Shared Tasks: In this division of responsibilities, each member of the team works on every, or most every, issue. You may then assign tasks by time: This week everyone works on marketing, next week everyone works on operations, and so forth. The advantage is that members of the team get a better understanding of all the issues facing the business, the topics may be covered more thoroughly since more people are working on them, and you may spark cross-functional creativity. The disadvantage is that it is very duplicative, takes more time, and may leave you with too little time to explore each area.

You can also work on some combination of this division: giving one person prime responsibility for a particular area over the course of the project but having the entire group work on each area for a short period.

Once you have figured out how you are going to divide tasks, you need to develop an assignment sheet, making clear whom each task is assigned to and due dates. ***The worksheet Assignment Sheet is on page 377.***

Reevaluating Assumptions

Toward the end of the planning process, prior to putting the written plan and presentation together, you'll want to revisit your original assumptions and assess which aspects of your business need to change. As a result of your research and data—and as you've become more familiar with the industry, market, and competition—you'll have a much better idea of what might actually succeed. This is the time to come together, as a group, to reevaluate your original assumptions and readjust your business concept or strategy.

Give yourself time in your planning process to have such an assessment meeting; it's easy to find yourself running up to your due date with only time to put the plan together. In some classes, the professor may require you to do a reassessment as part of the assignment.

Be willing to change. It may be difficult—once you've got sections of your business plan written and you just want to turn it in and be done with it—to go back and rethink or rewrite part of your plan and your business strategy, but it's worth it. You'll find you not only plan a more realistic business, but you've also got a better chance of getting a good grade or winning a competition.

Integrating the Work:
Preparing and Presenting the Plan

Once all the assignments have been finished, and the individual sections of the plan developed by individual team members, you'll need to prepare the actual written business plan and/or computer presentation. Even though each member of the team may be required to write their section of the plan, you're far from finished when they turn their sections in.

You'll likely find that you have a very uneven document: some sections more thorough than others, some more clearly written than others. You'll first have to determine how the group will handle those sections that are deemed to be insufficient. Typically your future is tied together with your teammates, whether for a grade or a competition prize, so you probably won't want to let one section be noticeably weaker than the others. Put one, or at most two, team members in charge of completing the written plan. It's difficult to write an excellent document by committee. Others can be in charge of the graphics, computer slide presentation, and the like.

Finally, decide who will be giving the presentation of the plan, if an oral presentation is required or an option (take it!), and then practice that presentation. You don't want to be caught fumbling at the last minute, figuring out who is going to stand up.

More details on preparing and presenting your plan are provided in Chapter 18, and you may also want to prepare your "Elevator Pitch" as described in Chapter 19.

Special Considerations for Classes

Many business, finance, or entrepreneurship classes require you to develop a business plan, often as part of the "capstone" or concluding course of your entire curriculum. The process of putting together a compelling business plan is designed to demonstrate that you can integrate the knowledge you've gained from your various courses and can relate them to one another and to a real-world situation.

Generally, the issues for preparing a successful business plan for a class—and getting a good grade—are the same for preparing any business plan. There are a few areas where plans for classes differ. Professors and teachers are likely to place more emphasis on the following:

- How well integrated the different sections of the plan are.

- How well documented the sources of information are.

- How realistic the plan is; how well it reflects an accurate assessment of the real- world situation.

- Whether you've included a clear statement of assumptions, and whether those assumptions are realistic.

- Whether the assessment of risk is adequate, reflecting real-world constraints.

In a class, you're also likely to be judged by how well the team has worked together—how well you've managed the process of putting together the plan—so pay particular attention to your group dynamics.

Finally, in a class, the quality of your written plan is always critical. Don't be sloppy. Pay attention not only to the content of the plan—making certain you've covered all sections thoroughly—but also to the look and quality of the written document itself. Refer back to Chapters 3 and 18 on how to make your plan compelling.

Special Considerations for Business Plan Competitions

There are hundreds of business plan competitions sponsored throughout the country. Many are conducted by leading universities and business schools, such as the Massachusetts Institute of Technology (MIT), Stanford University, Brigham Young University, the University of Texas, and the University of California, Berkeley, to name just a few. Some are sponsored by private industry or consulting firms; others are conducted by Small Business Development Centers, business associations, and even business magazines.

> " Business can be a lot more fun, inspiring, and powerful than business school suggests."
>
> Seth Goldman
> Cofounder, Honest Tea

Most of these competitions give cash prizes to the winning entries. The stakes in some competitions can be substantial sums of money. But perhaps even more important than the prize money, leading business plan competitions attract the attention of venture capitalists and corporations on the lookout for promising new enterprises in which to invest. Success in a business plan competition may lead directly to success in getting your company funded.

Each business plan competition has its own rules and requirements. Most business school competitions require either some or all of the company's team members to be students (or perhaps former students). Some competitions may be limited only to new businesses; others may allow plans from entrepreneurs who are already running their businesses but wish to expand.

Tricks for Improving Your Chances in Business Plan Competitions

- **Understand the nature of the competition.** A competition sponsored for business plans by MIT will have a different emphasis (and group of judges) than a competition sponsored to help small businesses get started.

- **Put together a cross-functional team.** Find team members with complementary backgrounds and skills. Judges often look to see if you have the depth of expertise needed. If your background is in marketing, balance your team with team members who are skilled in other functions, such as technology, operations, or finance.

- **For an annual competition, talk to past winners or entrants, if possible.** They can give you insight into how the competition really works and what the judges look for. If the competition sponsor shares examples of previous years' winning plans, look at a number of entries—not just the first-prize winner; you'll get a better feel for how they distinguish among entries.

- **Research the judges.** What areas of interest and expertise do they have? If they are investors themselves (e.g., venture capitalists), what types of businesses do they invest in? Such information gives you a sense of the level of industry and technology knowledge they'll bring to their judging.

- **For university competitions, call on alumni members for advice or information.** In fact, this may be the perfect opportunity to get a personal meeting with a potential funder (or employer) who happens to be an alumnus or alumna of your university or business school.

- **Be real.** Unless the competition is specifically seeking plans for visionary businesses, judges are much more likely to be impressed with a concept that has a good chance of succeeding in the real world, even if it is on a smaller scale than a totally groundbreaking concept.

> " I had won the Yale Business Plan competition for a different company, but I wasn't passionate about it. At Honest Tea, I'm on a mission."
>
> *Seth Goldman*
> *Cofounder, Honest Tea*

Team Process Checklist

In the space below, describe specifics and set dates for accomplishing each step in the team process. This is much like setting milestones for your business — except that you are setting milestones for your team to ensure a great outcome in the class or competition!

TASK	SPECIFICS	DATE COMPLETED
Choose Team Members		
Devise a Decision-Making Process		
Select the Business		
Identify Key Issues		
Assign Tasks (see assignment sheet on page 377)		
Reevaluate Assumptions		
Integrate the Work and then Prepare and Present the Plan		

Assignment Sheet

Use this worksheet to indicate assignments to team members and due dates for each task.

TASK	ASSIGNED TO	DUE DATE	COMPLETED
Industry			
Market			
Competition			
Strategy			
Marketing			
Operations			
Technology			
Management			
Social Responsibility			
Development			
Financials			

Chapter Summary

Preparing a business plan for a class or competition is very much like preparing a plan in the "real world." However, you are more likely to be working with a team, and so you face the challenges of group decision-making and managing the team process. The quality of your written document is particularly important in classes, even more than in the real world. Be as realistic as possible; you'll improve your chances for getting a good grade—or winning a competition—if your business plan reflects the real-world situation. Good luck!

CHAPTER 21

Internal Planning for Existing Businesses & Corporations

Planning isn't just what you do to go into business;
it's what you have to do to stay in business.

If You Have an Existing Business

While the entire business planning process described in this book is aimed at both new and existing businesses, companies already in operation have the ability, and need, to examine key marketing, operating, and financial activities more closely. This in-depth analysis particularly benefits those companies undertaking the business planning process for internal planning purposes rather than as a method of securing outside funding.

Ongoing internal planning is a must for any business; it enables you to stay competitive. A thorough planning process forces you to look closely at the dynamics of the current market situation rather than rely on old assumptions. Regular, ongoing planning enables a company to more quickly adapt to new market forces and incorporate new technological advances.

Internal planning provides you with the opportunity to examine ways to keep costs down and increase your profitability. In the constant press of day-to-day business, taking time out to think about what you do and in which direction your company is headed gives you more control over your company's future and better information on which to base crucial business decisions.

The Purpose of Internal Planning

When undertaking your internal planning process, you must first assess the goals and purpose of the process for your company.

Generally, internal planning can take one of three forms:

- **Evaluating.** To provide information on company performance.
- **Goal Setting.** To establish annual or periodic objectives.
- **Problem Solving.** To address a particular issue or concern.

These types of plans differ only in their objectives and scope; the process in each case is relatively similar. All three require that you assemble or develop sufficient information to enable you to evaluate and assess current company conditions; choose the necessary personnel to be involved in the evaluation of the data compiled; and have the ability to bring an honest and critical eye to the examination of your company's situation.

The Evaluational Plan

An evaluational plan provides management with the information needed to make decisions. Data gathering and assessment, rather than the recommendation of specific actions or the setting of specific performance objectives, are emphasized in this type of plan.

Such a plan particularly benefits a company that has not made a close examination of its operations or the market conditions for some time, or it may be used annually by a company that wants to do an in-depth analysis of these factors on a regular basis. An evaluational plan might be the most appropriate type for a company in which all decisions are made at upper levels of management only, and where the input of middle management and staff is given relatively little weight.

The Goal-Setting Plan

Probably the most widely used type of corporate business plan is that with the purpose of annual or periodic goal setting.

The function of this plan is not only to evaluate current and past conditions within the company and its environment, but to establish the specific, measurable objectives that departments and/or individuals are expected to achieve.

Some of the areas in which specific objectives may be set are below.

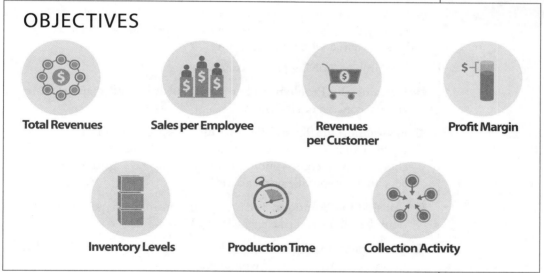

OBJECTIVES

Total Revenues   Sales per Employee   Revenues per Customer   Profit Margin

Inventory Levels   Production Time   Collection Activity

Many companies set performance objectives in these and other areas annually, based on past performance and projections of future conditions.

Performance objectives should be:

- **Measurable.** With specific numbers or dollar figures attached rather than merely subjective qualities or quantities.

- **Reasonable.** Based on a fair assessment of current and past activity and a temperate projection of future conditions rather than on an unreachable ideal.

- **Time Specific.** Delineating a clear time frame in which the objectives are to be achieved.

- **Motivational.** Neither impossible to reach nor too easily accomplished, either of which will reduce employee motivation.

The Problem-Solving Plan

Another option for internal planning is to narrow the planning process to a few key issues to be addressed. This type of problem-solving process focuses on the top priorities for operational improvement rather than on an overall evaluation of company performance. Planning for problem solving, however, should not take the place of more-comprehensive planning; you still need to look at your complete operations. But it offers you a method of focusing resources and creativity on one or two areas in order to make significant gains in performance.

A problem to be solved can be assigned to a department or division, but often it is advisable instead to assemble a task force to tackle the issue. Such a task force allows management to bring together staff across divisional or departmental lines.

Keep in mind that to a large extent whom you choose to participate in the task force will determine the outcome. If the task force is composed only of staff members who have been with the company for 20 or more years, it is unlikely you will come up with fresh approaches to the problem. If the members are too inexperienced, on the other hand, they will not have the necessary knowledge of the realities of the business nor will their recommendations be viewed with much authority.

The problem-solving process consists of:

- **Defining the Problem.** Either management or staff may delineate the areas of concern or challenges.

- **Assembling the Team.** Limit the number of people involved and bring together only those whose contribution will move the process forward; choose team members more for their intelligence, attitude, and knowledge than for job title or data access.

- **Considering Solutions.** Persistent problems often require creative solutions; be willing to make changes to achieve results.

- **Recommending Specific Activities.** Suggest the changes or enhancements necessary to solve the problem.

Large Corporations

Many, if not most, larger corporations now develop business plans annually on a company-wide, divisional, departmental, or team level. *Successful Business Plan: Secrets and Strategies* serves as a guidebook for developing a plan at any of these levels, whether corporate-wide or for an individual team. For departmental or team planning, some sections may require modification to accommodate specific circumstances or may not be applicable at all.

As you work through the book, use the described process and worksheets but adapt the material to your specific situation and needs. While the term "you" is used throughout the book, particular actions might be carried out by a subordinate, research department, or other members of the planning team. Nevertheless, the person making the final decisions should be sufficiently informed about the planning process and have access to raw data

> "The trials and tribulations and the fun of it all comes from getting in tough places and then figuring out how to scramble out of them."
>
> *Kay Koplovitz*
> *Chair, Kate Spade*

enabling him or her to competently evaluate the action plans recommended by others.

If yours is a particularly large or complex business, you may want to separate your business plan into two sections, one containing the specific financial performance objectives and the other examining more-strategic and long-term issues facing the company.

Bottom-Up/Top-Down

The business planning process in large corporations is most successful when conducted as a cooperative effort between those on the top of the decision-making ladder and those who actually carry out the decisions. A one-way planning process without the involvement of both management and staff leads to a company-wide lack of commitment to the plan and inevitably undermines its effectiveness.

In establishing and participating in the business planning process, management has these responsibilities:

- Clearly communicating the specific goals and importance of the planning process.

- Establishing the time frame for completion and execution.

- Assembling the appropriate personnel and making time available for them to participate.

- Bringing in additional outside expertise if necessary.

- Making available the necessary resources for the planning process.

- Being open and responsive to results and recommendations of the plan.

Likewise, staff has certain responsibilities in the process:

- Identifying areas of concern and specific problems.

- Defining the resources and outside expertise required for the planning process.

- Providing the necessary data and information.

- Honestly and diligently evaluating the data gathered.

- Viewing the planning process as necessary and beneficial.

- Realizing the limitations of their roles in decision-making.

Ratio Analysis

You may be surprised by how much you can learn about your company and its profitability from a few relatively simple calculations. Even if you think "number crunching" is only for bleary-eyed accountants, you will discover that figures are vital business tools. Particularly useful are the **key ratios** indicating how one activity or figure relates to another.

For instance, the key ratio of return on equity compares total net profit after taxes to the total amount of money invested in the company. Dividing profit by the amount of equity allows you to see exactly how much each

> " What holds a lot of small business owners back is themselves. The fear — the fear of mistakes, of getting out of their comfort zone, of talking to someone who's an expert."
>
> *Bill Rancic*
> *Serial Entrepreneur*

> " The danger of drinking your own Kool-Aid is that no one else likes the flavor of it."
>
> *Premal Shah*
> *President, Kiva*

invested dollar earned. This is a critical number for your business as it shows how effectively you used the money you had to spend. The return-on-equity ratio is particularly important for investors who want to know how efficiently the money they invested is being used to create profits.

When evaluating these ratios and using them as a planning tool, you want to look for ways to increase productivity by decreasing the amount of assets necessary to generate sales, reducing your debt, and increasing the amount of profitability made on each sale.

The principal value of computing ratios for your company is in comparing them from one time period to another. In this way, you can assess both the progress your company is making in controlling costs and increasing profitability and the trends you see developing in these areas.

Another important way to use this information is to compare these key ratios in your company with the ratios of other similar companies in your industry. These figures are available in financial publications such as the annual review by Dun & Bradstreet, the *Almanac of Business and Industrial Financial Ratios* (published by Prentice-Hall), and reports from industry trade associations. A comparison of your ratios with those of other leading companies will give you a better sense of your company's performance and competitive position.

The Key Ratio Analysis worksheet on pages 388–389 shows how to calculate many of the most important measurements of your business. The ratios included on this worksheet help you better understand the profitability of your company and specific operations, how well your company manages the assets it has at its disposal, and your cash flow situation. A brief discussion of the four ratios you will find on the Key Ratios Analysis worksheet is provided below.

Liquidity Ratios

Liquidity ratios show the extent of the readily available assets, indicating your company's ability to meet short-term debts. Generally, you want to try to increase **liquidity** and decrease amounts tied up in inventory. Specific types of liquidity ratios include:

- **Current.** How capable the company is to cover short-term debts with short-term assets. (Be certain to use current rather than total assets and liabilities from balance sheets.)

- **Quick or "Acid Test."** How well the company could cover short-term debts without selling inventory; this ratio should always be greater than one.

- **Inventory to Net Working Capital.** How much of the company's cash is tied up in inventory.

Profitability Ratios

Profitability ratios show how much the company has earned and the profits made on sales. Your goal is to have the percentages as high as possible. Profitability ratios include:

- **Profit to Sales.** Relationship of total sales to actual profitability after all expenses.

- **Return on Equity.** Profitability in comparison to the investment of stockholders.

- **Return on Assets.** Profitability in comparison to both investment and loans; how productive the company's total assets are in producing profit.

- **Gross Profit Margin.** Income after the direct costs of sales are deducted.

- **Net Profit Margin.** Income after all expenses are deducted.

- **Earnings per Share.** Amount of income expressed in terms of each share of common stock held.

Debt Ratios

Debt ratios show the extent of the company's debt and its capacity for engaging in additional borrowing; generally, the lower the percentages, the stronger the company's financial position. Debt ratios include:

- **Debt to Assets.** How much the company has relied on borrowing to finance its operations.

- **Debt to Equity.** How much the company owes creditors in comparison to the value owned by stockholders.

Activity Ratios

Activity ratios show how productively the company uses its assets, and how much value the company gets for the inventory or other assets it maintains. The greater the ratio value, the further each dollar goes (except with the Average Collection Period, which ideally is a low figure). Activity ratios include:

- **Inventory Turnover.** Dollar value of the inventory it takes the company to generate sales.

- **Inventory Utilization.** Average amount of money the company has invested in inventory.

- **Inventory Units Turnover.** How much inventory the company has on hand in relation to inventory sold.

- **Fixed Asset Utilization.** Amount of plant and equipment used to generate sales.

- **Total Asset Utilization.** Amount of all assets required to generate the company's sales.

- **Average Collection Period.** Length of time that the company's income is tied up in accounts receivable.

Key Customers

In most businesses, the "80-20 rule" applies to revenues. This rule states that 80% of your income comes from 20% of your customers. This means that a relatively small number of customers are often crucial in determining your success.

80-20 RULE:

80% of your income comes from 20% of your customers

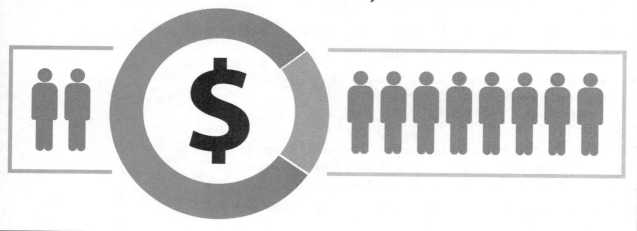

In most cases, this 20% is composed of actual individual customers. However, in some cases, it may be a specific type of customer who makes up the bulk of your business.

If indeed your business is dominated by a few key customers (or types of customers), you should take a careful look at their buying patterns and motivation. These customers are vital to your ongoing financial well-being; you want to gain as much insight into their purchasing behavior as possible.

Additionally, you can gain a much better understanding of your customers by examining the significant customers you have recently gained and the important customers you have recently lost. This type of examination of trends in your customer base gives you a sense of how the market views your company and the future direction of your company's sales.

The Key Customer Analysis worksheet on page 390, assists you in evaluating the activity of your key customers.

Touching Base with Your Plan

In corporate business planning, a natural tendency exists to spend a great deal of time and energy putting together a business or annual plan, and then, once the planning process is finished, forget the conclusions reached and go back to business as usual. This not only wastes a great deal of resources, it also creates a high level of cynicism about the importance and value of the planning process.

To make your business plan a meaningful working document, schedule periodic evaluation meetings to get back in touch with the plan. Perhaps once a month at a staff meeting, the plan can be reviewed and progress assessed. At the very least, the plan should be reviewed quarterly with both management and staff participating in the evaluation. Don't let your business plan gather dust; use it.

Chapter Summary

Existing businesses require business planning as much as start-up enterprises do. Planning is a necessity for any company aiming to improve its operations, increase its profitability, or maintain or enlarge its market share. Planning is a regular part of your business, not a once-in-a-business or once-in-a-decade undertaking. Long-term success depends on proper planning: It's the only way to keep up with the competition.

> Milestones are critical. If we do a $1 million deal, we'll only give them $500,000 at first, and then once they hit their quarterly goal, we'll look at the plan and give them 20% more, and so on."
>
> *Damon Doe*
> *Managing Partner*
> *Montage Capital*

Key Ratio Analysis

Liquidity Ratios

$$\text{Current} = \frac{\text{Current Assets}}{\text{Current Liabilities}}$$

$$\text{Quick or "Acid Test"} = \frac{\text{Current Assets} - \text{Inventory}}{\text{Current Liabilities}}$$

$$\text{Inventory to Net Working Capital} = \frac{\text{Inventory}}{\text{Current Assets} - \text{Current Liabilities}}$$

Profitability Ratios

$$\text{Profit to Sales} = \frac{\text{Net Income after Taxes}}{\text{Sales}}$$

$$\text{Return on Equity} = \frac{\text{Net Income after Taxes}}{\text{Equity}}$$

$$\text{Return on Assets} = \frac{\text{Net Income after Taxes}}{\text{Average Total Assets}}$$

$$\text{Gross Profit Margin} = \frac{\text{Sales} - \text{Cost of Sales}}{\text{Sales}}$$

$$\text{Net Profit Margin} = \frac{\text{Net Income after Taxes}}{\text{Sales}}$$

$$\text{Earnings per Share} = \frac{\text{Net Income after Taxes}}{\text{Number of Common Shares Outstanding}}$$

Debt Ratios

$$\text{Debt to Assets} = \frac{\text{Total Debt}}{\text{Total Assets}}$$

$$\text{Debt to Equity} = \frac{\text{Total Debt}}{\text{Total Equity}}$$

Activity Ratios

$$\text{Inventory Turnover} = \frac{\text{Cost of Sales}}{\text{Ending Inventory}}$$

$$\text{Inventory Utilization} = \frac{\text{Cost of Goods Sold}}{\text{Average Inventory at Cost}}$$

$$\text{Inventory Turnover in Units} = \frac{\text{Total Number of Units Sold}}{\text{Average Number of Units in Inventory}}$$

$$\text{Fixed Asset Utilization} = \frac{\text{Sales}}{\text{Average Net Fixed Assets}}$$

$$\text{Total Asset Utilization} = \frac{\text{Sales}}{\text{Average Total Assets}}$$

$$\text{Average Collection Period} = \frac{\text{Accounts Receivable Annual Sales}}{365}$$

Key Customer Analysis

Describe purchasing patterns and motivations of past, current, and new customers.

Key Current Customers

Customer	Products/Services Purchased	Number of Units Purchased	Sales $ This Year	Sales $ Last Year	Sales $ Prior Year
1.					
2.					
3.					
4.					
5.					
6.					
7.					

Major New Customers

Customer	Reason for Purchase	How Sale Was Secured	Sales $ This Year	Sales $ Last Year	Sales $ Potential
1.					
2.					
3.					
4.					
5.					
6.					
7.					

Major Lost Customers

Customer	Products/Services Purchased	Reason for Loss	Potential for Regain	Last Annual Purchase $	Previous $ High Annual
1.					
2.					
3.					
4.					
5.					
6.					
7.					

CHAPTER

22

Time-Saving Tips

*I've been on a calendar,
but I've never been on time.*

Speeding the Process

Developing a business plan takes time. It's not unusual for the entire process, from business concept to finished plan, to consume many months, especially for a new business. A plan for a such a business takes considerably longer than a plan for expansion or growth of an existing company.

Nevertheless, there are a number of shortcuts that can save you time and get your plan finished faster. Remember, you don't want to rush the process, but you don't want to spend so much time preparing a plan that you never get your business going.

Sometimes you have to have a business plan quickly, and you may only have time to put together an abbreviated overview of your business. While that is not an ideal way to present your business plan, there are occasions when you have no other choice. The section "When You're Really, Really in a Hurry" (on page 394) outlines how to prepare your business plan very quickly.

General Time-Saving Tips

Here are ways to make your business planning process quicker and easier:

■ **Prioritize the most important areas.** Not all sections of your plan are equally important. Make certain you have enough time to spend on those aspects of your business that most affect your long-term success or your chances of getting funded (if that's what you're using your business plan for). Don't squander time on areas that you already understand well or that are relatively less crucial to your goals. At the beginning of your plan preparation, identify which topics are the most important and address those first.

■ **Develop a research plan.** During the course of your plan preparation, you need to gather a lot of information. While you'll likely start online, you'll soon have to make many excursions away from your office or home, such as to industry meetings, interviews with other entrepreneurs, or visits with potential suppliers. You can avoid having to repeat these tasks over and over again if you outline all the information you're likely to need at the beginning of your business planning process. For instance, vendors not only may be able to tell you about the kinds and costs of goods, but they may know a lot about your potential competition and also about customer preferences. You'll want to ask about all of those in one meeting, rather than going back.

So start your research plan by making a list of all the information you want and potential sources of that information. Then put them in a logical order. As you go along, you'll find you need additional information, of course, but a research plan will reduce the amount of times you'll have to go back to the same source and will keep you moving forward.

■ **Organize all that paper!** You will amass an amazing amount of paper during the process of developing a business plan. Searching for information through stacks of reports, notes, and brochures will consume a great deal of time. So right from the start, organize your material so you can refer back to it quickly and easily. Set aside a separate file drawer or file box for your planning materials. Create individual files that correspond to the sections of your business plan, such as target market, competition, and operations, plus sections for miscellaneous material and possible appendices. One trick is to use a notebook binder or binders with tabs separating the sections of your plan. When you find important information online, save the pages to the appropriate file on your computer and/or print the relevant pages and put them in your file. Keep all your material together in one place, and start filing papers in their appropriate sections right away.

■ **Keep track of the most important information as you go along.** As you research your business, you're going to come across important data that you will want to use in your plan. Some of these will just be tidbits, such as U.S. Census Bureau figures on target market size, industry growth statistics, and so on. Avoid having to go back and read through entire papers or research reports by setting up a tracking system to file important items of information as you come across them. The best way to do this is by creating a separate computer file in your word processing program for each section of your business plan (plus miscellaneous information) and enter important data into the applicable file as you come across it. These can simply be notes; they don't have to be whole sentences or blocks of information. But be absolutely certain to indicate where the information came from, so you can give the necessary attribution without having to go back and look up the source. When not using a computer, use a colored highlighter to indicate the important information in each document, transfer that data to its appropriate computer file as soon as possible, and then place the material in the related file of your file drawer. You may have to photocopy some items because many documents will relate to more than one section of your plan. This method will really save you time. When you start to write your plan, you'll have almost all the information you need at your fingertips, in exactly the right place. And you'll be able to see which sections are missing sufficient detail.

■ **Use a spreadsheet.** A computerized spreadsheet (e.g., Microsoft's Excel) will make it easier and quicker to make the constant, necessary changes in your financial projections. To make this process even faster, you can purchase an Excel-based Business Plan Financials package as a supplement to this book. Visit www.PlanningShop.com to purchase and download these worksheets. If working with a spreadsheet is impractical, using even some simple bookkeeping software (e.g., Quicken) will make refiguring your financials faster.

■ **Get help.** It's not necessary to do every part of your business plan yourself. You can save a lot of time by spending a little money to hire a consultant to help. Many professional services can move your business planning process forward faster and improve the quality of the finished product. You may want to use the assistance of a professional business plan consultant and/ or research services (see Chapter 2). Although it may be somewhat costly, if you don't understand financial forms, are seeking funds from highly sophisticated investors, or are an existing business, consider using an accounting firm to prepare your financials. This often saves time, but more importantly, it increases investor confidence in your numbers.

When You're Really, Really in a Hurry

Sometimes you just don't have much time at all, and the thoroughness of the plan isn't as important as the speed with which it is prepared. What if a potential investor asks to see your business plan before she leaves town next week? What if a planning department needs your business plan before it can approve your building permit?

It's never a good idea to overly rush putting a business plan together, so you should try to avoid it if at all possible. (Can you ask the potential investor if you can give her your plan when she returns?) But sometimes you have no choice. In those instances, you can use the steps below to streamline the process:

1. **Figure out which information is most important.** If you're looking for an investor, generally the most critical issues are: the business concept, the size and nature of the market, what's happening with the competition, what kind of growth you project, and who's on your team.

INVESTOR CRITICAL ISSUES

The business concept | **The size and nature of the market** | **What's happening with the competition** | **What kind of growth you project** | **Who's on your team**

Concentrate on addressing those issues first.

2. *Go to the plan preparation forms at the end of most chapters and complete them.* These forms act as an outline for the text of your plan.

3. *Go to the financial forms in Chapter 16.* The three essential financial forms are the income statement, cash flow, and balance sheet. Concentrate on those. If you're stumped on where to get figures, refer back to the Flow-Through Financial forms. A list of these is in Chapter 16. These

forms will give you a structure for figuring out the information you need to complete all your financial forms.

4. ***Go back to Chapter 18.*** You'll find tips on how to lay out the plan for the best presentation and how to prepare an electronic presentation (which you may also need to do in a hurry).

5. ***If you're looking for funding, prepare your "Elevator Pitch" (Chapter 19).*** That will help you know how to explain your business quickly and confidently.

These steps will enable you to prepare a plan swiftly—possibly even in a weekend! But remember, you don't want to rush the process so much that the plan is not a good reflection of you and your business—you never get a second chance to make a first impression.

What to Avoid

One of the worst ways to save time on a business plan is by purchasing a computer program with standardized text or boilerplates, where you just add your company's name, industry, and financials. This can be tempting, because it seems as if most of the work has been done for you. But this "cookie-cutter" approach can be counterproductive, especially if you're using your business plan to raise money. Potential funders may ask you some tough questions, and they'll want to see that you understand what's behind the information you've put on paper.

Remember, the most important part of developing a business plan is the planning. You have to ask yourself the questions and work through the issues so that you understand which factors are most important to your success.

> If it looks like someone did one of those online 'fill in the blank' business plans, that's just lame."
>
> **Lauren Flanagan**
> **Cofounder and Managing Director, BELLE Capital USA**

Chapter Summary

It's natural to be intimidated by the prospect of preparing a business plan if you've never created one before. But that intimidation can easily lead to procrastination, which wastes a lot of time. Try to let go of your fear and take the process one step at a time. On the other hand, you don't want to rush through the business plan process merely to produce a written document. You need to know what's behind the words you put on paper.

Remember: A business plan doesn't have to be perfect; no plan is. You simply have to make an honest, best effort. You need not anticipate every possible situation, and it's not necessary to make revision after revision until you get it absolutely right. No plan written has ever been truly finished. Every plan could be improved, and every plan continues to change even after it's supposedly completed. So don't let the process overwhelm you. As the ad says, "Just do it!"

SECTION IV

References & Resources

Outline of a Business Plan

I.   Executive Summary

II. Company Description
  A. Company Name
  B. Mission Statement/Objectives
  C. Form of Business
  D. Trademarks, Copyrights, and Other Legal Issues
  E. Products or Services
  F. Management/Leadership
  G. Location and Geographical Information
  H. Development Stage
  I. Milestones Achieved to Date
  J. Specialty Business Information
  K. Financial Status

III. Industry Analysis & Trends
  A. Size and Growth Rate of Industry
  B. Industry Maturity
  C. Sensitivity to Economic Cycles
  D. Seasonal Factors
  E. Technological Factors
  F. Regulation/Certification
  G. Supply and Distribution
  H. Financial Characteristics
  I. Anticipated Changes and Trends in Industry
  J. Global Industry Concerns

IV. The Target Market
  A. Demographics/Geographics
  B. Lifestyle and Psychographics
  C. Purchasing Patterns
  D. Buying Sensitivities
  E. Market Size and Trends

> Every business plan varies. You may not necessarily have these same components in the following order in your plan. Use this outline as a guide.

V. The Competition

    A. Competitive Position
    B. Market Share Distribution
    C. Global Competition
    D. Future Competition
    E. Barriers to Entry

VI. Strategic Position & Risk Assessment

    A. Industry Trends
    B. Target Market
    C. Competitive Environment
    D. Company Strengths
    E. Risks Assessment
    F. Definition of Strategic Position

VII. Marketing Plan & Sales Strategy

    A. Company's Message
    B. Marketing Strategy
    C. Marketing Tactics
    D. Strategic Partnerships
    E. Online Marketing Tactics
    F. Sales Force and Structure

VIII. Operations

    A. Plant and Facilities
    B. Manufacturing/Production Plan
    C. Labor Requirements
    D. Capacity Utilization
    E. Quality Control
    F. Equipment and Furniture
    G. Inventory Management
    H. Supply and Distribution
    I. Order Fulfillment and Customer Service
    J. Research and Development
    K. Financial Control
    L. Contingency Planning
    M. Other Operational Concerns

IX. Technology Plan
A. Technology Goals and Position
B. Internet Goals and Plan
C. Software Needs
D. Hardware Needs
E. Telecommunications Needs
F. Technology Personnel Needs

X. Management & Organization
A. Key Employees/Principals
B. Compensation and Incentives
C. Board of Directors/Advisory Committee
D. Consultants/Specialists
E. Management to Be Added
F. Organizational Chart
G. Management Style/Corporate Culture

XI. Social Responsibility & Sustainability
A. Social Responsibility Goals
B. Company Policy
C. Social Responsibility Certifications
D. Community Involvment
E. Sustainability

XII. Development, Milestones & Exit Plan
A. Long-Term Company Goals
B. Growth Strategy
C. Milestones
D. Risk Evaluation
E. Exit Plan

XIII. The Financials
A. Income Statements
B. Cash Flow Projections
C. Balance Sheet
D. Sources and Use of Funds
E. Plan Assumptions
F. Break-Even Analysis

XIV. Appendix

Business Terms Glossary

Accrual-Basis Accounting. An accounting method whereby income and expenses are entered on the books at the time of contract or agreement rather than at the time of payment or receipt of funds.

Advisory Committee. A nonofficial group of advisors; has no legal authority or obligation.

Angel. A private individual who invests their own money in new enterprises.

Barriers to Entry. Those conditions that make it difficult or impossible for new competitors to enter the market: Two barriers to entry are patents and high start-up costs.

Board of Directors. The members of the governing body of an incorporated company. They have legal responsibility for the company.

Business Model. Describes what a company does and the structure it puts into place to make money. Examples of business models include designing and manufacturing a product that is sold to other businesses (B2B); or providing access to a software application online and selling it on a subscription basis.

Business Model Canvas. A tool for describing some elements of a new business in a one-page, visual format. It was originally created by Swiss management consultant Alexander Osterwalder.

Capacity. The amount of goods or work that can be produced by a company, given its level of equipment, labor, and facilities.

Capital. The funds necessary to establish or operate a business.

Cash-Basis Accounting. An accounting method whereby income and expenses are entered on the books at the time of actual payment or receipt of funds.

Cash Flow. The movement of money into and out of a company; actual income received and actual payments made out.

Cloud Computing. A way of delivering computing power and applications over the Internet as a service rather than a product that the end-user purchases and maintains in-house. Software, memory, and storage space are all shared and provided to computers and devices as a utility (much like the way electricity is provided).

Collateral. Assets pledged in return for loans.

Conventional Financing. Financing from established lenders, such as banks, rather than from investors; debt financing.

Convertible Debt. Loans made to a company that can be repaid with stock ownership (or a combination of stock and cash), usually at the lender's option.

Copyright. Legal rights covering any type of work that is "fixed" and "tangible" and granting protection from others who would copy, imitate, or steal that work.

Corporate Venture Capital. Venture capital funds established by corporations.

Crowdfunding. A method of raising money from a large number of people (the "crowd") for a new venture, cause, artistic endeavor, or product. Typically, the funds are raised through online, crowdfunding "platforms."

dba. "Doing business as..." a company's trade name rather than the name by which it is legally incorporated; a company may be incorporated under the name XYZ Corporation but do business as "The Dew Drop Inn."

Debt Financing. Raising funds for a business by borrowing, often in the form of bank loans.

Debt Service. Money being paid on a loan; the amount necessary to keep a loan from going into default.

Disbursements. Money paid out.

Distributor. Company or individual who arranges for the sale of products from manufacturer to retail outlets; the proverbial "middleman."

Downside Risk. The maximum amount that can be lost in an investment.

Due Diligence. The process undertaken by venture capitalists, investment bankers, or others to thoroughly investigate a company before financing; required by law before offering securities for sale.

Ecommerce. Conducting sales and transactions on the Internet.

Elevator Pitch. A concise summary of a company's service, business, or product idea that can be delivered in a very short time.

Equity. Shares of stock in company; ownership interest in a company.

Event. Investors or others may speak of an "event" taking place, usually a time at which value can be liquidated from the company. Commonly , it's a funding round, an acquisition, or an IPO.

Exit Plan. The strategy for leaving an investment and realizing the profits of such investment.

Funding Rounds. The number of times a company goes to the investment community to seek financing; each funding round is used to reach new stages of company development.

Go Public. To issue an initial public offering (see below).

Initial Public Offering (IPO). The first time the company's stock is sold to the general public (other than by a limited offering) through stock market or over-the-counter sales.

Key Ratio. A simple calculation that assesses the performance of a certain aspect of a company. Key ratios include liquidity ratios, profitability ratios, and debt ratios.

Leasehold Improvements. The changes made to a rented store, office, or plant, to suit the tenant and make the location more appropriate for the conduct of the tenant's business.

Letter of Intent. A letter or other document by a customer indicating the customer's intention to buy from a company.

Licensing. The granting of permission by one company to another to use its products, trademark, or name in a limited, particular manner.

Liquidity. The ability to turn assets into cash quickly and easily; widely traded stocks are usually a liquid asset.

Market Share. The percentage of the total available customer base captured by a company.

Milestone. A particular business achievement by which a company can be judged.

Mind Share. A relative sense of the awareness level a company has achieved in its target market versus the recognition and awareness of its competition.

Minimal Viable Product. A product that has been created quickly in order to get it to market as soon as possible. Over time, and based on the experience of actual customers, the product is improved on and refined.

Net Worth. The total ownership interest in a company, represented by the excess of the total amount of assets minus the total amount of liabilities.

Offshoring. Using outside vendors located in another country or transferring your own company's operations to another country, usually to reduce costs. Offshoring also includes setting up an independent subsidiary in another country to both lower costs and reduce taxes.

Options. The right to buy stock in a company at a later date, usually at a preset price; if the stock rises higher than the original price, an option holder is likely to exercise these options.

Outsourcing. To have certain tasks, jobs, manufacturing, and so on, produced by another company on a contract basis rather than having the work done by one's own company "in-house."

Partnership. A legal relationship of two or more individuals to run a company.

Patent. A government-issued protection of an invention, protecting the inventor for an extended period from letting others copy or sell imitations of the invention.

Profit Margin. The amount of money earned after the cost of goods (gross profit margin) or all operating expenses (net profit margin) are deducted; usually expressed in percentage terms.

Proprietary Technology or Information. Technology or information belonging to a company; private information not to be disseminated to others.

Receipts. Funds coming in to the company; the actual money paid to the company for its products or services; not necessarily the same as a company's real revenues.

Search Engine Marketing (SEM). The practice of purchasing ads to increase your website's ranking and visibility on relevant search engine results pages—often called paid search.

Search Engine Optimization (SEO). Optimizing your website by planning content and design that leads to high rankings on search engine results pages when a user searches for relevant keywords.

Social Media. Content created by individuals and disseminated online through networking sites such as blogs, YouTube, and Facebook. Used for awareness, marketing, and customer communication and retention.

Social Ventures. Companies whose primary mission is to address a social problem, using entrepreneurial approaches, while still earning a profit.

Sole Proprietorship. Company owned and managed by one person.

Strategic Partnership. An agreement with another company to undertake business endeavors together or on each other's behalf; can be for financing, sales, marketing, distribution, or other activities.

Strategic Position. A company's distinct identity that separates it from the competition and helps it focus on its activities.

Trademark (or Service Mark). A word, phrase, symbol, or design (or a combination of these) that identifies and distinguishes the maker of a product (or service) from makers of other, similar, products (or services).

Venture Capitalist. Individual or firm that invests money in new enterprises; typically this is money invested in the venture capital firm by others, particularly institutional investors.

Working Capital. The cash available to the company for the ongoing operations of the business.

Funding Sources

Angels, Venture Capitalists, and Lenders

Angel Capital Association

www.angelcapitalassociation.org

Directory of groups of angel investors throughout the United States and Canada.

The Angels' Forum LLC

www.angelsforum.com

A group of angels that invests, mentors, and advises start-ups in Silicon Valley. Works with early-stage companies from the seed stage through to the exit stage.

British Venture Capital Association

www.bvca.co.uk

The BVCA represents the vast majority of private venture-capital firms in the United Kingdom.

Dow Jones Financial Information Services

www.dowjones.com/privateequityventurecapital

Dow Jones Financial Information Services provides news on Venture Capital, both in the U.S. and abroad.

European Private Equity and Venture Capital Association

www.evca.eu

The EVCA represents over 950 venture capital firms in Europe.

Investors' Circle

www.investorscircle.net

A network of investors making private investments to socially responsible companies. It circulates proposals (for a fee) to its members.

Mid-Atlantic Venture Association

www.mava.org

MAVA represents private equity and venture capital firms with investment interests in the Mid-Atlantic region and beyond.

The National Association of Government Guaranteed Lenders

www.naggl.org

NAGGL is the association of banks and lending institutions that are active in offering SBA loans.

National Venture Capital Association

www.nvca.org

The NVCA represents the venture capital industry in the U.S. A list of member venture-capital firms is available from the site.

Small Business Investor Alliance

www.sbia.org

Small Business Investment Companies (SBICs) invest in small businesses. A list of member companies is available from the site.

State or City Offices of Business or Economic Development

Many states and cities maintain offices to encourage business expansion and increased employment opportunities. Generally, these offices only offer advice and perhaps some lists of resources. However, in certain cases, actual loans or grants may be available, particularly for job creation in economically stressed areas.

U.S. Small Business Administration (SBA)

www.sba.gov

The SBA maintains lists of banks and other lending institutions most active in making loans to small businesses in each geographical area. It also provides a loan guarantee program (not actual loans) to existing businesses, and direct loans limited to special categories such as Vietnam-era veterans and the disabled.

Western Association of Venture Capitalists

www.wavc.net

This association of more than 140 members represents virtually all of the professionally managed venture capital firms in the western United States.

Westlake Securities

www.westlakesecurities.com

Westlake Securities provides a full range of investment banking and financial advisory services to emerging growth and established privately held and publicly traded companies.

Publications

Galante's Venture Capital and Private Equity Directory

published by Alternative Investor

This directory lists over 2,000 American and international venture-capital and angel investors. It is very expensive to purchase, so check for availability at a good library.

Pratt's Guide to Private Equity and Venture Capital Sources

published by Thomson Financial/Venture Economics
www.prattsguide.com

This long-standing annual directory lists more than 20,000 venture capital sources around the world. It lists contact information, recent investments, and capital under management, and is cross-referenced by investment preferences, investment stage, and other key information. It is very expensive to purchase—either in print or through online access—so check for availability at a good library.

The Red Herring

www.redherring.com

Website that tracks venture investing. Good insight and background on the venture capital community and recent deals.

Business Plan Competitions

MIT Entrepreneurship Competition

www.mit100k.org

Since 1989, MIT has awarded cash prizes to student teams of entrepreneurs competing in its annual business plan competition. Many of the participants go on to build extremely successful companies.

New York Times Business Plan Competition Guide

**www.nytimes.com/interactive/2009/11/11/business/smallbusiness/
competitions-table.html**

The *New York Times* regularly updates this comprehensive list of business plan competitions, including information on prizes and deadlines.

Stanford University

http://bases.stanford.edu

Stanford conducts both an entrepreneur's business plan competition and a social entrepreneur's business plan competition for socially conscious for-profit and not-for-profit companies.

Research Sources

U.S. and Canadian Government Resources

These research sources supplement those listed in Chapter 2, on pages 23–32.

Government Printing Office

www.gpo.gov

Information from the U.S. Government on federal laws, governmental departments, and the like.

Publications.USA.gov

http://publications.usa.gov

Search for "Small Business" in the list of categories for publications on topics such as trademark, copyright, health care, and federal programs for the Americans with Disabilities Act.

Canadian Census

http://www12.statcan.gc.ca

The entry page for the Canadian Census, which is conducted every five years.

General Business & Industry Resources

American Management Association

www.amanet.org

Offers reports and studies on general business and industry-specific issues, including best practices in selected industries.

Columbia Books *National Trade and Professional Associations of the United States*

Lists over 7,800 professional and trade organizations in the United States. Available in most major libraries.

Kantar Media SRDS

www.srds.com

Reliable source of information on all publications and media outlets, including business publications, consumer magazines, online advertising, direct marketing lists, radio, cable, and television.

ProQuest Dialog

www.dialog.com

Paid database and research service. Used extensively in business.

Redbooks

www.redbooks.com

This directory contains detailed profiles of over 10,000 U.S. and 15,000 international advertising agencies, including accounts and brand names represented, fields of specialization, gross billings, and contact information on agency personnel.

Risk Management Association

www.rmahq.org

This association that serves the banking industry produces the most relied-on study of financial performance and ratios of over 600 industries. Its Annual Studies are available online on a per-industry basis for a small fee.

Human Resources

Advanced HR

www.advanced-hr.com

Provides salaries and stock options for pre-IPO companies. Fee based. But offers free limited access for start-ups.

Manufacturing

American Society for Quality

www.asq.org

A global organization that provides information on quality standards. It also trains and certifies professionals in the quality field.

ISO 9001 International Quality Standards

www.easy9001.com

Provides companies with solutions for implementing ISO 9001 standards.

National Association of Manufacturers (NAM)

www.nam.org

The largest manufacturing association in the United States.

Marketing

Advertising Age

www.adage.com

Provides information, data, and research on the advertising industry.

American Marketing Association

www.marketingpower.com

Worldwide marketing association with over 30,000 members.

Social Responsibility Resources

BSR

www.bsr.org

A global association of member companies interested in implementing responsible corporate policies and practices. BSR provides information on corporate leadership practices, conducts research and education workshops, develops practical business tools, and provides consulting services and technical assistance to its member companies.

Computer Professionals for Corporate Responsibility

www.cpsr.org

Promotes the responsible use of information and communications technology.

Social Venture Network (SVN)

www.svn.org

www.svneurope.com — Social Venture Europe

A membership organization of successful business and social entrepreneurs dedicated to changing the way the world does business. Provides opportunities for them to exchange ideas, share problems and solutions, and collaborate on an ad hoc basis with their peers.

Social Venture Partners

www.svpi.org

An organization uniting and encouraging the establishment of local social-venture partner organizations (SVPs) in the U.S. and internationally. SVPs enable entrepreneurs and other professionals to use their entrepreneurial skills to assist nonprofit causes.

VolunteerMatch

www.volunteermatch.org

A nonprofit organization dedicated to increasing volunteerism through the Internet.

Entrepreneurs' Sources

PlanningShop

555 Bryant Street, #180
Palo Alto, CA 94301
phone: (650) 364-9120
fax: (650) 364-9125
www.PlanningShop.com

PlanningShop, the publisher of this book, is the central resource for business planning information and advice. At the site, you can find a downloadable template of Excel spreadsheets to match the financial worksheets in this book.

Other Resources

America's SBDC

www.asbdc-us.org

Over 1,000 Small Business Development Centers exist around the United States, many located at community colleges. SBDCs are a partnership of private enterprise, the government, higher education, and industry. SBDCs offer individual counseling and assistance, seminars, technical help, libraries, and the like. Services are generally free. An outstanding, often overlooked, source of information for entrepreneurs.

Better Business Bureaus/Better Business Bureau Online

www.bbb.org
www.bbb.org/online

A long-respected organization of businesses that agree to adhere to certain standards. BBBOnline offers a certification program for Internet sites to increase users' confidence in sites' reliability or privacy policies.

Edward Lowe Foundation

www.edwardlowe.org

A nonprofit organization dedicated to assisting entrepreneurs. Extensive website of resources and articles.

Entrepreneurship.org

www.entrepreneurship.org

Run by the Kauffman Foundation, a nonprofit organization dedicated to assisting entrepreneurs. Extensive website of resources.

FWE — Forum for Women Entrepreneurs

www.fwe.ca

Founded in 1993, the Forum for Women Entrepreneurs (FWE) serves entrepreneurial women who are building or leading high-growth technology and life science companies. Started and headquartered in the San Francisco Bay Area, FWE has chapters in Seattle, San Diego/Orange County, Los Angeles, and Paris.

Inc. Magazine and Website

www.inc.com

Leading magazine for growing businesses. Website offers substantial archive of articles on business issues.

Intuit Community

www.community.intuit.com

Resources and peer-to-peer information sharing on small business topics, created by Intuit, maker of Quickbooks.

NASE — National Association for the Self-Employed

www.nase.org

Membership organization providing a number of services to self-employed and small businesses, including insurance and discounts.

NAWBO: National Association of Women Business Owners

www.nawbo.org

Membership group of women-owned businesses, with many local chapters around the country.

SBA — Small Business Administration of the U.S. Government

www.sba.gov

U.S. government agency dedicated to assisting and advocating for small businesses. Primary responsibility is administering guaranteed loan program. Offers resources or links to resources on various entrepreneurial issues. Maintains offices in larger cities throughout the country. Website is an excellent link to government sources to assist businesses.

SCORE — Service Corps of Retired Executives

www.score.org

Provides retired business owners as counselors for assistance to individual entrepreneurs and conducts workshops on business skills topics.

Startup America

www.s.co

Hundreds of founders, entrepreneurs, investors, mentors, and business executives work together to nurture start-ups throughout the U.S. Members become part of an extensive support network of start-ups, and gain access to valuable deals and resources from partner organizations.

SVForum

www.svforum.org

Long-standing, well-regarded Silicon Valley group of entrepreneurs, primarily, but not exclusively, in high tech. Sponsors or co-sponsors many seminars and programs on general entrepreneurship and start-up issues. Conducts one-on-one meetings with venture capitalists.

Women in Technology International

www.witi.com

An organization devoted to increasing the number of women in executive roles in technology and technology-based companies. More oriented to employees than to entrepreneurs, but still a good source of information and excellent conferences. Regional chapters.

Index

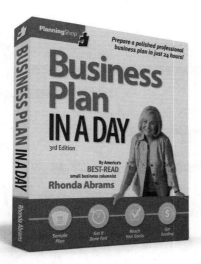

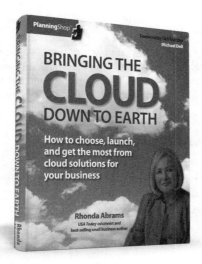
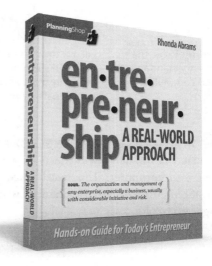

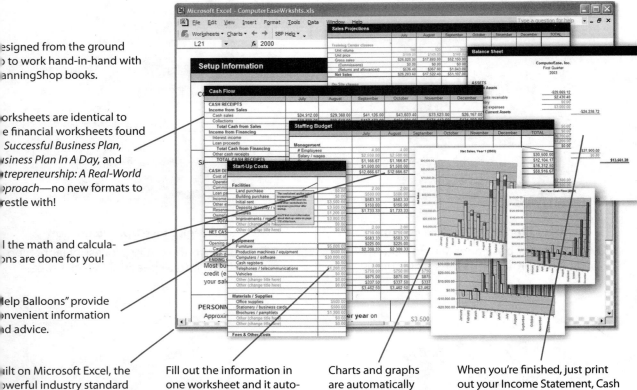